Other Books and Series by Jeff Bowen

Applications for Enrollment of Chickasaw Newborn Act of 1905
Volumes I thru VII

Cherokee Intermarried White 1906 Volume I thru X

Applications for Enrollment of Creek Newborn Act of 1905
Volumes I, II, III, IV, V, VI, VII, VIII, IX, X & XI

Visit our website at **www.nativestudy.com** to learn more about these and other books and series by Jeff Bowen

APPLICATIONS FOR ENROLLMENT OF CREEK NEWBORN ACT OF 1905
VOLUME XII

TRANSCRIBED BY
JEFF BOWEN
NATIVE STUDY
Gallipolis, Ohio
USA

Other Books and Series by Jeff Bowen

Turtle Mountain Reservation Chippewa Indians 1932 Census with Births & Deaths, 1924-1932

Chickasaw By Blood Enrollment Cards 1898-1914 Volume I thru V

Cherokee Descendants East An Index to the Guion Miller Applications Volume I
Cherokee Descendants West An Index to the Guion Miller Applications Volume II (A-M)
Cherokee Descendants West An Index to the Guion Miller Applications Volume III (N-Z)

Applications for Enrollment of Seminole Newborn Freedmen, Act of 1905

Eastern Cherokee Census, Cherokee, North Carolina, 1915-1922, Taken by Agent James E. Henderson
    Volume I (1915-1916)
    Volume II (1917-1918)
    Volume III (1919-1920)
    Volume IV (1921-1922)

Complete Delaware Roll of 1898

Eastern Cherokee Census, Cherokee, North Carolina, 1923-1929, Taken by Agent James E. Henderson
    Volume I (1923-1924)
    Volume II (1925-1926)
    Volume III (1927-1929)

Applications for Enrollment of Seminole Newborn Act of 1905 Volumes I & II

North Carolina Eastern Cherokee Indian Census 1898-1899, 1904, 1906, 1909-1912, 1914 Revised and Expanded Edition

1932 Hopi and Navajo Native American Census with Birth & Death Rolls (1925-1931) Volume 1 - Hopi
1932 Hopi and Navajo Native American Census with Birth & Death Rolls (1930-1932) Volume 2 - Navajo

Western Navajo Reservation Navajo, Hopi and Paiute 1933 Census with Birth & Death Rolls 1925-1933

Cherokee Citizenship Commission Dockets 1880-1884 and 1887-1889 Volumes I thru V

Other Books and Series by Jeff Bowen

1901-1907 Native American Census Seneca, Eastern Shawnee, Miami, Modoc, Ottawa, Peoria, Quapaw, and Wyandotte Indians (Under Seneca School, Indian Territory)

1932 Census of The Standing Rock Sioux Reservation with Births And Deaths 1924-1932

Census of The Blackfeet, Montana, 1897- 1901 Expanded Edition

Eastern Cherokee by Blood, 1906-1910, Volumes I thru XIII

Choctaw of Mississippi Indian Census 1929-1932 with Births and Deaths 1924-1931 Volume I
Choctaw of Mississippi Indian Census 1933, 1934 & 1937, Supplemental Rolls to 1934 & 1935 with Births and Deaths 1932-1938, and Marriages 1936-1938 Volume II

Eastern Cherokee Census Cherokee, North Carolina 1930-1939 Census 1930-1931 with Births And Deaths 1924-1931 Taken By Agent L. W. Page Volume I
Eastern Cherokee Census Cherokee, North Carolina 1930-1939 Census 1932-1933 with Births And Deaths 1930-1932 Taken By Agent R. L. Spalsbury Volume II
Eastern Cherokee Census Cherokee, North Carolina 1930-1939 Census 1934-1937 with Births and Deaths 1925-1938 and Marriages 1936 & 1938 Taken by Agents R. L. Spalsbury And Harold W. Foght Volume III

Seminole of Florida Indian Census, 1930-1940 with Birth and Death Records, 1930-1938

Texas Cherokees 1820-1839 A Document For Litigation 1921

Choctaw By Blood Enrollment Cards 1898-1914 Volumes I thru XVII

Starr Roll 1894 (Cherokee Payment Rolls) Districts: Canadian, Cooweescoowee, and Delaware Volume One
Starr Roll 1894 (Cherokee Payment Rolls) Districts: Flint, Going Snake, and Illinois Volume Two
Starr Roll 1894 (Cherokee Payment Rolls) Districts: Saline, Sequoyah, and Tahlequah; Including Orphan Roll Volume Three

Cherokee Intruder Cases Dockets of Hearings 1901-1909 Volumes I & II

Indian Wills, 1911-1921 Records of the Bureau of Indian Affairs Books One thru Seven;
Native American Wills & Probate Records 1911-1921

Copyright © 2012
by Jeff Bowen

ALL RIGHTS RESERVED
No part of this publication may be reproduced
or used in any form or manner whatsoever without
previous written permission from the copyright holder
or publisher.

Originally published:
Baltimore, Maryland
2012

Reprinted by:

Native Study LLC
Gallipolis, OH
www.nativestudy.com
2020

Library of Congress Control Number: 2020917992

ISBN: 978-1-64968-091-4

Made in the United States of America.

This series is dedicated to the descendants of the
Creek newborn listed in these applications.

DEPARTMENT OF THE INTERIOR.

Commissioner to the Five Civilized Tribes.

NOTICE.

Opening of Land Office at Wewoka,
IN THE SEMINOLE NATION, INDIAN TERRITORY.

Notice is hereby given that on Monday, September 4, 1905, the Commissioner to the Five Civilized Tribes will establish a land office at Wewoka, in the Seminole Nation, Indian Territory, for the purpose of allowing citizens and freedmen of the Seminole Nation to select allotments of land for their minor children enrolled under the Act of Congress approved March 3, 1905 (33 Stat. L 1060), and for the further purpose of allowing citizens and freedmen of the Seminole Nation, whose allotments are incomplete, to select additional land in order to bring the value of their allotments up to the standard of $309.09, as nearly as may be practicable.

Each child whose enrollment in accordance with the Act of March 3, 1905, has been duly approved by the Secretary of the Interior, is entitled to receive an alllotment of forty acres without regard to the character or value of the land selected.

Selection of allotments for minor children must be made by their citizen or freedmen parents or by a duly appointed guardian, or curator, or by a duly appointed administrator.

TAMS BIXBY,
Commissioner.

Muskogee, Indian Territory,
July 29, 1905.

This particular notice makes mention of the Act of 1905. The Creek and Seminole were closely related tribes. Both tribes' notices were similar in nature.

DEPARTMENT OF THE INTERIOR,
Commission to the Five Civilized Tribes.

Closing of Citizenship Rolls
OF THE MUSKOGEE OR CREEK NATION.

WHEREAS, on June 13, 1904, the Secretary of the Interior, under the authority in him vested by the provisions of the act of Congress approved March 3, 1901, (31 Stat., 1058) ordered that September 1, 1904, be and the same is hereby fixed as the time when the rolls of the Muskogee or Creek Nation shall be closed:

Notice is hereby given that the Commission to the Five Civilized Tribes will, at its office in Muskogee, Indian Territory, up to and inclusive of September 1, 1904, receive applications for the enrollment of citizens and freedmen of the Muskogee or Creek Nation, and that after that date the application of no person whomsoever for enrollment as a citizen or freedman of said nation will be received by the Commission.

Commission to the Five Civilized Tribes,
TAMS BIXBY, Chairman,
T. B. NEEDLES,
C. R. BRECKINRIDGE,
Commissioners.

Muskogee, Indian Territory,
June 25, 1904.

A notice like this was printed in newspapers and posted throughout Indian Territory.

INTRODUCTION

This series concerns Applications for Enrollment of Creek Newborn, National Archive film M-1301 (Act of 1905), as described in the National Archives publication *American Indians*. It falls under the heading Applications for Enrollment of the Commission to the Five Civilized Tribes, 1898-1914, M-1301 and is transcribed from microfilm rolls 414-419. This shows the application forms filled out by individuals applying for enrollment in the Five Civilized Tribes under the Dawes Commission. These applications contain additional information that wasn't abstracted to the census cards that you find in series M-1186. This particular roll (Creek by Birth) contains its own series of numbers separate from M-1186. To find each party's roll number you would have to reference M-1186. On July 25, 1898, there was an Indian Territory Division created in the Office of the Department of Interior. This division was created because of the increased work caused by what was called the Curtis Act, named after Senator Charles Curtis. Basically, this law stated that the tribal rolls needed to be descriptive and pointed out that each tribal roll was without description and had to be redone. At this point there was such a struggle among the Creeks to accept that the Government was going to change their way of life, again, that their leaders were refusing to cooperate in handing over their census information. The Commission had found that enrolling the Creeks was a difficult task not only because the Creek feared what was coming but also because their tribal structure was consistent with being a confederacy with forty-four different bands whose tribesmen lived in different towns of which each had a king that was supposed to keep track of their citizenry. The Commission reported that there was very little evidence of any census that existed and what there was had been kept carelessly. There were attempts and tribal conflicts along the way, but the Curtis Act would make it so they had to do it again no matter what effort from the past. In 1899, Agent Wesley Smith educated Washington to the fact that it was difficult to verify Creek eligibility. The acts passed by the Creeks themselves concerning enrollment since 1893 had been strewn amongst the archives of the Creek Council in Muskogee, I.T., and there was no provision ever approved for the printing of the those enrollments. There was confusion and difficulty let alone the fact that surnames were practically unknown among the Creek. But there was no confusion on March 9, 1905, when the Commission stated they would come to seven towns in the Creek Nation and accept applications that had to be made on a standardized blank form and contain a notarized affidavit from the mother and the attending doctor or midwife. A few by mail, but most of them were offered to a field party led by Commissioner Needles. The Commission took in applications for 2,410 children by the deadline of midnight, May 2, 1905.

This series contains applications and correspondence from 1,171 of those claimants. Realizing there were over 2,400 applicants originally, it is understood that not all were accepted. Also included are names of doctors, lawyers, mid-wives, and others who attended to the Creek Nation before and during this time in history.

Jeff Bowen
Gallipolis, Ohio
NativeStudy.com

Applications for Enrollment of Creek Newborn
Act of 1905   Volume XII

DEPARTMENT OF THE INTERIOR,

COMMISSION TO THE FIVE CIVILIZED TRIBES.

Wewoka, Indian Territory, May 8, 1905.

In the matter of the application for the enrollment of Gussie Bowlegs as a citizen of the Creek Nation.

Robert Bowlegs, being duly sworn, testified as follows:

Q What is your name? A Robert Bowlegs.
Q How old are you? A 33.
Q What is your post office? A Tidmore.
Q You are the father of Gussie Bowlegs? A Yes sir.
Q What is her mother's name? A Lula Bowlegs.
Q Of what Nation are you a citizen A Seminole.
Q Application has been made for the enrollment of Gussie Bowlegs as a citizen of the Creek Nation? A Yes sir.
Q You do not desire to make application for the enrollment of Gussie Bowlegs as a citizen of the Seminole Nation? A No sir.
Q You relinquish all rights she may have as a citizen of the Seminole Nation? A Yes sir.
Q And desire to select her allotment in the Creek Nation? A Yes sir.
Q This relinquishment of her rights as a Seminole is made in consideration of application having been made for her enrollment as a citizen of the Creek Nation? A Yes sir.

Frank C. Sabouris, being duly sworn, states that he is a stenographer for the Commission to the Five Civilized Tribes, and that the above and foregoing is a true transcript of his stenographic notes taken in said case on said date.

Frank C. Sabouris

Subscribed and sworn to before me this 9th day of May, 1905.

(Seal)

Chas E. Webster
Notary Public,

My Com expires April 28-1909

1

Applications for Enrollment of Creek Newborn
Act of 1905   Volume XII

DEPARTMENT OF THE INTERIOR.
COMMISSION TO THE FIVE CIVILIZED TRIBES.

In the matter of the death of   Gussie Bowlegs   a citizen of the Creek Nation, who formerly resided at or near   Tidmore   , Ind. Ter., and died on the   23rd   day of April   , 1904

AFFIDAVIT OF RELATIVE.

UNITED STATES OF AMERICA, Indian Territory,
Western   DISTRICT.

I,   Robert Bowlegs   , on oath state that I am   33   years of age and a citizen by (blood) freedman   , of the Seminole   Nation; that my postoffice address is   Tidmore   , Ind. Ter.; that I am   father   of   Gussie Bowlegs   who was a citizen, by blood   , of the   Creek   Nation and that said   Gussie Bowlegs   died on the   23   day of April   , 1904

Robert Bowlegs

Witnesses To Mark:
{

Subscribed and sworn to before me this 28 day of October, 1905.

Frank J Van Buskirk
Notary Public.

AFFIDAVIT OF ACQUAINTANCE.

UNITED STATES OF AMERICA, Indian Territory,
Western   DISTRICT.

I,   Douglas Rentie   , on oath state that I am   28   years of age, and a citizen by blood   of the Seminole   Nation; that my postoffice address is   Tidmore   , Ind. Ter.; that I was personally acquainted with   Gussie Bowlegs   who was a citizen, by blood, of the   Creek   Nation; and that said   Gussie Bowlegs   died on or about the   23   day of   April   , 1904

Douglas Rentie

Witnesses To Mark:
{

Subscribed and sworn to before me this 28 day of October, 1905.

Frank J Van Buskirk
Notary Public.

Applications for Enrollment of Creek Newborn
Act of 1905   Volume XII

BIRTH AFFIDAVIT.

DEPARTMENT OF THE INTERIOR,
COMMISSION TO THE FIVE CIVILIZED TRIBES.

IN RE Application for Enrollment, as a citizen of the Creek Nation, of Gussie Bowlegs, born on the 27 day of September, 1902

Name of Father: Robert Bowlegs   a citizen of the   Seminole   Nation.
Name of Mother: Lula Bowlegs   a citizen of the   Creek   Nation.

Post-office: *(blank)*

AFFIDAVIT OF MOTHER.

UNITED STATES OF AMERICA,
INDIAN TERRITORY.
Western   District.

I, Lula Bowlegs, on oath state that I am 32 years of age and a citizen by Blood, of the Creek Nation; that I am the lawful wife of Robert Bowlegs, who is a citizen, by Adoption of the Seminole Nation; that a Female child was born to me on 27th day of September, 1902, that said child has been named Gussie Bowlegs, and is now ~~living~~. Dead

Lula Bowlegs

WITNESSES TO MARK:

Subscribed and sworn to before me this 28th day of April, 1905.

J C Johnson
NOTARY PUBLIC.

AFFIDAVIT OF ATTENDING PHYSICIAN OR MID-WIFE.

UNITED STATES OF AMERICA,
INDIAN TERRITORY.
Western   District.

I, Rina Philips, a Midwife, on oath state that I attended on Mrs. Lula Bowlegs, wife of Robert Bowlegs on the 27th day of September, 1902; that there was born to her on said date a Female child; that said child is now ~~living~~ Dead and is said to have been named Gussie Bowlegs

her
Rina x Philips
mark

3

Applications for Enrollment of Creek Newborn
Act of 1905   Volume XII

WITNESSES TO MARK:
{ *(Name Illegible)*
{ J C Johnson

Subscribed and sworn to before me this 28th day of April , 1905.

J C Johnson
NOTARY PUBLIC.

NC 922   JLD

DEPARTMENT OF THE INTERIOR
COMMISSIONER TO THE FIVE CIVILIZED TRIBES.

In the matter of the application for the enrollment of Gussie Bowlegs, deceased, as a citizen by blood of the Creek Nation.

. . . .

STATEMENT AND ORDER.

The record in this case shows that on May 2, 1905, application was made, in affidavit form, supplemented by sworn testimony taken May 8, 1905, for the enrollment of Gussie Bowlegs, deceased, as a citizen of the Creek Nation, under the provisions of the act of Congress approved March 3, 1905.

It appears from the evidence filed in this matter that said Gussie Bowlegs, deceased, was born September 27, 1902 and died April 23, 1904.

The Act of Congress approved March 3, 1905, (33 Stats., 1048), provides:

"That the Commission to the Five Civilized Tribes is authorized for sixty days after the date of the approval of this act to receive and consider applications for enrollment, of children, <u>born subsequent to May twenty-fifth, nineteen hundred and one, and prior to March fourth, nineteen hundred and five, and living on said latter date</u>, to citizens of the Creek tribe of Indians whose enrollment has been approved by the Secretary of the Interior prior to the approval of this act; and to enroll and make allotments to such children."

It is, therefore, ordered that the application for the enrollment of said Gussie Bowlegs, deceased, as a citizen by blood of the Creek Nation be, and the same is, hereby dismissed.

Tams Bixby Commissioner.

Muskogee, Indian Territory.

Applications for Enrollment of Creek Newborn
Act of 1905   Volume XII

COMMISSIONERS:
TAMS BIXBY,
THOMAS B. NEEDLES,
C.R. BRECKINBRIDGE.

WM. O. BEALL
Secretary

DEPARTMENT OF THE INTERIOR,
COMMISSIONER TO THE FIVE CIVILIZED TRIBES.

HGH
REFER IN REPLY TO THE FOLLOWING:

Gussie Bowlegs

ADDRESS ONLY THE
COMMISSION TO THE FIVE CIVILIZED TRIBES.

Muskogee, Indian Territory, May 2, 1905.

Lula Bowlegs,
    Care of Robert Bowlegs,
        Tidmore, Indian Territory.

Dear Madam:

    The Commission is in receipt of an affidavit relative to the birth of your minor child, Gussie Bowlegs. It is stated in said affidavit that you are a citizen by blood of the Creek Nation, and that your husband, the father of said child, is a citizen by adoption of the Seminole Nation.

    You are hereby notified to appear before the Commission, at its office, in Muskogee, Indian Territory, for the purpose of electing in which Nation you desire said Gussie Bowlegs to be enrolled, in case it should be found that she is entitled to enrollment in either of said Nations.

                      Respectfully,
                            Tams Bixby   Chairman.

NC. 922.

Muskogee, Indian Territory, July 15, 1905.

Chief Clerk,
    Seminole Enrollment Division,
        Muskogee, Indian Territory.

Dear Sir:

    May 2, 1905, application was made to the Commission to the Five Civilized Tribes for the enrollment of Gussie Bowlegs, born September 27, 1902, as a citizen by blood of the Creek Nation. It is stated in said application that the father of said child is Robert Bowlegs, a citizen of the Seminole Nation, and that the mother is Lula Bowlegs, a citizen of the Creek Nation.

    You are requested to inform the Creek Enrollment Division as to whether application has been made for the enrollment of said Gussie Bowlegs, as a citizen of the Seminole Nation, and if so, what disposition has been made of the same.

Applications for Enrollment of Creek Newborn
Act of 1905 Volume XII

Respectfully,
Commissioner.

W.F.

DEPARTMENT OF THE INTERIOR.
COMMISSION TO THE FIVE CIVILIZED TRIBES.

Muskogee, Indian Territory, July 19, 1905.

Chief Clerk,
    Creek Enrollment Division.

Dear Sir:

    Receipt is hereby acknowledged of your letter of July 15, 1905, (NC-922) stating that application was made to the Commission to the Five Civilized Tribes for the enrollment of Gussie Bowlegs, born September 27, 1902, child of Robert Bowlegs, a citizen of the Seminole Nation, and Lula Bowlegs, a citizen of the Creek Nation, as a citizen by blood of the Creek Nation and requesting to be advised as to whether application has been made for the enrollment of said child as a citizen of the Seminole Nation.

    In reply to your letter you are advised that it does not appear from an examination of the records of this office that any application was made for the enrollment of said Gussie Bowlegs as a citizen of the Seminole Nation.

Respectfully,
Tams Bixby   Commissioner.

N.C. 922

Muskogee, Indian Territory, October 20, 1905.

Lula Bowlegs,
    Care Robert Bowlegs,
        Tidmore, Indian Territory.

Dear Madam:

    In the matter of the application for the enrollment of Gussie Bowlegs, born September 27, 1902, as citizens by blood of the Creek Nation, it is stated in your affidavit and the affidavit of Rina Philips, the midwife who attended at the birth of said child, executed April 28, 1905, that said Gussie Bowlegs was then dead.

Applications for Enrollment of Creek Newborn
Act of 1905   Volume XII

There is herewith enclosed blank form of death affidavit which you are requested to have executed before notary public, care being taken that he affix his name and notarial seal, and return it to this office in the enclosed envelope.

Respectfully,
Commissioner.

DA
Env.

NC 922.

Muskogee, Indian Territory, January 17, 1907.

Lula Bowlegs,
    c/o Robert Bowlegs,
        Tidmore, Indian Territory.

Dear Madam:

There is herewith enclosed one copy of the Statement and Order of the Commissioner to the Five Civilized Tribes, dated January 15, 1907, dismissing the application made by you for the enrollment of your minor child Gussie Bowlegs, deceased, as a citizen by blood of the Creek Nation.

Respectfully,
Commissioner.

LH-76.

NC 923   JLD

DEPARTMENT OF THE INTERIOR,
COMMISSIONER TO THE FIVE CIVILIZED TRIBES.

In the matter of the application for the enrollment of Selie Graham, deceased, as a citizen by blood of the Creek Nation.

. . . .

STATEMENT AND ORDER.

The record in this case shows that on May 2, 1905, application was made, in affidavit form, for the enrollment of Selie Graham, deceased, as a citizen by blood of the Creek Nation, under the provisions of the act of Congress approved March 3, 1905.

Applications for Enrollment of Creek Newborn
Act of 1905   Volume XII

It appears from the affidavit filed in this matter that Selie Graham, deceased, was born September 30, 1902, and died December 9, 1904.

The Act of Congress approved March 3, 1905, (33 Stats., 1048), provides:
"That the Commission to the Five Civilized Tribes is authorized for sixty days after the date of the approval of this act to receive and consider applications for enrollment, of children, <u>born subsequent to May twenty-fifth, nineteen hundred and one, and prior to March fourth, nineteen hundred and five, and living on said latter date,</u> to citizens of the Creek tribe of Indians whose enrollment has been approved by the Secretary of the Interior prior to the approval of this act; and to enroll and make allotments to such children."

It is, therefore, ordered that the application for the enrollment of said , deceased, as a citizen by blood of the Creek Nation be, and the same is, hereby dismissed.

                        Tams Bixby Commissioner.

Muskogee, Indian Territory.
JAN 4 – 1907

BIRTH AFFIDAVIT.

DEPARTMENT OF THE INTERIOR.
COMMISSION TO THE FIVE CIVILIZED TRIBES.

IN RE APPLICATION FOR ENROLLMENT, as a citizen of the Creek Nation, of Selie Graham, born on the 30 day of Sept, 1902

Name of Father: Louis Graham	a citizen of the	Choctaw Nation.
Name of Mother: Millie Graham	a citizen of the	Creek Nation.

                  Postoffice   Bearden IT

AFFIDAVIT OF MOTHER.

UNITED STATES OF AMERICA, Indian Territory, ⎫
    Western   DISTRICT. ⎭

I, Millie Graham , on oath state that I am 21 years of age and a citizen by Blood , of the Creek Nation; that I am the lawful wife of Louis Graham , who is a citizen, by Adoption of the Choctaw Nation; that a Female child was born to me on 30 day of Sept , 1902 , that said child has been named Selie , ~~and was living March 4, 1905~~.

                                      her
                            Millie x Graham
Witnesses To Mark: mark
   { C.W. Holmes
     Frank Cheatham

Applications for Enrollment of Creek Newborn
Act of 1905   Volume XII

Subscribed and sworn to before me this 1 day of May, 1905.

                     C.W. Holmes
                             Notary Public.

AFFIDAVIT OF ATTENDING PHYSICIAN OR MID-WIFE.

UNITED STATES OF AMERICA, Indian Territory, ⎫
     Western   DISTRICT.   ⎬

I, Louvena Chief , a Midwife , on oath state that I attended on Mrs. Millie Graham , wife of Louis Graham on the 30 day of Sept , 1902 ; that there was born to her on said date a Female child; that said child was living March 4, 1905, and is said to have been named Selie   her

                             Louvena x Chief
Witnesses To Mark: mark
   { C.W. Holmes
      Frank Cheatham

Subscribed and sworn to before me this 1 day of May, 1905.

                     C.W. Holmes
                             Notary Public.

DEPARTMENT OF THE INTERIOR.
COMMISSION TO THE FIVE CIVILIZED TRIBES.

In the matter of the death of Selie Graham a citizen of the Creek Nation, who formerly resided at or near Bearden , Ind. Ter., and died on the 4 day of Dec., 1904

AFFIDAVIT OF RELATIVE.

UNITED STATES OF AMERICA, Indian Territory, ⎫
     Western   DISTRICT.   ⎬

I, Louis Graham , on oath state that I am 27 years of age and a citizen by Adoption , of the Choctaw Nation; that my postoffice address is Bearden , Ind. Ter.; that I am Father of Selie Graham who was a citizen, by Blood , of the Creek Nation and that said Selie Graham died on the 9 day of December , 1904

                             Louis Graham

Applications for Enrollment of Creek Newborn
Act of 1905 Volume XII

Witnesses To Mark:
{

Subscribed and sworn to before me this 1 day of May, 1905.

C.W. Holmes
Notary Public.

AFFIDAVIT OF ACQUAINTANCE.

UNITED STATES OF AMERICA, Indian Territory,
Western DISTRICT.

I, Louvena Chief , on oath state that I am 45 years of age, and a citizen by Blood of the Choctaw Nation; that my postoffice address is Bearden , Ind. Ter.; that I was personally acquainted with Selie Graham who was a citizen, by Blood , of the Creek Nation; and that said Selie Graham died on the 9 day of Dec. , 1904

her
Louvena x Chief
mark

Witnesses To Mark:
{ C.W. Holmes
  Frank Cheatham

Subscribed and sworn to before me this 1 day of May, 1905.

C.W. Holmes
Notary Public.

N.C. 923

Muskogee, Indian Territory, October 6, 1905.

Lewis Graham,
  Bearden, Indian Territory.

Dear Sir:

Receipt is acknowledged of your communication of September 30, 1905, relative to the application for the enrollment of your minor children, Sissie and Selie Graham, deceased, as citizens by blood of the Creek Nation.

You also ask that a plat showing the vacant land in the entire Creek Nation be sent you.
  In reply you are advised that this office desires the affidavits of two disinterested witnesses who know the date of the birth of said Sissie Graham and also the affidavit of

Applications for Enrollment of Creek Newborn
Act of 1905   Volume XII

yourself or of your wife making an election as to the nation, Choctaw or Creek, in which you desire said child to be enrolled.

You are further advised that this office is unable to identify your wife, Millie Graham, on its roll of citizens of the Creek Nation and you are requested to state her maiden name, the names of her parents, the Creek Indian town to which she belongs, and, if possible, the numbers which appear on her deeds to land in the Creek Nation.

Further replying to your letter, you are advised that this office has no plats showing vacant land in the entire Creek Nation, for distribution but that you may examine such plats at this office or plats of any designated township will be mailed to you upon request.

       Respectfully,

           Commissioner.

       Muskogee, Indian Territory, October 6, 1905.

Lewis Graham,
  Bearden, Indian Territory.

Dear Sir:

Receipt is acknowledged of your letter of October 12, 1905, in the matter of the application for the enrollment of your minor child, Sissie Graham, born November 30, 1903, as a citizen by blood of the Creek Nation; you state that the name of your wife, Millie Graham, appears on the roll as Millie Chief.

In reply you are advised that this office is still unable, with the information at hand, to positively identify your said wife on the final roll of citizens by blood of the Creek Nation and you are requested to advise this office as to the names of the father and mother of said Millie Graham and also as to whether or not she was ever known by the name of Millie Anderson.

This matter should receive your prompt attention.

       Respectfully,

           Commissioner.

Applications for Enrollment of Creek Newborn
Act of 1905   Volume XII

NC 923

Muskogee, Indian Territory, November 13, 1906.

Chief Clerk,
    Choctaw-Chickasaw Enrollment Division,
        General Office,

Dear Sir:

    You are hereby advised that the name of Sissie Graham born November 30, 1903 to Lewis Graham an alleged citizen of the Choctaw Nation, and Millie Lewis a citizen by blood of the Creek Nation, is contained in schedule of minor citizens by blood of the Creek Nation, approved by the Secretary of the Interior, January 4, 1906, opposite Roll number 1003.

                Respectfully,

                                  Commissioner.

BIRTH AFFIDAVIT.

DEPARTMENT OF THE INTERIOR.
COMMISSION TO THE FIVE CIVILIZED TRIBES.

    IN RE APPLICATION FOR ENROLLMENT, as a citizen of the Creek Nation, of Exie Fife , born on the 29 day of July, 1903

Name of Father: Elijah Fife   a citizen of the   Creek   Nation.
Okfusky[sic] Canadian Town
Name of Mother: Millie Fife   a citizen of the   Creek   Nation.
Quassarte[sic] No. 1 Town

                  Postoffice   Eufaula, Ind. Ter.

AFFIDAVIT OF MOTHER.

UNITED STATES OF AMERICA, Indian Territory, }
    Western   DISTRICT.

    I, Millie Fife , on oath state that I am about 35 years of age and a citizen by blood , of the Creek   Nation; that I am the lawful wife of   Elijah Fife , who is a citizen, by blood of the Creek   Nation; that a female   child was born to me on 29

Applications for Enrollment of Creek Newborn
Act of 1905   Volume XII

day of July , 1903 , that said child has been named Exie Fife , and was living March 4, 1905.

Witnesses To Mark:
{ Alex Posey
  T. F. *(Illegible)*

Millie Fife x̄ mark (her mark)

Subscribed and sworn to before me this 15th day of April , 1905.

Thos. F. *(Illegible)*
Notary Public.

Aug 1-1906

AFFIDAVIT OF ATTENDING PHYSICIAN OR MID-WIFE.

UNITED STATES OF AMERICA, Indian Territory,
        Western   DISTRICT.

I, Lucy , a midwife , on oath state that I attended on Mrs. Millie Fife , wife of Elijah Fife on the 29 day of July , 1903 ; that there was born to her on said date a *(blank)* child; that said child was living March 4, 1905, and is said to have been named Exie Fife

Witnesses To Mark:
{ Alex Posey
  T. F. *(Illegible)*

Lucy x̄ mark (her mark)

Subscribed and sworn to before me this 15th day of April , 1905.

Thos. F. *(Illegible)*
Notary Public.

Aug 1-1906

Applications for Enrollment of Creek Newborn
Act of 1905   Volume XII

N.C. 925

DEPARTMENT OF THE INTERIOR,
COMMISSIONER TO THE FIVE CIVILIZED TRIBES.
Muskogee, Indian Territory, April 20, 1906.

In the matter of the application for the enrollment of Martha Anderson as a citizen by blood of the Creek Nation.

DAVID A. BARNETT, being duly sworn, testified as follows:

Q What is your name? A David. Barnett.
Q What is your age? A Fifty two.
Q What is your post office address? A Barnard.
Q Do you know Willie Anderson and his wife Sissy? A Yes, sir
Q Willie was once the husband of Sissy? A Yes, sir.
Q What was the name of Sissy's father do you know? A Yarnie.
Q What was the name of her mother? A Melar.
Q Do you know whether Sissy is enrolled and got her deed? A Yes, sir.
Q What name was she enrolled under? A Sissy Jim.
Q Did she have a son named Deer, do you know? A One named Israel Deer.
Q Has she a newborn child named Martha? A Martha Anderson.
Q Is that child living? A Yes, sir

The mother of said Martha Anderson is identified as Sissy Jim opposite Creek Indian roll No. 7303.

Q You are requested to tell Sissy when you see her that this office requires the affidavit of two disinterested witnesses about this child Martha for which I have given you a blank today, in place of the midwife who you say is dead? A Yes, sir

---

I, Anna Garrigues, on oath state that the above is a true and correct transcript of my stenographic notes as taken in said cause on said date.

Anna Garrigues

Subscribed and sworn to before me
this 20 day of April 1906.

Henry G. Hains
Notary Public.

Applications for Enrollment of Creek Newborn
Act of 1905   Volume XII

AFFIDAVIT OF DISINTERESTED WITNESSES.

United States of America,
   Western District,
      Indian Territory.

We, the undersigned, on oath state that we are personally acquainted with Sissie Jessie[sic],   formerly the wife of   Willie Anderson   ; that there was born to a female child on or about   1st   ~~day~~ week of   January   190 3 ; that the said child has been named   Martha Anderson   and was living March 4, 1905.

We further state that we have no interest in this case.

                                        James *(Illegible)*

                                        Robert Benson

Subscribed and sworn to before me this 21st day of April 1906

                                        D A Barnett
My Commission expires Oct 10th 1906   Notary Public.

AFFIDAVIT OF TWO DISINTERESTED WITNESSES.

United States of America, (
Western Judicial District, (ss
   Indian Territory.   (

We, the undersigned, on oath state that we are personally acquainted with Sissy Jim   not the wife of   Willie Anderson   ; and that there was born to her a female child on or about the 10 day of January, 1903; that said child has been named Martha Anderson and was living March 4, 1905.

We further state that we have no interest in this case.

Witnesses to mark.	her Hettie x McGirt mark
J McDermott	her
J McDermott	Massey x Jesse mark
Jim Cantrell	
Jim Cantrell	

Subscribed and sworn to before me this 4th day of Dec, 1906.

15

Applications for Enrollment of Creek Newborn
Act of 1905 Volume XII

My Commission expires
July 25' , 1907.

J McDermott
Notary Public.

BIRTH AFFIDAVIT.

DEPARTMENT OF THE INTERIOR.
COMMISSION TO THE FIVE CIVILIZED TRIBES.

IN RE APPLICATION FOR ENROLLMENT, as a citizen of the Creek Nation, of Martha Anderson, born on the 1st week of January, 1903

Name of Father: Willie Anderson   a citizen of the   Creek   Nation.
  (Illegible) Town
Name of Mother: Sissy Jessie   a citizen of the   "   Nation.
  Tulmochus
                          Postoffice   Carson I.T.

(Child present)

AFFIDAVIT OF MOTHER.

UNITED STATES OF AMERICA, Indian Territory,
     Western   DISTRICT.

I, Sissy Jessie , on oath state that I am 25 years of age and a citizen by blood , of the Creek   Nation; that I was formerly ~~am the~~ lawful wife of Willie Anderson , who is a citizen, by blood of the Creek Nation; that a female child was born to me on 1st week ~~day~~ of January , 1903 , that said child has been named Martha Anderson , and was living March 4, 1905.

                                    her
                             Sissy x Jessie
Witnesses To Mark: mark
  { H.G. Hains
  { Alex Posey

Subscribed and sworn to before me this 24" day of April , 1905.

                        H.G. Hains
                             Notary Public.

Applications for Enrollment of Creek Newborn
Act of 1905 Volume XII

BIRTH AFFIDAVIT.

DEPARTMENT OF THE INTERIOR.
COMMISSION TO THE FIVE CIVILIZED TRIBES.

IN RE APPLICATION FOR ENROLLMENT, as a citizen of the Creek Nation, of Martha Anderson, born on the 10 week of January, 1903

Name of Father: Willie Anderson	a citizen of the	Creek Nation.
Name of Mother: Sissy Jim	a citizen of the	Creek Nation.

Postoffice   Carson I.T.

AFFIDAVIT OF MOTHER.

UNITED STATES OF AMERICA, Indian Territory,
Western DISTRICT.

I, Sissy Jim, on oath state that I am about 26 years of age and a citizen by blood, of the Creek Nation; that I am not the lawful wife of Willie Anderson, who is a citizen, by blood of the Creek Nation; that a female child was born to me on 10 day of January, 1903, that said child has been named Martha Anderson, and was living March 4, 1905. and died in March 1906

           her
           Sissy x Jim
Witnesses To Mark: mark
 { J McDermott
  Jim Cantrell

Subscribed and sworn to before me this 4th day of December, 1906.

My Com   J McDermott
Ex July 25" 1907   Notary Public.

NC 925

        Muskogee, I T October 20 1905

Sissy Jessie
  Carson I T

Dear Madam:

  In the matter of the application for the enrollment of your minor child, Martha Anderson, born the first week in January 1903, as a citizen by blood of the Creek Nation; this office is unable to identify you on its final roll of citizens by blood of the Creek

Applications for Enrollment of Creek Newborn
Act of 1905 Volume XII

Nation, you are requested to state all the names by which you have been known, the names of your parents, the Creek Indian town to which you belong and the numbers which appear on your deeds and allotment certificate.

    This office desires affidavit of the midwife or physician who attended you at the birth of said Martha Anderson and a blank for that purpose is herewith inclosed.

    In the event that there was no physician or midwife in attendance when said child was born, it will be necessary for you to furnish this office with the affidavits of two disinterested witnesses relative to her birth. Said affidavits must set forth the name of said child, the date of her birth, the names of her parents and whether or not she was living on March 4, 1905.

                      Respt
                      Comr

                                                  JWH

N C 925

                    Muskogee, Indian Territory, March 1, 1907.

Sissy Jim,
    % Willie Anderson,
        Carson, Indian Territory.

Dear Madam :--

    You are hereby advised that on February 15, 1907, the Secretary of the Interior approved the enrollment of your minor child, Martha Anderson, as a citizen by blood of the Creek Nation, and that the name of said child appears upon the roll of New Born citizens by blood of the Creek Nation, enrolled under the Act of Congress approved March 3, 1905, as number 1180.

    This child is now entitled to allotment and application therefor should be made without delay at the Creek Land Office, Muskogee, Indian Territory.

                      Respectfully,
                              Commissioner.

Applications for Enrollment of Creek Newborn
Act of 1905   Volume XII

BIRTH AFFIDAVIT.

DEPARTMENT OF THE INTERIOR.
COMMISSION TO THE FIVE CIVILIZED TRIBES.

IN RE APPLICATION FOR ENROLLMENT, as a citizen of the Creek Nation, of Larley Cummings, born on the 28 day of July, 1901

Thomas Cummings (de'd)
Name of Father: ~~Alex Harjo~~ (Fish Pond)   a citizen of the   Creek   Nation.
Name of Mother: Martha Harjo   a citizen of the   "   Nation.
(Tookpafka)

Postoffice   Okemah, I.T.

(Child present)

AFFIDAVIT OF MOTHER.

UNITED STATES OF AMERICA, Indian Territory,
Western   DISTRICT.

I, Martha Harjo, on oath state that I am about 23 years of age and a citizen by blood, of the Creek Nation; that I am the lawful wife of Thomas Cummings (de'd), who is a citizen, by blood of the Creek Nation; that a female child was born to me on 28" day of July, 1901, that said child has been named Larley Cummings, and was living March 4, 1905.

Martha Harjo

Witnesses To Mark:
{

Subscribed and sworn to before me this 26" day of April, 1905.

Henry G. Hains
Notary Public.

Uncle
AFFIDAVIT OF ~~ATTENDING PHYSICIAN OR MID-WIFE~~.

UNITED STATES OF AMERICA, Indian Territory,
Western   DISTRICT.

my sister
I, Alex Harjo, a --- --- ---, on oath state that I attended on ~~Mrs~~. Martha Harjo, wife of Thomas Cummings (de'd) on the 28" day of July, 1901; that there was born to her on said date a female child; that said child was living March 4, 1905, and is said to have been named Larley Cummings

Alex Harjo

Witnesses To Mark:
{

Subscribed and sworn to before me this 26" day of April, 1905.

19

Applications for Enrollment of Creek Newborn
Act of 1905   Volume XII

Henry G. Hains
Notary Public.

DEPARTMENT OF THE INTERIOR.
COMMISSION TO THE FIVE CIVILIZED TRIBES.

In the matter of the death of   Larley Comie   a citizen of the Muskogee or Creek Nation, who formerly resided at or near   Okemah   , Ind. Ter., and died on the 5th day of October , 1905

AFFIDAVIT OF RELATIVE.

UNITED STATES OF AMERICA, Indian Territory,
Western   DISTRICT.

I, Martha Comie , on oath state that I am 23 years of age and a citizen by Blood , of the Muskogee Nation; that my postoffice address is   Okemah   , Ind. Ter.; that I am   Mother   of   Larley Comie   who was a citizen, by   Blood   , of the Muskogee   Nation and that said   Larley Comie   died on the   5th day of October   , 1905

Martha Comie

Witnesses To Mark:
{

Subscribed and sworn to before me this 7 day of November, 1905.

Geo. A Harvison
Notary Public.

AFFIDAVIT OF ACQUAINTANCE.

UNITED STATES OF AMERICA, Indian Territory,
Western   DISTRICT.

I, Aaron Grayson , on oath state that I am 34   years of age, and a citizen by Adoption Freedman of the Muskogee   Nation; that my postoffice address is Okemah , Ind. Ter.; that I was personally acquainted with   Larley Comie   who was a citizen, by Blood , of the Muskogee Nation; and that said   Larley Comie   died on the   5th day of October   , 1905

Aaron Grayson

Witnesses To Mark:
{

Applications for Enrollment of Creek Newborn
Act of 1905 Volume XII

Subscribed and sworn to before me this 7 day of November, 1905.

                               Geo. A Harvison
                               Notary Public.

BIRTH AFFIDAVIT.

DEPARTMENT OF THE INTERIOR.
COMMISSION TO THE FIVE CIVILIZED TRIBES.

IN RE APPLICATION FOR ENROLLMENT, as a citizen of the CREEK Nation, of Larley Comie, born on the 28th day of July, 1901

Name of Father: Thomas Comie (Fishpond Town)a citizen of the CREEK Nation. His allotment Deed Commission NO 20667 and Creek Roll NO 6570.
Name of Mother: Martha Comie   a citizen of the CREEK Nation.
(Tookpafka Town)
                     Postoffice Okemah, Creek Nation, IND. TERR.

AFFIDAVIT OF MOTHER.

UNITED STATES OF AMERICA, Indian Territory,
    Western Judicial   DISTRICT.   Creek Indian roll no. 6473

     I, Martha Comie, on oath state that I am 23 years of age and a citizen by Blood, of the Creek Nation; that I am the lawful wife of Thomas Comie, who is a citizen, by Blood of the Creek Nation; that a Female child was born to me on 28th day of July, 1901, that said child has been named Larley Comie, and was living March 4, 1905.

                             Martha Comie

Witnesses To Mark:

Subscribed and sworn to before me this 7th day of November, 1905.

                             Geo A Harvison
                             Notary Public.

Applications for Enrollment of Creek Newborn
Act of 1905   Volume XII

AFFIDAVIT OF ATTENDING PHYSICIAN OR MID-WIFE.

UNITED STATES OF AMERICA, Indian Territory,
   Western Judicial   DISTRICT.

                                                                                        are personally acquainted
We, the undersigned , a , on oath state that We ~~attended on Mrs~~. with Martha Comie, wife of Thomas Comie on or about the 28th day of July , 1901 ; that there was born to her on said date a female child; that said child was living March 4, 1905, and is said to have been named Larley Comie

                                        Aaron Grayson
                                            her
Witnesses To Mark: Silby x Harjo
  { M.C. Jones   mark
  { Geo. A. Harvison

Subscribed and sworn to before me this 7 day of November, 1905.

                                        Geo A Harvison
                                          Notary Public.

N.C. 926

                            Muskogee, Indian Territory, October 20, 1905.

Martha Harjo,
      Care Alex Harjo,
            Okemah, Indian Territory.

Dear Madam:

      In the matter of the application for the enrollment of Larley Cummings, born July 28, 1902, as a citizen by blood of the Creek Nation, it will be necessary for you to furnish this office with the affidavits of two disinterested witnesses relative to her birth. Said affidavits must set forth said child's name, the date of her birth, the names of her parents and whether or not she was living on March 4, 1905.

      You state in your affidavit executed April 26, 1905, relative to the birth of said Larley Cummings, that you are the lawful wife of Thomas Cummings; it therefore necessarily follows that your name is Martha Cummings and not Martha Harjo.

      There is herewith enclosed blank form of birth affidavit which has been properly filled out; if it correctly states the facts, you are requested to have same executed before a notary public and re it to this office in the enclosed envelope.

      This office is unable to identify your husband, Thomas Cummings, on the final roll of citizens by blood of the Creek Nation; you are requested to state the names of his

Applications for Enrollment of Creek Newborn
Act of 1905   Volume XII

parents, the Creek Indian town to which he belongs and the numbers which appear on his deeds and allotment certificate.

Respectfully,
Commissioner.

N.C. 926

Muskogee, Indian Territory, October 30, 1905.

Martha Harjo,
    Care Alex Harjo,
        Okemah, Indian Territory.

Dear Madam:

    There is herewith enclosed a form of birth affidavit which has been properly filled out; if the same correctly states the facts in the matter of the application for the enrollment of your minor child, Larley Cummings, born July 28, 1901, as a citizen by blood of the Creek Nation, you are requested to have same executed in accordance with instructions contained in the letter of this office of October 20, 1905, from which this affidavit was omitted.

Respectfully,
Commissioner.

AG-5

DEPARTMENT OF THE INTERIOR,
COMMISSION TO THE FIVE CIVILIZED TRIBES.
April 29, 1905, Sapulpa, I.T.

Beaver (?)

    In the matter of the application for the enrollment of _____ Brown, _____ Brown, Wisey Long, Suka Long, Martha Conner and Mary Pinehill, as citizens by blood of the Creek Nation.

    Ben W. Wadsworth, being duly sworn, testified as follows by E.C. Griesel, a Notary Public, testified as follows:

By Commission:

Q What is your name? A Ben W. Wadsworth.
Q What is your age? A 34.

Applications for Enrollment of Creek Newborn
Act of 1905 Volume XII

Q What is your post office? A Bristow.
Q To what town do you belong? A Hickory Ground.
Q You are employed by the Commission under special instructions to secure data relative to children born subsequent to May 25, 1901, and prior to March 4, 1905, and living on said latter date, to citizens of the Creek tribe of Indians whose enrollment has been approved by the Secretary of the Interior prior to the date of the approval of said act, were you? A Yes.
Q You wish to make application for the enrollment of six children the parents of whom are commonly known as Snake Indians? A Yes.
Q How did you obtain this information? A You better take them up one at a time and then I can explain what I had to do in each case.

Mr. Wadsworth here presents a memorandum upon which appear the names of the children, the names of the parents, the probable age etc., upon which the applications were made.

By Commission:
Q The first one you have here is _____ Brown; who are the parents of this _____ Brown? A Jim and Loda Brown.
Q Are they both living? A Yes
Q To what town do they belong? A Euchee.
Q How old is this child whose first name is unknown to you? A About two years old.
Q You saw the child, did you? A Yes sir.
Q Did you converse with the parents.[sic] A I tried to but they refused to talk to me.
Q Did they understand the purpose of your visit? A Yes, I suppose they did, for I told them I wanted to enroll their children for them.
Q Did they give you the information you wished? A No sir.
Q How did you get this information? A I got the information from Lewis and Henry Long, brothers-in-law of Jim Brown, they are neighbors of Jim Brown.
Q The neighbors could not give you the names of the children? A Well they knew but they would not give them to me, they said the father ought to give them to me.
Q When did you see this child? A Day before yesterday.
Q Did these parents have another child? A Yes.
Q How old was that child? A About a year old.
Q You saw the child at the same time? A Yes sir. I was able to see them for a little while only, for the mother took them and ran to the woods with them. Shortly afterwards the father left me too, with the remark that he had to work on a house.

Q Who are the parents of Suka Long? A Lewis and Nancy Long.
Q Are they citizens of the Creek Nation? A Yes.
Q Are they living? A Yes sir.
Q Is this child Suka living? A Yes, sir.
Q How old is this child? A It was born April 22, 1903.
Q How did you get the exact date? A I got it from the father.
Q Who gave you the information? A I worried with the father two hours trying to explain the matter and that the child ought to get the allotment and that an application must be made before May the 1st, 1905, and he finally submitted and gave it to me.

Applications for Enrollment of Creek Newborn
Act of 1905 Volume XII

Q You saw the child yourself, did you? A Yes sir.

Q Who are the parents of Wisey Beaver? A Wattie and Nancy Beaver.
Q Are they living? A Yes sir.
Q They are citizens of the Creek Nation, are they? A Yes sir.
Q When was this child born? A The child is about two years old.
Q You saw the child? A Yes.
Q How did you get your information? A They would not give me the necessary information.
Q How did you get it? A I got it from one Tom Tiger. He did not know the age of the child but he gave me its name, and the name of the father and mother, but he guessed it was about two years old.
Q You saw the child, did you? A Yes sir.

Q Who are the parents of Martha Conner? A George and Jeannetta Conner.
Q Are they living? A Yes sir.
Q Are they citizens of the Creek Nation? A Yes sir.
Q Did you see this child, Martha Conner? A Yes.
Q When was it born? A They said it was about 30 months old, that was all the information I got. They gave me some information but not sufficient; I got the rest from Hattie Grayson, Indian Territory a neighbor.

Q Who are the parents of Mary Pinehill? A Lasley and Sallie Pinehill
Q Both are living are they? And are citizens of the Creek Nation? A Yes sir.
Q Did you see the child Mary? A Yes sir.
Q About how old is that child? A I would judge it to be about eight months old.
Q Did you have any difficulty in getting the information? A I worried with them about two hours, they would not give me any information at all, but Hattie Grayson, Indian Territory a neighbor gave me the information.

Q These people are all Snakes are they? A Yes sir.
Q You saw these children and got all the information you have furnished us, last week? A Yes sir.
Q Now Mr. Wadsworth, have you any statements to make to the Commission relative to the enrollment of these children? A Yes sir; Their reason was that that[sic] there would be plenty of time to enroll their children, and they would not be in any hurry at all; that the land belongs to the Creek people and the government could not beat them out of it; as far as the government has already went ahead and enrolled and allotted us Indians without our consent we just let the government finished[sic] them up. That we would not help them finish the matter as the government had gone ahead so far and whatever the end may be we will live and die on it. They claim that as the government has enrolled and allotted them without their consent and now we let the government go ahead and take care of the children; they won't help in any way. Are just sitting back and refuse to give the government any help.
Q You explained the intent and purpose of the Act under which we are now acting, did you? A Yes.
Q You were out among them all week, were you? A Oh yes.

Applications for Enrollment of Creek Newborn
Act of 1905 Volume XII

E.C. Griesel, being duly sworn, on his oath, states that the above and foregoing is a true and correct transcript of his stenographic notes as taken in said cause on said date.

Edw C Griesel

Subscribed and sworn to before me this 5 day of May, 1905.

Drennan C Skaggs
Notary Public.

BIRTH AFFIDAVIT.

DEPARTMENT OF THE INTERIOR,
COMMISSIONER TO THE FIVE CIVILIZED TRIBES.

ENROLLMENT OF MINORS. ACT OF CONGRESS, APPROVED APRIL 26, 1906.

IN RE APPLICATION FOR ENROLLMENT, as a citizen of the Creek Nation, of Sa-ke Long, born on the 21 day of April, 1903

Name of Father: Lewis Long (Roll No. 8109)   a citizen of the   Creek   Nation.
Name of Mother: Lannie Long (Roll No. 8110)   a citizen of the   Creek   Nation.

Tribal enrollment of father   Euche   Tribal enrollment of mother   Euche

Postoffice   Newby, Indian Territory

AFFIDAVIT OF MOTHER.

UNITED STATES OF AMERICA, Indian Territory,
    Western   District.   Child present

I, Lannie Long, on oath state that I am about 31 years of age and a citizen by blood, of the Creek Nation; that I am the lawful wife of Lewis Long, who is a citizen, by blood of the Creek Nation; that a female child was born to me on 21 day of April, 1903, that said child has been named Sa-ke Long, and was living March 4, 1906.

her
Lannie x Long
mark

WITNESSES TO MARK:
   Alex Posey
   DC Skaggs

Subscribed and sworn to before me this 22 day of June, 1906.

Alex Posey
Notary Public.

Applications for Enrollment of Creek Newborn
Act of 1905   Volume XII

AFFIDAVIT OF ATTENDING PHYSICIAN OR MID-WIFE.

UNITED STATES OF AMERICA, Indian Territory, } Western District.

I, Co-ah , a midwife , on oath state that I attended on Lannie Long   , wife of Lewis Long on the   21 day of April , 1903 ; that there was born to her on said date a female   child; that said child was living March 4, 1906, and is said to have been named Sa-ke Long

                                               her
                                          Co-ah x
WITNESSES TO MARK: mark
{ Alex Posey
  D C Skaggs

Subscribed and sworn to before me this 22   day of   June , 1906.

                                       Alex Posey
                                             Notary Public.

BIRTH AFFIDAVIT.
(Snake)   **DEPARTMENT OF THE INTERIOR.**
                      COMMISSION TO THE FIVE CIVILIZED TRIBES.

    (Snake)
IN RE APPLICATION FOR ENROLLMENT, as a citizen of the Creek Nation, of Suka Long, born on the 21 day of April , 1903

Name of Father: Louis Long (37)   a citizen of the   Creek   Nation.
(Euchee)
Name of Mother: Nancy "   (30)   a citizen of the   "   Nation.
(Euchee)
                               Postoffice   Bristow

                      AFFIDAVIT OF ~~MOTHER~~.   Acquaintance

UNITED STATES OF AMERICA, Indian Territory, } Western DISTRICT.

I, Ben W. Wadsworth , on oath state that I am 34 years of age and a citizen by blood , of the Creek   Nation; that I am ~~the lawful wife of~~ acquaintance of Louis and Nancy Long , who ~~is a~~ are citizens, by blood of the Creek   Nation; that a female child was born to ~~me~~ them on 21 day of April , 1903 , that said child has been named Suka Long, and was living March 4, 1905.
                                         BW Wadsworth

Applications for Enrollment of Creek Newborn
Act of 1905   Volume XII

Witnesses To Mark:

{

    Subscribed and sworn to before me this 29 day of April , 1905.

(Seal)   Edw C Griesel
                                                                Notary Public.

                                                                                                 HGH

REFER IN REPLY TO THE FOLLOWING:	**DEPARTMENT OF THE INTERIOR,**
N.C. 927	**COMMISSIONER TO THE FIVE CIVILIZED TRIBES.**

                                  Muskogee, Indian Territory, October 20, 1905.

Nancy Long,
       Care Lewis Long,
              Bristow, Indian Territory.

Dear Madam:

    In the matter of the application for the enrollment of your minor child, Suka Long, said to have been born April 21, 1903, as a citizen by blood of the Creek Nation, this office desires your affidavit and affidavit of the midwife or physician in attendance at the birth of said child and a blank for that purpose is enclosed herewith.

    In the event that there was no physician or midwife in attendance when said child was born, it will be necessary for you to furnish this office with the affidavits of two disinterested witnesses relative to her birth. Said affidavits must set forth the name of said child, the date of her birth, the names of her parents and whether or not she was living on March 4, 1905.

    This office is unable to identify you on its final roll of citizens by blood of the Creek Nation; you are requested to state the names of your parents, the Creek Indian town to which you belong, your maiden name and whether you were ever know by the name Lannie Long; also the numbers which appear on your deeds to lands in the Creek Nation.

    This matter should receive your immediate attention.

                                  Respectfully,
                                               Tams Bixby
                                                         Commissioner.

B A
Env.

Applications for Enrollment of Creek Newborn
Act of 1905   Volume XII

HGH

REFER IN REPLY TO THE FOLLOWING:
———————————

DEPARTMENT OF THE INTERIOR,
COMMISSIONER TO THE FIVE CIVILIZED TRIBES.

Muskogee, Indian Territory, October 24, 1906.

Nancy Long,
   c/o Lewis Long,
      Bristow, Indian Territory.

Dear Madam:

    You are hereby advised that the name of your minor child, Suke Long, is contained in the partial list of citizens by blood of the Creek Nation, approved by the Secretary of the Interior October 15, 1906, and that a selection of land in the Creek Nation may now be made for said child at the Creek Land Office in Muskogee, Indian Territory.

    This matter should receive your prompt attention.

                    Respectfully,

                              Tams Bixby
                                  Commissioner.

BIRTH AFFIDAVIT.

DEPARTMENT OF THE INTERIOR.
COMMISSION TO THE FIVE CIVILIZED TRIBES.

    IN RE APPLICATION FOR ENROLLMENT, as a citizen of the Creek Nation, of Sagie Bucktrot , born on the ----- day of March, 1903

Name of Father: Con-char-char Bucktrot (dec)   a citizen of the   Creek   Nation. Euchee
Name of Mother: Mattie Bucktrot   a citizen of the   Creek   Nation. (Euchee)

                  Postoffice   Kellyville

Applications for Enrollment of Creek Newborn
Act of 1905   Volume XII

AFFIDAVIT OF MOTHER.   Child <u>Present</u>

UNITED STATES OF AMERICA, Indian Territory, ⎱
   Western   DISTRICT.   ⎰

     I, Mattie Bucktrot, on oath state that I am 30 (?) years of age and a citizen by blood, of the Creek Nation; that I am the lawful wife of Con-char-char Bucktrot, (dec), who is a citizen, by blood of the Creek Nation; that a female child was born to me on ----- day of March, 1903, that said child has been named Sagie Bucktrot, and was living March 4, 1905.

Her
Mattie x Bucktrot
mark

Witnesses To Mark:
  ⎰ Davis Shelby
  ⎱ Jesse McDermott

    Subscribed and sworn to before me this 1 day of May, 1905.

(Seal)   Edw C Griesel
Notary Public.

AFFIDAVIT OF ATTENDING PHYSICIAN OR MID-WIFE.

UNITED STATES OF AMERICA, Indian Territory, ⎱
   Western   DISTRICT.   ⎰

     I, Nannie Littlehead, a Midwife, on oath state that I attended on Mrs. Mattie Bucktrot, wife of Con-char-char Bucktrot on the ----- day of Mar, 1903; that there was born to her on said date a female child; that said child was living March 4, 1905, and is said to have been named Sagie Bucktrot

Her
Nannie x Littlehead
mark

Witnesses To Mark:
  ⎰ Davis Shelby
  ⎱ Jesse McDermott

    Subscribed and sworn to before me this 1 day of May, 1905.

(Seal)   Edw C Griesel
Notary Public.

Applications for Enrollment of Creek Newborn
Act of 1905 Volume XII

N.C. 931

DEPARTMENT OF THE INTERIOR,
COMMISSIONER TO THE FIVE CIVILIZED TRIBES.
Tulsa, Indian Territory, September 1, 1906.

In the matter of the application for the enrollment of Jay and William Sullivan as citizens by blood of the Creek Nation.

MAMIE SULLIVAN, being duly sworn, testified as follows:
BY COMMISSIONER:

Q What is your name? A Mamie Sullivan.
Q What is your age? A Twenty five.
Q What is your postoffice address? A No. 1014 East 12th Street, Kansas City, Mo.
Q Are you a citizen of the Creek Nation? A Yes sir.
Q Have you selected your allotment of land? A Yes sir.
Q Have you the deed to your allotment? A Yes sir.

The witness presents allotment deed issued to Mamie Perryman Creek Roll No. 2828.

Q Have you two children for whom you made application for enrollment in the Creek Nation? A Yes sir.
Q What are their names? A Jay and William.
Q Which one is the older? A Jay.
Q When was he born? A July 19th 1901.
Q Is he living? A Yes sir.
Q When was William born? A August 31st 1904.
Q Who is the father of these children? A P. P. Sullivan.
Q Is he a Creek citizen? A No sir.

There are two affidavits on file at the office of the Commissioner to the Five Civilized Tribes executed by you on April 27, 1905, stating that the names of these children are Jay and William Frick and that their father is J.L. Frick.

Q Do you recollect signing such affidavits? A Yes sir.
Q Did the father of these children have two names? A Yes sir.
Q Were you lawfully married to the father of these children when they were born? A Yes sir.
Q To whom were the marriage license issued by which you married the father of these children? A To P. P. Sullivan.
Q Well, why did you state that J.L. Frick was their father in your original affidavits?
A Because that was his right name. P.P. Sullivan is only an adopted name that he had when we were married.
Q What was his reason for adopting that name? A He told me that an Insurance Company in Chicago had him employed as an agent and that that Company got into a mixup some way and got him to change his name to P. P. Sullivan.

Applications for Enrollment of Creek Newborn
Act of 1905 Volume XII

Q Do you know that to be a fact? A Yes sir, that very same Company use to send him money first of every month when we lived in Little Rock.
Q Can you produce, the marriage license and certificate between you and P. P. Sullivan? A Yes, but I would have to send to Little Rock for them.
Q Will you make an effort to get the license and sent them to the Commissioner to be considered in this matter. A Yes sir.
Q Where were you living when these children were born? A In Little Rock, Arkansas.
Q Are you living with your husband now? A No sir, we have been separated nearly two years, will be two years next October.
Q Do you know the postoffice address of your husband? A He is in New York.
Q In New York City or New York state? A In New York state.
Q Can you furnish the Commissioner the names and addresses of the physicians who attended on you when these children were born? A Yes sir, Dr Flynn of Little Rock, Arkansas attended on me when Jay was born. Dr Lowery of Luxora, Arkansas attende[sic] on me when William was born.
Q Both of these children are living are they? A Yes sir.

I, Jesse McDermott, on oath state that the above and foregoing is a full and true transcript of my notes as taken in said cause on said date.

Jesse McDermott

Subscribed and sworn to before me this 5th day of November, 1906.

My com. expires Dec 12-1906

MZ Flesher
Notary Public.

B. W. FLINN, M. D.
OFFICE.
120 MAIN STREET.

NC 931

L<small>TTLE</small>[sic] R<small>OCK</small> A<small>RK</small>. March 4<u>th</u>   190 5

To Whom it May Concern

This is to certify that I attended Mrs. Mayme Perryman Frick - Wife of J.L. Frick in confinement, at 1611 East 4<u>th</u> St. Little Rock, Ark, July 19<u>th</u> 1902 a male child was born (Jay Frick).

B. W. Flinn M.D.

Applications for Enrollment of Creek Newborn
Act of 1905   Volume XII

REFER IN REPLY TO THE FOLLOWING:

N.C. 931

DEPARTMENT OF THE INTERIOR,
COMMISSIONER TO THE FIVE CIVILIZED TRIBES.

Bristow, Indian Territory, September 6, 1906.

Commissioner to the Five Civilized Tribes,
    Muskogee, Indian Territory.

Dear Sir:

    There are herewith enclosed two affidavits executed by Mamie Sullivan (nee Perryman) in the matter of the application for the enrollment of her two minor children Jay and William Sullivan as citizens by blood of the creek[sic] nation[sic]. Her original application show the names of the children Jay and William Frick. I took testimony from her relative to the change of names and she fully explains the cause.

    She also states in her testimony that her marriage license and certificate are in Little Rock, Arkansas and that she would get them and sent them to you.

                  Respectfully,
                               Jesse McDermott
                               Clerk in Charge

N.C. 931.   F.H.W.

DEPARTMENT OF THE INTERIOR,
COMMISSIONER TO THE FIVE CIVILIZED TRIBES.

    In the matter of the application for the enrollment of Jay Frick and William Frick as citizens by blood of the Creek Nation.

DECISION.

    The record in this case shows that an application was filed, in affidavit form, on May 10, 1905, for the enrollment of Jay and William Frick as citizens by blood of the Creek Nation. Further proceedings were had before a Creek enrollment field party at Tulsa, Indian Territory, on September 1, 1906. Supplemental affidavits as to the birth of the said applicants filed May 10, 1905, and September 6, 1906, are attached to and made a part of the record herein.

    The evidence show that on the supplemental affidavits filed September 6, 1906, the surname of the parents and that of the applicants appears as Sullivan but it being clearly shown in evidence that "Frick" is the correct name of the father, reference to the applicants is herein made under the surname Frick.

    The evidence further shows that Jay and William Frick are the children of J. L. Frick, a non citizen, and Mayme (Mamie) Frick, who is identified as Mamie Perryman on

Applications for Enrollment of Creek Newborn
Act of 1905   Volume XII

a partial schedule of citizens by blood of the Creek Nation, approved by the Secretary of the Interior March 13, 1902, opposite roll No. 2628."

It is further established in evidence that the said Jay Frick was born July 19, 1902, that the said William Frick was born August 31, 1904, and that both were living March 4, 1905.

The Act of Congress approved March 3, 1905, (33 Stats. 1048) provides in part as follows:

"That the Commission to the Five Civilized Tribes is authorized for sixty days after the date of the approval of this act to receive and consider applications for enrollments of children born subsequent to May twenty five, nineteen hundred and one, and prior to March fourth, nineteen hundred and five, and living on said latter date, to citizens of the Creek tribe of Indians whose enrollment has been approved by the Secretary of the Interior prior to the date of the approval of this Act; and to enroll and make allotments to such children."

It is therefore, ordered and adjudged that said Jay Frick and William Frick are entitled to be enrolled as citizens by blood of the Creek Nation, in accordance with the provisions of law above quoted, and the application for their enrollment as such is accordingly granted.

Tams Bixby COMMISSIONER.

Muskogee, Indian Territory.
JAN 18 1907

BIRTH AFFIDAVIT.

DEPARTMENT OF THE INTERIOR,
COMMISSIONER TO THE FIVE CIVILIZED TRIBES.

IN RE APPLICATION FOR ENROLLMENT, as a citizen of the Creek Nation, of William Frick, born on the 31" day of August, 1904

Name of Father: J. L. Frick   a citizen of the   U.S.   Nation.
Name of Mother: Mayme Frick   a citizen of the   Creek   Nation.

Postoffice   Tulsa Ind. Ter

AFFIDAVIT OF MOTHER.

UNITED STATES OF AMERICA, Indian Territory, }
Western Judicial   District.

I, Mayme Frick, on oath state that I am 24 years of age and a citizen by Blood, of the Creek Nation; that I am the lawful wife of J. L. Frick, who is a citizen, by Blood of the U. S. Nation; that a Male child was born to me on 31" day of August, 1904, that said child has been named William Frick, and was living March 4, 1905.

Applications for Enrollment of Creek Newborn
Act of 1905 Volume XII

Mayme Frick

Witness to Mark:

}

Subscribed and sworn to before me this   27 day of   April , 1905.

Com Ex 7/3/1906   Robert E. Lynch
                                                              Notary Public.

AFFIDAVIT OF ATTENDING PHYSICIAN OR MID-WIFE.

UNITED STATES OF AMERICA, ~~Indian Territory,~~
State of Ark. Cn of Miss   ~~District.~~ }

I, Sydney A Lowry M.D. , a physician of Luxora Ark   , on oath state that I attended on Mrs. J. L. Frick , wife of J. L. Frick at Luxora Ark on the 31st day of August , 1904 ; that there was born to her on said date a   male   child; that said child was living March 4, 1905, and is said to have been named   William Frick

                                            Sydney A Lowry Phy. M.D.
Witness to Mark:
    RB Sanders   }
    Wm Wood

Subscribed and sworn to before me this   25 day of   April , 1905.

                                            J M. Landman
                                                              Notary Public.
MY COMMISSION EXPIRES
SEPT. 20, 1905.

BIRTH AFFIDAVIT.
DEPARTMENT OF THE INTERIOR.
COMMISSION TO THE FIVE CIVILIZED TRIBES.

IN RE APPLICATION FOR ENROLLMENT, as a citizen of the Creek Nation, of   William Sullivan, born on the 31" day of August, 1904

Name of Father: P. P. Sullivan   a citizen of the   U S   Nation.
Name of Mother: Mamie Sullivan   a citizen of the   Creek   Nation.
    Roll #2628
                              Postoffice   Kansas City, Mo.

Applications for Enrollment of Creek Newborn
Act of 1905   Volume XII

AFFIDAVIT OF MOTHER.

UNITED STATES OF AMERICA, Indian Territory,
　Western　　　　　　DISTRICT.

　　I, Mamie Sullivan (nee Perryman) , on oath state that I am 25 years of age and a citizen by blood , of the Creek Nation; that I am the lawful wife of P. P. Sullivan , who is a citizen, by ----- of the U.S. Nation; that a male child was born to me on 31" day of August , 1904 , that said child has been named William Sullivan , and was living March 4, 1905.

　　　　　　　　　　　　　　　　Mamie Sullivan

Witnesses To Mark:
{

　　Subscribed and sworn to before me this 4th day of Sept. , 1906.

My Commission　　　　　　　　　J McDermott
Expires July 25" 1907　　　　　　　Notary Public.

BIRTH AFFIDAVIT.

DEPARTMENT OF THE INTERIOR,
COMMISSIONER TO THE FIVE CIVILIZED TRIBES.

　　IN RE APPLICATION FOR ENROLLMENT, as a citizen of the Creek Nation, of Jay Frick , born on the 19" day of July , 1902

Name of Father: J. L. Frick　　　　a citizen of the　U.S.　　Nation.
Name of Mother: Mayme Frick　　　a citizen of the　Creek　Nation.

　　　　　　　Postoffice　　Tulsa I.T.

AFFIDAVIT OF MOTHER.

UNITED STATES OF AMERICA, Indian Territory,
　Western Judicial　　　　District.

　　I, Mayme Frick , on oath state that I am 24 years of age and a citizen by Blood , of the Creek Nation; that I am the lawful wife of J. L. Frick , who is a citizen, by Blood of the U. S. Nation; that a Male child was born to me on 19 day of July , 1902 , that said child has been named Jay Frick, and was living March 4, 1905.

　　　　　　　　　　　　　　　　Mayme Frick

Witness to Mark:
}

Applications for Enrollment of Creek Newborn
Act of 1905   Volume XII

Subscribed and sworn to before me this   27 day of April , 1905.

Com Ex 7/3/1906   Robert E. Lynch
                                    Notary Public.

AFFIDAVIT OF ATTENDING PHYSICIAN OR MID-WIFE.

UNITED STATES OF AMERICA, Indian Territory,
Western Judicial   District.

I, B. W. Flynn , a Physician , on oath state that I attended on Mrs. Mayme Frick , wife of J. L. Frick   on the   19" day of July , 1902 ; that there was born to her on said date a   Male   child; that said child was living March 4, 1905, and is said to have been named   Jay Frick

                                    B. W. Flinn, M.D.
Witness to Mark:

Subscribed and sworn to before me this First   day of   May , 1905.

                        J.F. Riegle
                                    Notary Public.

My Commission expires July 19, 1905

BIRTH AFFIDAVIT.

                    Copy

DEPARTMENT OF THE INTERIOR.
COMMISSION TO THE FIVE CIVILIZED TRIBES.

IN RE APPLICATION FOR ENROLLMENT, as a citizen of the Creek Nation, of Jay Frick, born on the 19th day of July, 1902

Name of Father: JL Frick	a citizen of the U.S.	Nation.
Name of Mother: Mayme Frick	a citizen of the Creek	Nation.

                Postoffice   *(blank)*

AFFIDAVIT OF MOTHER.

UNITED STATES OF AMERICA, Indian Territory,
Western Judicial   DISTRICT.

I,   Mayme Frick , on oath state that I am   24   years of age and a citizen by Blood, of the Creek   Nation; that I am the lawful wife of   J. F. Frick , who is a citizen,

Applications for Enrollment of Creek Newborn
Act of 1905   Volume XII

by Blood of the U.S. Nation; that a male child was born to me on 19 day of July, 1902, that said child has been named Jay Frick, and was living March 4, 1905.

                                        Mayme Frick

Witnesses To Mark:
{

    Subscribed and sworn to before me this 2" day of May, 1905.

Com Ex 7/3/906   Robert E. Lynch
                                            Notary Public.

BIRTH AFFIDAVIT.
DEPARTMENT OF THE INTERIOR.
COMMISSION TO THE FIVE CIVILIZED TRIBES.

IN RE APPLICATION FOR ENROLLMENT, as a citizen of the Creek Nation, of Jay Frick, born on the 19 day of July, 1902

Name of Father: J.L. Frick   a citizen of the   U.S.   Nation.
Name of Mother: Mayme Frick   a citizen of the   Creek   Nation.

                            Postoffice   Tulsa IT

AFFIDAVIT OF MOTHER.

UNITED STATES OF AMERICA, Indian Territory,
    Wtn Judicial   DISTRICT.

    I, Mayme Frick, on oath state that I am 24 years of age and a citizen by Blood, of the Creek Nation; that I am the lawful wife of J.L. Frick, who is a citizen, by Blood of the U.S. Nation; that a male child was born to me on 19 day of July, 1902, that said child has been named Jay Frick, and was living March 4, 1905.

                                        Mayme Frick

Witnesses To Mark:
{

    Subscribed and sworn to before me this 27" day of April, 1905.

Com 7/3/06   Robert E. Lynch
                                              Notary Public.

Applications for Enrollment of Creek Newborn
Act of 1905   Volume XII

AFFIDAVIT OF ATTENDING PHYSICIAN OR MID-WIFE.

UNITED STATES OF AMERICA, Indian Territory,
Western Judicial   DISTRICT.

I, B. W. Flynn, a Physician, on oath state that I attended on Mrs. Mamie Frick, wife of J.L. Frick on the 19 day of July, 1902; that there was born to her on said date a male child; that said child was living March 4, 1905, and is said to have been named Jay Frick

B. W. Flynn M.D.

Witnesses To Mark:
{

Subscribed and sworn to before me 1st day of May, 1905.

My Com Ex July 19-05   J.F. Riegle
                                                    Notary Public.

BIRTH AFFIDAVIT.

DEPARTMENT OF THE INTERIOR.
COMMISSION TO THE FIVE CIVILIZED TRIBES.

IN RE APPLICATION FOR ENROLLMENT, as a citizen of the Creek Nation, of William Frick, born on the 31" day of August, 1904

Name of Father: J.L. Frick   a citizen of the   U.S.   Nation.
Name of Mother: Mayme Frick   a citizen of the Creek NationNation.

Postoffice   Tulsa Ind. Ter.

AFFIDAVIT OF MOTHER.

UNITED STATES OF AMERICA, Indian Territory,
Western Judicial   DISTRICT.

I, Mayme Frick, on oath state that I am 24 years of age and a citizen by blood, of the Creek Nation; that I am the lawful wife of J.L. Frick, who is a citizen, by blood of the U.S. Nation; that a male child was born to me on 31" day of August, 1904, that said child has been named William Frick, and was living March 4, 1905.

Mayme Frick

Witnesses To Mark:
{

Applications for Enrollment of Creek Newborn
Act of 1905   Volume XII

Subscribed and sworn to before me this 27" day of April , 1905.

Com Ex 7/3/06   Robert E Lynch
                              Notary Public.

AFFIDAVIT OF ATTENDING PHYSICIAN OR MID-WIFE.

UNITED STATES OF AMERICA, Indian Territory,
State of Ark. Co of Miss.   DISTRICT.

   I, Sydney A Lowry M.D. , a physician at Luxora Ark , on oath state that I attended on Mrs. J.L. Frick , wife of J.L. Frick at Luxora Ark   on the 31st day of August , 1904 ; that there was born to her on said date a male child; that said child was living March 4, 1905, and is said to have been named William Frick

                              Sydney A. Lowry - Phy. M.D.

Witnesses To Mark:
 RB Sanders
 Wm Wood

   Subscribed and sworn to before me 25" day of April, 1905.

My Com   J.M. Landman
Ex Sept 25 1905   Notary Public.

BIRTH AFFIDAVIT.
DEPARTMENT OF THE INTERIOR,
COMMISSIONER TO THE FIVE CIVILIZED TRIBES.

   IN RE APPLICATION FOR ENROLLMENT, as a citizen of the Creek Nation, of Jay Frick , born on the 19 day of July , 1902

Name of Father: J. L. Frick   a citizen of the   U.S.   Nation.
Name of Mother: Mayme Frick   a citizen of the   Creek   Nation.

                Postoffice   *(blank)*

                AFFIDAVIT OF MOTHER.

UNITED STATES OF AMERICA, Indian Territory,
   Western Judicial   District.

   I, Mayme Frick , on oath state that I am 24 years of age and a citizen by Blood , of the Creek   Nation; that I am the lawful wife of J. L. Frick   , who is a citizen, by

Applications for Enrollment of Creek Newborn
Act of 1905 Volume XII

Blood of the U. S. Nation; that a Male child was born to me on 19" day of July, 1902, that said child has been named Jay Frick, and was living March 4, 1905.

Mayme Frick

Witness to Mark:

}

Subscribed and sworn to before me this 2" day of May, 1905.

Com Ex 7/3/1906　　　　　　　　　　Robert E. Lynch
Notary Public.

N C 931.

Muskogee, Indian Territory, March 7, 1907.

Mamie Frick (or Mamie Perryman),
　　　Tulsa, Indian Territory.

Dear Madam:

　　You are advised that on March 2, 1907 the Secretary of the Interior approved the enrollment of your minor children, Jay Frick and William Frick, as citizens by blood of the Creek Nation, and that the names of said children appear upon the roll of new born citizens by blood of the Creek Nation enrolled under the Act of Congress approved March 3, 1905, as numbers 1237 and 1238, respectively.

　　These children are now entitled to allotments and application therefor should be made without delay at the Creek Land Office, Muskogee, Indian Territory.

Respectfully,
Commissioner.

Muskogee, Indian Territory, May 29, 1905.

Mamie Frick,
　　　Tulsa, Indian Territory.

Dear Madam:

　　The Commission is in receipt of your letter of May 22, in which you ask if your children Jay and Willie Frick are enrolled.

　　In reply you are advised that it on May 10, 1905, an affidavit relative to the birth of your new born child, Jay Frick was received.

Applications for Enrollment of Creek Newborn
Act of 1905   Volume XII

You are further advised that the rolls of the Creek Nation were closed September 1, 1904, by order of the Secretary of the Interior, and the Commission is now without authority to receive applications for enrollment as citizens of said Nation.

> Respectfully,
> Com
> Chairman.

NC 931.

> Little Rock, Ark. March 4th, 1905.

To whom it May Concern:

This is to certify that I attended on Mrs. Mayme Perryman Frick, wife of J.L. Frick, in confinement at 1611 East 4th St. Little Rock, Ark., July 19th, 1902, a make[sic] child was born (Jay Frick).

> B.W. Flinn, M.D.

> Tulsa, I.T. May 1st, 1905.

J Blair Shoenfelt,
  Muskogee.

Enclosed find 2 enrollment application for my children Jay and Willie Frick I attach to my blank a certificate from Dr Flynn and have sent a blank for him to sign on your regular form but it has not returned yet and when it does I will send to your office.

> Respt. Mayme Frick,
> Per R.E. Lynch.

NC 931.

> Muskogee, Indian Territory, October 20, 1905.

Mayme Frick,
  Care J.L. Frick,
    Tulsa, Indian Territory.

Dear Madam:

In the matter of the application for the enrollment of your minor children, Jay Frick, born July 19, 1902, and William Frick, born August 31, 1904, as citizens by blood of the Creek Nation; this office is unable to identify you on its final roll of citizens of said Nation, you are requested to state your maiden name, the names of your parents, the

Applications for Enrollment of Creek Newborn
Act of 1905   Volume XII

Creek Indian town to which you belong and the numbers on your deeds to lands in the Creek Nation.

Respectfully,

Commissioner.

N.C. 932   I.D.

DEPARTMENT OF THE INTERIOR,
COMMISSIONER TO THE FIVE CIVILIZED TRIBES.

In the matter of the application for the enrollment of Nellie Owen as a citizen by blood of the Creek Nation.

ORDER

The record in yes case shows that on May 4, 1905, there was filed with the Commission to the Five Civilized Tribes at Muskogee, Indian Territory, the application of Elva Owen for the enrollment of her minor child, Nellie Owen, as a citizen by blood of the Creek Nation blood of the Creek Nation. Further proceedings were had August 22, 1905.

The evidence shows that said Nellie Owen was born November 15, 1903, and that she was living March 4, 1905.

An examination of the records of this Office shows that no application was made for the enrollment of said Nellie wen prior to May 4, 1905.

The Act of Congress approved March 3, 1905, (Public No. 212) provides:

> "That the Commission to the Five Civilized Tribes is authorized for sixty days after the date of the approval of this act to receive and consider applications for enrollments of children born subsequent to May twenty five, nineteen hundred and one, and prior to March fourth, nineteen hundred and five, and living on said latter date, to citizens of the Creek tribe of Indians whose enrollment has been approved by the Secretary of the Interior prior to the date of the approval of this Act; and to enroll and make allotments to such children."

Applications for Enrollment of Creek Newborn
Act of 1905   Volume XII

It is, therefore, ordered that there is no authority of law for the enrollment of said Nellie Owen as a citizen by blood of the Creek Nation, and that the application for her enrollment as such shall be and the same is hereby dismissed.

Commissioner.

Muskogee, Indian Territory.

N.C. 932

Muskogee, Indian Territory, October 9, 1905.

Butts and Bliss,
    Attorney for Elva Owen,
        Muskogee, Indian Territory.

Gentlemen:

Receipt is acknowledged of your letter of September 30, 1905, transmitting affidavit of Elva Owen in the matter of the application for the enrollment of her minor child, Nellie Owen, as a citizen by blood of the Creek Nation.

You state that there is enclosed with your letter a brief in behalf of the child's enrollment.

You are advised that the brief referred to was not enclosed with your letter.

Respectfully,
Commissioner.

Applications for Enrollment of Creek Newborn
Act of 1905   Volume XII

DEPARTMENT OF THE INTERIOR,
COMMISSION TO THE FIVE CIVILIZED TRIBES.
April 29, 1905, Sapulpa, I.T.

In the matter of the application for the enrollment of _____ Brown, _____ Brown, Wisey Long, Suka Long, Martha Conner and Mary Pinehill, as citizens by blood of the Creek Nation.

Ben W. Wadsworth, being duly sworn, testified as follows by E.C. Griesel, a Notary Public, testified as follows:

By Commission:

Q What is your name? A Ben W. Wadsworth.
Q What is your age? A 34.
Q What is your post office? A Bristow.
Q To what town do you belong? A Hickory Ground.
Q You are employed by the Commission under special instructions to secure data relative to children born subsequent to May 25, 1901, and prior to March 4, 1905, and living on said latter date, to citizens of the Creek tribe of Indians whose enrollment has been approved by the Secretary of the Interior prior to the date of the approval of said act, were you? A Yes.
Q You wish to make application for the enrollment of six children the parents of whom are commonly known as Snake Indians? A Yes.
Q How did you obtain this information? A You better take them up one at a time and then I can explain what I had to do in each case.

Mr. Wadsworth here presents a memorandum upon which appear the names of the children, the names of the parents, the probable age etc., upon which the applications were made.

By Commission:
Q The first one you have here is _____ Brown; who are the parents of this _____ Brown? A Jim and Loda Brown.
Q Are they both living? A Yes
Q To what town do they belong? A Euchee.
Q How old is this child whose first name is unknown to you? A About two years old.
Q You saw the child, did you? A Yes sir.
Q Did you converse with the parents.[sic] A I tried to but they refused to talk to me.
Q Did they understand the purpose of your visit? A Yes, I suppose they did, for I told them I wanted to enroll their children for them.
Q Did they give you the information you wished? A No sir.
Q How did you get this information? A I got the information from Lewis and Henry Long, brothers-in-law of Jim Brown, they are neighbors of Jim Brown.
Q The neighbors could not give you the names of the children? A Well they knew but they would not give them to me, they said the father ought to give them to me.
Q When did you see this child? A Day before yesterday.

Applications for Enrollment of Creek Newborn
Act of 1905   Volume XII

Q Did these parents have another child? A Yes.
Q How old was that child? A About a year old.
Q You saw the child at the same time? A Yes sir. I was able to see them for a little while only, for the mother took them and ran to the woods with them. Shortly afterwards the father left me too, with the remark that he had to work on a house.

Q Who are the parents of Suka Long? A Lewis and Nancy Long.
Q Are they citizens of the Creek Nation? A Yes.
Q Are they living? A Yes sir.
Q Is this child Suka living? A Yes, sir.
Q How old is this child? A It was born April 22, 1903.
Q How did you get the exact date? A I got it from the father.
Q Who gave you the information? A I worried with the father two hours trying to explain the matter and that the child ought to get the allotment and that an application must be made before May the 1st, 1905, and he finally submitted and gave it to me.
Q You saw the child yourself, did you? A Yes sir.

Q Who are the parents of Wisey Beaver? A Wattie and Nancy Beaver.
Q Are they living? A Yes sir.
Q They are citizens of the Creek Nation, are they? A Yes sir.
Q When was this child born? A The child is about two years old.
Q You saw the child? A Yes.
Q How did you get your information? A They would not give me the necessary information.
Q How did you get it? A I got it from one Tom Tiger. He did not know the age of the child but he gave me its name, and the name of the father and mother, but he guessed it was about two years old.
Q You saw the child, did you? A Yes sir.

Q Who are the parents of Martha Conner? A George and Jeannetta Conner.
Q Are they living? A Yes sir.
Q Are they citizens of the Creek Nation? A Yes sir.
Q Did you see this child, Martha Conner? A Yes.
Q When was it born? A They said it was about 30 months old, that was all the information I got. They gave me some information but not sufficient; I got the rest from Hattie Grayson, Indian Territory a neighbor.

Q Who are the parents of Mary Pinehill? A Lasley and Sallie Pinehill
Q Both are living are they? And are citizens of the Creek Nation? A Yes sir.
Q Did you see the child Mary? A Yes sir.
Q About how old is that child? A I would judge it to be about eight months old.
Q Did you have any difficulty in getting the information? A I worried with them about two hours, they would not give me any information at all, but Hattie Grayson, Indian Territory a neighbor gave me the information.

Q These people are all Snakes are they? A Yes sir.

Applications for Enrollment of Creek Newborn
Act of 1905   Volume XII

Q You saw these children and got all the information you have furnished us, last week?
A Yes sir.
Q Now Mr. Wadsworth, have you any statements to make to the Commission relative to the enrollment of these children? A Yes sir; Their reason was that that[sic] there would be plenty of time to enroll their children, and they would not be in any hurry at all; that the land belongs to the Creek people and the government could not beat them out of it; as far as the government has already went ahead and enrolled and allotted us Indians without our consent we just let the government finished[sic] them up. That we would not help them finish the matter as the government had gone ahead so far and whatever the end may be we will live and die on it. They claim that as the government has enrolled and allotted them without their consent and now we let the government go ahead and take care of the children; they won't help in any way. Are just sitting back and refuse to give the government any help.
Q You explained the intent and purpose of the Act under which we are now acting, did you? A Yes.
Q You were out among them all week, were you? A Oh yes.

      E.C. Griesel, being duly sworn, on his oath, states that the above and foregoing is a true and correct transcript of his stenographic notes as taken in said cause on said date.

Edw C Griesel

Subscribed and sworn to before me this 5 day of May, 1905.

Drennan C Skaggs
Notary Public.

BIRTH AFFIDAVIT.

DEPARTMENT OF THE INTERIOR.
COMMISSION TO THE FIVE CIVILIZED TRIBES.

(Snake)

    IN RE APPLICATION FOR ENROLLMENT, as a citizen of the Creek Nation, of Martha Conner, born during the spring of , 1903

Name of Father: George Conner (Concharte)	a citizen of the	Creek	Nation.
Name of Mother: Jennetta " (Tookapacha)	a citizen of the	"	Nation.

Postoffice   Bristow

Applications for Enrollment of Creek Newborn
Act of 1905   Volume XII

AFFIDAVIT OF ~~MOTHER~~.   Acquaintance

UNITED STATES OF AMERICA, Indian Territory, ⎫
   Western   DISTRICT.   ⎬

    I, Ben W. Wadsworth , on oath state that I am 34 years of age and a citizen by blood , of the Creek Nation; that I am ~~the lawful wife~~ an acquaintance of George and Jennetta Conner , who ~~is a~~ are citizens, by blood of the Creek Nation; that a female child was born to ~~me on~~ them during the spring of , 1903 , that said child has been named Martha Conner , and was living March 4, 1905.

                              BW Wadsworth

Witnesses To Mark:
{

    Subscribed and sworn to before me this 29 day of April , 1905.

(Seal)   Edw C Griesel
                                  Notary Public.

BIRTH AFFIDAVIT.
Snake   DEPARTMENT OF THE INTERIOR.
                COMMISSION TO THE FIVE CIVILIZED TRIBES.

    IN RE APPLICATION FOR ENROLLMENT, as a citizen of the Creek Nation, of Martha Conner, born in the spring of , 1903

Name of Father: George Conner   a citizen of the   Creek   Nation.
(Concharte)
Name of Mother: Jennetta Conner   a citizen of the   Creek   Nation.
(Tookapacha)
                          Postoffice   Bristow

                               Acquaintances
                 AFFIDAVIT OF ~~MOTHER~~.

UNITED STATES OF AMERICA, Indian Territory, ⎫
   Western   DISTRICT.   ⎬
                                                          we are
    We , George Island and Callie Island , on oath state that ~~I am~~ 32 & 30 years of age respectively and a citizen by blood , of the Creek Nation; that ~~I am the lawful wife~~ we are acquaintances of Jennetta Conner & George Conner , who ~~is a~~ are citizens, by blood of the Creek Nation; that a female child was born to ~~me~~ them during the Spring of , 1903 , that said child has been named Martha Conner , and was living March 4, 1905.

Applications for Enrollment of Creek Newborn
Act of 1905   Volume XII

Witnesses To Mark:
{ David Shelby
  Jesse McDermott

His
George x Island
mark
Her
Callie x Island
mark

Subscribed and sworn to before me this 27 day of April, 1905.

(Seal)

Edw C Griesel
Notary Public.

(The above Birth Affidavit given again.)

N.C. 933   F.H.W.
DEPARTMENT OF THE INTERIOR,
COMMISSIONER TO THE FIVE CIVILIZED TRIBES.

In the matter of the application for the enrollment of Martha Biggs as a citizen by blood of the Creek Nation.

DECISION.

The record in this case shows that on April 29, 1905, Ben Wadsworth, employed by the Commission under special instructions, appeared before a Creek enrollment field party to make application for certain minor children whose parents were members of the Snake or disaffected faction of Creek Indians. In the said testimony occurs the name of Martha Conner. Inasmuch as the records of this office identify the father of said Martha Conner under the surname of Biggs, the said testimony is herein considered an original application for the enrollment of Martha Biggs as a citizen by blood of the Creek Nation in order that the rights of the applicant be protected. Supplemental affidavits as to the birth of the applicant filed May 2, 1905 are attached to and made a part of the record herein.

The evidence and the records in the possession of this office show that the said Martha Biggs is the child of George C. Biggs and Jeannetta Biggs, whose names appear on a partial schedule of citizens by blood of the Creek Nation, approved by the Secretary of the Interior November 14, 1902, opposite roll Nos. 9058 and 9059, respectively.

It further appears that the said Martha Biggs was born some time during the spring of 1903 and was living March 4, 1905.

The Act of Congress approved March 3, 1905, (33 Stats. 1048) provides in part as follows:

"That the Commission to the Five Civilized Tribes is authorized for sixty days after the date of the approval of this act to receive and consider applications for enrollment, of children, <u>born subsequent to May twenty-fifth, nineteen hundred and one, and prior to March fourth, nineteen hundred and five, and living on said</u>

Applications for Enrollment of Creek Newborn
Act of 1905   Volume XII

latter date, to citizens of the Creek tribe of Indians whose enrollment has been approved by the Secretary of the Interior prior to the approval of this act; and to enroll and make allotments to such children."

It is, therefore, ordered and adjudged that the said Martha Biggs is entitled to be enrolled as a citizen by blood of the Creek Nation, in accordance with the provisions of law above quoted, and the application for her enrollment as such is accordingly granted.

Tams Bixby   COMMISSIONER.

Muskogee, Indian Territory.
JAN 22 1907

REFER IN REPLY TO THE FOLLOWING:
N.C. 933

DEPARTMENT OF THE INTERIOR,
COMMISSIONER TO THE FIVE CIVILIZED TRIBES.

Bristow, Indian Territory, September 12, 1906.

Commissioner to the Five Civilized Tribes,
Muskogee, Indian Territory

Dear Sir:

I have the honor to report that the parents of Martha Conner refuse to furnish any proof in the matter of the application for her enrollment as a citizen by blood of the Creek Nation.

Respectfully,
Jesse McDermott
In Charge.

N C 933.

Muskogee, Indian Territory, March 7, 1907.

Jeannetta Biggs,
  Care of George C. Biggs,
    Bristow, Indian Territory.

Dear Madam:

You are hereby advised that on March 2, 1907, the Secretary of the Interior approved the enrollment of your minor child, Martha Biggs, as a citizen by blood of the Creek Nation and that the name of said child appears upon the roll of new born citizens by blood of the Creek Nation enrolled under the Act of Congress approved March 3, 1905, as number 1239.

Applications for Enrollment of Creek Newborn
Act of 1905 Volume XII

This child is now entitled to allotment and application therefor should be made without delay at the Creek Land Office, Muskogee, Indian Territory.

Respectfully,

Commissioner.

DEPARTMENT OF THE INTERIOR,
COMMISSION TO THE FIVE CIVILIZED TRIBES.
April 29, 1905, Sapulpa, I.T.

In the matter of the application for the enrollment of _____ Brown, _____ Brown, Wisey Long, Suka Long, Martha Conner and Mary Pinehill, as citizens by blood of the Creek Nation.

Ben W. Wadsworth, being duly sworn, testified as follows by E.C. Griesel, a Notary Public, testified as follows:

By Commission:

Q What is your name? A Ben W. Wadsworth.
Q What is your age? A 34.
Q What is your post office? A Bristow.
Q To what town do you belong? A Hickory Ground.
Q You are employed by the Commission under special instructions to secure data relative to children born subsequent to May 25, 1901, and prior to March 4, 1905, and living on said latter date, to citizens of the Creek tribe of Indians whose enrollment has been approved by the Secretary of the Interior prior to the date of the approval of said act, were you? A Yes.
Q You wish to make application for the enrollment of six children the parents of whom are commonly known as Snake Indians? A Yes.
Q How did you obtain this information? A You better take them up one at a time and then I can explain what I had to do in each case.

Mr. Wadsworth here presents a memorandum upon which appear the names of the children, the names of the parents, the probable age etc., upon which the applications were made.

By Commission:
Q The first one you have here is _____ Brown; who are the parents of this _____ Brown? A Jim and Loda Brown.

Applications for Enrollment of Creek Newborn
Act of 1905 Volume XII

Q Are they both living? A Yes
Q To what town do they belong? A Euchee.
Q How old is this child whose first name is unknown to you? A About two years old.
Q You saw the child, did you? A Yes sir.
Q Did you converse with the parents.[sic] A I tried to but they refused to talk to me.
Q Did they understand the purpose of your visit? A Yes, I suppose they did, for I told them I wanted to enroll their children for them.
Q Did they give you the information you wished? A No sir.
Q How did you get this information? A I got the information from Lewis and Henry Long, brothers-in-law of Jim Brown, they are neighbors of Jim Brown.
Q The neighbors could not give you the names of the children? A Well they knew but they would not give them to me, they said the father ought to give them to me.
Q When did you see this child? A Day before yesterday.
Q Did these parents have another child? A Yes.
Q How old was that child? A About a year old.
Q You saw the child at the same time? A Yes sir. I was able to see them for a little while only, for the mother took them and ran to the woods with them. Shortly afterwards the father left me too, with the remark that he had to work on a house.

Q Who are the parents of Suka Long? A Lewis and Nancy Long.
Q Are they citizens of the Creek Nation? A Yes.
Q Are they living? A Yes sir.
Q Is this child Suka living? A Yes, sir.
Q How old is this child? A It was born April 22, 1903.
Q How did you get the exact date? A I got it from the father.
Q Who gave you the information? A I worried with the father two hours trying to explain the matter and that the child ought to get the allotment and that an application must be made before May the 1st, 1905, and he finally submitted and gave it to me.
Q You saw the child yourself, did you? A Yes sir.

Q Who are the parents of Wisey Beaver? A Wattie and Nancy Beaver.
Q Are they living? A Yes sir.
Q They are citizens of the Creek Nation, are they? A Yes sir.
Q When was this child born? A The child is about two years old.
Q You saw the child? A Yes.
Q How did you get your information? A They would not give me the necessary information.
Q How did you get it? A I got it from one Tom Tiger. He did not know the age of the child but he gave me its name, and the name of the father and mother, but he guessed it was about two years old.
Q You saw the child, did you? A Yes sir.

Q Who are the parents of Martha Conner? A George and Jeannetta Conner.
Q Are they living? A Yes sir.
Q Are they citizens of the Creek Nation? A Yes sir.
Q Did you see this child, Martha Conner? A Yes.

Applications for Enrollment of Creek Newborn
Act of 1905 Volume XII

Q When was it born? A They said it was about 30 months old, that was all the information I got. They gave me some information but not sufficient; I got the rest from Hattie Grayson, Indian Territory a neighbor.

Q Who are the parents of Mary Pinehill? A Lasley and Sallie Pinehill
Q Both are living are they? And are citizens of the Creek Nation? A Yes sir.
Q Did you see the child Mary? A Yes sir.
Q About how old is that child? A I would judge it to be about eight months old.
Q Did you have any difficulty in getting the information? A I worried with them about two hours, they would not give me any information at all, but Hattie Grayson, Indian Territory a neighbor gave me the information.

Q These people are all Snakes are they? A Yes sir.
Q You saw these children and got all the information you have furnished us, last week? A Yes sir.
Q Now Mr. Wadsworth, have you any statements to make to the Commission relative to the enrollment of these children? A Yes sir; Their reason was that that[sic] there would be plenty of time to enroll their children, and they would not be in any hurry at all; that the land belongs to the Creek people and the government could not beat them out of it; as far as the government has already went ahead and enrolled and allotted us Indians without our consent we just let the government finished[sic] them up. That we would not help them finish the matter as the government had gone ahead so far and whatever the end may be we will live and die on it. They claim that as the government has enrolled and allotted them without their consent and now we let the government go ahead and take care of the children; they won't help in any way. Are just sitting back and refuse to give the government any help.
Q You explained the intent and purpose of the Act under which we are now acting, did you? A Yes.
Q You were out among them all week, were you? A Oh yes.

    E.C. Griesel, being duly sworn, on his oath, states that the above and foregoing is a true and correct transcript of his stenographic notes as taken in said cause on said date.

Edw C Griesel

Subscribed and sworn to before me this 5 day of May, 1905.

Drennan C Skaggs
Notary Public.

Applications for Enrollment of Creek Newborn
Act of 1905 Volume XII

BIRTH AFFIDAVIT.

DEPARTMENT OF THE INTERIOR.
COMMISSION TO THE FIVE CIVILIZED TRIBES.

IN RE APPLICATION FOR ENROLLMENT, as a citizen of the Creek Nation, of John Brown, born on the 12th day of March, 1904

Name of Father: Com-pe-sen-ney Brown   a citizen of the   Creek   Nation.
Name of Mother: Loda Brown   a citizen of the   Creek   Nation.

Postoffice   Newby I.T.

AFFIDAVIT OF MOTHER.

UNITED STATES OF AMERICA, Indian Territory,
    Western   DISTRICT.

     I, Loda Brown , on oath state that I am about 35 years of age and a citizen by blood , of the Creek Nation; that I am the lawful wife of Com-pe-sen-ney Brown , who is a citizen, by blood of the Creek Nation; that a male child was born to me on 12th day of March , 1904 , that said child has been named John Brown , and was living March 4, 1905.   her

                                      Loda Brown x

Witnesses To Mark: mark
    { L.M. Calloway
      W.L. Cheatham

     Subscribed and sworn to before me this 8th day of January , 1906.

                                 W^m L Cheatham
                                 Notary Public.

AFFIDAVIT OF ATTENDING PHYSICIAN OR MID-WIFE.

UNITED STATES OF AMERICA, Indian Territory,
    Western   DISTRICT.

     I, Lannie Long , a midwife , on oath state that I attended on Mrs. Loda Brown , wife of Com-pe-sen-ney Brown on the 12th day of March , 1904 ; that there was born to her on said date a male child; that said child was living March 4, 1905, and is said to have been named John Brown   her

                                Lannie Long x

Witnesses To Mark: mark
    { L.M. Calloway
      W.L. Cheatham

Applications for Enrollment of Creek Newborn
Act of 1905   Volume XII

Subscribed and sworn to before me this 8th day of January, 1906.

W^m L Cheatham
Notary Public.

BIRTH AFFIDAVIT.

DEPARTMENT OF THE INTERIOR.
COMMISSION TO THE FIVE CIVILIZED TRIBES.

IN RE APPLICATION FOR ENROLLMENT, as a citizen of the Creek Nation, of Willie Brown, born on the 21st day of April, 1902

Name of Father: Com-pe-sen-ney Brown	a citizen of the	Creek	Nation.
Name of Mother: Loda Brown	a citizen of the	Creek	Nation.

Postoffice   Newby I.T.

AFFIDAVIT OF MOTHER.

UNITED STATES OF AMERICA, Indian Territory, }
   Western   DISTRICT.

I, Loda Brown, on oath state that I am about 35 years of age and a citizen by blood, of the Creek Nation; that I am the lawful wife of Com-pe-sen-ney Brown, who is a citizen, by blood of the Creek Nation; that a male child was born to me on 21st day of April, 1902, that said child has been named Willie Brown, and was living March 4, 1905.

                                        her
                               Loda Brown x
Witnesses To Mark: mark
{ L.M. Calloway
  W.L. Cheatham

Subscribed and sworn to before me this 8th day of January, 1906.

W^m L Cheatham
Notary Public.

AFFIDAVIT OF ATTENDING PHYSICIAN OR MID-WIFE.

UNITED STATES OF AMERICA, Indian Territory, }
   Western   DISTRICT.

I, Lannie Long, a midwife, on oath state that I attended on Mrs. Loda Brown, wife of Com-pe-sen-ney Brown on the 21st day of April, 1902; that there was born

Applications for Enrollment of Creek Newborn
Act of 1905   Volume XII

to her on said date a male child; that said child was living March 4, 1905, and is said to have been named Willie Brown

                                                                                      her
                                           Lannie Long x

Witnesses To Mark: mark
  { L.M. Calloway
    W.L. Cheatham

      Subscribed and sworn to before me this 8th day of January , 1906.

                                                 W^m L Cheatham
                                                    Notary Public.

BIRTH AFFIDAVIT.

DEPARTMENT OF THE INTERIOR.
COMMISSION TO THE FIVE CIVILIZED TRIBES.

(Snake)

      IN RE APPLICATION FOR ENROLLMENT, as a citizen of the Creek Nation, of Willie Brown, born during the year , 1903

Name of Father: Jim Brown   a citizen of the   Creek   Nation.
(Euchee)   Com-pe-cin-ny
Name of Mother: Loda Brown   a citizen of the   "   Nation.
(Euchee)

                          Postoffice   Bristow

                      AFFIDAVIT OF ~~MOTHER~~.   Acquaintance

UNITED STATES OF AMERICA, Indian Territory,
     Western   DISTRICT.

      I, Ben W. Wadsworth , on oath state that I am 34 years of age and a citizen by blood , of the Creek   Nation; that I am ~~the lawful wife~~ an acquaintance of   Jim and Loda Brown , who ~~is a~~ are citizens, by blood of the Creek Nation; that a male   child was born to ~~me~~ them during the year 1903 , that said child has been named   Willie Brown , and was living March 4, 1905.

                                          BW Wadsworth

Witnesses To Mark:
  {

      Subscribed and sworn to before me this 29 day of April , 1905.

(Seal)   Edw C Griesel
                                             Notary Public.

Applications for Enrollment of Creek Newborn
Act of 1905   Volume XII

BIRTH AFFIDAVIT.

DEPARTMENT OF THE INTERIOR.
COMMISSION TO THE FIVE CIVILIZED TRIBES.

(Snake)

      IN RE APPLICATION FOR ENROLLMENT, as a citizen of the Creek Nation, of John Brown, born during latter part of , 1904

              Com-pe-cin-ny

Name of Father: Jim Brown	a citizen of the Creek	Nation.
Name of Mother: Loda Brown	a citizen of the "	Nation.

              Postoffice   Bristow

              AFFIDAVIT OF ~~MOTHER~~.   Acquaintance

UNITED STATES OF AMERICA, Indian Territory,
    Western   DISTRICT.

      I, Ben W. Wadsworth , on oath state that I am 34 years of age and a citizen by blood , of the Creek Nation; that I am ~~the lawful wife~~ an acquaintance of Jim and Loda Brown , who ~~is a~~ are citizens, by blood of the Creek Nation; that a male child was born to ~~me~~ them during the latter part of 1904 , that said child has been named John Brown , and was living March 4, 1905.

                                        BW Wadsworth

Witnesses To Mark:

      Subscribed and sworn to before me this 29 day of April , 1905.

(Seal)   Edw C Griesel
                                      Notary Public.

N.C. 934

                            Muskogee, Indian Territory, October 20, 1905.

Loda Brown,
    Care Con-pe-sin-ney (or Jim) Brown,
        Bristow, Indian Territory.

Dear Madam:

      In the matter of the application for the enrollment of your minor children, John Brown, said to have been born during the year 1904, and Willie Brown, said to have been born during the year 1903, as citizens by blood of the Creek Nation, this office desires the

Applications for Enrollment of Creek Newborn
Act of 1905   Volume XII

affidavit of yourself and the midwife or physician in attendance at the birth of said children and a blank for that purpose is inclosed herewith.

In the event that there was no physician or midwife in attendance when said children were born, it will be necessary for you to furnish this office with the affidavits of two disinterested witnesses relative to their birth. Said affidavits must set forth the name of said children, the date of their birth, the names of her parents and whether or not they were living on March 4, 1905.

Respectfully,

BC-Env.   Commissioner.

Muskogee, Indian Territory, December 16, 1905.

Con-pe-sin-ney Brown,
    Care Jesse Allen,
        Bristow, Indian Territory.

Dear Sir:

In the matter of the application for the enrollment of your minor children, John Brown, said to have been born during the year 1904 and Willie Brown, said to have been born during the year 1903, as citizens by blood of the Creek Nation; this office desires the affidavit of your wife, Loda Brown, the mother of said children and of the midwife or physician in attendance at the births of said children and blanks for that purpose are enclosed herewith.

In the event that there was no midwife or physician in attendance when said children were born, it will be necessary for you to furnish this office with the affidavits of two disinterested witnesses relative to their birth; said affidavits must set forth the names of said children, the dates of their birth, the names of their parents and whether or not they were living on March 4, 1905.

In executing affidavits care should be taken that the notary affixes his signature and notarial seal; that all blanks are properly filled out; that the witnesses sign the affidavits and that each signature by mark is attested by two witnesses.

This matter should receive your immediate attention.

Respectfully,

Commissioner.

2 B A
4 Dis.

Applications for Enrollment of Creek Newborn
Act of 1905 Volume XII

HGH

REFER IN REPLY TO THE FOLLOWING:

DEPARTMENT OF THE INTERIOR,
COMMISSIONER TO THE FIVE CIVILIZED TRIBES.

Muskogee, Indian Territory, October 24, 1906.

Loda Brown,
    c/o Jim Brown,
        Bristow, Indian Territory.

Dear Madam:

    You are hereby advised that the names of your minor children, Willie and John Brown, are contained in the partial list of citizens by blood of the Creek Nation, approved by the Secretary of the Interior October 15, 1906, and that selections of land in the Creek Nation may now be made for said children at the Creek Land Office in Muskogee, Indian Territory.

    This matter should receive your prompt attention.

                Respectfully,
                      Tams Bixby   Commissioner.

Cr BA-2381-B

Muskogee, Indian Territory, May 5, 1905.

R. R. Bruner,
    Beggs, Indian Territory.

Dear Sir:

    The Commission is in receipt of your letter of April 29, 1905, enclosing affidavit of Georgia Bruner, relative to the birth of her minor child, Ruby Bruner; you state that you have been unable to secure affidavit of the midwife or doctor in attendance at the birth of said child and ask to be allowed further time within which to secure such evidence.

Applications for Enrollment of Creek Newborn
Act of 1905   Volume XII

In reply you are advised that you will be allowed thirty days from date within which to file with the Commission affidavit of the midwife or doctor in attendance at the birth of Ruby Bruner.

       Respectfully,
            Chairman.

NC 935

       Muskogee, Indian Territory, October 20, 1905.

Georgia Bruner,
  Care Pinkey Bruner,
    Edna, Indian Territory.

Dear Madam:

  In the matter of the application for the enrollment of Ruby Bruner, born March 3, 1905, as a citizen by blood of the Creek Nation, you are hereby notified to appear before this office within fifteen days from date with the midwife who attend[sic] you at the birth of said Ruby Bruner.

  If for any reason you are unable to secure the evidence of said midwife, you will then appear before this office within the time specified with two disinterested witnesses who know the exact day and time of day on which said Ruby Bruner was born.

       Respectfully,
            Commissioner.

N C 935.

       Muskogee, Indian Territory, September 21, 1906.

Georgia Bruner,
  c/o Mr. Ghant,
    Bixby, Indian Territory.

Dear Madam:

  In the matter of the application for the enrollment of your minor child, Ruby Bruner, as a citizen of the Creek Nation, you are hereby notified to appear at this Office within fifteen days from date with the midwife or physician who attended on you at the birth of said child.

       Respectfully,
            Commissioner.

Applications for Enrollment of Creek Newborn
Act of 1905 Volume XII

BIRTH AFFIDAVIT.

DEPARTMENT OF THE INTERIOR.
COMMISSION TO THE FIVE CIVILIZED TRIBES.

IN RE APPLICATION FOR ENROLLMENT, as a citizen of the Creek Nation, of Ruby Bruner, born on the 3 day of March, 1905

Name of Father: Pinkey   a citizen of the Creek Nation.
Name of Mother: Georgia Bruner   a citizen of the United States Nation.

Postoffice   Edna I.T.

AFFIDAVIT OF MOTHER.

UNITED STATES OF AMERICA, Indian Territory,
     Western   DISTRICT.

I, Georgia Bruner, on oath state that I am 19 years of age and a citizen by marriage, of the Creek Nation; that I am the lawful wife of Pinkey Bruner, who is a citizen, by blood of the Creek Nation; that a male[sic] child was born to me on 3rd day of March, 1905, that said child has been named Ruby Bruner, and was living March 4, 1905.

                                   Georgia Bruner

Witnesses To Mark:

Subscribed and sworn to before me this 27th day of April, 1905.

My Commission expires March 25th 1909   Richard J. Hill
                                                  Notary Public.

Applications for Enrollment of Creek Newborn
Act of 1905   Volume XII

COMMISSIONERS:
TAMS BIXBY,
THOMAS B. NEEDLES,
C.R. BRECKINBRIDGE.

WM. O. BEALL
Secretary

DEPARTMENT OF THE INTERIOR,
COMMISSIONER TO THE FIVE CIVILIZED TRIBES.

HGH

REFER IN REPLY TO THE FOLLOWING:

ADDRESS ONLY THE
COMMISSION TO THE FIVE CIVILIZED TRIBES.

Muskogee, Indian Territory, June 30, 1905.

Taylor Bruner,
    Wetumka, Indian Territory.

Dear Sir:

    In compliance with your request of June 24, 1905, there is herewith enclosed blank form of birth affidavit.

                            Respectfully,
1 DA   Tams Bixby   Chairman.

REFER IN REPLY TO THE FOLLOWING:
N.C. 936

DEPARTMENT OF THE INTERIOR,
COMMISSIONER TO THE FIVE CIVILIZED TRIBES.

HGH

Muskogee, Indian Territory, August 4, 1905.

Ilsey Bruner,
    Wetumka, Indian Territory.

Dear Madam:

    July 10, 1905, there was filed with this office an affidavit in which it is stated that Turner Bruner died September 27, 1904; the names of the parents of said Turner Bruner are not given.

    There is herewith enclosed a blank for proof of birth which should be properly executed before a notary public; care being taken that he affixes his signature and official seal to same.

    You are advised that this office is unable to identify said Turner Bruner as a citizen by blood of the Creek Nation and you are requested to state the names of his parents, the Creek Indian town to which they belong and, if possible, the numbers which appear on their deeds to land in the Creek Nation.

                            Respectfully,
1 B A   Tams Bixby   Commissioner.

Applications for Enrollment of Creek Newborn
Act of 1905   Volume XII

N.C. 936.

Muskogee, Indian Territory, August 30, 1905.

Taylor Bruner,
    Wetumka, Indian Territory.

Dear Sir:

July 10, 1905, there was filed with this office an affidavit in which it is stated that Turner Bruner died September 27, 1904; the names of the parents of said Turner Bruner are not given.

There is herewith enclosed a blank for proof of birth which should be properly executed before a notary public; care being taken that he affixes his signature and official seal to same.

You are advised that this office is unable to identify said Turner Bruner as a citizen by blood of the Creek Nation and you are requested to state the names of his parents, the Creek Indian town to which they belong and, if possible, the numbers which appear on their deeds to land in the Creek Nation.

Respectfully,

1 B A

Commissioner.

NC 937

Muskogee, Indian Territory, October 27, 1905.

Lydia Cates,
    Joseph Cates,
        Bristow, Indian Territory.

Dear Madam:

In the matter of the application for the enrollment of Governor Cates, born July 19, 1903, as a citizen by blood of the Creek Nation; you state in your affidavit relative to the birth of said child that you are a citizen by birth of the Creek Nation. This office is unable to identify you on the final roll of either the freedmen or citizens by blood of the

Applications for Enrollment of Creek Newborn
Act of 1905   Volume XII

Creek Nation; you are requested to state your maiden name, the names of your parents, the Creek Indian town to which you belong the numbers on your deeds to lands in the Creek Nation.

In the event that you are not in fact a citizen of the Creek Nation, it will be necessary for you to supply evidence of your marriage which may consist of either the original or a certified copy of your marriage license an certificate.

Respectfully,
Commissioner.

NC-937   (Copy)

Bristow, Ind Terr, Nov 14th, 1905.

Commission to the Five Civilized Tribes,
    Muskogee, I. T.

Sir:-

Answering you communication of Oct 20th last, in which I am advised that you are unable to identify me, in the matter of the enrollment of my new born child, Governor Cates, etc.

You are advised that my name appears on the Indian Roll, as Lydia Barnett, Creek Roll No 8845. Commission Roll No. 5040, am a member of Tuskeegee[sic] Town.

My homestead it the N 1/2 of the N 1/2 of the SE 1/4 of Sec 1, Twp 15 N, R & E.

Trusting that this will be sufficient to establish my identity to satisfy the Commission.

I am yours very respectfully yours,

(signed) LYDIA (her x mark) CATES, nee BARNETT.

Applications for Enrollment of Creek Newborn
Act of 1905 Volume XII

BIRTH AFFIDAVIT.

DEPARTMENT OF THE INTERIOR,
COMMISSION TO THE FIVE CIVILIZED TRIBES.

In Re Application for Enrollment, as a citizen of the Creek Nation, of Governor Cates, born on the 19 day of July, 1903

Name of Father: Joseph Cates   a citizen of the   Creek   Nation.
Name of Mother: Lydia Cates   a citizen of the   Creek   Nation.

Post-office   Bristow Ind Tey

AFFIDAVIT OF MOTHER.

UNITED STATES OF AMERICA,
  INDIAN TERRITORY,
  Western   District.

I, Lydia Cates, on oath state that I am 35 years of age and a citizen by birth, of the Creek Nation; that I am the lawful wife of Joseph Cates, who is a citizen, by birth of the Creek Nation; that a male child was born to me on 19 day of July, 1903, that said child has been named Governor Cates, and is now living.

                                   her
                             Lydia x Cates
WITNESSES TO MARK: mark
  C.C. DonCarlos
  J.A. Helton

Subscribed and sworn to before me this 29 day of April, 1905.

                             E.W. Sims
                             NOTARY PUBLIC.

AFFIDAVIT OF ATTENDING PHYSICIAN OR MID-WIFE.

UNITED STATES OF AMERICA,
  INDIAN TERRITORY,
  Western   District.

I, Lizzie Harry, a Midwife, on oath state that I attended on Mrs. Lydia Cates, wife of Joseph Cates on the 19 day of July, 1903; that there was born to her on said date a male child; that said child is now living and is said to have been named Governor Cates

Applications for Enrollment of Creek Newborn
Act of 1905   Volume XII

                                her
                         Lizzie x Harry

WITNESSES TO MARK: mark

{ M.C. Flournay
{ C.C. DonCarlos

Subscribed and sworn to before me this 29 day of   April , 1905.

                                E.W. Sims
                                NOTARY PUBLIC.

NC 938.

                        Muskogee, Indian Territory, January 18, 1907.

Sissie Lee,
    c/o Gano Lee,
        Sapulpa, Indian Territory.

Dear Madam:

    There is herewith enclosed one copy of the Statement and Order of the Commissioner to the Five Civilized Tribes, dated January 18, 1907, dismissing the application made by you for the enrollment of your minor children, John and Joseph Lee, both deceased, as citizens of the Creek Nation.

                        Respectfully,
                                      Commissioner.

LM-?02.

Applications for Enrollment of Creek Newborn
Act of 1905   Volume XII

BIRTH AFFIDAVIT.

DEPARTMENT OF THE INTERIOR.
COMMISSION TO THE FIVE CIVILIZED TRIBES.

IN RE APPLICATION FOR ENROLLMENT, as a citizen of the Creek Nation, of Johnson Lee, born on the 31 day of March, 1902

Name of Father: Gano Lee   a citizen of the   Creek   Nation.
(Coweta)
Name of Mother: Sissie "   a citizen of the   "   Nation.
(Cussehta)

Postoffice   Sapulpa

AFFIDAVIT OF MOTHER.

UNITED STATES OF AMERICA, Indian Territory,
     Western   DISTRICT.

I, Sissie Lee, on oath state that I am 26 years of age and a citizen by blood, of the Creek Nation; that I am the lawful wife of Gano Lee, who is a citizen, by blood of the Creek Nation; that a male child was born to me on 31 day of March, 1902, that said child has been named Johnson Lee, and ~~was living March 4, 1905~~. died April 1, 1902

                                    Her
                              Sissie x Lee
Witnesses To Mark: mark
  { David Shelby
  { Jesse McDermott

Subscribed and sworn to before me this 29 day of April, 1905.

(Seal)   Edw C Griesel
                                       Notary Public.

AFFIDAVIT OF ~~ATTENDING PHYSICIAN OR MID-WIFE~~.
                                      Father

UNITED STATES OF AMERICA, Indian Territory,
     Western   DISTRICT.

I, Gano Lee, ~~a (blank)~~, on oath state that I attended on Mrs. Sissie Lee, my wife ~~of~~ *(blank)* on the 31 day of March, 1902; that there was born to her on said date a   male   child; that said child ~~was living March 4, 1905~~, and is said to have been named Johnson Lee   died April 1, 1902
                                       His
                                   Gano x Lee
                                       mark

Applications for Enrollment of Creek Newborn
Act of 1905   Volume XII

Witnesses To Mark:
  { David Shelby
  { Jesse McDermott

Subscribed and sworn to before me this 29 day of April, 1905.

(Seal)   Edw C Griesel
                                         Notary Public.

BIRTH AFFIDAVIT.

DEPARTMENT OF THE INTERIOR.
COMMISSION TO THE FIVE CIVILIZED TRIBES.

IN RE APPLICATION FOR ENROLLMENT, as a citizen of the Creek Nation, of Joseph Lee, born on the 31 day of October, 1904

Name of Father: Gano Lee   a citizen of the   Creek   Nation.
(Coweta)
Name of Mother: Sissie Lee   a citizen of the   "   Nation.
(Cussehta)

Postoffice   Sapulpa

AFFIDAVIT OF MOTHER.

UNITED STATES OF AMERICA, Indian Territory, }
     Western   DISTRICT.   }

I, Sissie Lee, on oath state that I am 26 years of age and a citizen by blood, of the Creek Nation; that I am the lawful wife of Gano Lee, who is a citizen, by blood of the Creek Nation; that a male child was born to me on 31 day of October, 1904, that said child has been named Joseph Lee, and ~~was living March 4, 1905~~. died Nov 6, 1904

                                         Her
                                   Sissie x Lee
Witnesses To Mark: mark
  { David Shelby
  { Jesse McDermott

Subscribed and sworn to before me this 29 day of April, 1905.

(Seal)   Edw C Griesel
                                         Notary Public.

Applications for Enrollment of Creek Newborn
Act of 1905   Volume XII

AFFIDAVIT OF ~~ATTENDING PHYSICIAN OR MID-WIFE~~.
                                                                Father
UNITED STATES OF AMERICA, Indian Territory, ⎱
       Western   DISTRICT.   ⎰

    I, Gano Lee , ~~a (blank)~~ , on oath state that I attended on Mrs. Sissie Lee , my wife ~~of (blank)~~ on the 31 day of October , 1904 ; that there was born to her on said date a   male   child; that said child ~~was living March 4, 1905~~, and is said to have been named Joseph Lee   died Nov 6 1904

His
Gano x Lee
mark

Witnesses To Mark:
  ⎰ David Shelby
  ⎱ Jesse McDermott

    Subscribed and sworn to before me this 29 day of April , 1905.

(Seal)   Edw C Griesel
                                                 Notary Public.

N.C. 938.   J.L.De
DEPARTMENT OF THE INTERIOR,
COMMISSIONER TO THE FIVE CIVILIZED TRIBES.

    In the matter of the applications for the enrollment of Johnson Lee, deceased, and Joseph Lee, deceased, as citizens by blood of the Creek Nation.

STATEMENT AND ORDER.

    The record in this case shows that on May 2, 1905, applications were made, in affidavit form, for the enrollment of Johnson Lee, deceased and Joseph Lee, deceased, as citizens by blood of the Creek Nation, under the Act of Congress approved March 3, 1905.
    It appears from the affidavits filed in this matter that said Johnson Lee and Joseph Lee were born March 31, 1902, and October 31, 1904, respectively, and died April 1, 1902, and November 6, 1904, respectively.

    The Act of Congress approved March 3, 1905, (33 Stats., 1048), in part, provides:

    "That the Commission to the Five Civilized Tribes is authorized for sixty days after the date of the approval of this act to receive and consider applications for enrollment, of children, born subsequent to May twenty-fifth, nineteen hundred and one, and prior to March fourth, nineteen hundred and five, and living on said latter date, to citizens of the Creek tribe of Indians whose enrollment has been approved by the

Applications for Enrollment of Creek Newborn
Act of 1905   Volume XII

Secretary of the Interior prior to the approval of this act; and to enroll and make allotments to such children."

It is, therefore, ordered that the applications for the enrollment of said Johnson Lee, deceased, and Joseph Lee, deceased, as citizens by blood of the Creek Nation be, and the same are hereby dismissed.

Tams Bixby COMMISSIONER.

Muskogee, Indian Territory.
JAN 18 1907

BIRTH AFFIDAVIT.

DEPARTMENT OF THE INTERIOR.
COMMISSION TO THE FIVE CIVILIZED TRIBES.

IN RE APPLICATION FOR ENROLLMENT, as a citizen of the Creek Nation, of Modie Hay, born on the 3 day of December, 1903

Name of Father: John Hay   a citizen of the   Creek   Nation.
(Euchee)
Name of Mother: Eggie "   a citizen of the   "   Nation.
(Euchee)

Postoffice   Kellyville

AFFIDAVIT OF MOTHER.

Child Present

UNITED STATES OF AMERICA, Indian Territory, ⎫
    Western   DISTRICT.   ⎬
                                               ⎭

I, Eggie Hay, on oath state that I am 22 years of age and a citizen by blood, of the Creek Nation; that I am the lawful wife of John Hay, who is a citizen, by blood of the Creek Nation; that a male child was born to me on 3 day of December, 1903, that said child has been named Modie Hay, and was living March 4, 1905.

Her
Eggie x Hay
mark

Applications for Enrollment of Creek Newborn
Act of 1905   Volume XII

Witnesses To Mark:
  { David Shelby
  { Jesse McDermott

   Subscribed and sworn to before me this 1 day of May, 1905.

(Seal)   Edw C Griesel
                                                   Notary Public.

AFFIDAVIT OF ATTENDING PHYSICIAN OR MID-WIFE.

UNITED STATES OF AMERICA, Indian Territory, }
   Western   **DISTRICT.**

   I, Polly Char co te ten na, a Midwife, on oath state that I attended on Mrs. Eggie Hay, wife of John Hay on the 3 day of Dec, 1903; that there was born to her on said date a male child; that said child was living March 4, 1905, and is said to have been named Modie Hay
                                                     Her
                                          Polly x Char co te ten na
Witnesses To Mark: mark
   David Shelby
   Jesse McDermott

   Subscribed and sworn to before me this 1 day of May, 1905.

(Seal)   Edw C Griesel
                                                   Notary Public.

N.C. 941.   DEPARTMENT OF THE INTERIOR,
            COMMISSIONER TO THE FIVE CIVILIZED TRIBES.
                   Muskogee, I. T., February 8, 1906.

   In the matter of the application for the enrollment of of Ella Char co-te-ten-na as a citizen by blood of the Creek Nation.

          Katie Char-co-te-ten-na, being duly sworn, testified as follows:

   Through S. W. Brown, who was duly sworn as Euche Interpreter:

Applications for Enrollment of Creek Newborn
Act of 1905   Volume XII

BY THE COMMISSIONER:
Q What is your name? A Katie Char-co-te-ten-na.
Q How old are you? A I am about twenty-five.
Q What is your post office address? A Kellyville.
Q Have you a new born child? A Yes, sir.
Q What is its name? A Ella.
Q We have a[sic] affidavit here in which you give the name of the child as Ellen. That is not correct is it? A That is not correct.
Q We have affidavits here which give different dates of the birth. What month was this child born? A She was born on the 5th day of May, two years ago. Will be two years old next May.
Q Is Ella living? A Yes, sir.
Q What is the name of the father of the child? A He-ca-tah.
Q Has he recieved[sic] his allotment in the Creek Nation? A Yes, sir.
Q Under what name? A I don't know.
Q Do you know whether his English name is Anderson Johnson? A Yes, sir, it is.
Q That is the child there is it? A Yes, sir.
Q Were you married to He-ca-tah? A No, sir.
Q So you call the child after yourself, do you? A Yes, sir.
Q You are sure it was born in May and not in April, are you? A Yes, sir.

---oooOOOooo---

I, D. C. Skaggs, on oath state that the above and foregoing is a full and thre[sic] transcript of my stenographic notes as taken in said cause on said date.

D. C. Skaggs

Subscribed and sworn to before me this 12 day of February, 1906.

J McDermott
Notary Public.

IN THE DEPARTMENT OF THE INTERIOR.

Hon. Tams Bixby,

COMMISSIONER TO THE FIVE CIVILIZED TRIBES

The undersigned, John Hay, whose residence is near Kelleyville[sic], I.T., and who filed an affidavit with the Department some months ago, about the 1st. day of May, 1905, touching the birth of the little daughter of His sister, Katie Char-co-te-ten-na, in which there was a mistake as it appears therein that affiant stated that he was the father of said child, Ellen Char-co-te-ten-na, this must have been misinterpreted or a mistake of the Notary Public or the party who drew up said affidavit, as the father of said child was an Indian He-ca-tah, who is now dead, to whom my sister was never married.

Applications for Enrollment of Creek Newborn
Act of 1905   Volume XII

There is also another mistake in said affidavit or the proofs filed with reference to the date of the birth of said child, Ellen Char-co-te-ten-na, as she was born on the 5th. day of May, 1904, and was named Ellen instead of Ella.

John Hay

Subscribed and sworn to before me this 7th. day of November, 1905.

Notary Public Western District of
Indian Territory.

BIRTH AFFIDAVIT.

DEPARTMENT OF THE INTERIOR,
COMMISSION TO THE FIVE CIVILIZED TRIBES.

IN RE Application for Enrollment, as a citizen of the   Creek   Nation, of Ellen Char-co-te-ten-na, born on the 5th day of May, 1904 now

Name of Father: He-ca-tah (dead)   a citizen of the   Creek   Nation.
Name of Mother: Katie Char-co-te-ten-na   a citizen of the   Creek   Nation.

Post-office: Kelleyville[sic], I.T.

AFFIDAVIT OF MOTHER.

UNITED STATES OF AMERICA, ⎫
   INDIAN TERRITORY.   ⎬
  Western   District.   ⎭

I, Katie Char-co-te-ten-na , on oath state that I am about 21 years of age and a citizen by blood , of the Creek Nation; that I am not the lawful wife of He-ca-tah (now dead) , who is a citizen, by blood of the Creek Nation; that a female child was born to me on 5th day of May , 1904 , that said child has been named Ellen Char-co-te-ten-na, and is now living.

her
Katie x Car-co-te-ten-na
mark

WITNESSES TO MARK:
  { S.W. Brown
    F.L. Mars

Subscribed and sworn to before me this 7th *day of* Nov , *1905.*

My commission expires May 7, 1908.   James J. Mars
NOTARY PUBLIC.

Applications for Enrollment of Creek Newborn
Act of 1905   Volume XII

AFFIDAVIT OF ATTENDING PHYSICIAN OR MID-WIFE.

UNITED STATES OF AMERICA,
  INDIAN TERRITORY.
  Western   District.

I, Polly Char-co-te-ten-na , a midwife , on oath state that I attended on ~~Mrs.~~ Katie Char-co-te-ten-na , wife of ----- on the 5th day of May , 1904 ; that there was born to her on said date a female child; that said child is now living and is said to have been named Ellen Char-co-te-ten-na

her
Polly x Char-co-te-ten-na
mark

WITNESSES TO MARK:
{ S.W. Brown
{ F.L. Mars

Subscribed and sworn to before me this 7th *day of* Nov , 1905.

James J. Mars
NOTARY PUBLIC.

My commission expires May 7, 1908.

BIRTH AFFIDAVIT.

DEPARTMENT OF THE INTERIOR.
COMMISSION TO THE FIVE CIVILIZED TRIBES.

IN RE APPLICATION FOR ENROLLMENT, as a citizen of the   Creek   Nation, of   Ella Char-co-te-ten-na , born on the 5 day of April , 1904

Name of Father: Unknown   a citizen of the ----------- Nation.
Name of Mother: Katie Char-co-te-ten-na   a citizen of the   Creek   Nation.
(Euchee)
                        Postoffice   Kellyville

AFFIDAVIT OF ~~MOTHER~~. Acquaintance
&
Uncle

UNITED STATES OF AMERICA, Indian Territory,
  Western   DISTRICT.

I, John Hay , on oath state that I am 27 years of age and a citizen by blood , of the Creek Nation; that I am ~~the lawful wife~~ the Brother of Katie Char-co-te-ten-na , who is a citizen, by blood of the Creek   Nation; that a female   child was born to me

Applications for Enrollment of Creek Newborn
Act of 1905   Volume XII

on 5 day of   April , 1904 , that said child has been named Ella Char-co-te-ten-na ,
and was living March 4, 1905.

             John Hay

Witnesses To Mark:

    Subscribed and sworn to before me this 1 day of May, 1905.

(Seal)   Edw C Griesel
               Notary Public.

AFFIDAVIT OF ATTENDING ~~PHYSICIAN~~ OR MID-WIFE. (& Grandmother)

UNITED STATES OF AMERICA, Indian Territory,
  Western   **DISTRICT.**

  I, Polly Char-co-te-ten-na , a Midwife , on oath state that I attended on Mrs. Katie Char-co-te-ten-na , ~~wife of~~ on the 5 day of April , 1904 ; that there was born to her on said date a female child; that said child was living March 4, 1905, and is said to have been named Ella Char-co-te-ten-na

             Her
           Polly x Char-co-te-ten-na
Witnesses To Mark: mark
 David Shelby
 Jesse McDermott

  Subscribed and sworn to before me this 1 day of May, 1905.

(Seal)   Edw C Griesel
               Notary Public.

Mother too sick to come in -

Applications for Enrollment of Creek Newborn
Act of 1905   Volume XII

HGH

REFER IN REPLY TO THE FOLLOWING:

NC 941

DEPARTMENT OF THE INTERIOR,
COMMISSIONER TO THE FIVE CIVILIZED TRIBES.

Muskogee, Indian Territory, October 20, 1905.

Katie Char-co-te-ten-na,
    Care John Hay,
        Kellyville, Indian Territory.

Dear Madam:

    In the matter of the application for the enrollment of your minor child, Ella Char-co-te-ten-na, born April 5, 1904, as a citizen by blood of the Creek Nation, this office desires your affidavit relative to the date of the birth of said child, the names of her parents and whether or not she was living March 4, 1905.

    In the affidavit of your brother, John Hay, executed May 1, 1905, he states that he is the father of said child. If that statement is incorrect, it will be necessary for you to file with this office the affidavit of said John Hay stating that he is not the father of said child and that said statement in his affidavit was an error on his part or on the part of the notary by whom said affidavit was written.

    This matter should receive your prompt attention.

                Respectfully,
                Tams Bixby   Commissioner.

N.C. 941

Muskogee, Indian Territory, December 16, 1905.

Katie Char-co-te-ten-na,
    Care John Hay,
        Kellyville, Indian Territory.

Dear Madam:

    In the matter of the application for the enrollment of your minor child, Ellen Char-co-te-ten-na, as a citizen by blood of the Creek Nation, this office is unable to identify He-ca-tah, who you state is the father of said child, on the final roll of citizens by blood of the Creek Nation. You are requested to state the names of his parents, the Creek Indian town to which he belongs and his roll number as the same appears on his deeds and allotment certificate; also state if He-ca-tah was ever known as He-tah-oo-oo-tan.

    This matter should receive your prompt attention.

Applications for Enrollment of Creek Newborn
Act of 1905   Volume XII

                    Respectfully,

                                  Commissioner.

(The letter below typed as given.)

57103
N.C. 941

                    COPY

                    Sapulpa, Ind. Ter., Dec. 26th. 1905.

Hon. Tams Bixby,
      Muskogee, I.T.

Dear Sir:-

    Answering your attached letter will say, He-ca-tah means in English Anderson Johnson, and is now dead, he was a son of Andres Johnson, whose name is on the roll, also Katie Charcote tenna, is daughter of Polly Char-co-te-ten-na is on the roll, He-ca-tah or Anderson Johnson and Katie Char-co-te-ten-na were the parents of Ellen Char-co-te-ten-na, (Illegitimate).

                    Yours truly,
                          Katie Char-co-te-ten-na
                              per M.

                                              JWH

N C 941

                Muskogee, Indian Territory, March 1, 1907.

Katie Char-co-te-ten-na,
      Kellyville, Indian Territory.

Dear Madam :--

    You are hereby advised that on February 15, 1907, the Secretary of the Interior approved the enrollment of your minor child, Ella Char-co-te-ten-na, as a citizen by blood of the Creek Nation, and that the name of said child appears upon the roll of New Born citizens by blood of the Creek Nation, enrolled under the Act of Congress approved March 3, 1905, as number 1181.

    This child is now entitled to allotment and application therefor should be made without delay at the Creek Land Office, Muskogee, Indian Territory.

                    Respectfully,
                                Commissioner.

Applications for Enrollment of Creek Newborn
Act of 1905 Volume XII

HGH

REFER IN REPLY TO THE FOLLOWING:
N.C. 942

DEPARTMENT OF THE INTERIOR,
COMMISSIONER TO THE FIVE CIVILIZED TRIBES.

Muskogee, Indian Territory, October 21, 1905.

Jemima Rogers,
    Care Chepon Rogers,
        Sapulpa, Indian Territory.

Dear Madam:

    In the matter of the application for the enrollment of your minor child, Lucy Rogers, born May 20, 1904, as a citizen by blood of the Creek Nation, this office is unable to identify you on its roll of citizens by blood of the Creek Nation; you are requested to state your maiden name, the names of your parents, the Creek Indian town to which you belong and the numbers which appear on your deeds to lands in the Creek Nation.

                Respectfully,

                              Tams Bixby
                              Commissioner.

Lucy   2994
Town SE 1/4 32-19-11

BIRTH AFFIDAVIT.

DEPARTMENT OF THE INTERIOR,
COMMISSION TO THE FIVE CIVILIZED TRIBES.

    IN RE Application for Enrollment, as a citizen of the Creek Nation, of Lucy Rogers , born on the 20th day of May A.D. , 1904

Name of Father: Chepon Rogers   a citizen of the   Creek   Nation.
(Tuskegee)
Name of Mother: Jemima Rogers   a citizen of the   Creek   Nation.
(Lochopocha)

                        Post-office: Sapulpa I.T.

Applications for Enrollment of Creek Newborn
Act of 1905   Volume XII

AFFIDAVIT OF MOTHER.

UNITED STATES OF AMERICA,
    INDIAN TERRITORY.
Western   District.

    I,   Jemima Rogers   , on oath state that I am 25   years of age and a citizen by blood , of the   Creek   Nation; that I am the lawful wife of   Chepon Rogers , who is a citizen, by blood of the Creek   Nation; that a   female child was born to me on 20th day of   May A.D. , 1904 , that said child has been named   Lucy Rogers , and is now living.

Jemima Rogers

WITNESSES TO MARK:
  Vergie *(Illegible)*
  Sandy Johnson

Subscribed and sworn to before me this 3rd *day of*   April A.D. , 1905.

F.L. Mars

My Commission expires July 11, 1908.   **NOTARY PUBLIC.**

AFFIDAVIT OF ATTENDING PHYSICIAN OR MID-WIFE.

UNITED STATES OF AMERICA,
    INDIAN TERRITORY.
Western   District.

    I, Lizzie Cosar , a   midwife   , on oath state that I attended on Mrs. Jemima Rogers , wife of Chepon Rogers on the 20th day of May, A.D. , 1904 ; that there was born to her on said date a female child; that said child is now living and is said to have been named Lucy Rogers

Lizzie Cosar

WITNESSES TO MARK:
  Sandy Johnson

Subscribed and sworn to before me this 3rd *day of*   April A.D. , 1905.

F.L. Mars

My Commission expires July 11, 1908.   **NOTARY PUBLIC.**

Applications for Enrollment of Creek Newborn
Act of 1905   Volume XII

BIRTH AFFIDAVIT.

DEPARTMENT OF THE INTERIOR.
COMMISSION TO THE FIVE CIVILIZED TRIBES.

IN RE APPLICATION FOR ENROLLMENT, as a citizen of the Creek Nation, of Lucy Rogers, born on the 20 day of May, 1904

Name of Father: Chepon Rogers   a citizen of the Creek   Nation. Tuskegee
Name of Mother: Jemima Rogers   a citizen of the   "   Nation. Lochopocha

                            Postoffice   Sapulpa

AFFIDAVIT OF ~~MOTHER~~. Father

UNITED STATES OF AMERICA, Indian Territory,
        Western   DISTRICT.

  I, Chepon Rogers, on oath state that I am 44 years of age and a citizen by blood, of the Creek Nation; that I am the lawful ~~wife~~ Husband of Jemima Rogers, who is a citizen, by blood of the Creek Nation; that a female child was born to me on 20 day of May, 1904, that said child has been named Lucy Rogers, and was living March 4, 1905.
                                         His
                              Chepon x Rogers
Witnesses To Mark: mark
    David Shelby
    Jesse McDermott

   Subscribed and sworn to before me this 1 day of May, 1905.

(Seal)   Edw C Griesel
                                         Notary Public.

Applications for Enrollment of Creek Newborn
Act of 1905 Volume XII

BIRTH AFFIDAVIT.

DEPARTMENT OF THE INTERIOR.
COMMISSION TO THE FIVE CIVILIZED TRIBES.

IN RE APPLICATION FOR ENROLLMENT, as a citizen of the Creek Nation, of Noah Ispokogee, born on the 13 day of Aug, 1902

Name of Father: Belcher Ispokogee   a citizen of the   Creek   Nation.
Cussehta
Name of Mother: Jennie   "   a citizen of the   "   Nation.
(Lochopaka)
                             Postoffice   Sapulpa

AFFIDAVIT OF MOTHER.

UNITED STATES OF AMERICA, Indian Territory,
    Western   DISTRICT.

     I, Jennie Ispogee[sic], on oath state that I am 23 years of age and a citizen by blood, of the Creek Nation; that I am the lawful wife of Belcher Ispokogee, who is a citizen, by blood of the Creek Nation; that a male child was born to me on 13 day of Aug, 1902, that said child has been named Noah Ispokogee, and was living March 4, 1905.

                             Jennie Ispogee[sic]
Witnesses To Mark:

     Subscribed and sworn to before me this 29 day of April, 1905.

(Seal)   Edw C Griesel
                                    Notary Public.

AFFIDAVIT OF ATTENDING ~~PHYSICIAN~~ OR MID-WIFE.

UNITED STATES OF AMERICA, Indian Territory,
    Western   DISTRICT.

     I, Mary Hutke, a Midwife, on oath state that I attended on Mrs. Jennie Ispokogee, wife of Belcher Ispokogee on the 13 day of Aug, 1902; that there was born to her on said date a male child; that said child was living March 4, 1905, and is said to have been named Noah Ispokogee   Her
                                    Mary x Hutke
Witnesses To Mark: mark
    David Shelby
    Jesse McDermott

Applications for Enrollment of Creek Newborn
Act of 1905   Volume XII

Subscribed and sworn to before me this 29 day of April, 1905.

(Seal)   Edw C Griesel
                                    Notary Public.

NF-561

Muskogee, Indian Territory, September 15, 1905.

Julia Hogan,
    Care of Robert Hogan,
        Beggs, Indian Territory.

Dear Madam:

    In the matter of the application for the enrollment of your minor child, Willie D. Hogan, as a Creek Freedman, you are advised that this Office is unable to identify you on its rolls of Creek Freedmen.

    You are requested to wrote this Office at an early date, giving your maiden name, the names of your parents, the Creek Indian Town to which you belong, and, if possible, your name and roll number as same appear on your deeds to land in the Creek Nation.

    Your name is spelled in the body of the birth affidavit, in the matter of the birth of said child, as Julia Hogan, while you signed the affidavit "Julia A. Hogans." You are requested to write this Office at once as to the correct spelling [sic] your name.

                Respectfully,

                              Acting Commissioner.

Applications for Enrollment of Creek Newborn
Act of 1905   Volume XII

(The letter below typed as given.)

RICHARD JOSEPH HILL
(CREEK CITIZEN)
Attorney and Counselor at Law

PRACTICE BEFORE SUPREME
COURT WASHINGTON, D. C.

PROMPT AND RELIABLE SERVICES

BEGGS, I. T. 9/19 **190**5

Department of the Interior

In the matter of the application for the enrollment of application for the enrollment of the minor child Willie D Hogan

Yours of 15th isnt return with proper correction

I am on Creek Roll

Name of my parents are Mother Millie San-go Father Samson Brown (dead) the town to which I belong is Thoelecco
Deed or certificate of allotment not in my possession at present
My maiden name is Julia Brown it apeare on my Deed the same

My name is at present Julia Hogan
I hope this will gave requored infomatio   Respetfully yours

　　　　　　　　　　　　　Julia Hogan
in *(illegible)* of Robt Hogan
　　　　　　　　　　　　　　　　　Beggs

BIRTH AFFIDAVIT.

DEPARTMENT OF THE INTERIOR.
COMMISSION TO THE FIVE CIVILIZED TRIBES.

IN RE APPLICATION FOR ENROLLMENT, as a citizen of the CREEK Nation, of Willie D. Hogan, born on the 27 day of Jan, 1905

Name of Father: Robert Hogan　　　　a citizen of the   U.S.   Nation.
Name of Mother: Julia   "   　　　　a citizen of the   Creek   Nation.

　　　　　　　　Postoffice   ~~Musk~~ Beggs

Applications for Enrollment of Creek Newborn
Act of 1905   Volume XII

(Child present)

AFFIDAVIT OF MOTHER.

UNITED STATES OF AMERICA, Indian Territory,
WESTERN   DISTRICT.

I, Julia Hogan , on oath state that I am 20 years of age and a citizen by Freedman , of the Creek Nation; that I am the lawful wife of Robert Hogan , who is a citizen, by ------- of the U.S. Nation; that a female child was born to me on 27 day of January , 1905 , that said child has been named Willie D. Hogans , and is now living.

Julia A. Hogans

Witnesses To Mark:

Subscribed and sworn to before me this 20" day of March , 1905.

Edw C Griesel
Notary Public.

AFFIDAVIT OF ATTENDING ~~PHYSICIAN~~ OR MID-WIFE.

UNITED STATES OF AMERICA, Indian Territory,
WESTERN   DISTRICT.

I, Ann McQueen , a Midwife , on oath state that I attended on Mrs. Julia Hogan, wife of Robert Hogan on the 26 day of Jan , 1905 ; that there was born to her on said date a female child; that said child is now living and is said to have been named Willie D. Hogan

Her
Ann x McQueen
mark

Witnesses To Mark:
  Jesse McDermott
  EC Griesel

Subscribed and sworn to before me this 8 day of April, 1905.

Edw C Griesel
Notary Public.

Applications for Enrollment of Creek Newborn
Act of 1905 Volume XII

N.C. 946.

DEPARTMENT OF THE INTERIOR,
COMMISSIONER TO THE FIVE CIVILIZED TRIBES.
Muskogee, I. T., January 10, 1906.

In the matter of the application for the enrollment of Tom Davis as a citizen by blood of the Creek Nation.

Ja-tah-ko-co-cah-ney, being duly sworn, testified as follows:

Through Amos Roland who was duly sworn as Euche interpreter:

BY THE COMMISSIONER:
Q What is your name? A Ja-tah-ko-con-cah-ney.
Q What is the name of your father? A Ah-la-con-tay.
Q What wa the name of your mother? A Po-con-we-ney. (Interpreter states that it may be Po-ko-con-we-ney)
Q How old are you? A About thirty.
Q what is your post office address? A Kelleyville[sic].
Q We have here a affidavit signed, by mark, Nancy Davis Wolf. Is that you? A Yes, sir.
Q Is that your name or is Ja-tah-ke-con-cah-ney your proper name? A Nancy Davis Brown is my English name and Ja-tah-ke-con-cah-ney is my Euche name.

Witness is identified as Ja-tah-ko-con-cah-ney opposite Creek Indian Roll No. 7910.

Q Have you a child named Tom Davis? A Yes, sir.
Q Is that child living? A Yes, sir.
Q When was it born? A It is a little over three years old.
Q What month was it born in? A It was born in July.
Q Do you mean that it will be three years old next July o was it three years old last July? A It will be three years old next July.
W We have here an affidavit signed, by mark, by Nancy Davis Wolf, in which it is stated that Tom Davis was born July 10, 1903, which would make him three years old next July. Is that correct? A Yes, sir. I can't tell exactly.
Q What is the correct name of that child? A Tom Davis.
Q What is the name of the father of Tom Davis? A Addie Davis. (The interpreter explains "that is the way an Euche calls Eddie")
Q He is not enrolled as Eddie is he? A He is on the roll as De-con-sac.
Q Is De-con-sac living? A Yes, sir.
Q What is the name of his father? A Sal-con-cah-ney.
Q What is the name of his mother? A Ta-san-kay-nay.

The father of said child is identified under the name of De-con-sac opposite Roll No. 790*(illegible)*.

Applications for Enrollment of Creek Newborn
Act of 1905   Volume XII

Q Is De-con-sac's English name Eddie Davis? A Yes, sir.
Q And you want this child enrolled as Tom Davis? A Yes, sir, that is his name.

The child is present and appears to be a little over two years of age.

I, D. C. Skaggs, on oath state that the above and foregoing is a full and true transcript of my stenographic notes as taken in said cause on said date.

D. C. Skaggs

Subscribed and sworn to before me this 11 day of Jan, 1906.

J McDermott
Notary Public.

Western District
Indian Territory   SS

We, the undersigned, on oath state that we are personally acquainted with Nancy Davis Wolf (Ja-tah-ko-con-cah-ney)   wife of De-con-sac ; and that on or about the 10 day of July 1903 , a   male   child was born to them and has been named Tom Davis   ; that said child was living March 4, 1905.

We further state that we have no interest in the above case.

Miller Barnett
her
Linda x Barnett
mark

Witness to mark:
H.G. Hains
Alex Posey

Subscribed and sworn to before
me this 10 day of Jan. 1906

H.G. Hains
Notary Public.

Applications for Enrollment of Creek Newborn
Act of 1905   Volume XII

BIRTH AFFIDAVIT.

DEPARTMENT OF THE INTERIOR.
COMMISSION TO THE FIVE CIVILIZED TRIBES.

IN RE APPLICATION FOR ENROLLMENT, as a citizen of the Creek Nation, of Tom Davis, born on or about the 10 day of July, 1903

Name of Father: Addie Davis   a citizen of the   Creek   Nation.
(Euchee)
Name of Mother: Nancy Davis Wolf   a citizen of the   "   Nation.
(Euchee)   ~~Sat-ah-co-con-coh-ny~~
    Ja-tah-ko-con-cah-ney   Postoffice   Kellyville

AFFIDAVIT OF MOTHER.
Child Present

UNITED STATES OF AMERICA, Indian Territory,
    Western   DISTRICT.

I, Nancy Davis Wolf, on oath state that I am 30 years of age and a citizen by blood, of the Creek Nation; that I ~~am~~ was formerly the lawful wife of Addie Davis, who is a citizen, by blood of the Creek Nation; that a male child was born to me on 10 day of July, 1903, that said child has been named Tom Davis, and was living March 4, 1905.
                                           Her
                             Nancy Davis x Wolf
Witnesses To Mark: mark
   { David Shelby
     Jesse McDermott

Subscribed and sworn to before me this 24 day of April, 1905.

                                 Edw C Griesel
                                 Notary Public.

AFFIDAVIT OF ATTENDING PHYSICIAN OR MID-WIFE.

UNITED STATES OF AMERICA, Indian Territory,
.... DISTRICT.

I, ..., a ...., on oath state that I attended on Mrs. ...., wife of .... on the .... day of ...., 1.........; that there was born to her on said date a .... child; that said child was living March 4, 1905, and is said to have been named ....

Witnesses To Mark: No one else present.
   { ....
     ....

Applications for Enrollment of Creek Newborn
Act of 1905 Volume XII

Subscribed and sworn to before me this .... day of ...., 1 ....

....
Notary Public.

NC 946

Muskogee, Indian Territory, October 20, 1905.

Nancy Davis Wolf,
Kellyville, Indian Territory.

Dear Madam:

    In the matter of the application for the enrollment of Tom Davis, born July 10, 1903, as a citizen by blood of the Creek Nation, this office is unable to identify you or Addie Davis, the father of said child, on its final roll of citizens by blood of the Creek Nation; you are requested to state your maiden name, the names of the parents of yourself and of said Addie Davis, the Creek Indian town to which you belong and the numbers which appear on your deeds to lands in the Creek Nation.

                          Respectfully,
                                       Commissioner.

NC-946

Muskogee, Indian Territory, December 16, 1905.

Nancy Davis Wolf,
Kellyville, Indian Territory.

Dear Madam:

    In the matter of the application for the enrollment of your minor child, Tom Davis, born July 10, 1903, as a citizen by blood of the Creek Nation, this Office is unable to identify you or Addie Davis, the father of said child, on its final rolls of citizens of the Creek Nation. It is necessary that you should be so identified before the right to enrollment of said child can be determined.

    You are requested to write this Office at an early date, giving your maiden name, the names of your parents and those of said Addie Davis, the Creek Indian Town to which each of you belongs, and, if possible, your names and roll numbers as same appear on your allotment certificate or deeds to land in the Creek Nation.

    It is also necessary that you furnish this Office with the affidavits of two disinterested persons relative to said child's birth, and a blank for that purpose is herewith enclosed.

Applications for Enrollment of Creek Newborn
Act of 1905   Volume XII

Dis

Respectfully,

Commissioner.

(The letter below does not belong to this applicant.)

N.C. 957.

Muskogee, Indian Territory, January 12, 1906.

William F. A. Gierkey[sic],
   Beggs, Indian Territory.

Dear Sir:

   Receipt is acknowledged of your letter of January 6, 1906, relative to the enrollment of Willie Friday as a citizen of the Creek Nation. You request that an affidavit on file in this office, to which you failed to affix your notarial seal, be returned you for correction. You state that the mid-wife has left the country.

   You are advised that the defective affidavit referred to is not that of the mid-wife but of the mother, Jennie Friday, and same cannot be remedied in the manner requested by you for the reason that her affidavit, having been executed in 1902, does not state whether her child was living March 4, 1905, as is required.

   You are requested to have said Jennie Friday appear before a notary public and execute an affidavit, stating the name of her child, the names of its parents, the date of its birth and whether it was living March 4, 1905, taking care that same is properly signed by the affiant and dated, signed and sealed by the notary public. A blank form for that purpose is herewith inclosed.

Respectfully,

1-BA.

Commissioner.

Applications for Enrollment of Creek Newborn
Act of 1905 Volume XII

N.C. 947

DEPARTMENT OF THE INTERIOR,
COMMISSION TO THE FIVE CIVILIZED TRIBES.
April 24, 1905.

In the matter of the application for the enrollment of certain new borns as citizens of the Creek Nation.

Alex Posey, being duly sworn, testified as follows:

By Commission:
Q What is your name, age and post office address? A Alex Posey, 31, Muskogee.
Q Are you a citizen of the Creek Nation? A Yes sir
Q Got your land, have you? A Yes sir.
Q You have been engaged recently in the field for the Dawes Commission securing evidence about Creek citizens or new borns? A Yes sir.
Q Have you a list of children for whom application could not be made and about whom you have succeeded in obtaining some information? A Yes sir.
Q You may state the conditions and the names of these children? You desire to make application for them? A Yes sir.
Q Name them.
A   July Proctor, Weogufky Town, Sukey Proctor, Weogufky Town, have two children --one about three years old and one about six months old. Post office, Hanna, Indian Territory.
    Jacob Bullet, about three years old. Parents: Maxey Bullet, Seminole, and Hannah Bullet, Hillabbee[sic]. Post Office, Hannah, Indian Territory.
    Connie Hawkins, Hillabee Town, Sabella Hawkins, Okchiye, have two children--one about three years old and a younger child. Post Office, Hanna, Indian Territory.
    Willie Fisher, Hickory Ground Town, Lussee Fisher, Okfusky[sic] Canadian Town, have two children--one about three years old and a baby. Post Office, Slumpker, Indian Territory.
    Lizzie Lasley, about three years old, Sam Lasley, born in either August or September, 1904. Parents: Sam Lasley, Okchiye, Wisey Lasley, Weogufky. Post Office, Hanna, Indian Territory.
    Jim Haynes (or Sangee), Okchiye Town, Folotkokee, Weogufky Town have a male child about three years old named Joe. Post Office, Hanna, Indian Territory.
    Taylor Foley, Weogufky, Melinda Foley, Okchiye, have a child about two years old. Post Office, Skumpka[sic], Indian Territory.
    Phillip Lindsey, Tuckabatchee, Cilla Lindsey, Hillabee, have a child about three years old. Post Office, Hanna, Indian Territory.
    Big William (or William Thlocco), Okchiye Town, Cinda Williams, Weogufky Town, have two children -- one about three years old-- one born in February 1905. Post Office Hanna, Indian Territory.
    Freeland Lindsey, Tuckabctshee[sic] or Hillabee, Nancy Proctor, Tullahassoche, have a child about two years old. Post Office, Hanna, Indian Territory.
    Timonthluppy George, Weogufky Town, Nellie George, Pukon Tullahassee[sic], have a child about three years old. Post Office, Slumpkaer[sic], Indian Territory.

Applications for Enrollment of Creek Newborn
Act of 1905   Volume XII

Walter Simmons, Weogufky, Chippie Simmons, Pukon Tulahassee[sic], have a child about one years old. Post Office, Hannah, Indian Territory.

Jacob Larney (or Green), Arbeka Tulledega Town, Bettie Larney, (or Green), Hillabee Town, have a child. Post Office, Hanna, Indian Territory.

John Hill, Okchiye, Millie Hill, Weogufky, have a child about three months old. Post Office, Hanna, Indian Territory.

Jim Pigeon, Okchiye Town, Jennie Pigeon, Okchiye Town, have a child about five months old. Post Office, Hanna, Indian Territory.

Thomas Deo, Okchiye Town, Nancy Deo, Fish Pond Town, have a child about three months old. Post Office, Hanna, Indian Territory.

Jack Buckner, born December 17, 1904. Parents: Wiley Buckner, Okchiye, Susie Buckner, Cussehta. Post Office, Hanna, Indian Territory.

Q This is the information you received from relatives right around there on April 24, 1905? A Yes sir.

Q Were you informed that the parents of these children were unwilling to make application for their enrollment? A Yes sir.

Q This was the only way that the rights of these children would be saved? A Yes sir. I made every effort to obtain direct information from the parents but in every instance they refused to give their testimony.

Lona Merrick being duly sworn, states that the above and foregoing is a true and correct transcript of his stenographic notes as taken in said cause on said date.

Lona Merrick

Subscribed and sworn to before me this 9th day of May, 1905.

Edw C Griesel
Notary Public.

2448-B.
DEPARTMENT OF THE INTERIOR,
COMMISSION TO THE FIVE CIVILIZED TRIBES.
Carson, I. T., June 14, 1905.

In the matter of the application for the enrollment of a child of Freeland Lindsey and Nancy Proctor.

SHAWNEE HARPER, being duly sworn, testified as follows:

Through Alex Posey Official Interpreter:

BY COMMISSION:
Q What is your name? A Shawnee Harper.
Q How old are you? A Between thirty and thirty-one.
Q What is your post office address? A Carson.

Applications for Enrollment of Creek Newborn
Act of 1905   Volume XII

Q Are you a citizen of the Creek Nation? A Yes, sir.
Q To what town do you belong? A Hillabee.
Q Do you know Freeland Lindsey and Nancy Proctor? A Yes, sir, I am well acquainted with both of them.
Q Have they a new-born child for whom they have made no application? A I am not certain that Freeland Lindsey is the father of the child which Nancy has. I have never heard who the father was.
Q Were Freeland Lindsey and Nancy Proctor ever married? A I do not think they were ever married.
Q Do you know the name of the child? A No, sir.
Q Do you know when the child was born? A The child was born in 1904, I do not know in what month.
Q Was the child born in the Spring, Summer, Fall or Winter? A Sometime in the Fall--I think in September.
Q Is the child living? A Yes, sir.
Q Is it a boy or girl? A I do not know.
Q Do you know any one who could give more deffinite[sic] information about this child? A Hullie Proctor would perhaps know when the child was born.

LUMBER PROCTOR, being duly sworn, testified as follows:

Through Alex Posey Official Interpreter:

BY COMMISSION:
Q What is your name? Lumber Proctor.
Q How old are you? A About twenty-eight.
Q What is your post office address? A Dustin.
Q Are you a citizen of the Creek Nation? A Yes, sir.
Q To what town do you belong? A Weogufke.
Q Do you know Nancy Proctor? A Yes, sir, she is my sister.
Q Has she a new-born child? A Yes, sir.
Q What is the child's name? A Columbia.
Q Who is the father of the child? A Freeland Lindsey.
Q Is Freeland Lindsey the lawful husband of Nancy Proctor? A No, sir.
Q Do you know whether or not he acknowledges the child as his own? A Yes, sir.
Q Does he contribute towards the support of the child? A I think not.
Q Do you know when Columbia was born? A The grand-mother of the child told me the other day that the child was born on the 15th day of February, 1904.
Q Is the child over a year old? A Yes, sir, the child is just about able to walk.
Q To what town does the mother belong? A Tallahassoche.
Q To what town does the father belong? A Tuckabatche.
Q Do you know why Nancy has not made application for the enrollment of this child? A She was dis-suaded[sic] from doing so by her father who is opposed to allotment.

---oooOOOooo---

Applications for Enrollment of Creek Newborn
Act of 1905   Volume XII

I, D. C. Skaggs, on oath state that the above and foregoing is a full and true transcript of my stenographic notes as taken in said cause on said date.

D. C. Skaggs

JUL 17 1905

Subscribed and sworn to before me this ____ day of _____ 1905.

Edw C Griesel
Notary Public.

Dustin, Indian Territory, June 17, 1905.

Commission to the Five Civilized Tribes,
    Muskogee, Indian Territory.

Gentlemen:

There is enclosed herewith testimony in the matter of the application for the enrollment of a child of Freeland Lindsey and Nancy Proctor (No. 2444-B) as a citizen by blood of the Creek Nation; I find it impossible to secure further evidence about said child.

Respectfully,
Alex Posey
Clerk in Charge Creek Field Party.

See 2448 B testimony
    taken Apr 24-05 at Eufaula -
            Gr.

N.C. 947.   F.H.W.

DEPARTMENT OF THE INTERIOR,
COMMISSIONER TO THE FIVE CIVILIZED TRIBES.

In the matter of the application for the enrollment of Columbia Lindsey as a citizen by blood of the Creek Nation.

DECISION.

The record in this case shows that on April 24, 1905, Alex Posey, clerk in charge of a Creek enrollment field party, appeared before the Commission to the Five Civilized Tribes, at Muskogee, Indian Territory, and testified in the matter of the application for enrollment of and accounting for certain new-born children of duly enrolled Creek citizens members of the Snake faction. In the said testimony appears the name of Columbia Lindsey and the said testimony is herein considered as an application for the enrollment of the said Columbia Lindsey as a citizen by blood of the Creek Nation, in

Applications for Enrollment of Creek Newborn
Act of 1905   Volume XII

order that the rights of the said applicant be protected. Further proceedings were ad June 14, 1905.

The evidence shows that Columbia Lindsey is the illegitimate child of Freeland Lindsey and Nancy Proctor, whose names appear on partial schedules of citizens by blood of the Creek Nation approved by the Secretary of the Interior March 28, 1902, and March 13, 1902, opposite Nos. 8059 and 3714 respectively.

The evidence further shows that said Columbia Lindsey was born February 15, 1904 and was living June 14, 1905.

The Act of Congress approved March 3, 1905, (33 Stats. 1048) provides in part as follows:

"That the Commission to the Five Civilized Tribes is authorized for sixty days after the date of the approval of this act to receive and consider applications for enrollment, of children, born subsequent to May twenty-fifth, nineteen hundred and one, and prior to March fourth, nineteen hundred and five, and living on said latter date, to citizens of the Creek tribe of Indians whose enrollment has been approved by the Secretary of the Interior prior to the approval of this act; and to enroll and make allotments to such children."

It is therefore, ordered and adjudged that said Columbia Lindsey is entitled to be enrolled as a citizen by blood of the Creek Nation, in accordance with the provisions of law above quoted, and the application for her enrollment as such is accordingly granted.

                              Tams Bixby Commissioner.
Muskogee, Indian Territory.

    January 14-1907

                                                                    JWH
NC 947
                        Muskogee, Indian Territory, March 1, 1907.

Nancy Proctor,
    Freeland Lindsey,
              Carson, Indian Territory.

Dear Madam :--

You are hereby advised that on February 15, 1907, the Secretary of the Interior approved the enrollment of your minor child, Columbia Lindsey, as a citizen by blood of the Creek Nation, and that the name of said child appears upon the roll of New Born citizens by blood of the Creek Nation, enrolled under the Act of Congress approved March 3, 1905, as number 1182.

                        Respectfully,
                                        Commissioner.

Applications for Enrollment of Creek Newborn
Act of 1905 Volume XII

40103

(C O P Y.) DEPARTMENT OF THE INTERIOR

Land-F.T. Office of Indian Affairs
31064-22 Washington
C G P
Error on citizenship roll APR 21 1922
as to designation of sex.

The Honorable

    The Secretary of the Interior.

Sir:

    I have the honor to transmit herewith a report of April 12, 1922, from the Superintendent for the Five Civilized Tribes, and other papers relative to an error appearing on the final approved roll of New Born citizens by blood of the Creek Nation in reference to the designation of the sex of Columbia Lindsey, whose name appears opposite No. 1182 on said roll. It appears that Columbia Lindsey was designated on said roll as a female and should have been designated as a male.

    The Office therefore recommends that the letter "F" appearing in the sex column opposite the name of Columbia Lindsey at No. 1182, on the final approved roll of new Born citizens by blood of the Creek Nation be cancelled and that the letter "M" be substituted therefore, and that this Office and the Superintendent for the Five Civilized Tribes be authorized to make a similar correction upon the copies of the rolls in their possession.

                    Respectfully,

                            E.B. Meritt,
Approved: APR 21 1922   Assistant Commissioner.
    F. M. Goodwin
        Assistant Secretary.

Applications for Enrollment of Creek Newborn
Act of 1905   Volume XII

2215 B

DEPARTMENT OF THE INTERIOR,
COMMISSION TO THE FIVE CIVILIZED TRIBES.
April 24, 1905, Sapulpa, I.T.

  In the matter of the application for the enrollment of Andy Downing as a citizen by blood of the Creek Nation.

  Mahala Downing being duly sworn by E.C. Griesel, a Notary Public, testified as follows: Through official Interpreter, J. McDermott.

By Commission:

Q What is your name? A Mahala Downing.
Q What is your age? A 25.
Q What is your post office? A Kelleyville[sic].
Q You are a citizen of the Creek Nation? A Yes sir.
Q To what town do you belong to? A Euchee Town.
Q You wish to make application for the enrollment of Andy Downing as a citizen by blood of the Creek Nation? A Yes sir.
Q Are you the mother of Andy Downing? A Yes sir.
Q Who is the father of this child? A James Downing.
Q Is he a citizen of the Creek Nation? A Yes.
Q When was this child born? A November 3, 1903.
Q Are you living with James Downing now? A No sir.
Q When did you separate? A Last year.
Q What time last year? A I don't know.
Q What month? A I don't know.
Q Was it in the summer, fall or winter? A In the fall.
Q How long after the birth of this child did he continue to live with you? A Did not live with him a month.
Q Did you live with him after the birth of this child? - No.
Q You swear that this child was born November 3, 1903, and that he left you last year, how do you account for this? A No I mean before 1904.
Q How long did you live with James Downing? A Pretty near a year.
Q When were you married to James Downing? A don't just remember.
Q How long did you live together as man and wife? A About a year.
Q Did you ever live with any one else? After James Downing left you? A No sir.
Q Did you ever have anything to do with anyone after he left you? A No sir.

-----------------------oOo-----------------------

Applications for Enrollment of Creek Newborn
Act of 1905   Volume XII

     James Downing being duly sworn, by E.C. Grisel[sic], a Notary Public, testified as follows, Through Official Interpreter.

By Commission:
Q What is your name? A James Downing.
Q How old are you? A 20.
Q What is your post office? A Kelleyville[sic].
Q Are you a citizen of the Creek Nation? A Yes, sir.
Q To what town do you belong to? A Euchee Town.
Q Are you married? A I have been married but I have separated, and now trying to get a divorce.
Q What was the name of your wife? A Mahala Brown.
Q Was Mahala Brown ever known as Mahala Harris? A Don't know.
Q How long did you live with your wife, Mahala Downing? A We didn't live together for two months when someone else interfered when I left her.
Q When were you married to her? A October, 1902.

     Witness here exhibits marriage license issued by R.P. Harrison, Clerk of U.S. Court, dated October 9, 1902. Marriage certificate to the effect that the ceremoney[sic] was performed by O. M. Irelan, deputy clerk, U.S. Court, October 9, 1902.

Q You say you only lived with her two months after this ceremony was performed? A Not quite two months.
Q You swear positovely[sic] that you did not have anything to do with her after the two months? A No, I went back but another man wouldn't allow me to do anything with her.
Q According to your statement you separated in September, 1902, is that true or not? A Yes, that is right.
Q You were present when Mahala gave her testimony for the application for the enrollment of her infant child and heard it? A Yes I heard it.
Q You heard her statement that you were the father of Andy Downing when she made application for the child? A Yes I heard it.
Q Is that statement true, and are you the father of Andy Downing? A I couldn't say that I was the father of that child when I left her after two months and the child was born December, 1903.
Q She has testified that Andy Downing was born in November, 1903, and you testified that your separated[sic] that you separated in November, 1902. Now did you have anything to do with her after December, 1902? A No sir.
Q Do you deny that you are the father of Andy Downing? A Yes sir.
Q Did you have any personal knowledge of the birth of this child Andy Downing? A No sir, I did not pay any attention and was not interested.
Q Do you know the day and month and year? A No sir.
Q Do you know whether she gave birth to a male child in November, 1903? A I heard that there was a child born then.

-----oOo-----

Applications for Enrollment of Creek Newborn
Act of 1905   Volume XII

April 25, 1905, Sapulpa, Indian Territory.

William H. Whiteman, being duly sworn by E.C. Griesel, a Notary Public, testified as follows:

By Commission:
Q What is your name? A William H. Whiteman.
Q What is your age? A 63.
Q What is your post office? A Sapulpa.
Q Are you a citizen of the Creek Nation? A No sir.
Q Do you know Mahala Downing? A Yes sir.
Q How long have you known her? A Eight or nine months.
Q Do you know Andy Downing, a child of hers? A Yes.
Q When was it born? A It was born November 3, 1903.
Q How do you know this date? A They sent for me to get a doctor, and call, and he told me to go out to Mahala's house and see if enyerthing[sic] was alright and if so he would not need to go.
Q You were at Mahala's house when Andy Downing was born? A No, sir, the child was born when I got there.
A She was sitting up and I put her to bed and got some warm water and washed the child?
Q Is that Mahala? (Pointing to Mahala) A Yes sir.
Q Is that Andy Downing (Also indicating), she is holding in her lap? A Yes. When I was at the house I found she had no clothes for the child and returned to town and got some clothes and sent them to her.
Q This all occurred in 1903? A Yes, 4th of November.

-------------------oOo-------------------

E.C. Griesel, being duly sworn, on his oath states that the above and foregoing is a true and complete transcript of his stenographic notes as taken in said cause on said date.

Edw C Griesel

Subscribed and sworn to before me this 5 day of May, 1905.

Zera E. Parrish.
Notary Public.

Applications for Enrollment of Creek Newborn
Act of 1905   Volume XII

BIRTH AFFIDAVIT.

DEPARTMENT OF THE INTERIOR.
COMMISSION TO THE FIVE CIVILIZED TRIBES.

IN RE APPLICATION FOR ENROLLMENT, as a citizen of the Creek Nation, of Andy Snap, born on the 3 day of November, 1903

Name of Father: James Snap	a citizen of the Creek	Nation.
Name of Mother: Mahele Snap	a citizen of the Creek	Nation.

Postoffice   Kellyville, I. T.

AFFIDAVIT OF MOTHER.

UNITED STATES OF AMERICA, Indian Territory,
Western   DISTRICT.

I, Mahele Snap, on oath state that I am 25 years of age and a citizen by blood, of the Creek Nation; that I am the lawful wife of James Snap, who is a citizen, by blood of the Creek Nation; that a male child was born to me on 3 day of November, 1903, that said child has been named Andy Snap, and was living March 4, 1905. There was no physician or midwife or other person present

             Mahele Snap

Witnesses To Mark:
  { Harry Campbell
   William H. Whiteman

Subscribed and sworn to before me this 14th day of November, 1905.

             Harry Campbell
             Notary Public.

Applications for Enrollment of Creek Newborn
Act of 1905 Volume XII

BIRTH AFFIDAVIT.

Testimony taken.

DEPARTMENT OF THE INTERIOR.
COMMISSION TO THE FIVE CIVILIZED TRIBES.

IN RE APPLICATION FOR ENROLLMENT, as a citizen of the Creek Nation, of Andy Downing, born on the 3 day of Nov, 1903

Name of Father: James (Downing) Snap   a citizen of the   Creek   Nation.
(Euchee)   (nee Harris)
Name of Mother: Mahala Downing   a citizen of the   Creek   Nation.
(Euchee)

Postoffice   Kellyville

AFFIDAVIT OF MOTHER.

Child Present

UNITED STATES OF AMERICA, Indian Territory,
Western   DISTRICT.

I, Mahala Downing, on oath state that I am 25 years of age and a citizen by blood, of the Creek Nation; that I am the lawful wife of James Downing, who is a citizen, by blood of the Creek Nation; that a male child was born to me on 3 day of Nov, 1903, that said child has been named Andy Downing, and was living March 4, 1905.

Mahele Snap

Witnesses To Mark:

Subscribed and sworn to before me this 24 day of April, 1905.

Edw C Griesel
Notary Public.

AFFIDAVIT OF ATTENDING PHYSICIAN OR MID-WIFE.

UNITED STATES OF AMERICA, Indian Territory,
DISTRICT.

I, ..., a ...., on oath state that I attended on Mrs. ...., wife of .... on the .... day of ...., 1......; that there was born to her on said date a .... child; that said child was living March 4, 1905, and is said to have been named ....

Witnesses To Mark: No one else present.

Applications for Enrollment of Creek Newborn
Act of 1905   Volume XII

Subscribed and sworn to before me this ....day of................, 1........ .

....
Notary Public.

United States of America,)
)
Indian Territory) SS.
)
Western District)

  Timmie Brown, on oath, states that he is a citizen of the Creek Nation of Indians, and lives at Olive, Indian Territory; that he is twenty-one years of age, and speaks and understands the English language.

  Affiant further states that he is acquainted with one, James Snap, who is a citizen of the Creek Nation by blood and has known him nearly all his life; that he is usually known as James Downing; that he is acquainted with the wife of the said James Snap; that he[sic] names[sic] is Mahale Snap, but is usually called and known as Mahale Downing; that she is the sister of this affiant, and he has known her all his life.

  That in the latter part of October and the first part of November 1903, affiant was staying with his sister, the said Mahale Snap, about seven miles south west of Sapulpa, Indian Territory where she lived.

  That on the second or third day of November 1903, the said Mahale Snap became sick, and affiant went to Sapulpa to get a physician for her; after arriving there he asked one, William H. Whiteman, who had her allottment[sic] leased to get a doctor for the said Mahale, telling him that she was sick, and that he thought she was going to have a baby; that they could not get a physician, and that the said Whiteman went with the affiant on his return to Mahale's home; that they reached there sometime in the night; that they found that a male child was born to me on day of , 190, that said child has been named , and was living March 4, 1905. had been born just before they got there; that it was lying on the floor, and Mahale was sitting in front of the fire place by the child; that there was no other person there except another child of Mahale's about five years of age; that the said Whiteman put Mahale to bed, washed the child, wrapped it in an old dress skirt and put it to bed; that the said Whiteman reamined[sic] there till morning when he returned to Sapulpa; that the child was named Andy, and is usually called Anday[sic] Downing, but he is the son of James Snap and Mahale Snap aforesaid; that said child is still living; that the said James Snap and Mahale Snap were not living together at the time of the birth of said child; that they had separated some time before that time.

               Timmie Brown

Applications for Enrollment of Creek Newborn
Act of 1905   Volume XII

Subscribed and sworn to before me this 14th day of November 1905.

         Harry Campbell
         Notary Public.

United States of America,)	
)	
Indian Territory,)	SS.
)	
Western District.)	

  William H. Whiteman, on oath, states that he is a citizen of the United States and is is[sic] sixty three years of age; that he resides at Sapulpa, Indian Territory; that he is acquainted with James Snap, usually known as James Downing; that he is a citizen by blood of the Creek Nation; that he is acquainted with the wife of the said James Snap; that her name is Mahale, and is usually known as Mahale Downing; that he has known said James Snap and his said wife for about nine years; that the said Mahale Snap or Downing is a citizen by blood of the Creek Nation.

  That on the second or third day of November 1903, the affiant is not certain which, one Timmie Brown, a citizen of the Creek Nation, and a brother of the said Mahale Snap or Downing came to affiant in Sapulpa and told affiant the said Mahale was sick, and he (Timmie Brown) wanted affiant to get a doctor to go to her her[sic] home about six or seven miles south west of Sapulpa; affiant tried to get a doctor to go out, but could not get one; that affiant and the said Timmie Brown went to the home of the said Mahale Downing or Snap that night and reached there possibly about eight or nine o'clock P. M.; that they went into the house which was dark, there being no light except the light made by the fire in the fire place; that affiant and the said Timmie Brown found that the said Mahale Snap or Downing was alone except she had a child which has evidently been born but a few minutes and another child about five years of age; that the said Mahale was sitting on the floor by the fireplace, and the child was lying on the floor; that affiant put the said Mahale Downing or Snap to bed, and washed the baby, and there being no clothes for the baby he wrapped same in an old dress skirt, and put it to bed with Mahale. Affiant remained there all night, and next morning went to Sapulpa and sent some clothes out for the baby. Affiant had the allottment[sic] of the said Mahale Snap or Downing leased at that time, and the said Mahale and her brother looked to him for help; there was no physician or midwife there that night.

  Affiant further states that he still has the allottment[sic] of said Mahale leased, and sees her and the child frequently; that said child has been named Andy Snap or Downing; that he is usually known as Andy Downing.

  Affiant further states that said child is still living, and is a male child.

  Affiant further states that he is well acquainted with all said Indians, but that said James Snap has been known to him as James Downing, and that said Mahale Snap has

Applications for Enrollment of Creek Newborn
Act of 1905   Volume XII

been known to him as Mahale downing, and that said Andy Snap has been known to him as Andy Downing; that the said Mahale is a citizen of the Creek Nation, and has an allottment[sic], and that he knows the said child belongs to her and he knows he is still living. That the child named Andy was the child born the night of November 2nd or 3rd 1903.

William H. Whiteman

Subscribed and sworn to before me this 14th day of November 1905.

Harry Campbell
Notary Public.

N.C. 948

Muskogee, Indian Territory, October 20, 1905.

Mahele Downing (or Snap),
    Care James Downing (or Snap),
        Kellyville, Indian Territory.

Dear Madam:

    In the matter of the application for the enrollment of Andy Downing, born November 3, 1903, as a citizen by blood of the Creek Nation, you state in your affidavit relative to the birth of said child, executed April 24, 1905, that you are the lawful wife of James Downing, that the name of your said child is Andy Downing, and you sign said affidavit Mahele Downing. In the caption of the affidavit it is stated that the name of the father of said child is James (Downing) Snap and he is identified on the final roll of citizens by blood of the Creek Nation as James Snap. If James Snap is the correct name of the father of said child it follows that the correct name of said child is Andy Snap, and if you are the lawful wife of James Snap, as stated in your affidavit, it necessarily follows that your surname is Snap.

    This office desires the affidavit of yourself and the midwife or physician in attendance at the birth of said child and a blank for that purpose, partially filled out, is enclosed herewith.

    In the event that there was no physician or midwife in attendance when said child was born, it will be necessary for you to furnish this office with the affidavits of two disinterested witnesses relative to his birth. Said affidavits must set forth said child's name, the date of his birth, the names of his parents and whether or not he was living on March 4, 1905.

Respectfully,
Commissioner.

1-3

Applications for Enrollment of Creek Newborn
Act of 1905   Volume XII

NC-948 (Copy)

Nov. 14th, 1905.

Hon. Tams Bixby, Commissioner.
Muskogee, I. T.

Dear Sir:

I hereby enclose additional proff[sic] of the birth of my child Andy Snap or Downing, as requested in your letter of the 20th of October.

Yours Truly,
Mahale Snap (Downing)

F484

DEPARTMENT OF THE INTERIOR,
COMMISSION TO THE FIVE CIVILIZED TRIBES.
Holdenville, I. T., March 31, 1905.

In the matter of the application for the enrollment of Nora Johnson as a Creek Freedman.

DELILA SANGO, being duly sworn, testified as follows:

BY COMMISSION:
Q What is your name? A Delila Sango.
Q How old are you? A 27.
Q What is your post office? A Holdenville.
Q Are you a citizen of the Creek Nation? A No, sir, I am a Seminole.
Q Seminole Fredman[sic]? A Yes, sir.
Q Do you make application for the enrollment of your minor child, Nora Johnson, as a Creek Freedman? A Yes, sir.
Q What is the name of her father? A Johnnie Johnson.
Q Is he a citizen of the Creek Nation? A Yes, sir.
Q To what town does he belong? A Canadian Colored.
Q Is he your lawful husband? A No, sir.
Q Were you ever married to him? A No, sir
Q Did you ever live with him as man and wife? A No, sir.
Q Does he recornize[sic] Nora Johnson as his child? A Yes, sir.

Applications for Enrollment of Creek Newborn
Act of 1905   Volume XII

Q Does he support the child? A Yes, sir.
Q What has he bought for the child? A Everything she needs.
Q Just state what he has bought for the child. Did he buy food and clothing for her? A Yes, sir.
Q When was the last time he bought anything for that child? A Last year.
Q Has he contributed to the support of that child since that time? A No, sir.
Q Does he come to see the child? A He is in the penitentiary now.
Q How long has he been there? A They sent him last Fall.
Q You were not living with him at the time the child was born? A No, sir.
Q Were you ever married to any one else? A Yes, sir, I was married before that child was born.
Q How long before? A About seven years I guess.
Q What was the name of your husband? A Jackson Sango. He got killed.
Q You never lived with any one else since Jackson Sango was killed? A No, sir.
Q How do you know that Nora Johnson is the child of Johnnie Johnson? A Because there was no other man come around me.
Q Wa Johnnie Johnson frequently at your house before and after the child was born? A Yes, sir.
Q Have you any other children besides Nora? A Yes, sir.
Q What are their names? A Timmie, Leah and Lucinda Sango and Rena Vann.
Q Who is the father of Timmie, Leah and Lucinda? A Jackson Sango.
Q Was he your lawful husband? A Yes, sir.
Q Was he a citizen of the Creek Nation? A Yes, sir.
Q Are those children enrolled in the Creek Nation? A No, sir, Seminole.
Q Who is the father of Rena Vann? A Billy Vann.
Q Was he your lawful husband? A No, sir.
Q Did you ever live with him as his wife? A No, sir.
Q Is Billy Vann a citizen of the Creek Nation? A Yes, sir.
Q To what town does he belong? A I don't know.
Q Where is Rena Vann enrolled? A In the Seminole Nation.
Q How old is she? A She will be six years old next month.
Q Did Johnnie Johnson contribute anything towards your support before Nora was born? A Yes, sir.
Q What did he contribute? A Everything.
Q Did he by you food and clothing? A Yes, sir.
Q Is Nora Johnson generally recognized in your neighborhood as the child of Johnnie Johnson? A Yes, sir.
Q Every one considers her his child? A Yes, sir.
Q If it should be found that your child Nora Johnson is entitled to enrollment in either the Creek or Seminole Nations in which nation do you desire to have her enrolled? A In the Creek Nation.

REDMAN HOLMES, being duly sworn, testified as follows:

BY COMMISSION:
Q What is your name? A Redman Holmes.
Q How old are you? A About thirty-seven.

Applications for Enrollment of Creek Newborn
Act of 1905   Volume XII

Q What is your post office address? A Wetumka.
Q Are you a citizen of the Creek Nation? A Yes, sir.
Q To what town do you belong? A Canadian Colored.
Q Do you know Johnnie Johnson and Delila Sango? A Yes, sir.
Q Do you know a child of their named Nora Johnson? A Yes, sir.
Q Is Johnnie Johnson the lawful husband of Delila Sango? A Not that I know of.
Q Did he ever live with her? A Yes, sir.
Q How long did he live with her? A I don't know just exactly how long.
Q According to your best recollection? A I guess he lived with her about six or eight months.
Q Live in the same house did he and contributed to her support? A Yes, sir.
Q How long ago has that been? A It has been about a year ago, I think. Near as I can think of it.
Q Was he living with her at the time Nora was born? A He wasn't there at that time. He was off.
Q How long had he been gone before the child was born? A I don't know just how long?
Q Was it as much as a year? A He had not been gone that long.
Q Was it as much as six or seven months? A I guess it was. I don't know exactly when he left. I didn't pay any attention to him, when he come or when he went and don't know.
Q Was Delila Sango recognized in the neighborhood as his wife? A I couldn't tell you anything about it. I never heard any one say anything about it.
Q Did any other man ever live with her? A Not that I know of.
Q What is her character in the neighborhood? A I never heard anything about her character.
Q You ought to know you live right in her neighborhood? A She has not got a good. I couldn't say while she was sitting' right there. (Delila Sango was told to leave the room) She has four sets of children. She has a set by Jackson Sango, she got one from Billy Vann and got one from Bill Davis and then this one here, Nora.
Q Is Jackson Sango a citizen of the Creek Nation? A Yes, sir, he was a citizen and was her lawful husband.
Q Was Vann a citizen of the Creek Nation? A Yes, sir.
Q Was Davis a citizen of the Creek Nation? A No, sir, he was a United States citizen.
Q When did he live with her? A Between four and five years ago.
Q Did any one lie with her before Johnnie Johnson? A No, sir, not for a year before I think. I live right close and pass her house often and never seen any one there, and never heard any one say anything about any one being there. There is always some one to tell about it you know.
Q Does Johnnie Johnson recognize Nora Johnson as his child? A Yes, sir.
Q Do you know whether or not he contributed anything towards her support? A Yes, sir, he did when he was out of the pen.
Q Is the child recognized in the neighborhood as his child? A Yes, sir.
Q Do you recognize the child as being the child of Johnnie Johnson? A Yes, sir.

---oooOOOooo---

Applications for Enrollment of Creek Newborn
Act of 1905   Volume XII

     I, D. C. Skaggs, on oath state that the above and foregoing is a full and true transcript of my stenographic notes as taken in said cause on said date.

D. C. Skaggs

Subscribed and sworn to before me this 20 day of July, 1905.

Edw C Griesel
Notary Public.

(The letter below typed as given.)
COPY

To the Hon. Tams Bixby Chairman
    of the Commission to the Five Civilized Tribes

Mr. Tams Bixby, Muscogee[sic] Ind. Ter dear Sir I am the father of Nora Johnson an I desire to have her put on the role with me. Nora Johnson Was Born May 1904. he mother is a cittenson of the Simmonole Nattion   Nora Johnson mother died Aug. 18, 1905. I am a Creek Indian Belong to Tuckparfka Town an I would like to have the child plase on the Creek Role with me as the child mother is dead. you will find my role No. ~~18~~ 1573. John Johnson is my name. Also Nora Johnson is in the Cair of her ant Kattie James near holdenville Ind Ter an I am now in prison at Ft. Leavenworth an I cant see after her just now so I would like for her and Katie James to select land for Nora Johnson in the Creek Nattion an file for her and to perform every thing nesecery to be done for the child untill my time expire here then I can see after it or help her to see after it from your respectly

Signed   John Johnson
                       Okise

BIRTH AFFIDAVIT.
DEPARTMENT OF THE INTERIOR.
COMMISSION TO THE FIVE CIVILIZED TRIBES.

     IN RE APPLICATION FOR ENROLLMENT, as a citizen of the Creek Nation, of Nora Johnson, born on the 2 day of May, 1904

Name of Father: Johnnie Johnson   a citizen of the   Creek   Nation.
Canadian Colored
Name of Mother: Delila Sango   a citizen of the Seminole   Nation.

Postoffice   Holdenville I.T.

Applications for Enrollment of Creek Newborn
Act of 1905   Volume XII

AFFIDAVIT OF MOTHER.   Child Present
Testimony 2/31/05

UNITED STATES OF AMERICA, Indian Territory, ⎱
   Western   DISTRICT.   ⎰

     I, Delila Sango , on oath state that I am 27 years of age and a citizen by adoption , of the Seminole Nation; that I am the lawful wife of Johnnie Johnson , who is a citizen, by adoption of the Creek Nation; that a female child was born to me on 2 day of May , 1902 , that said child has been named Nora Johnson , and was living March 4, 1905.

her
Delila x Sango
mark

Witnesses To Mark:
  ⎰ DC Skaggs
  ⎱ Alex Posey

     Subscribed and sworn to before me this 31 day of March , 1905.

Drennan C Skaggs
Notary Public.

AFFIDAVIT OF ATTENDING PHYSICIAN OR MID-WIFE.

UNITED STATES OF AMERICA, Indian Territory, ⎱
   Western   DISTRICT.   ⎰

     I, Jane James , a mid-wife , on oath state that I attended on Mrs. Delila Sango , ~~wife of~~ on the 2 day of May , 1904 ; that there was born to her on said date a female child; that said child was living March 4, 1905, and is said to have been named Nora Johnson

her
Jane x James
mark

Witnesses To Mark:
  ⎰ DC Skaggs
  ⎱ Alex Posey

     Subscribed and sworn to before me this 31 day of March , 1905.

Drennan C Skaggs
Notary Public.

Applications for Enrollment of Creek Newborn
Act of 1905   Volume XII

N.F. 484

Muskogee, Indian Territory, August 2, 1905.

Clerk in Charge,
    Seminole Enrollment Division.

Dear Sir:

    There is on file at this office an affidavit relative to the birth of Nora Johnson, child of Delila Sango, a citizen of the Seminole Nation, and Johnnie Johnson, a freedman of the Creek Nation.

    You are requested to advise the Creek Enrollment Division whether application has been made for her enrollment as a Seminole freedman. If application has been made, advise date when made and card number of same.

              Respectfully,

                           Commissioner.

W.F.

REFER IN REPLY TO THE FOLLOWING:

DEPARTMENT OF THE INTERIOR,
COMMISSIONER TO THE FIVE CIVILIZED TRIBES.

Muskogee, Indian Territory, August 4, 1905.

Clerk in Charge,
    Creek Enrollment Division.

Dear Sir:

    Receipt is hereby acknowledged of your letter of the 2nd instant (NF-484) asking to be advised if application has been made for the enrollment of Nora Johnson, child of Delila Sango, a citizen of the Seminole Nation, and Johnnie Johnson, a Creek freedman, as a Seminole freedman.

    In reply to your letter you are informed that it does not appear from an examination of the records of this office that any application has ever been made for the enrollment of said Nora Johnson as a citizen of the Seminole Nation.

              Respectfully,

                           Tams Bixby
                           Commissioner.

Applications for Enrollment of Creek Newborn
Act of 1905   Volume XII

NC-484.

Muskogee, Indian Territory, October 31, 1905.

Delila Sango,
    Holdenville, Indian Territory.

Dear Madam:

    In the matter of the application for the enrollment of your minor child Nora Johnson you stated in your testimony of March 31, 1905, that Johnnie Johnson, the father of said child, was then in the penitentiary.

    You are requested to advise this office in what penitentiary the said Johnnie Johnson is now confined, in order that his affidavit may be obtained in said case.

        Respectfully,

                              Commissioner.

NF-484

Muskogee, Indian Territory, December 26, 1905.

Katie Nevins,
    Holdenville, Indian Territory.

Dear Madam:

    Receipt is acknowledged of your letter of December 22, 1905, in which you ask when you will be allowed to come and file for your niece, Nora Johnson, daughter of Delilah Sango, your deceased sister; you state that the mother if said child has willed her to you.

    In reply you are advised that there are on file at this Office the affidavit of said Delilah Sango, a Seminole, and of Jane James, midwife, relative to the birth of Nora Johnson. It appears from said affidavit that said Delilah Sango was not married to Johnnie Johnson, who is a citizen of the Creek Nation.

    You are further advised that this Office requires the testimony of said Johnnie Johnson, and you are requested to advise this Office in what penitentiary said Johnnie Johnson is now confined in order that his affidavit may be obtained in said case.

    When the matter of the application for the enrollment of said child has been finally approved, the parties in interest will be duly notified with regard to filing.

        Respectfully,

                              Commissioner.

Applications for Enrollment of Creek Newborn
Act of 1905   Volume XII

(The letter below typed as given.)

COPY

Holdenville, I. T.
Feb-8-1906.

Daws commission dear Sir I Reciev a letter from John Johnson stating to me that he want his little girl nora Johnson inroll with him and he want me to file for her if she will be allowed to file in the creek nation so please let me no if I can file for her or not please let me no and oblige yous Respectfully

Katy Nevins
sometime Katie James.

here is the letter that John Johnson send to you.

NC 949.

Muskogee, Indian Territory, August 21, 1906.

Chief Clerk,
    Seminole Enrollment Division,
        Muskogee, Indian Territory.

Dear Sir:

Application has been made for the enrollment as a citizen of the Creek Nation of Nora Johnson, born May 2, 1904, to John Johnson, a citizen of the Creek Nation, and Delilah Sango, a citizen of the Seminole Nation.

You are requested to advise this office if application has been made for the enrollment of said child as a citizen of the Seminole Nation, and if so, please furnish the present status of said application.

Respectfully,

Commissioner.

Applications for Enrollment of Creek Newborn
Act of 1905 Volume XII

REFER IN REPLY TO THE FOLLOWING:
_____

DEPARTMENT OF THE INTERIOR,
COMMISSIONER TO THE FIVE CIVILIZED TRIBES.

Muskogee, Indian Territory, August 24, 1906.

Chief Clerk,
    Creek Enrollment Division,
        Muskogee, Indian Territory.

Dear Sr:

    Receipt is hereby acknowledged of your letter of August 21, 1906, asking if application has been made for the enrollment as a citizen of the Seminole Nation of Nora Johnson, child of John Johnson, a citizen of the Creek Nation, and Delilah Sango, a citizen of the Seminole Nation.

    In reply you are advised that it does not appear from the records of this office that application has been made by or on behalf of Nora Johnson for enrollment as a new born citizen of the Seminole Nation under the Act of Congress approved March 3, 1905.

                        Respectfully,
                          Wm. O. Beall
                          Acting Commissioner.

NC 949.

                  Muskogee, Indian Territory, October 31, 1906.

Chief Clerk,
    Seminole Enrollment Division,
        Muskogee, Indian Territory.

Dear Sir:

    There is on file in this office an application for the enrollment of Nora Johnson, born May 2, 1904, to Delila Sango, a deceased citizen of the Seminole Nation, and John Johnson, who is identified as a citizen of the Creek Nation, opposite Creek Indian roll number 1573.

    You are advised that the name of said child is contained in a partial list of new born citizens by blood of the Creek Nation, approved by the Secretary of the Interior October 15, 1906, opposite roll number 1090.

                        Respectfully,
                                  Commissioner.

Applications for Enrollment of Creek Newborn
Act of 1905   Volume XII

h.C. 951   Frank Grayson

Is the son of Isaac Washington & Lizzie Grayson who is the legal wife of Tom Grayson but who has lived with Isaac Washington for over three years. Frank Grayson is alive & is about 4 years old.

P.B. Ewing

NC 951

Muskogee, Indian Territory, October 21, 1905.

Lizzie Grayson
    Care Tom Grayson, Indian Territory
        Eufaula, Indian Territory.

Dear Madam:

In the matter of the application for the enrollment of your minor child, Frank Grayson, Indian Territory born December 27, 1903, as a citizen by blood of the Creek Nation, this office is unable to identify you on its roll of citizens by blood of the Creek Nation; you are requested to state your maiden name, the names of your parents, the Creek Indian town to which you belong and the numbers on your deeds to lands in the Creek Nation.

Respectfully,
Commissioner.

NC 951

Muskogee, I T Dec 18, 1905

Lizzie Grayson,
    Care Tom Grayson,
        Eufaula, I T
Dear Madam:

In the matter of the application for the enrollment of your minor child, Frank Grayson, Indian Territory born December 27, 1903, as a citizen by blood of the Creek Nation, this Office is unable to to[sic] identify you on its final roll of citizens by blood of the Creek Nation; you are requested to state your maiden name, the names of your parents, the Creek Indian town to which you belong and your roll number as the same appears on your deeds to land in the Creek Nation.

This matter should receive your prompt attention.

Resp
Comr

Applications for Enrollment of Creek Newborn
Act of 1905 Volume XII

HGH

REFER IN REPLY TO THE FOLLOWING:

NC 951

DEPARTMENT OF THE INTERIOR,
COMMISSIONER TO THE FIVE CIVILIZED TRIBES.

Muskogee, Indian Territory, January 18, 1907.

Lizzie Grayson,
    Care of Tom Grayson,
        Eufaula, Indian Territory.

Dear Madam:

    In the matter of the application for the enrollment of your minor child Frank Grayson as a citizen by blood of the Creek Nation this office is unable to identify you upon its rolls as a citizen by blood of the Creek Nation blood of said nation.

    You are requested to write this office within ten days furnishing information as to your maiden name, the names of your parents, the Creek Indian town to which you belong and your roll number as the same appears on your deeds to land in the Creek Nation. Before the right to enrollment as a citizen of the Creek Nation of said child can be adjudicated it is necessary that you be identified as a citizen thereof. This matter should receive your prompt attention.

                Respectfully,
                Tams Bixby
                        Commissioner.

        Department of the Interior,
COMMISSION TO THE FIVE CIVILIZED TRIBES.

In re application for enrollment, as a citizen of the Creek Nation, of   Frank Grayson born on the 27 day of December A.D. 190 3.
                            United States
Name of father   Tom Grayson   a citizen of the ~~Creek Nation~~.
Name of Mother   Lizzie Grayson   a citizen of the Creek Nation.

                Postoffice   Eufaula I.T.

                Affidavit of Mother.

United States of America, Indian Territory, "
Western District.   "
                              "

I,   Lizzie Grayson   , on oath state that I am   Thirty nine   years of age and a citizen by   blood   of the Creek Nation, that I am the lawful wife of   Tom Grayson   who is a

Applications for Enrollment of Creek Newborn
Act of 1905   Volume XII

citizen, by   blood   , of the   United   ~~Nation~~,   States that a   male   child was born to me   27th day of   December   190 3   that said child has been names   Frank Grayson and was living March 4th., 1905.

Lizzie Grayson

Witness to mark.
Fannie Morris
E I O'Reilly

Subscribed and sworn to before me this 27 day of April 1905.

E.I. O'Reilly
Notary Public.

Affidavit of attending physician or mid-wife.

UNITED STATES OF AMERICA,
   INDIAN TERRITORY
   WESTERN DISTRICT.

   I   F.B. Morris   a   physician   on oath state that I attended on Mrs.   Lizzie Grayson   wife of   Tom Grayson   on the   27   day of   Dec 1903 that there was born to her on said date a   male   child; that said child was living March 4, 1905, and is said to have been named   Frank Grayson

FB Morris

Subscribed and sworn to before me this 27 day of April 1905.

E.I. O'Reilly Notary Public.

Applications for Enrollment of Creek Newborn
Act of 1905   Volume XII

NC 952.

DEPARTMENT OF THE INTERIOR,
COMMISSIONER TO THE FIVE CIVILIZED TRIBES.
MUSKOGEE, INDIAN TERRITORY.
JUNE 4, 1906.

In the matter of the application for the enrollment of Frances Willard Crowell, as a citizen of the Creek Nation.

Edward L. Crowell Jr., being duly sworn, testified as follows:

Q What is your name? A Edward L. Crowell, Jr.
Q What is your age? A 28 years old.
Q What is your post office address? A Coweta will be from this on.
Q Have you ever lived at Graham, Texas? A Yes sir.
Q What Creek Indian Town do you belong to? A I don't know.
Q Have you a brother that was enrolled same time as you were? A Yes sir.
Q What is his name? A Theres[sic] Tom, Benn, Joe and Bob.
Q Robert A. appears here on the same card with you and your father? A Yes sir.

Witness is identified as Edward L. Crowell, Jr., opposite Creek Indian Roll No. 43.

Q What is the name of this little girl your wife has here? A Frances Willard Crowell.
Q When was she born? A February 10, 1905.
Q What is the name of her mother? A Ida May Crowell.
Q What was the name of the doctor or midwife? A Dr. J.W. Gallaher.
Q Are you married to Ida? A Yes sir.
Q When were you married, do you remember A July 23, 1903, I believe it was the 23rd.
Q Where were you married? A Bowling Green, Kentucky.
Q Who married you? A E.G. Vick.
Q Is he a Minister of the Gospel? A Yes sir.
Q Do you remember the names of the witnesses? A Pearl Hill, and Will Stamps.
Q Mr. Crowell, you present here a certificate of marriage which states that Mr. Eban G. Vick married Mr. T.E. Ross to Miss Ida Edwards, do you claim this as your marriage certificate? A Yes.
Q How does it come that your name in the certificate is written T.E. Ross? A I changed my name when I left there.
Q Was that just an alias? A Yes sir.
Q Have you any witnesses to prove that this is meant for you? A Well I could get the pastor to recognize me.
Q What circumstances cause you to change your name? A I got into some trouble in Berry County, Missouri, and left the country. The sheriff of Lincoln County, Oklahoma arrested me under the name of Ross and then turned me loose, I was released day before yesterday.
Q Well now I don't know whether it is necessary but in order to investigate further, you might tell us the nature of that first trouble for which you had to leave the country.

Applications for Enrollment of Creek Newborn
Act of 1905   Volume XII

A Well the sheriff is the best evidence ---
Q Was that the sheriff that cause[sic] you to change your name? A Well now my name was Crowell and he arrested me under the name Ross, he had a charge against me as Crowell, he knew me as Crowell and he arrested me under the name of Ross.
Q Where is your brother Robert? A He is out here at Bacone at the school.
Q Do you think he is in town today? A Yes sir, I think he is in town.

Ida May Crowell, being duly sworn, testified as follows:

Q What is your name? A Ida May Crowell.
Q What was your name before your marriage? A Ida May Edwards.
Q You don't claim to be a citizen of any of the Five Tribes? A No sir.
Q White woman? A Yes sir.
Q What is the name of this child you have in your arms? A Frances Willard Crowell.
Q How old are you? A 20 YEARS OLD.
Q What is your post office? A Will be Coweta.
Q Did you make application just a little over a year ago for the enrollment of this child? A Yes sir.
Q Did you have a doctor to make affidavit at the same time? A Yes sir.
Q What is his name? A J.W. Gullaher[sic].
Q You stated in that affidavit that the father of that child was Edward L. Crowell, was that correct? A Yes sir.
Q Was that this gentleman here? A Yes sir.
Q Your husband? A Yes sir.
Q You were married to him in Bowling Green, Kentucky? A Yes sir.
Q Under what name? A T.E. Ross.
Q Do you know that was just an assumed name? A Yes sir.
Q You knew that when you married him? A Yes sir.
Q This is the identical man here whose name is Edward L. Crowell? A Yes sir.
Q Lived with him ever since? A Yes sir.
Q How long have you been his wife? A Will be three years this coming July 23rd.
Q Where did you live at the time of your marriage? A Bowling Green, Kentucky.
Q Where did you live before that? A In Kentucky.
Q Where did your husband live? A He lied there too.
Q Where did he live before that? A I don't know, I got acquainted with him in Bowling Green.
Q Where did you go from there? A We went to Hot Spring[sic] and then to Graham, Texas.
Q Have you ever lived in any other town in Texas besides Graham? A No sir.
Q You have your marriage license? A No sir, the pastor kept that and he just gave me this. (Meaning a marriage certificate).

Robert A. Crowell, being duly sworn, testified as follows:

Q What is your name? A Robert A. Crowell.
Q How old are you? A 26.

Applications for Enrollment of Creek Newborn
Act of 1905 Volume XII

Q What is your post office address? A Muskogee, now, just graduated at the University at Bacone.
Q What is the name of your father? A J.A. Crowell.
Q What is the name of your mother? A Martha Crowell.
Q Did you have a brother enrolled with you at the same time? A I don't know whether he was enrolled with me at the same time.
Q What is his name? A Edward L. Crowell.
Q Do you know what Creek Indian town you belong to? A I voted in one town.
Q Indian Town, was it Big Springs? A Yes sir. We have lived in Tulsa the past 25 years.
Q Do you know this gentleman here? A Yes sir.
Q What is his name? A My brother, Edward L. Crowell.
Q Is he the son of the same parents as you are? A Yes sir
Q He hasben't[sic] been with you the last ten years? A No sir, he has not, however, I have been with him a few times.
Q You make a statement as to what his trouble was and how you have seem him the few times you say you have ------? A Well, I put in all their applications for him for the child, and we wrote to him in Texas, and then he went away from Texas. I have been corresponding with him under the name of tom Ross. I have written him a number of letters.
Q You were the only man probably in Muskogee that knew where he was? A Yes sir, I think so.
Q You knew that he went under the name of Ross? A Yes sir, I was going to school in Arkadelphia and he came there with his wife to visit and I saw him at Hot springs[sic] at two different times. He went under that name there all the time.
Q Everybody knew him by the name of Ross? A Yes sir
Q You think that he is the same person that is mentioned in this marriage certificate that he presents here? A Yes sir, he is the same person.
Q What is the name of the woman he married, you know her, don't you? A I couldn't say what her maiden name was.
Q What is her first name? A Ida.
Q That is the lady right here? A Yes sir, he had this woman in Arkadelphia and Hot Springs.
Q And this is his child by her? A Yes sir.
Q The application that you put in for him? A Yes sir.
Q He is your full brother? A Yes sir.

Lona Merrick, being duly sworn, states that the above and foregoing is a true and correct transcript of her stenographic notes as taken in said cause on said date.

Lona Merrick

Subscribed and sworn to before me this 5th day of June, 1906.

HGHains
Notary Public.

Applications for Enrollment of Creek Newborn
Act of 1905   Volume XII

THIS CERTIFIES THAT MR. T.E. Ross, of Weatherford, Texas, and Miss Ida May Edwards, of Bowling Green, Kentucky, were united in HOLY MATRIMONY on the 23rd day of July, A.D. Ninteen[sic] Hundred and Three, at Bowling Green, Ky. in accordance with the Laws of Kentucky. Dated this 23rd day of July, A.D. 1903.

(Signed) Eben G. Vick.

Witnesses:
Mr. Will Stamps
Miss Pearl Hills.

Lona Merrick, being duly sworn, states that the above and foregoing is a true and correct copy of the original.

Lona Merrick

Subscribed and sworn to before me
this 4th day of June, 1906.

HGHains
Notary Public.

BIRTH AFFIDAVIT.

DEPARTMENT OF THE INTERIOR,
COMMISSIONER TO THE FIVE CIVILIZED TRIBES.

IN RE APPLICATION FOR ENROLLMENT, as a citizen of the Creek Nation, of Francis Willion[sic] Crowell , born on the 10th day of February , 1905

Name of Father: Edward L Crowell   a citizen of the   Creek   Nation.
Name of Mother: Ida May Crowell   a citizen of the United States Nation.

Postoffice   Graham, Texas

AFFIDAVIT OF MOTHER.

UNITED STATES OF AMERICA, Indian Territory,
State of Texas
Young County   District.

I, Ida May Crowell , on oath state that I am twenty (20) years of age and a citizen by birth , of the United States   Nation; that I am the lawful wife of Edward L Crowell , who is a citizen, by blood of the Creek Nation; that a female   child was born to me on   10th   day of February , 1905 , that said child has been named Francis Willard Crowell , and was living March 4, 1905.

Ida May Crowell

Witness to Mark:
   (Name Illegible)
   J.C. Vaughan

Applications for Enrollment of Creek Newborn
Act of 1905   Volume XII

Subscribed and sworn to before me this 22⁴ day of April , 1905.

                          (Name Illegible)
                              Notary Public.
                 (Illegible) Notary Public
               In and for Young County, Texas

AFFIDAVIT OF ATTENDING PHYSICIAN OR MID-WIFE.

UNITED STATES OF AMERICA, Indian Territory,
State of Texas, County of Young.
                 District.

I, J W Gallaher , a physician , on oath state that I attended on Mrs. Ida May Crowell , wife of Edward L Crowell on the 10 day of Feb , 1905 ; that there was born to her on said date a Female child; that said child was living March 4, 1905, and is said to have been named Francis Willard Crowell

                                 J W Gallaher

Witness to Mark:
R O Payne
(Illegible) Morris

Subscribed and sworn to before me this 22 day of April , 1905.

                          (Name Illegible)
                              Notary Public.
                 (Illegible) Notary Public
               In and for Young County, Texas

                                            HGH

REFER IN REPLY TO THE FOLLOWING:	**DEPARTMENT OF THE INTERIOR,**
NC 952	**COMMISSIONER TO THE FIVE CIVILIZED TRIBES.**

Muskogee, Indian Territory, October 21, 1905.

Ida May Crowell,
    Care Edward L. Crowell,
        Graham, Texas.

Dear Madam:

    In the matter of the application for the enrollment of your minor child, Frances Willard Crowell, born February 10, 1905, as a citizen by blood of the Creek Nation, this office desires proof of you marriage to said Edward L. Crowell, the father of said child;

Applications for Enrollment of Creek Newborn
Act of 1905   Volume XII

this proof may consist of either the original or a certified copy of your marriage license and certificate.

This matter should receive your prompt attention.

                        Respectfully,
                            Tams Bixby   Commissioner.

N.C. 952

                      Muskogee, Indian Territory, December 18, 1905.

Ida May Crowell,
    Care Edward L. Crowell,
        Graham, Texas.

Dear Madam:

    In the matter of the application for the enrollment of your minor child, Frances Willard Crowell, born February 10, 1905, as a citizen by blood of the Creek Nation, you are again advised that this office desires proof of your marriage to Edward L. Crowell, the father of said child. Such proof may consist of either the original or a certified copy of your marriage license and certificate.

    This matter should receive your immediate attention.

                        Respectfully,
                            Commissioner.

                                                            JWH

N C 952

                      Muskogee, Indian Territory, March 1, 1907.

Edward L. Crowell, Jr.,
    Coweta, Indian Territory.

Dear Sir :--

    You are hereby advised that on February 15, 1907, the Secretary of the Interior approved the enrollment of your minor child, Francis Willard Crowell, as a citizen by blood of the Creek Nation, and that the name of said child appears upon the roll of New Born citizens by blood of the Creek Nation, enrolled under the Act of Congress approved March 3, 1905, as number 1183.

    This child is now entitled to allotment and application therefor should be made without delay at the Creek Land Office, Muskogee, Indian Territory.

Applications for Enrollment of Creek Newborn
Act of 1905   Volume XII

Respectfully,

Commissioner.

NC 953

OCH
CM

DEPARTMENT OF THE INTERIOR,
COMMISSIONER TO THE FIVE CIVILIZED TRIBES.

In the matter of the application for the enrollment of Eucongodalie as a citizen by blood of the Creek Nation.

STATEMENT AND ORDER.

The record in this case shows that on December 14, 1905, a communication was addressed to this office by James Tiger relative to one Eucongodalie and He-co-con-thla Tiger, which is herein considered in the nature of an original application for the enrollment of said Eucongodalie as a citizen by blood of the Creek Nation. Certain other letters and copies of letters relative to Eucongodalie and He-co-con-thla Tiger are made a part of this record.

The records of this office show that on January 9, 1907, the application for the enrollment as a citizen by blood of the Creek Nation of He-co-con-thla Tiger, aged thirteen years, was granted by the Commissioner, and he has been regularly listed for enrollment on Creek Indian card No. 4691.

This office has by letter, and by interviews at this office of prominent Creek citizens of extensive acquaintance, made every effort to obtain further information as to the right of said Eucongodalie to enrollment as a citizen by blood of the Creek Nation.

It is believed that said Eucongodalie and said He-co-con-thla Tiger is the same person, or that Eucongodalie is the same person as some member of the family of said James Tiger, who has already been duly enrolled as a citizen of the Creek Nation.

In view of the foregoing, I am of the opinion that the application herein should be dismissed and it is so ordered.

Tams Bixby COMMISSIONER.

Muskogee, Indian Territory,
FEB 20 1907

Applications for Enrollment of Creek Newborn
Act of 1905   Volume XII

(The letter below typed as given.)

COPY.

55965.   Sapulpa, Ind. Ter.
                                                                                Dec. 14, 1905.
Dawes Commission,

Recieved your letter in few days ago. will say that relative to the right to enrollment of my minor child Eucongodalie as a citizen by the blood of the Creek Nation I am writting another letter to the department He.co.con.thla Tiger is another person but he is not my child. I will send in my papers as you can see yourself. I am willing to appear in person any time you call on me and bring the boy with me that has no allotment yet. and the two witness that knows he h has no fileing yet. this is nothing true. Your truly

James Tiger.

COPY

Muskogee, Indian Territory, December 22, 1905.

James tiger,
    Sapulpa, Indian Territory.

Dear Sir:

    Receipt is acknowledged of your letter of December 14, 1905, relative to the right to enrollment of your minor child, Eucongodalie, as a citizen by blood of the Creek Nation.

    In reply you are advised that it does not appear from the records of this office that application has been made for enrollment of said Eucongodalie as a citizen of the Creek Nation.

    You are further advised that the rolls of the Creek Nation for new-born children were closed May 2, 1905, and this office is now without authority to receive applications for enrollment as citizens of said Nation.

Respectfully,
Commissioner.

Applications for Enrollment of Creek Newborn
Act of 1905   Volume XII

(The letter below typed as given)

(COPY)

Sapulpa, I. T.
January 25, 1906.

Mr. Wm. O. Beall,
    Muskogee, I. T.

Dear Sir :--

    Yours of last 22nd November, 1905, requested whether or not He con con thla Tiger or Eucongodalie is the same name has never received his allotment he is 12 years old and he is dually entidly to allotment and he is living and he is in school today at the Euchee Institute Sapulpa I. T.

                Very respectfully,
                (Signed) Saml. W. Brown.

Please look into this it will be favorable to James Tiger.

(COPY)

Sapulpa, I. T.,
Feby. 1st, 1906.

Mr. W. O. Bealls[sic],
    Muskogee, I. T.

Dear Sir :--

    In reply of yours of 27th last is at hand in regard to He con con Tiger or Ucodalia is the same name or not I will furnish you the following list of the Family, to wit:

1	Yah con pn con thla
2	King
3	Ah la co con thla my
4	Willie
5	Jimmie
6	You lon wa thla

    I am coming down next week I will make effort stay few days correct some of the names.

                Yours truly,
                (Signed) S. W. Brown

Applications for Enrollment of Creek Newborn
Act of 1905 Volume XII

(COPY)

NC 953.

Muskogee, Indian Territory, January 24, 1907.

James Tiger,
    Sapulpa, Indian Territory.

Dear Sir :--

    You are requested to appear before this office as once to give testimony in the matter of the application for the enrollment of Eucongodalie, as a citizen of the Creek Nation. There is information on file tending to show that said person is your child.

                Respectfully,

                            Commissioner.

(COPY)

Jacket
I. 3475.

Muskogee, Indian Territory, January 27, 1906.

Samuel W. Brown,
    Sapulpa, Indian Territory.

Dear Sir :--

    Receipt is acknowledged of your letter of January 20, 1906, in which you state "Yours of last 22, November, 1905, requested whether or not He con con thla Tiger or U co dalie is the same name has never received his allotment"; you state that he is twelve years old, is entitled to an allotment and is living and attending school at the Euchee institute, Sapulpa, Indian Territory today. You state that if this matter is looked into it will be favorable to James Tiger.

    You are advised that there is proof on file in this office that He con con thla died prior to April 1, 1900, and is therefore, not entitled to an allotment in the Creek Nation.

                Respectfully,

                            Acting Commissioner.

Applications for Enrollment of Creek Newborn
Act of 1905   Volume XII

NC 953.

Muskogee, Indian Territory, February 21, 1907.

James Tiger,
   Sapulpa, Indian Territory.

Dear Sir:

   There is herewith enclosed one copy of the statement and order of the Commissioner to the Five Civilized Tribes, dated February 20, 1907, dismissing the application made by you for the enrollment of your minor child, Eucongodalie, as a citizen by blood of the Creek Nation.

Respectfully,

Commissioner.

Register.
LM-32.

NC 954

En. 919.

DEPARTMENT OF THE INTERIOR,
COMMISSIONER TO THE FIVE CIVILIZED TRIBES.
Muskogee, Indian Territory, January 3, 1906.

   In the matter of the application for the enrollment of Joseph Charles Beaver as a citizen of the Creek Nation.

   Ella Beaver being duly sworn testified as follows:

Q What is your name? A Ella Beaver.
Q What is your age? A About twenty three.
Q What is your post office address? A Bristow.
Q You have testified about this child before? A Yes, sir.
Q What is the name of this little child here? A Joseph Charles Beaver.
Q In what month was he born? A Sixth of January. This 6th of January he will be four years old.
Q He must have been born in 1902? A Yes, sir.
Q We have your affidavit made out March 1, 1902 and your testimony given March 15, 1905 and the testimony of John Beaver, the father of the child, that says this boy was born January 6, 1902, that is correct is it? A Yes, sir.

Applications for Enrollment of Creek Newborn
Act of 1905   Volume XII

Q We have here an affidavit signed by F.A. Henshaw on January 1, 1902, that the child was born January 6, 1902, he couldn't make an affidavit the child was born before he was born?[sic] A Yes, sir a mistake.
Q Later on on the 19th of April at Bristow you and John Beaver and F.A. Henshaw made out affidavits that this child was born January 6, 1901, is that correct? A No, sir.
Q Because that would make the child five years old? A Yes, sir.
Q How do you explain making out this affidavit making it 1901? A Dr. Henshaw said when he came in the office at Bristow that that was a mistake, that he didn't have the book his age was on that he wasn't sure and he would give in[sic] the best he knew.
Q And so he gave 1901 because you and your husband gave 1901? A Yes, sir.
Q And you are now sure 1901 is a mistake? A Yes, sir.
Q We will have you and John make a new affidavit and give the right year as you now believe is correct. The child is here present and appears to be about four years old. The only thing is we want to get the correct age.

John Beaver being duly sworn testified as follows:

Q What is your name? A John Beaer.
Q What is your age? A I don't know my age, about fifty.
Q You are a citizen of the Creek Nation? A Yes, sir.
Q What was the name of your father? A He had an Indian name but his name on the roll is John Beaver.
Q To what town did he belong? A Tuskegee.
Q You are a full blood are you? A Yes, sir.
Q What is the name of this boy you have in your lap? A John Charles Beaver.
Q How old is he? A Four years this 6th of January.
Q Did you make a mistake when you made an affidavit he was born in 1901? A Yes, sir. The Dr. had the dates and I just went by him and supposed he had it right when I did that.
Q You see now you made a mistake? A Yes, sir.

I, Anna Garrigues, on oath state that the above and foregoing is a true and correct transcript of my stenographic notes as taken in said cause on said date.

Anna Garrigues

Subscribed and sworn to before me this 5 day of January 1906.

J McDermott
Notary Public.

Applications for Enrollment of Creek Newborn
Act of 1905   Volume XII

BA- 4.

DEPARTMENT OF THE INTERIOR,
COMMISSIONER TO THE FIVE CIVILIZED TRIBES.
MUSKOGEE, INDIAN TERRITORY, MARCH 15, 1905

-ooOoo-

In the matter of the application for the enrollment of Joseph Charles Beaver, as a citizen by blood of the Creek Nation.

ELLA BEAVER, being duly sworn, testified as follows:

EXAMINATION BY COMMISSION:
Q What is your name? A Ella Beaver.
Q How old are you? A 23.
Q What is your postoffice address? A Beggs.
Q Are you a citizen of the Creek Nation? A No, sir.
Q Are you the mother of Joseph Charles Beaver? A Yes, sir.
Q Who is the father of that child? A John Beaver--he is sometimes called Hecton Beaver.
Q When was Joseph Charles Beaver born? A The 6th of January.
Q What year? A (No answer).
Q How old was he last January? A Three years.
Q Then he was born January 6, 1902? A Yes, sir.
Q Is Joseph Charles Beaver living now? A Yes, sir.
   (Child is present and appears to be about the age indicated.
Q Who was present when that child was born? A Mrs. Fuller.
Q Was there a doctor present? A Yes, sir.
Q What is his name? A Henshaw.
Q F. A. Henshaw? A Yes, sir.

JOHN BEAVER, being duly sworn, testified as follows:

EXAMINATION BY COMMISSION:
Q What is your name? A John Beaver.
Q How old are you? A I don't know, sir. (Witness appears to be about forty-five).
Q What is your postoffice address? A Bristow.
Q Are you the husband of Ella Beaver? A Yes, sir.
Q You do not live together do you? A No.
Q Were you living together in 1902? A Yes.
Q Are you the father of a child of hers born on the 6th of January, 1902? A Yes, sir.
Q What is the name of that child? A Joseph Charles Beaver.
Q Are you a citizen of the Creek Nation? A I am.

Witness if identified on Creek Indian Card, Field Number 1875, and his name is contained in the partial list of citizens by blood, approved by the Secretary of the Interior, March 28, 1902, Roll Number 5924.

Applications for Enrollment of Creek Newborn
Act of 1905 Volume XII

Q Is Joseph Charles Beaver living? A Yes, sir, that is him there.

Zera Ellen Parrish, being sworn on her oath states that as stenographer to the Commission to the Five Civilized Tribes she reported the above case and that this is a full, true and correct transcript of her stenographic notes in same.

Zera Ellen Parrish

Subscribed and sworn to before me this 17 day of March, 1905.

Edw C Griesel
Notary Public.

N.C. 954.   I.S.N.

DEPARTMENT OF THE INTERIOR,
COMMISSIONER TO THE FIVE CIVILIZED TRIBES.
-:o:-

In the matter of the application for the enrollment of Joseph Charles Beaver, as a citizen by blood of the Creek Nation.

DECISION

The record in this case shows that on March 3, 1902, there was filed in the office of the Commission to the Five Civilized Tribes, in Muskogee, Indian Territory, an affidavit in the matter of the birth of Joseph Charles Beaver and such affidavit is considered as an original application for his enrollment as a citizen by blood of the Creek Nation blood of the Creek Nation. Further proceedings were had on March 15, 1905, and January 3, 1906.

The evidence shows that said Joseph Charles Beaver was born January 6, 1902, and was living on the date of the last proceedings herein.

The evidence further shows that said Joseph Charles Beaver is the minor child of John Beaver and Ella Beaver, his non-citizen wife. It also appears from the evidence and the records in this office that the name of John Beaver is contained in a partial list of citizens by blood of the Creek Nation approved by the Secretary of the Interior March 28, 1902, opposite number 5924.

It is, therefore, ordered and adjudged that said Joseph Charles Beaver is entitled to be enrolled as a citizen by blood of the Creek Nation in accordance with the provisions of the act of Congress approved March 3, 1905, (33 Stats., 1060) and the application for his enrollment as such is accordingly granted.

Tams Bixby
Commissioner.

Applications for Enrollment of Creek Newborn
Act of 1905 Volume XII

Muskogee, Indian Territory,
MAR 11 1906

BIRTH AFFIDAVIT.

DEPARTMENT OF THE INTERIOR.
COMMISSION TO THE FIVE CIVILIZED TRIBES.

IN RE APPLICATION FOR ENROLLMENT, as a citizen of the Creek Nation, of Joseph Charles Beaver, born on the 6 day of Jan., 1902

Name of Father: John Beaver   a citizen of the   Creek   Nation.
Name of Mother: Ella Beaver   a citizen of the   "   Nation.

Postoffice   Bristow I.T.

AFFIDAVIT OF MOTHER.

UNITED STATES OF AMERICA, Indian Territory,
Western   DISTRICT.

     I, John Beaver, on oath state that I am about 50 years of age and a citizen by blood, of the Creek Nation; that I ~~am~~ was the lawful ~~wife~~ husband of Ella Beaver, (we are now separated) who is a citizen, by --------- of the U. S. ~~Nation~~; that a male child was born to ~~me~~ her on 6" day of January, 1902, that said child has been named Joseph Charles Beaver, and was living March 4, 1905.

                       John x Beaver

Witnesses To Mark:
   { H.G. Hains
     Jesse McDermott

Subscribed and sworn to before me this 3" day of January, 1906.

                       H.G. Hains
                       Notary Public.

Applications for Enrollment of Creek Newborn
Act of 1905 Volume XII

BIRTH AFFIDAVIT.

DEPARTMENT OF THE INTERIOR.
COMMISSION TO THE FIVE CIVILIZED TRIBES.

IN RE APPLICATION FOR ENROLLMENT, as a citizen of the Creek Nation, of Joseph Charles Beaver, born on the 6 day of Jan., 1902

Name of Father: John Beaver	a citizen of the	Creek	Nation.
Name of Mother: Ella Beaver	a citizen of the	non ~~Creek~~	Nation.

Postoffice   Bristow I.T.

AFFIDAVIT OF MOTHER.

UNITED STATES OF AMERICA, Indian Territory,}
  Western   DISTRICT.

I, Ella Beaver, on oath state that I am 23 years of age and a citizen ~~by~~ U. S., of the U. S. ~~Nation~~; that I ~~am~~ was the lawful wife of John Beaver (We have been separated about a year), who is a citizen, by blood of the Creek Nation; that a male child was born to me on 6 day of January, 1902, that said child has been named Joseph Charles Beaver, and was living March 4, 1905.

                                her
                        Ella x Beaver
Witnesses To Mark: mark
 { H.G. Hains
 { Jesse McDermott

Subscribed and sworn to before me this 3" day of Jan., 1906.

                        H.G. Hains
                            Notary Public.

BIRTH AFFIDAVIT.

DEPARTMENT OF THE INTERIOR,
COMMISSION TO THE FIVE CIVILIZED TRIBES.

IN RE Application for Enrollment, as a citizen of the Creek Nation, of Joseph Charles Beaver, born on the *(blank)* day of *(blank)*, 1*(blank)*

Name of Father: John Beaver	a citizen of the	Creek	Nation.
Name of Mother: Ella Beaver	a citizen of the	U. S.	Nation.

Applications for Enrollment of Creek Newborn
Act of 1905   Volume XII

Post-office: Bristow I.T.

AFFIDAVIT OF MOTHER.

UNITED STATES OF AMERICA,
    INDIAN TERRITORY.
Western   District.

I,   Ella Beaver   , on oath state that I am   25   years of age and a citizen by *(blank)* , of the U.S. ~~Nation~~; that I am the lawful wife of   John Beaver , who is a citizen, by blood of the   Creek 2 Nation; that a   male child was born to me on   6th day of January , 1902 , that said child has been named   Joseph Charles Beaver , and is now living.

                              her
                      Ella Beaver x
WITNESSES TO MARK: mark
{ Joe Mackin
  John E. *(Illegible)*

Subscribed and sworn to before me this   First   *day of*   March , 1902.

                      T. W. Flynn
                        NOTARY PUBLIC.

AFFIDAVIT OF ATTENDING PHYSICIAN OR MID-WIFE.

UNITED STATES OF AMERICA,
    INDIAN TERRITORY.
Western   District.

I,   F. A. Henshaw , a   Physician   , on oath state that I attended on Mrs. Ella Beaver , wife of   John Beaver   on the   6th day of   January , 1902 ; that there was born to her on said date a male child; that said child is now living and is said to have been named Joseph Charles Beaver

                      F. M. Henshaw
WITNESSES TO MARK:
{

Subscribed and sworn to before me this   First   *day of*   March , 1902.

                      T. W. Flynn
                        NOTARY PUBLIC.

Applications for Enrollment of Creek Newborn
Act of 1905 Volume XII

BIRTH AFFIDAVIT.

Cr En 919.

DEPARTMENT OF THE INTERIOR,
COMMISSION TO THE FIVE CIVILIZED TRIBES.

In Re- Application for Enrollment, as a citizen of the Creek Nation, of Joseph Charles Beaver , born on the 6th day of January , 1902

Name of Father: John Beaver   a citizen of the   Creek   Nation.
Name of Mother: Ella Beaver   a citizen of the   U.S.   Nation.

Post-office   Bristow, Ind. Terr.

AFFIDAVIT OF MOTHER.

UNITED STATES OF AMERICA,
   INDIAN TERRITORY,
  Western   District.

    I, Ella Beaver , on oath state that I am 24 years of age and a citizen ~~by~~ of the U.S. , of the *(blank)* Nation; that I am the lawful wife of John Beaver , who is a citizen, by blood of the Creek Nation; that a male child was born to me on sixth day of January , 1902 , that said child has been named Joseph Charles Beaver , and is now living.

                                                    her
                                    Ella Beaver x
Witnesses To Mark: mark
    J.J. Elliott
    Joseph Liston

    Subscribed and sworn to before me this 30th day of December, 1905. , 190 .

                                      T. W. Flynn
                                            Notary Public.

AFFIDAVIT OF ATTENDING PHYSICIAN OR MID-WIFE.

UNITED STATES OF AMERICA,
   INDIAN TERRITORY,
  Western   District.

    I, F. A. Henshaw , a Physician , on oath state that I attended on Mrs. Ella Beaver , wife of John Beaver on the 6th day of January, 1902. , 1 ; that there was born to her on said date a male child; that said child is now living and is said to have been named Joseph Charles Beaver

                                     F.A. Henshaw M.D.

Applications for Enrollment of Creek Newborn
Act of 1905   Volume XII

Witnesses To Mark:
- J.J. Elliott
- Joseph Liston

Subscribed and sworn to before me this 30th day of December, 1905. , 190 .

T. W. Flynn
Notary Public.

BIRTH AFFIDAVIT.

See Enrollment Case

DEPARTMENT OF THE INTERIOR.
COMMISSION TO THE FIVE CIVILIZED TRIBES.

IN RE APPLICATION FOR ENROLLMENT, as a citizen of the Creek Nation, of Joseph Charles Beaver, born on the 6 day of Jan , 1901

Name of Father: John Beavers   a citizen of the   Creek   Nation.
 Tuskegee
Name of Mother: Ella Beaver   a citizen of the   U.S.   Nation.

Postoffice   Bristow

AFFIDAVIT OF MOTHER.

Child Present

UNITED STATES OF AMERICA, Indian Territory,
   Western   DISTRICT.

I, John Beaver , on oath state that I am 55 years of age and a citizen by blood , of the Creek Nation; that I am the lawful ~~wife~~ Husband of Ella Beaver , who is a citizen, by -------- of the U. S. Nation; that a male child was born to me on 6 day of Jan , 1901 , that said child has been named Joseph Charles Beaver , and is now living.

His
John x Beaver
mark

Witnesses To Mark:
- Jesse McDermott
- EC Griesel

Subscribed and sworn to before me this 19 day of April , 1905.

Edw C Griesel
Notary Public.

Applications for Enrollment of Creek Newborn
Act of 1905 Volume XII

AFFIDAVIT OF ATTENDING PHYSICIAN OR MID-WIFE.

UNITED STATES OF AMERICA, Indian Territory,
    Western   DISTRICT.

    I, F. A. Henshaw , a Physician , on oath state that I attended on Mrs. Ella Beaver , wife of John Beaver on the 6 day of Jan. , 1901 ; that there was born to her on said date a male child; that said child is now living and is said to have been named Joseph Charles Beaver

                                 F.A. Henshaw

Witnesses To Mark:

    Subscribed and sworn to before me this 19 day of April , 1905.

                                Edw C Griesel
                                   Notary Public.

BIRTH AFFIDAVIT.
                        See Enrollment Case

DEPARTMENT OF THE INTERIOR.
COMMISSION TO THE FIVE CIVILIZED TRIBES.

    IN RE APPLICATION FOR ENROLLMENT, as a citizen of the Creek Nation, of Joseph Charles Beaver, born on the 6 day of Jan , 1901

Name of Father: John Beavers   a citizen of the   Creek   Nation.
    Tuskegee
Name of Mother: Ella Beaver   a citizen of the   U.S.   Nation.

                        Postoffice   Bristow

AFFIDAVIT OF MOTHER.
                                      Child Present

UNITED STATES OF AMERICA, Indian Territory,
    Western   DISTRICT.

    I, Ella Beaver , on oath state that I am 23 years of age and a citizen by -------- , of the U. S. Nation; that I am the lawful wife of John Beaver , who is a citizen, by blood of the Creek Nation; that a male child was born to me on 6 day of Jan , 1901, that said child has been named Joseph Charles Beaver , and is now living.
                                    Her
                             Ella x Beaver
                                mark

Applications for Enrollment of Creek Newborn
Act of 1905   Volume XII

Witnesses To Mark:
{ Jesse McDermott
{ EC Griesel

    Subscribed and sworn to before me this 19 day of April, 1905.

    (Seal)   Edw C Griesel
                                          Notary Public.

HGH

COMMISSIONERS:
TAMS BIXBY,
THOMAS B. NEEDLES,
C.R. BRECKINRIDGE.

DEPARTMENT OF THE INTERIOR,
COMMISSIONER TO THE FIVE CIVILIZED TRIBES.

REFER IN REPLY TO THE FOLLOWING:

NC 9.

WM. O. BEALL
Secretary

ADDRESS ONLY THE
COMMISSION TO THE FIVE CIVILIZED TRIBES.

Muskogee, Indian Territory, May 19, 1905.

John Beaver,
    Beggs, Indian Territory.

Dear Sir:

    The Commission desires further evidence in the matter of the application for the enrollment of your minor child, Joseph Charles Beaver, as a citizen of the Creek Nation.

    You are hereby notified that it will be necessary for your wife, Ella Beaver, to appear before the Commission, at its office, in Muskogee, Indian Territory, with the midwife who attended on her at the birth of said child, and give testimony under oath as to the exact date on which said child was born.

                                  Respectfully,
                                  Tams Bixby
                                      Chairman.

Register.

Applications for Enrollment of Creek Newborn
Act of 1905   Volume XII

HGH

REFER IN REPLY TO THE FOLLOWING:
~~Cr En 919~~
NC 954

DEPARTMENT OF THE INTERIOR,
COMMISSIONER TO THE FIVE CIVILIZED TRIBES.

Muskogee, Indian Territory, December 28, 1905.

Ella Beaver,
    Bristow, Indian Territory.

Dear Madam:

    Receipt is acknowledged of your letter of December 23, 1905, relative to the application for the enrollment of your minor children, Earnest and Joseph Charlie Beaver, as citizens of the Creek Nation.

    March 3, 1902, there were filed in this Office your affidavit and the affidavit of F. A. Henshaw, physician, in the matter of the application for the enrollment of Joseph Charles Beaver, born January 6, 1902; on March 15, 1905, you and John Beaver, father of said child, appeared and testified under oath that said Joseph Charles Beaver was born January 6, 1902, and that he was living on said date; April 19, 1905, you and the father of said child, and F. A. Henshaw, said physician, made affidavits stating that said child was born January 6, 1901.

    You are requested to furnish this Office with your affidavit and the affidavit of said physician giving the correct date of the birth of said child.

    You are advised that the name of your minor child, Earnest Beaver is contained in a partial list of Creek citizens approved by the Secretary of the Interior August 22, 1905, and that an application for a selection of land in the Creek Nation may now be made at this Office for said child by John Beaver, his citizen parent.

                  Respectfully,

                              Tams Bixby
                              Commissioner.

Applications for Enrollment of Creek Newborn
Act of 1905   Volume XII

NC 956

OCH
JCL

DEPARTMENT OF THE INTERIOR,
COMMISSIONER TO THE FIVE CIVILIZED TRIBES.

In the matter of the application for the enrollment of Mamie Chisholm as a citizen by blood of the Creek Nation.

STATEMENT AND ORDER.

The records of this office show that on March 27, 1903, a communication was addressed to this office on behalf of Susan Skahkah, stating that she desired to have her granddaughter, Mamie Chisholm, the infant child of her daughter, Jennie Chisholm, deceased, placed upon the rolls. This communication is herein considered in the nature of an original application for the enrollment of said Mamie Chisholm as a citizen by blood of the Creek Nation.

It appears from the records of this office that the name of said Jennie Chisholm, deceased, the mother of said Mamie Chisholm, was included in a schedule of citizens by blood of the Creek Nation, approved by the Secretary of the Interior, November 14, 1902, opposite number 9189, and that thereafter her name was stricken from said approved roll, under authority of the Secretary of the Interior, for the reason that an allotment had been made to her as an Eastern Shawnee.

The application herein, and subsequent correspondence, copies of which are made a part of this record, fail to show the name of the father of said child.

In view of the foregoing, I am of the opinion, that there is no authority of law for the enrollment of said Mamie Chisholm as a citizen by blood of the Creek Nation, and the application for her enrollment is accordingly dismissed.

Tams Bixby   COMMISSIONER.

Muskogee, Indian Territory,
FEB 26 1907

(COPY)

First State Bank.
Paden, Ind. Ter.

A. I. Stewart, President.
W. Y. Dilley, Vice Pres.

Paden, I.T.   3/27/03.

Hon. Tams Bixby, Chairman,
   Muskogee, I. T.

Dear Sir :--

Mrs. Susan Skahkah, who was formerly Susan Tomahawk Chisholm, wished to have placed on the rolls, so that an allotment can be selected, the name of Mamie

Applications for Enrollment of Creek Newborn
Act of 1905 Volume XII

Chisholm, the infant daughter of Jennie Chisholm, deceased. Mamie Chisholm is the granddaughter of Susan Skahakah, and the latter is also the legally appointed guardian of the child. Please place the name on file and send instructions to the guardian at this place.

Very truly Yrs.
W. Y. Dilley

(COPY)

Creek I. 3992.

Muskogee, Indian Territory, April 4, 1903.

Susan Skahkah,
    Paden, Indian Territory.

Dear Madam :--

    Referring to a letter addressed to the Commission, under date of March 27, 1903, by W. Y. Dilley, of Paden, Indian Territory, in regard to selecting an allotment of land for your grandchild, Mamie Chisholm, you are advised that if you will furnish the Commission with the date of the birth of said Mamie Chisholm, and if not living, the date of her death, you will be given the information you desire.

    It appearing from said letter that your daughter Jennie Chisholm, the mother of said Mamie Chisholm, is dead, information is now desired as to the exact date of her death. Blank death affidavit for this purpose is herewith inclosed, which please have properly filled out and signed and sworn to before a notary public by yourself and one other person who known[sic] when said Jennie Chisholm died, and return same to this office in the enclosed envelope, which requires no postage.

    You are also requested to advise the Commission whether said Jennie Chisholm ever received an allotment is[sic] the Quapaw reservation as an Eastern Shawnee, Oklahoma and if so, whether said allotment was ever cancelled.

Respectfully,

D.C. Skaggs   Commissioner in Charge.

Applications for Enrollment of Creek Newborn
Act of 1905   Volume XII

(The letter below typed as given.)

(C O P Y)

Paden, I. T., April 27, 03.

Commission 5 Civilized Trebes,
    Muscogee, I. T.

Sirs :--

    Replying to your letter Creek I. 3992 permit me to say that I enclose herewith affidavit of the death of Jennie Chisholm. Mamie Chisholm, her child, was born July 20th, 1902, and still living. Jennie Chisholm received an allotment in the Quapaw reservation as an Eastern Shawnee and said allotment was never cancelled. Please advise if can have Mamie Chisholm enrolled and select an allotment for her in the Creek Nation.

                  Yours truly,
                        (Signed) Susan Skah-kah

                                      J.J.B

Creek I-3992.

Muskogee, Indian Territory, May 4, 1903.

Susan Skah-kah,
    Paden, Indian Territory.

Dear Madam:

    The Commission is in receipt of your letter of April 27, 1903, inclosing affidavit in the matter of the death of Jennie Chisholm. You ask if her child, Mamie Chisholm, born July 20, 1902, can be enrolled as a citizen of the Creek Nation.

    In reply you are advised that a child born July 20, 1902, cannot be enrolled as a citizen of the Creek Nation.

                  Respectfully,
                              Chairman.

Applications for Enrollment of Creek Newborn
Act of 1905   Volume XII

(The letter below typed as given.)

(COPY)

Paden, I. Ter., Dec. 25, 1905.

Commissioner,

   Sir:

   I will write and tell you about this her name is Manie Cone her mother was name Jennie Chisholm but that man had separated from before she died Jennie Chisholm my Daughter and this is her little girl I will tell you that I never made no application for her and I will close for this time hope to hear from you again so that I would no what you can do for her about getting her land. he memie Coone.

(Signed) Susie Skahkah

NC 956

(COPY)

Muskogee, Indian Territory, January 23, 1907.

Alex Posey,
   Clerk in Charge Creek Field Party,
      Paden, Indian Territory.

Dear Sir :--

   There is inclosed herewith certain data with reference to one Mamie Chisholm or Mamie Cone.

   You are directed to obtain information as to who was the father of this child and any other information that will help to identify you as a citizen of the Creek Nation. information bearing on its right to enrollment as a citizen of the Creek Nation.

Respectfully,

Commissioner.

Inc. CM-23-1

(Handwritten note)

FEB 20 1907

Chances are 100 to 1 that child's father was not a Creek citizen but apparently no efforts were ever made to find out. Do you wish anything further done?

A.N.C.

Applications for Enrollment of Creek Newborn
Act of 1905   Volume XII

(Below is memo to the employees of the telegraph company.)

ALL MESSAGES TAKEN BY THIS COMPANY ARE SUBJECT TO THE FOLLOWING TERMS:

To guard against mistakes or delays, the sender of a message should order it REPEATED ; that is, telegraphed back to the originating office for comparison. For this, one-half the regular rate is charged in addition. It is agreed between the sender of the following message and this Company, that said Company shall not be liable for mistakes or delays in the transmission or delivery, or for non-delivery of any UNREPEATED message, beyond the amount received for sending the same ; nor for mistakes or delays in the transmission or delivery, or for non-delivery of any REPEATED message, beyond fifty times the sum received for sending the same, unless specially insured, nor in any case for delays arising from unavoidable interruption in the working of its lines, or for errors in cipher or obscure messages. And this Company is hereby made the agent of the sender, without liability, to forward any message over the lines of any other Company when necessary to reach its destination.

Correctness in the transmission of a message to any point on the lines of this Company can be INSURED by contract in writing, stating agreed amount of risk, and payment of premium thereon, at the following rates, in addition to the usual charge for repeated messages, viz, one per cent. for any distance not exceeding 1,000 miles, and two per cent, for any greater distance. No employee of the Company is authorized to vary the foregoing.

No responsibility regarding messages attaches to this Company until the same are presented and accepted at one of its transmitting offices ; and if a message is sent to such office by one of the Company's messengers, he acts for that purpose as the agent of the sender.

Messages will be delivered free within the established free delivery limits of the terminal office. For delivery at a greater distance, a special charge will be made to cover the cost of such delivery.

The Company will not be liable for damaged or statutory penalties in any case where the claim is not presented in writing within sixty days after the message is filed with the Company for transmission.

ROBERT C. CLOWRY, President and General Manager.

Applications for Enrollment of Creek Newborn
Act of 1905 Volume XII

THE WESTERN UNION TELEGRAPH COMPANY.
----------INCORPORATED----------
23,000 OFFICES IN AMERICA.   CABLE SERVICE TO ALL THE WORLD.
ROBERT C. CLOWRY, President and General Manager.

Receiver's No.	Time Filed	Check
		Of. B. Govt. Rate. Pd.

SEND the following message subject to the terms on back hereof, which are hereby agreed to.

February 21, 1907.

(NC 956)

Susan Skah-kah,
Paden, I. T.

You are requested to furnish this office immediately the name and citizenship of father of Mamie Chisholm, and also evidence as to his marriage to Jennie Chisholm.

BIXBY, Commissioner.

READ THE NOTICE AND AGREEMENT ON BACK

NC 956

(C O P Y)

Paden, Ind. Ter. Feb. 26, 1907.

Dawes Commission,
    Muskogee, Indian Territory.

Dear Sir:-

In reply to your telegram that was received a few days ago will say that the father of Mamie Chisholm was George Coon, and the said George Coon was a member of the Shawnee tribe and had taken his allotment in the Shawnee Nation, in Pottawatomie county.

Coon married my daughter Jennie Chisholm in the year 1901, this child Mamie Chisholm was born July 20th, 1902, Coon had left my daughter Jennie Chisholm before the child was born. Was married according to the Indian custom.

(Signed) Susie Skah-kah.

Endorsed on back.

Commissioner to Five Tribes.
No. 11529. Received Mar. 1, 1907.

Applications for Enrollment of Creek Newborn
Act of 1905   Volume XII

JWH

N C 956

Muskogee, Indian Territory, March 1, 1907.

Susan Skah-kah,
    Paden, Indian Territory.

Dear Madam :--

    There is enclosed herewith copy of statement and order of the Commissioner to the Five Civilized Tribes, dated February 26, 1907, dismissing the application made by you for the enrollment of your grandchild, Mamie Chisholm, as a citizen by blood of the Creek Nation.

                         Respectfully,

                                      Commissioner.

Registered.
JWH 1-1

BA-NE-28.

DEPARTMENT OF THE INTERIOR,
COMMISSION TO THE FIVE CIVILIZED TRIBES.
MUSKOGEE, INDIAN TERRITORY, MAY 10, 1905.

-ooOoo-

    In the matter of the application for the enrollment of Willie Friday as a Creek Freedman.

    JENNIE NASH, being duly sworn, testified as follows:

EXAMINATION BY THE COMMISSION:

Q What is your name? A Jennie Friday it was, but it is Jennie Nash now.
Q How old are you? A Twenty-two.
Q What is your postoffice address? A Beggs.
Q Are you a citizen of the Creek Nation? A Yes.
Q What is the name of the father of Willie Friday? A Berry Friday.
Q Is he a citizen of the Creek Nation? A Yes, he is a Freedman.
Q Creek Freedman is he? A Yes.
Q And so you are a Creek Freedman also? A I am Indian and Freedman

Applications for Enrollment of Creek Newborn
Act of 1905   Volume XII

Q Have you got your land? A Yes, I have got my land; he sold his.
Q Is this child, Willie Friday, living? A Yes, he is living; I am going to bring him in here.
Q He was living when you left home as he A Yes, he was living when I left home.
Q Are you positive of that? A Yes, I am positive of it.
Q What is the name of your father? A Eli Jacob.
Q What is the name of your mother? A Sissie Bruner.

      The name of Berry Friday, father of Willie Friday, appears on Creek Freedman Card, Field Number 318, Roll Number 1189.
      The name of Jennie Friday, mother of said Willie Friday, appears on Creek Indian Card, Field Number 1742, and her name is contained in the partial list of Creek Indians by blood, approved by the Secretary of the Interior, March 28, 1902, opposite Roll Number 5582.

Q You are positive, are you, that your child, Willie Friday, was living on March 4, of this year? A Yes.
Q You are sure that he was living on March 4, 1905? a Yes.

      Affidavit heretofore referred to is made a part of the record herein.

      Zera Ellen Parrish, being sworn on her oath states that as a stenographer to the Commission to the Five Civilized Tribes she reported the above case and that this is a full, true and correct transcript of her stenographic notes in same.

                                          Zera Ellen Parrish

Subscribed and sworn
to before me this 10th day
of May, 1905.

                                          Edw C Griesel
                                                Notary Public.

BIRTH AFFIDAVIT.

DEPARTMENT OF THE INTERIOR.
COMMISSION TO THE FIVE CIVILIZED TRIBES.

      IN RE APPLICATION FOR ENROLLMENT, as a citizen of the cREEK[sic] Nation, of WILLIE FRIDAY, born on the First day of October, 1901

Name of Father: Berry Friday	a citizen of the	Creek	Nation.
Name of Mother: Jennie Friday	a citizen of the	Creek	Nation.

                              Postoffice   Haskell, Ind. Ter.

Applications for Enrollment of Creek Newborn
Act of 1905 Volume XII

AFFIDAVIT OF MOTHER.

UNITED STATES OF AMERICA, Indian Territory, }
Western DISTRICT.

    I, Jennie Friday, on oath state that I am 23 years of age and a citizen by Blood, of the Creek Nation; that I am the lawful wife of Berry Friday, who is a citizen, by Blood of the Creek Nation; that a male child was born to me on First day of October, 1901, that said child has been named Willie Friday, and was living March 4, 1905.

                                                her
                                      Jennie x Friday

Witnesses To Mark: mark
  { Wm F.A. Gierkes
    James K. Kepley

Subscribed and sworn to before me this 17th. day of January, 1906.

My commission expires 6-29-1908.   Wm FA Gierkes
                                             Notary Public.

BIRTH AFFIDAVIT.

DEPARTMENT OF THE INTERIOR,
COMMISSION TO THE FIVE CIVILIZED TRIBES.

IN RE Application for Enrollment, as a citizen of the Creek Nation, of Willie Friday, born on the 1st day of October, 1901

Name of Father: Berry Friday   a citizen of the   Creek   Nation.
Name of Mother: Jennie Friday   a citizen of the   Creek   Nation.

                    Post-office: Beggs Ind. Ter.

AFFIDAVIT OF MOTHER.

UNITED STATES OF AMERICA, }
    INDIAN TERRITORY.
  Western   District.

    I, Jennie Friday, on oath state that I am 25 years of age and a citizen by birth, of the Creek Nation; that I am the lawful wife of Berry Friday, who is a citizen, by Birth of the Creek Nation; that a male child was born to me on 1st day of October, 1901, that said child has been named Willie Friday, and is now living.

                                                her
                                    Jennie x Friday
                                      mark

Applications for Enrollment of Creek Newborn
Act of 1905   Volume XII

WITNESSES TO MARK:
{ W.H. Anine
 Lucindia Peters

Subscribed and sworn to before me this 4th *day of* October , *1902.*

W.H. Anine
NOTARY PUBLIC.

AFFIDAVIT OF ATTENDING PHYSICIAN OR MID-WIFE.

UNITED STATES OF AMERICA,
  INDIAN TERRITORY.
Western   District.

I, Patient Grayson , a midwife , on oath state that I attended on Mrs. Jennie Friday , wife of Berry Friday on the 1st day of October , 1901 ; that there was born to her on said date a male child; that said child is now living and is said to have been named Willie Friday
                                her
                        Patient x Grayson
WITNESSES TO MARK: mark
{ W.H. Anine
  Lucindia Peters

Subscribed and sworn to before me this 4th *day of* October , *1902.*

W.H. Anine
NOTARY PUBLIC.

BIRTH AFFIDAVIT.
DEPARTMENT OF THE INTERIOR.
COMMISSION TO THE FIVE CIVILIZED TRIBES.

IN RE APPLICATION FOR ENROLLMENT, as a citizen of the Creek Nation, of Willie Friday, born on the 1st day of Oct, 1901

Name of Father: Berry Friday   a citizen of the   Creek   Nation.
Name of Mother: Jennie Nash (nee Friday) a citizen of the   Creek   Nation.

Postoffice   Edna I.T.

Applications for Enrollment of Creek Newborn
Act of 1905   Volume XII

AFFIDAVIT OF ATTENDING PHYSICIAN OR MID-WIFE.

UNITED STATES OF AMERICA, Indian Territory,
    Western   DISTRICT.

    I, Patience Grayson , a midwife , on oath state that I attended on Mrs. Jennie Nash (nee Friday) , wife of Frank Nash, formerly of Berry Friday on the First day of October , 1901 ; that there was born to her on said date a male child; that said child is now living and is said to have been named Willie Friday

                                                her
                                     Patience x Grayson
Witnesses To Mark: mark
    { Wm FA Gierkes
      Samuel Bright

    Subscribed and sworn to before me this Sixth day of November, 1905.

                                      W^{m}FA Gierkes
                                      NOTARY PUBLIC
                               My Commission Expires June 29, 1908

C 957

                        Muskogee, Indian Territory, October 21, 1905.

Jennie Nash,
    Beggs, Indian Territory.

Dear Madam:

    In the matter of the application for the enrollment of Willie Friday, born October 1, 1901, as a citizen by blood of the Creek Nation, this office desires affidavit of the midwife or physician in attendance at the birth of said child and a blank for that purpose is enclosed herewith.

    In the event that there was no physician or midwife in attendance when said child was born, it will be necessary for you to furnish this office with the affidavits of two disinterested witnesses relative to his birth. Said affidavits must set forth said child's name, the date of his birth, the names of his parents and whether or not he was living on March 4, 1905.

                        Respectfully,
                                        Commissioner.

BC
Env.

Applications for Enrollment of Creek Newborn
Act of 1905 Volume XII

N.C. 957

Muskogee, Indian Territory, December 18, 1905.

Jennie Nash,
    Beggs, Indian Territory.

Dear Madam:

In the matter of the application for the enrollment of your minor child, Willie Friday, born October 1, 1901, as a citizen by blood of the Creek Nation, your affidavit relative to the birth of said child, on file in this office, is defective, inasmuch as the notary public before whom the same was sworn to, did not affix there to his official seal.

There is herewith enclosed blank form of birth affidavit which you are requested to have executed before a notary public, care being taken that he affixes his name and notarial seal, and return to this office in the enclosed envelope.

                    Respectfully,

                                      Commissioner.

BA
Env.

Cr DA-116.
DEPARTMENT OF THE INTERIOR,
COMMISSION TO THE FIVE CIVILIZED TRIBES.

In the matter of the application for the enrollment of Charles Tiger as a citizen by blood of the Creek Nation.

(NO APPEARANCE)

Jennetta Tiger, being duly sworn, testified as follows:

EXAMINATION BY THE COMMISSION.
Q What is your name? A Jennetta Tiger.
Q How old are you? A 37.
Q What's your postoffice? A Kellyville.
Q Are you a citizen of the Creek Nation? A Yes sir.
Q Got your land? A Yes sir.

Applications for Enrollment of Creek Newborn
Act of 1905   Volume XII

Q To what Town do you belong? A I don't know; Caochee[sic], I guess.
Q Doyyou[sic] know a person named Charlie Tiger? A Yes, that's a woman's baby; she's dead; the baby is dead too.
Q What's her name? A Kakana.
Q She is dead? A Yes sir.
Q How long has she been dead--when did she die? A I don't know when she died. She died before Christmas.
Q Before last Christmas? A Died two or three weeks before Christmas.
Q Is Charles Tiger dead too? A Yes sir.
Q When did he die? A 1903. I don't know what month. I was there when the child died. It was in the fall when the child died.
Q What was the name of of[sic] his father? A Dave Tiger.
Q Is he living? A Yes sir.
Q Where does he live? A This side of Kellyville.
Q Kellyville is his postoffice address? A Yes sir.
Q Is he enrolled? A Yes sir.
Q In what Creek Indian Town? A Euchee.
Q What was the name of Charles' mother? A Kakana.
Q Is she enrolled? A Enrolled in --- ---
Q Do you know what land she filed on? A I don't remember what land; it was filed five miles southwest from me, six miles from Kellyville.
Q Are you sure she died as much as three years ago? A No, she died a little before Christmas.
Q Were you present when she died? A No sir.
Q How long after you heard? A Two weeks after the undertaker come to fine out how to get his pay.
Q That was before Christmas? A Yes sir.
Q What was the name of the undertaker? A Man from Sapulpa.
Q Is he there now? A Yes, Huffington Bros.
Q How old was Charles Tiger when he died? A About a year old, I guess. It was born in August and died the next fall.
Q Are you positive that he died a little before Christmas--last Christmas? A He died in 1903; I don't know what months[sic]. The child was in my house all the time just a little before Christmas.
Q Born in the fall of 1902 and died in 1903? A Yes sir.
Q Do you know whether there was a record made of the date of the birth of this child? A No sir.
Q When did the mother die? A 1904.
Q Just last Chretmas[sic]? A Yes sir.
Q 1904? A Yes sir.
Q Did you say Charley was two years old when he died? A No sir
Q Was he as much as a year or a year and half old? A Born in August and died the next Fall, born in 1902 and died 1903.
Q Born in 1902 and died in 1903? A Yes sir.

An affidavit relative to the death of Charles Tiger, filed February 26, 1903, made a part of the record herein.

Applications for Enrollment of Creek Newborn
Act of 1905   Volume XII

Arleka Cohoney, being duly worn, testified as follows (through S. W. Brown, sworn interpreter):

EXAMINATION BY THE COMMISSION:

Q What is your name? A Arleka Cohoney.
Q How old are you? A I must be past 40.
Q What is your postoffice address? A Kelleyville[sic].
Q Are you a citizen of the Creek Nation? A Yes sir.
Q What Creek Town do you belong to? A Euchee.
Q Did you know Charles Tiger? A Yes sir.
Q Is he living? A Not living.
Q What was the name of his father? A Dave Tiger.
Q Is Dave Tiger living? A Yes sir.
Q What is his postoffice address? A Kellyville.
Q About how old is Dave Tiger now? A I don't know exactly.
Q About 27 or 28, you think? A About 28.
Q Is he a Euchee? A Yes sir.
Q What was the name of Charles' mother? A Kakaney.
Q Is she living? A No sir.
Q Do you know when she died? A Yes sir; one day in the winter of last year. 1904.
Q When did Charles Tiger die? A Died in the fall.
Q Of the year before the mother died? A The year before.
Q How old was he when he died? A A little over a year old.

INDIAN TERRITORY, Western District.

I, J. Y. Miller, a stenographer to the Commission to the Five Civilized Tribes, do hereby certify upon oath that the above and foregoing is a true and complete translation of my notes as same appear in my stenographic report of this case.

JY Miller

Sworn to and subscribed
 before me this the
 21 day of March,
 1905.

Edw C Griesel
Notary Public.

Applications for Enrollment of Creek Newborn
Act of 1905 Volume XII

NC 959

ISN
CM

DEPARTMENT OF THE INTERIOR,
COMMISSIONER TO THE FIVE CIVILIZED TRIBES.

In the matter of the application for the enrollment of Charles Tiger, deceased, as a citizen by blood of the Creek Nation.

DECISION

The record in this case shows that on February 26, 1903, there was filed with the Commission to the Five Civilized Tribes an affidavit in the matter of the death of Charles Tiger, which said affidavit is considered as an original application for his enrollment as a citizen by blood of the Creek Nation. Further proceedings were had March 4, 1905.

It appears from the evidence and from the records in the possession of this office that said Charles Tiger, deceased, was the minor child of Dave Tiger and Ka-ke-ney Tiger, duly enrolled citizens of the Creek Nation, whose names appear upon a partial schedule of citizens by blood of said nation, approved by the Secretary of the Interior March 28, 1902, opposite Nos. 6150 and 6664 respectively.

It further appears that said applicant was born in the month of August, 1902, and though the evidence as to the date of death of said applicant is contradictory the weight of evidence establishes such date as sometime in the fall of the year 1903.

It is, therefore, ordered and adjudged that there is no authority of law for the enrollment of said Charles Tiger, deceased, as a citizen by blood of the Creek Nation, and the application for his enrollment as such is accordingly denied.

Tams Bixby   COMMISSIONER.

Muskogee, Indian Territory.
JAN 26 1907

HGH

REFER IN REPLY TO THE FOLLOWING:

NC 959.

DEPARTMENT OF THE INTERIOR,
COMMISSIONER TO THE FIVE CIVILIZED TRIBES.

Muskogee, Indian Territory, January 29, 1907.

Ka-ka-ney Tiger,
c/o Dave Tiger,
Kellyville, Indian Territory.

Dear Madam:

There is herewith enclosed one copy of the decision of the Commissioner to the Five Civilized Tribes in the matter of the application for the enrollment of your minor

Applications for Enrollment of Creek Newborn
Act of 1905   Volume XII

child, Charles Tiger, deceased, as a citizen by blood of the Creek Nation, denying said application.

The decision, with a copy of the proceedings had in the same, is this day transmitted to the Secretary of the Interior for his review and decision. The final decision of the Secretary will be made known to you as soon as the Commissioner is informed of the same.

Respectfully,
Tams Bixby
Commissioner.

Register.
LM-959.

NC 959.

Muskogee, Indian Territory, January 29, 1907.

M. L. Mott,
    Attorney for Creek Nation,
        Muskogee, Indian Territory.

Dear Sir:

There is herewith enclosed one copy of the decision of the Commissioner to the Five Civilized Tribes in the matter of the application for the enrollment of Charles Tiger, deceased, as a citizen by blood of the Creek Nation, denying said application.

The decision, together with a copy of the proceedings had in the same, is this day transmitted to the Secretary of the Interior for his review and decision. The final decision of the Secretary will be made known to you as soon as the Commissioner is informed of the same.

Respectfully,
Commissioner.

LM-54.

NC 959.

Muskogee, Indian Territory, January 29, 1907.

The Honorable,
    The Secretary of the Interior.

Sir:

There is herewith transmitted the record of proceedings had in the matter of the application for the enrollment of Charles Tiger, deceased, as a citizen of the Creek Nation, including the decision of the Commissioner denying said application.

Applications for Enrollment of Creek Newborn
Act of 1905 Volume XII

Respectfully,

Commissioner.

LM-55.

Through the Commissioner
of Indian Affairs.

Refer in reply to the following:
Land 10332-1907

COPY

DEPARTMENT OF THE INTERIOR,
OFFICE OF INDIAN AFFAIRS,
WASHINGTON.

February 25, 1907.

The Honorable,
The Secretary of the Interior.

Sir:

I have the honor to transmit herewith a communication from the Commissioner to the Five Civilized Tribes, dated January 29, 1907, enclosing the record in the matter of the application for the enrollment of Charles Tiger, deceased, as a citizen of the Creek Nation, including the Commissioner's decision of January 26, 1907, denying the application.

It appears from the record that an affidavit in the matter of the death of Charles Tiger was filed with the Commission to the Five Civilized Tribes on February 26, 1903, which was considered as an original application for his enrollment as a citizen by blood of the Creek Nation blood. It further appears that Charles Tiger was the son of Dave Tiger and Ka-ka-ney Tiger, both duly enrolled citizens by blood of the Creek Nation. Testimony was taken in the matter on March 4, 1905. The applicant was born in August, 1902. The evidence as to the date of the death is not clear, it seems to be established that it occurred some time in the fall of 1903.

The office concurs in the opinion of the Commissioner to the Five Civilized Tribes that there is no authority of law for the enrollment of Charles Tiger, deceased, and it is recommended that the decision denying the application be affirmed.

Very Respectfully,
C. F. Larrabee,
Acting Commissioner.

EWE-C

Applications for Enrollment of Creek Newborn
Act of 1905   Volume XII

DEPARTMENT OF THE INTERIOR,　　　　　JF
WASHINGTON.　　　　　　　　　　　　FHE

LRS

I.T.D.   4850, 4890, 4904, 4960, 4962-07.
　　　　4964, 5082, 5166, 5202, 5328- "
　　　　5342, 5374, 5376, 5378, 5380- "
　　　　5396, 5398, 5400, 5402, 5404- "
　　　　5410, 5416, 5418, 5424, 5428- "
　　　　5466, 5488, 5498, 5548,　　- "
D.C.   12430-1907.
DIRECT.

Commissioner to the Five Civilized Tribes,
　　Muskogee, Indian Territory.

Sir:

　　Your decisions in the following Creek citizenship cases adverse to the applicants are hereby affirmed, viz:

Title of case.	Date of your letter of transmittal.
Rhoda Walker.	December 19, 1906
Josiah McIntosh	January 18, 1907
Tony Harlings	January 18, 1907
George Allen, (Freedman)	January 28, 1907
Henry Edwards, (Freedman)	January 28, 1907
Lewis Davis, deceased,	January 28, 1907
Robert Scott, deceased	October 19, 1906
Tom and Mattie Jeffries, deceased,	February 8, 1907
Emma Dodge, (Freedman)	February 8, 1907
Georgia Davis, deceased, (Freedman)	February 7, 1907
Thelma Maud Gibson,	February 7, 1907
Magie Nola Foe, (Freedman)	January 28, 1907
Nelson McIntosh,	January 19, 1907
Calley Ceasar, deceased,	January 28, 1907
Sarah Buck, deceased,	January 25, 1907
Willie Perryman, (Freedman)	January 28, 1907
Joshua Gentry, et al.	January 28, 1907
Dennis Taylor, (Freedman)	January 22, 1907
Paul and Pauline Bruner,	January 25, 1907
Gennie Sanders, (Freedman)	January 28, 1907
Eddie Levi, (Freedman	January 28, 1907
Gabriel Hawkins, (Freedman)	January 28, 1907
Lottie Dickson, (Freedman)	January 28, 1907
Charles Tiger, deceased,	January 29, 1907

Applications for Enrollment of Creek Newborn
Act of 1905   Volume XII

Herford Barnett, deceased,				January 28, 1907
Ceborn Holt, (Freedman)				February 7, 1907
Marguerite Scott, deceased, (Freedman)		January 31, 1907

Copies of Indian Office letters submitting your reports and recommending that the decisions be approved, are inclosed.

A copy hereof and all the papers in the above mentioned cases have been sent to the Indian Office.

>Respectfully,
>(Signed) Jesse E. Wilson,
>Assistant Secretary.

27 inc. and 61 for Ind. Of.

AFMc
3-1-07.

JWH

N C 959

Muskogee, Indian Territory, March 8, 1907.

Ka-Ka-Ney Tiger,
%Dave Tiger,
Kellyville, Indian Territory.

Dear Madam :--

You are hereby advised that under date of March 1, 1907, the Secretary of the Interior affirmed the decision of the Commissioner to the Five Civilized Tribes, denying the application for the enrollment of your minor child, Charles Tiger, as a citizen by blood of the Creek Nation.

>Respectfully,
>Commissioner.

Applications for Enrollment of Creek Newborn
Act of 1905   Volume XII

Witnesses To Mark:
{ Alex Posey
  DC Skaggs

                    her
        Sarah x Perryman
                    mark

Subscribed and sworn to before me this 10 day of April, 1905.

                          Drennan C Skaggs
                            Notary Public.

BA-73.

DEPARTMENT OF THE INTERIOR,
COMMISSION TO THE FIVE CIVILIZED TRIBES.

Muskogee, Indian Territory, March 7, 1905.

In the matter of the application for the enrollment of Minnie May Price as a citizen by blood of the Creek Nation.

M. B. Price, being duly sworn, testified as follows:

EXAMINATION BY THE COMMISSION:
Q What is your name? A M. B. Price.
Q What is your name[sic]? A 34.
Q What is your postoffice? A Wagoner.
Q Have you a child named Minnie May Price? A Yes sir.
Q When was that child born? A August. Will be four years old coming August.
Q 1901? A Yes sir.
Q Remember the day of the month? A Yes sir.
Q What day? A The 22, somewhere like that.
Q Have you a child older than Minnie May? A Yes, names James Lawrence.

    Sallie Price, Indian Territory the mother of Minnie May Price, Indian Territory is identified on Creek Indian card, Field No. 713, and her name is contained in partial list of Creek citizens by blood approved by the Secretary of the Interior March 13, 1902, Roll No. 2331

Q Is Minnie May living? A Yes sir.
Q Did you have a physician in attendance when she was born? A Yes sir.

Applications for Enrollment of Creek Newborn
Act of 1905   Volume XII

Q What was his name? A Dr. Thompson.
Q What is his postoffice? A I declare I could of tell you. He went to Florida last fall, last we heard; he was at Jacksonville. I was talking with the other doctor his parner[sic]; he told me he got a letter from him; I could not tell he's somewhere in Florida.
Q Is this your wife's signature? A I suppose it is.

    A birth affidavit filed herein September 1, 1901, is made a part of the record in this case.

INDIAN TERRITORY, Western District.
    I, J. Y. Miller, a stenographer to the Commission to the Five Civilized Tribes, do hereby certify upon oath that the above and foregoing is a true and complete translation of my notes as same appear in my stenographic report of this case.

                                                   JY Miller
Sworn to and subscribed
  before me this the
  6 day of April, 1905.   Edw C Griesel
                                                      Notary Public.

UNITED STATES OF AMERICA,

INDIAN TERRITORY,

WESTERN DISTRICT.

    Ellen Marlow being duly sworn on her oath states, my age is thirty seven years; that my Post Office address is Wagoner, Indian Territory; I am personally acquainted with Mose B. Price and Sallie Price, his wife; I have lived within one mile of Mose B. Price and his wife Sallie Price for the past twelve years; I was at the home of the said Mose B. Price and Sallie Price on the 23rd day of August 1901 the day after their girl child, Minnie May Price, was born; that said Minnie May Price was born on the 22nd day of August, 1901; that she is the child of Mose B. Price and Sallie Price and is yet living.

    I further swear that I am in no way interested in the application for enrollment as a citizen by blood of the Creek Nation of the said Minnie May Price.

                                                  Ellen Marlow

Signed subscribed and sworn to before me this the 31st day of October, 1905.

                                                Chas G Watts
                                                Notary Public.
My Commission expires the 31st day of July, 1906.

Applications for Enrollment of Creek Newborn
Act of 1905 Volume XII

UNITED STATES OF AMERICA,

INDIAN TERRITORY,

WESTERN DISTRICT.

Millie Monroe being duly sworn on her oath states that her age is twenty four (24) years and that she is the wife of Lum Monroe; I am personally acquainted with Mose B. Price and his wife, Sallie Price, who live four miles southwest of Wagoner, Indian Territory and have known them for the past twelve years; I am now living on the farm controlled by Mose B. Price and have lived on said farm and in that immediate neighborhood for the past six years; I was at the home of Mose B. Price three or four days after their child, Minnie may Price was born which was August 22nd, 1901 and said Minnie May Price is yet living.

I further swear that I am not in any way interested in the enrollment as a Citizen of the Creek Nation of the said Minnie May Price.

Millie Monroe

Signed subscribed and sworn to before me this the 31st day of October, 1905.

Chas G Watts
Notary Public.

My Commission expires the 31st day of July, 1906.

BIRTH AFFIDAVIT.

DEPARTMENT OF THE INTERIOR,
COMMISSION TO THE FIVE CIVILIZED TRIBES.

IN RE Application for Enrollment, as a citizen of the Creek Nation, of Minnie May Price, born on the 22 day of August, 1901

Name of Father: M. B. Price	a citizen of the ----------	Nation.
Name of Mother: Sallie Price	a citizen of the Creek	Nation.

Post-office: Wagoner, I. T.

Applications for Enrollment of Creek Newborn
Act of 1905   Volume XII

AFFIDAVIT OF MOTHER.

UNITED STATES OF AMERICA,
   INDIAN TERRITORY.
Western   District.

    I, Sallie Price , on oath state that I am 23 years of age and a citizen by blood , of the Creek   Nation; that I am the lawful wife of M. B. Price , who is a citizen, by ------ of the ------- Nation; that a female   child was born to me on 22 day of August , 1901 , that said child has been named Minnie May Price , and is now living.

                                     Sallie Price

WITNESSES TO MARK:
  J P Clayton

    Subscribed and sworn to before me this 4$^{\underline{th}}$ day of September , 1901.

                                     J.P. Clayton
                                        NOTARY PUBLIC.

My Com Exp 6/24/1905

AFFIDAVIT OF ATTENDING PHYSICIAN OR MID-WIFE.

UNITED STATES OF AMERICA,
   INDIAN TERRITORY.
Western   District.

    I, William Thomson , a Physician , on oath state that I attended on Mrs. Sallie Price , wife of M.B. Price on the 22   day of August , 1901 ; that there was born to her on said date a female child; that said child is now living and is said to have been named Minnie May Price

                                  Wm Thomson MD

WITNESSES TO MARK:
  JP Clayton

    Subscribed and sworn to before me this 9$^{\underline{th}}$ day of September , 1901.

                                     J P Clayton
                                        NOTARY PUBLIC.

Applications for Enrollment of Creek Newborn
Act of 1905   Volume XII

NC 961

Muskogee, Indian Territory, October 21, 1905.

Sallie Price,
    Care Mose B. Price,
        Wagoner, Indian Territory.

Dear Madam:

    In the matter of the application for the enrollment of your minor child, Minnie May Price, born August 22, 1901, as a citizen by blood of the Creek Nation, there is on file at this office, the affidavit of William Thompson, the physician who attended you at the birth of your said child, Minnie May Price, executed September 9, 1901.

    It appears from said affidavit that said Minnie May Price was born on August 22, 1901 and that she was living September 9, 1901.

    This office desires the affidavit of the physician as to whether said child was living on March 4, 1905; in the event that you are unable to obtain the affidavit of the Physician, it will be necessary for you to furnish this office with the affidavits of two disinterested witnesses relative to her birth. Said affidavits must set forth said child's name, the date of her birth, the names of her parents and whether or not she was living on March 4, 1905.

                Respectfully,

                              Commissioner.

NC-961

Muskogee, Indian Territory, November 6, 1905.

Sallie Price,
    Care of Moses B. Price,
        Wagoner, Indian Territory.

Dear Madam:

    In the matter of the application for the enrollment of your minor child, Minnie May Price, born August 22, 1901, as a citizen by blood of the Creek Nation, this Office desires further proof that said child was living March 4, 1905.

    There is herewith enclosed form of birth affidavit which has been properly filled out. If said affidavit correctly states the facts, you are requested to have same executed and returned to this Office in the enclosed envelope.

                Respectfully,

                              Commissioner.

JYM-6-1

Applications for Enrollment of Creek Newborn
Act of 1905 Volume XII

BIRTH AFFIDAVIT.

DEPARTMENT OF THE INTERIOR.
COMMISSION TO THE FIVE CIVILIZED TRIBES.

IN RE APPLICATION FOR ENROLLMENT, as a citizen of the Creek Nation, of Eula Pearl Whetstone, born on the 10 day of May, 1902

Name of Father: James Whetstone   a citizen of the Creek Nation.
Ketchopatch Town
Name of Mother: Theodosia Whetstone   a citizen of the United States Nation.

Postoffice   Henryetta, Ind. Ter.

AFFIDAVIT OF MOTHER.

UNITED STATES OF AMERICA, Indian Territory,
Western   DISTRICT.   Child is present

I, Theodosia Whetstone, on oath state that I am 32 years of age and a citizen by *(blank)*, of the United States Nation; that I am the lawful wife of James Whetstone, who is a citizen, by blood of the Creek Nation; that a female child was born to me on 10 day of May, 1902, that said child has been named Eula Pearl Whetstone, and was living March 4, 1905.

                       Theodosia Whetstone

Witnesses To Mark:

Subscribed and sworn to before me this 10 day of April, 1905.

                       Drennan C Skaggs
                       Notary Public.

AFFIDAVIT OF ATTENDING PHYSICIAN OR MID-WIFE.

UNITED STATES OF AMERICA, Indian Territory,
Western   DISTRICT.

                                       my wife
I, James Whetstone, a~~—~~, on oath state that I attended on ^ Mrs. Theodosia Whetstone, ~~wife of~~ on the 10 day of May, 1902; that there was born to her on said

Applications for Enrollment of Creek Newborn
Act of 1905   Volume XII

date a female child; that said child was living March 4, 1905, and is said to have been named Eula Pearl Whetstone

            James Whetstone

Witnesses To Mark:
{

 Subscribed and sworn to before me 10 day of April, 1905.

           Drennan C Skaggs
           Notary Public.

BIRTH AFFIDAVIT.

DEPARTMENT OF THE INTERIOR.
COMMISSION TO THE FIVE CIVILIZED TRIBES.

 IN RE APPLICATION FOR ENROLLMENT, as a citizen of the Creek Nation, of Eula Pearl Whetstone, born on the 10th day of May, 1902

Name of Father: James Whetstone	a citizen of the Creek	Nation.
Name of Mother: Theodosia Whetstone	non a citizen of the *(blank)*	Nation.

      Postoffice Henryetta, Indian Territory

AFFIDAVIT OF MOTHER.

UNITED STATES OF AMERICA, Indian Territory, }
  Western   DISTRICT.

 I, Theodosia Whetstone, on oath state that I am 33 years of age and a citizen by *(blank)*, of the *(blank)* Nation; that I am the lawful wife of James Whetstone, who is a citizen, by Blood of the Creek Nation; that a female child was born to me on 10th day of May, 1902, that said child has been named Eula Pearl Whetstone, and was living March 4, 1905.

           Theodosia Whetstone

Witnesses To Mark:
{

 Subscribed and sworn to before me this 28th day of December, 1905.

           William B Morgan
           Notary Public.

My commission expires April 22, 1908.

Applications for Enrollment of Creek Newborn
Act of 1905   Volume XII

DEPARTMENT OF THE INTERIOR,
COMMISSION TO THE FIVE CIVILIZED TRIBES.

In re the application for the enrollment, as a citizen of the Creek Nation, of Eula Pearl Whetstone, born on the 10th, day of May, 1902., Name of father   James Whetstone a citizen of the Creek Nation, Name of mother Theodosia Whetstone. Post office, Henryetta Indian Territory.

United States of America,)	
)	Affidavit in re the marriage of
Indian Territory,)	James Whetstone and Theodosia Whetstone,
)	in the State Texas on the 8th, day of
Western Judicial District.)	September, 1889.

G.W. Smoot and his wife E.A. Smoot, both of lawful age being first duly sworn according to law state upon their oath each for themselves that they are acquainted with James Whetstone and Theodosia Whetstone and have been for the last twenty years; that they knew them in the State of Texas where they lived before coming to the Indian Territory, and that they were both present when the said James Whetstone and Theodosia Whetstone were married and that they witnessed the marriage cerimony[sic] and that the said James Whetstone and Theodosia Whetstone were duly married on the 8th, day of September, 1889, at the resident of the affiants, in Smith County Texas, that they have know[sic] them every since and know them to be husband and wife and are now living together,   And that a preacher by the name of Richardson whose first name is now unknown to affiants officiated at said wedding.

Affiant further states that they have not[sic] whatever in the above case.

<table>
<tr><td></td><td>his</td></tr>
<tr><td>Witnesses to mark</td><td>G W x Smoot</td></tr>
<tr><td>WB Morgan</td><td>mark</td></tr>
<tr><td>W R Hoyt</td><td>E A Smoot</td></tr>
</table>

Subscribed and sworn to before me this 29th day of December, 1905.

William B Morgan
Noary[sic] Public.

My commission expires April 22nd, 1908.

Applications for Enrollment of Creek Newborn
Act of 1905   Volume XII

Western District
Indian Territory   SS

    We, the undersigned, on oath state that we are personally acquainted with Theodisia[sic] Whetstone   wife of   James Whetstone   ; and that on or about the 10th day of   May   19 02 , a   female   child was born to them and has been named Eula Pearl Whetstone   ; that said child was living March 4, 1905.

    We further state that we have no interest in the above case.

                                       his
                                G W x Smoot
                                     mark
                                E A Smoot

Witness to mark:
WB Morgan
W R Hoyt

Subscribed and sworn to before
me this 29th day of December 1905.

                                    William B Morgan
                                        Notary Public.

My Com Ex April 22, 1908.

NC 963

                        Muskogee, Indian Territory, October 21, 1905.

Theodosia Whetstone,
      Care James Whetstone,
            Henryetta, Indian Territory.

Dear Madam:

    In the matter of the application for the enrollment of your minor child, Eula Pearl Whetstone, born May 10, 1902, as a citizen by blood of the Creek Nation, this office desires affidavit of the midwife or physician in attendance at the birth of said child and a blank for that purpose is inclosed herewith.

    In the event that there was no physician or midwife in attendance when said child was born, it will be necessary for you to furnish this office with the affidavits of two disinterested witnesses relative to her birth. Said affidavits must set forth said child's name, the date of her birth, the names of her parents and whether or not she was living on March 4, 1905.

Applications for Enrollment of Creek Newborn
Act of 1905   Volume XII

    This office desires proof of your marriage to James Whetstone; such proof may consist of either the original or a certified copy of your marriage license and certificate.

                        Respectfully,

NC-Env.   Commissioner.

N.C. 963

                      Muskogee, Indian Territory, December 18, 1905.

Theodosia Whetstone,
      Care James Whetstone,
           Henryetta, Indian Territory.

Dear Madam:

    In the matter of the application for the enrollment of your minor child, Eula Pearl Whetstone, born May 10, 1902, as a citizen by blood of the Creek Nation, this office desires affidavit of the midwife or physician in attendance at the birth of said child and a blank for that purpose is inclosed herewith.

    In the event that there was no physician or midwife in attendance when said child was born, it will be necessary for you to furnish this office with the affidavits of two disinterested witnesses relative to her birth and a blank for that purpose is also enclosed.

    It will also be necessary for you to furnish this office with proof of your marriage to James Whetstone, the father of said child; such proof may consist of either the original or a certified copy of your marriage license and certificate.

    This matter should receive your prompt attention.

                        Respectfully,

                                              Commissioner.

BA
Dis.

Applications for Enrollment of Creek Newborn
Act of 1905   Volume XII

NC 963 (Copy)

Henryetta, Indian Territory,
December 29th, 1905.

Commission to the Five Civilized Tribes,
Muskogee, Indian Territory.

Dear Sir:

Inclosed please find affidavit of Theodosia Whetstone, mother of Eula Pear[sic] Whetstone, also affidavit of G.W. and E.A. Smoot as to the birth of said child. Also affidavit of the same parties as to the marriage of James Whetstone and Theodosia Whetstone. My marriage certificate was detroyed[sic] bt[sic] fire and unless the inclosed affidavit will answer the purpose of the certificate and shall have to send to Quitman, county site of Wood County Texas and get a certified copy of the marraige[sic] certificate. Please let me know if this affidavit will do. If not I shall get the certified copy. All my children are on the roll and have filed.

Yours very truly,
(signed) JAMES WHETSTONE

Marriage License

United States of America,
INDIAN TERRITORY,   } ss.   No. **21**
Northern District.

To Any Person Authorized by Law to Solemnize Marriage---Greeting:

You are Hereby Commanded to Solemnize the Rite and publish the Banns of Matrimony between Mr.   Stephen C. Sanger   of   Okmulgee , in the Indian Territory, aged   24   years and Miss Viola Alford   of   Okmulgee   in the Indian Territory aged   20   years according to law, and do you officially sign and return this License to the parties therein named.

Applications for Enrollment of Creek Newborn
Act of 1905   Volume XII

  WITNESS my hand and official seal at Muscogee Indian Territory this   27   *day of*   January   *A.D. 190*0

Chas. A. Davidson
Clerk of the U.S. Court

By (Name Illegible)   Deputy

CERTIFICATE OF MARRIAGE.

United States of America,
  INDIAN TERRITORY,   } ss.
  Northern District.

  I, A. M. Lusk , *a Minister of the Gospel, DO HEREBY CERTIFY that on the* 30 *day of* January *A. D.* 1900, *I did duly and according to law as commanded in the foregoing License, solemnize the Rite and publish the Banns of Matrimony between the parties therein named.*

  WITNESS my hand this 31 *day of* January *A. D.* 1900

  My credentials are recorded in the office of the Clerk of the United States Court, Indian Territory, ~~Northern~~ Third *District, Book* A , *Page* 135 .

A. M. Lusk
A Minister of the Gospel

Note—This License and Certificate of Marriage must be returned to the Office of the Clerk of the United States Court in the Northern District, Indian Territory, from whence it was issued, within sixty days from the date thereof, or the party to whom the license was issued will be liable in the amount of the One Hundred Dollars ($100.00)

CERTIFICATE OF RECORD.

United States of America,
  INDIAN TERRITORY,   } ss.
  Northern District.

  I, **CHARLES A. DAVIDSON**, *Clerk of the United States Court in the Northern District, Indian Territory, do hereby certify that the instrument hereto attached was filed for record in my office the* 14 *day of* Feby. 1900 *at* 8 *A..M., and duly recorded in Book* 2 , *Marriage Record, Page* 225

  WITNESS my hand and seal of said Court at Muscogee, in said Territory, this 14 *day of* Feby. *A. D.* 1900

Applications for Enrollment of Creek Newborn
Act of 1905 Volume XII

                                Chas. A. Davidson   *Clerk.*
                        By..*Deputy.*

BIRTH AFFIDAVIT.

DEPARTMENT OF THE INTERIOR.
COMMISSION TO THE FIVE CIVILIZED TRIBES.

IN RE APPLICATION FOR ENROLLMENT, as a citizen of the Creek Nation, of Jaunitta Sanger, born on the 1st day of May, 1903

Name of Father: Stephen Sanger   a citizen of the   Creek   Nation.
Name of Mother: Viola Sanger   a citizen of the   U. S.   ~~Nation~~.

                         Postoffice   Okmulgee, I. T.

AFFIDAVIT OF MOTHER.

UNITED STATES OF AMERICA, Indian Territory,
    Western   DISTRICT.

    I, Viola Sanger, on oath state that I am 28 years of age and a citizen by marriage, of the Creek Nation; that I am the lawful wife of Stephen Sanger, who is a citizen, by blood of the Creek Nation; that a female child was born to me on 1st day of May, 1903, that said child has been named Jaunitta Sanger, and was living March 4, 1905.

                                  Viola Sanger
Witnesses To Mark:

    Subscribed and sworn to before me this 22nd day of March, 1905.

                                    Wesley M Dyson
                                    Notary Public.

AFFIDAVIT OF ATTENDING PHYSICIAN OR MID-WIFE.

UNITED STATES OF AMERICA, Indian Territory,
    Western   DISTRICT.

    I, W. M. Cott, a Physician, on oath state that I attended on Mrs. Viola Sanger, wife of Stephen Sanger on the 1st day of May, 1903 ; that there was born to her on said date a female child; that said child was living March 4, 1905, and is said to have been named Jaunitta Sanger

                                    WM Cott

Applications for Enrollment of Creek Newborn
Act of 1905   Volume XII

Witnesses To Mark:
{

    Subscribed and sworn to before me this 22 day of March, 1905.

                                 Wesley M Dyson
                                 Notary Public.

NC 964

                          Muskogee, Indian Territory, October 21, 1905.

Viola Sanger,
    Care Stephen Sanger,
        Okmulgee, Indian Territory.

Dear Madam:

    In the matter of the application for the enrollment of Jaunitta Sanger, as a citizen by blood of the Creek Nation blood, this office desires proof of your marriage to Stephen Sanger and it will be necessary for you to furnish either your marriage license and certificate or a certified copy of the same for the files in this case.

                               Respectfully,
                                          Commissioner.

                                                             NC-967

DEPARTMENT OF THE INTERIOR,
COMMISSIONER TO THE FIVE CIVILIZED TRIBES.

                Muskogee, Indian Territory, November 2, 1905.

    In the matter of the application for the enrollment of Susie Rose Sneed as a citizen by blood of the Creek Nation.

    George Sneed, being duly sworn, testified as follows:

EXAMINATION BY THE COMMISSIONER:
Q What is your name? A George Sneed.

Applications for Enrollment of Creek Newborn
Act of 1905   Volume XII

Q How old are you? A 33 past, if I make no mistake.
Q Are you a citizen of the Creek Nation? A Yes sir.
Q What is your postoffice address? A Muskogee.
Q What is the name of your father? A Charlie Sneed. He has been dead. I can just recollect him.
Q He was not a citizen of the Creek Nation, was he? A No sir, he was not.
Q He was an ordinary negro? A I don't know much about him.
Q What was the name of our mother? A Martha Sneed.
Q She is living? A She is dead.
Q Was she a citizen of the Creek Nation? A Yes sir.
Q To what Town did she belong, do you know? A Artusey Town.
Q You have some children enrolled; name them. A George Everett, Maron and Leonard.
Q What is the name of their mother? A Hannah Sneed.
Q Have you two new-born children by her? A I have got Larzar Sneed by her.
Q And the other one? A Susie Rose
Q This is also her child? A Yes sir.
Q You are enrolled here as George Sneed; why did you allow them to make affidavits about Susie Rose, your child, and put in George W.? A I have a middle name.
Q But your correct name is George Sneed, as you were enrolled? A Yes sir.
Q When you made the affidavit you put in-- A My name, George Washington Sneed.
Q You want it now the way you are enrolled? A I am scared to tell you whether it is George or George W. Sneed.
Q You mean you are reluctant to state which you want to give as your name, but you know that you are this party, do you? A I am the Sneed, yes, sir.

Witness is identified as George Sneed, and his name is contained in the partial list of citizens by blood of the Creek Nation opposite Roll No. 9825.

Q When was Susie Rose Sneed born? A Born in 1902, April 27.
Q Is she living? A Yes sir.
Q Is your child, Larzar, living? A Yes sir.
Q Have you endeavored to get the affidavit of the midwife who was present when Susie Rose was born? A Yes, I have sent it, but I haven't any reply.
The witness is advised that if he is unable to obtain the affidavit of the midwife who was present when Susie Rose was born, this Office requires the affidavits of two disinterested witnesses relative to its birth.

Q Hannah Sneed is not a citizen of any tribe in Indian Territory? A No sir.

INDIAN TERRITORY, WESTERN DISTRICT.
I, J. Y. Miller, a stenographer to the Commissioner to the Five Civilized Tribes, do hereby certify that the above and foregoing is a true and complete translation of my notes as same appear in my stenographic report of this case.

JY Miller

Applications for Enrollment of Creek Newborn
Act of 1905   Volume XII

Sworn to and subscribed before me
this the 10 day of November,
1905. Edw C Griesel
  Notary Public.

BIRTH AFFIDAVIT.

DEPARTMENT OF THE INTERIOR.
COMMISSION TO THE FIVE CIVILIZED TRIBES.

IN RE APPLICATION FOR ENROLLMENT, as a citizen of the Creek Nation, of Susie Rose Sneed, born on the 27 day of April, 1902
  W.
Name of Father: George ^ Sneed a citizen of the Creek Nation.
Artusse Town
Name of Mother: Hannah Sneed a citizen of the United States Nation.

  Postoffice Okmulgee, Ind. Terr.

AFFIDAVIT OF MOTHER.

UNITED STATES OF AMERICA, Indian Territory, ⎫
  Western DISTRICT. ⎭

I, Hannah Sneed, on oath state that I am 32 years of age and a citizen by -------, of the United States ~~Nation~~; that I am the lawful wife of George W. Sneed, who is a citizen, by blood of the Creek Nation; that a female child was born to me on 27 day of April, 1902, that said child has been named Susie Rose Sneed, and was living March 4, 1905. That the mid-wife in attendance is some place in Louisanna[sic]

  Hannah Sneed
Witnesses To Mark:

{

Subscribed and sworn to before me this 10 day of April, 1905.

  Drennan C Skaggs
  Notary Public.

Applications for Enrollment of Creek Newborn
Act of 1905   Volume XII

father
AFFIDAVIT OF ~~ATTENDING PHYSICIAN OR MID-WIFE~~.

UNITED STATES OF AMERICA, Indian Territory, ⎫
  Western   DISTRICT.   ⎭

I, George ^W^ Sneed , ~~a (blank)~~ , on oath state that I assisted the midwife who attended on my wife Mrs. Hannah Sneed , ~~wife of~~ *(blank)* on the 27 day of April , 1902 ; that there was born to her on said date a   female   child; that said child was living March 4, 1905, and is said to have been named Susie Rose Sneed

George ^W^ Sneed

Witnesses To Mark:
{

Subscribed and sworn to before me this 10 day of April, 1905.

Drennan C Skaggs
Notary Public.

BIRTH AFFIDAVIT.

DEPARTMENT OF THE INTERIOR.
COMMISSION TO THE FIVE CIVILIZED TRIBES.

IN RE APPLICATION FOR ENROLLMENT, as a citizen of the Creek Nation, of Susie Rose Sneed , born on the 27 day of Apr , 1902

Name of Father: George W. Sneed	a citizen of the Creek	Nation.
Name of Mother: Hannah Sneed	a citizen of the U. S.	Nation.

Postoffice   Okmulgee, I.T.

AFFIDAVIT OF MOTHER.

UNITED STATES OF AMERICA, Indian Territory, ⎫
  Western   DISTRICT.   ⎭

I, Hannah Sneed , on oath state that I am 32 years of age and a citizen by *(blank)* , of the U. S. ~~Nation~~; that I am the lawful wife of George W. Sneed , who is a citizen, by blood of the Creek Nation; that a female child was born to me on 27 day of April , 1902 , that said child has been named Susie Rose Sneed , and was living March 4, 1905.

her
Hannah x Sneed
mark

Witnesses To Mark:
{ George C. Beidleman
  J.E. *(Illegible)*

Applications for Enrollment of Creek Newborn
Act of 1905   Volume XII

Subscribed and sworn to before me this 6" day of November, 1905.

My Com. Exp, April 27-1908   George C. Bridleman
                                                     Notary Public.

AFFIDAVIT OF ATTENDING PHYSICIAN OR MID-WIFE.

UNITED STATES OF AMERICA, Indian Territory, }
     Western   DISTRICT. }

I, Julia Shelton, a Midwife, on oath state that I attended on Mrs. Hannah Sneed, wife of George W. Sneed on the 27 day of April, 1902; that there was born to her on said date a female child; that said child was living March 4, 1905, and is said to have been named Susie Rose Sneed

                                                      her
                                                  Julia x Shelton
Witnesses To Mark: mark
   { John Sneed
   { P.M. Qwlah

Subscribed and sworn to before me 2$\underline{nd}$ day of November, 1905.

                                                  John F. Slattery
                                                  Notary Public.

0967

                  STATE OF LOUISIANA--PARISH OF CADDO.

                             Proces Verbal of Marriage.

BE IT REMEMBERED, That by virtue of a License issued by the Clerk of the District Court of the Parish of Caddo, I, Sam Armstead, have celebrated Marriage between Mr. George Sneed and M Hanah Kary, and have joined them together in Holy Wedlock, according to law, this the 31st day of July, 1892.

                                               George Sneed.)
)   ) Parties.
   George Willis.)   Hanah Kary.)
   Vitter Thomas.) Witness.   )
   Flutcher Hason.)   Sam Armstead.
)

)
INDIAN TERRITORY.)   I, J. Y. Miller, a stenographer to the
Western District.   ) ss.   Commissioner to the Five Civilized
)   Tribes, do hereby certify that the above and foregoing is a true and complete copy of its original.

Applications for Enrollment of Creek Newborn
Act of 1905   Volume XII

JY Miller

Subscribed and sworn to before me
this the 8th day of November,
1905.

J. McDermott
Notary Public.

BIRTH AFFIDAVIT.

DEPARTMENT OF THE INTERIOR.
COMMISSION TO THE FIVE CIVILIZED TRIBES.

IN RE APPLICATION FOR ENROLLMENT, as a citizen of the Creek Nation, of Larzar Sneed, born on the 15 day of May , 1904

Name of Father: George Sneed   a citizen of the   Creek   Nation.
Artusse Town
Name of Mother: Hannah Sneed   a citizen of the United StatesNation.

Postoffice   Okmulgee, Ind. Terr

AFFIDAVIT OF MOTHER.

Child not present.

UNITED STATES OF AMERICA, Indian Territory,
Western   DISTRICT.

I, Hannah Sneed , on oath state that I am 32 years of age and a citizen by ----- , of the United States Nation; that I am the lawful wife of George Sneed , who is a citizen, by adoption of the Creek Nation; that a male child was born to me on 15 day of May , 1904 , that said child has been named Larzar Sneed , and was living March 4, 1905.

Hannah Sneed

Witnesses To Mark:

Subscribed and sworn to before me this 10 day of April , 1905.

Drennan C Skaggs
Notary Public.

Applications for Enrollment of Creek Newborn
Act of 1905   Volume XII

AFFIDAVIT OF ATTENDING PHYSICIAN OR MID-WIFE.

UNITED STATES OF AMERICA, Indian Territory, }
    Western   DISTRICT.

    I, Sylvia Tomlin , a midwife , on oath state that I attended on Mrs. Hannah Sneed, wife of George W Sneed on the 15 day of May , 1904 ; that there was born to her on said date a male child; that said child was living March 4, 1905, and is said to have been named Larzar Sneed

                              her
                          Sylvia x Tomlin
Witnesses To Mark: mark
  { George W Sneed
    Elijah P. Blakemore

    Subscribed and sworn to before me 10 day of Apr, 1905.

My Commission Expires Nov. 18, 1908.   Elijah P. Blakemore
                                            Notary Public.

NC 967

                          Muskogee, Indian Territory, October 21, 1905.

Hannah Sneed,
    Care George Sneed,
        Okmulgee, Indian Territory.

Dear Madam:

    In the matter of the application for the enrollment of your minor child, Rose Sneed, born April 27, 1902, as a citizen by blood of the Creek Nation, this office desires affidavit of the midwife or physician in attendance at the birth of said child and a blank for that purpose is inclosed herewith.

    In the event that there was no physician or midwife in attendance when said child was born, it will be necessary for you to furnish this office with the affidavits of two disinterested witnesses relative to her birth. Said affidavits must set forth said child's name, the date of her birth, the names of her parents and whether or not she was living on March 4, 1905.

    This office desires proof of your marriage to George Sneed and it will be necessary for you to furnish either the original or a certified copy of your marriage license license[sic] and certificate for the files in this case.

                          Respectfully,

BC   Commissioner.
Env.

Applications for Enrollment of Creek Newborn
Act of 1905   Volume XII

NC-967

Muskogee, Indian Territory, November 8, 1905.

George Sneed,
   Okmulgee, Indian Territory.

Dear Sir:

There is herewith returned your original certificate of marriage, a copy of which has been made for this Office in the matter of the application for the enrollment of your minor child, Susie Rose Sneed, as a citizen by blood of the Creek Nation.

Respectfully,

Commissioner.

JYM-8-4

Muskogee, Indian Territory, December 26, 1905.

George W. Sneed,
   Okmulgee, Indian Territory.

Dear Sir:

Receipt is acknowledged of your letter of December 21, 1905, in which you ask when you may be allowed to select allotments for your minor children, Susie, Rose and Larzar Sneed.

In reply you are advised that the matter of the application for the enrollment of said children is pending, and that when final action is had in same, you will be notified with regard to filing.

Respectfully,

Commissioner.

Applications for Enrollment of Creek Newborn
Act of 1905 Volume XII

N.C. 968　　　　　　　　　　　　　　　　　　　　　　　　　　I.D.

DEPARTMENT OF THE INTERIOR,
COMMISSIONER TO THE FIVE CIVILIZED TRIBES.

In the matter of the application for the enrollment of Charles Jackson Shields, Jr. as a citizen by blood of the Creek Nation.

......ORDER......

The record in this case shows that on April 15, 1905, there was filed with the Commission to the Five Civilized Tribes at Muskogee, Indian Territory, the application of Clara Williams Shields for the enrollment of her minor child, Charles Jackson Shields, Jr., as a citizen by blood of the Creek Nation.

The evidence shows that said Charles Jackson Shields Jr. was born July 22, 1902, and that he was living March 4, 1905.

The evidence further shows that said Charles Jackson Shields Jr. is the minor child of Charles J. Shields and Clara Williams Shields; and an examination of the records of this Office shows that the names of said Charles J. Shields and said Clara Williams Shields, or either of them, are not contained in the lists of citizens by blood of the Creek Nation whose enrollment has been approved by the Secretary of the Interior prior to March 3, 1905.

The act of Congress approved March 3, 1905, (Public No. 212), provides:

"That the Commission to the Five Civilized Tribes is authorized for sixty days after the date of the approval of this Act to receive and consider applications for enrollments of children born subsequent to May twenty five, nineteen hundred and one, and prior to March fourth, nineteen hundred and five, and living on said latter date, to citizens of the Creek tribe of Indians whose enrollment has been approved by the Secretary of the Interior prior to the date of the approval of this act; and to enroll and make allotments to such children."

It is, therefore, ordered that there is no authority of law for the enrollment of said Charles Jackson Shields, Jr. as a citizen by blood of the Creek Nation, and that the application for his enrollment as such should be and the same is hereby dismissed.

　　　　　　　　　　　　　　　　　　　　　　　　　　Commissioner.

Muskogee, Indian Territory.

Applications for Enrollment of Creek Newborn
Act of 1905 Volume XII

BIRTH AFFIDAVIT.

DEPARTMENT OF THE INTERIOR.
COMMISSION TO THE FIVE CIVILIZED TRIBES.

IN RE APPLICATION FOR ENROLLMENT, as a citizen of the Creek Nation, of Charles Jackson Shield, Jr. , born on the 22 day of July , 1902

Name of Father: Charles J. Shields   a citizen of the United States Nation.
Name of Mother: Clara Williams Shields   a citizen of the   Creek   Nation.
Hickory Ground Town
                Postoffice   Okmulgee, Ind. Ter.

AFFIDAVIT OF MOTHER.

UNITED STATES OF AMERICA, Indian Territory,
   Western   DISTRICT.   Child is present

    I, Clara Williams Shields , on oath state that I am 26 years of age and a citizen by blood , of the Creek   Nation; that I am the lawful wife of Charles J. Shields , who is a citizen, by *(blank)* of the United States   Nation; that a male   child was born to me on 22 day of July , 1902 , that said child has been named Charles Jackson Shields, Jr. , and was living March 4, 1905.

                          Clara Williams Shields

Witnesses To Mark:
{

    Subscribed and sworn to before me this 10 day of April , 1905.

                          Drennan C Skaggs
                          Notary Public.

AFFIDAVIT OF ATTENDING PHYSICIAN OR MID-WIFE.

UNITED STATES OF AMERICA, Indian Territory,
   Western   DISTRICT.

    I, W.C. Mitchener , a physician , on oath state that I attended on Mrs. Clara Williams Shields , wife of Charles J. Shields on the 22 day of July , 1902 ; that there was born to her on said date a male   child; that said child was living March 4, 1905, and is said to have been named Charles Jackson Shields, Jr.

                          W.C. Mitchener M.D.

Witnesses To Mark:
{

Applications for Enrollment of Creek Newborn
Act of 1905   Volume XII

Subscribed and sworn to before me 10 day of April, 1905.

Drennan C Skaggs
Notary Public.

Muskogee, Indian Territory, December 2, 1903.

Thomas West,
    Konawa, Indian Territory.

Dear Sir:

    Receipt is acknowledged of your letter of November 26, 1905, in which you state that you desire to have two children of Marpiyecher, Yamah aged eight and Josie aged six, enrolled as citizens of the Creek Nation. You state that neither of them has been allotted.

    In reply you are advised that it does not appear from the records of this office that application was ever made for the enrollment of said children within the time specified by law.

    You are further advised that the rolls of the Creek Nation were closed September 1, 1904 and for children born since May 21, 1901, on May 2, 1905; this office is now without authority to receive or consider applications for the enrollment of citizens of said nation.

Respectfully,

Acting Commissioner.

N.C. 969.

Muskogee, Indian Territory, June 22, 1906.

Thomas West,
    Konawa, Indian Territory.

Dear Sir:

    December 1, 1905, a letter was addressed to you by this office in reply to your letter of November 26, 1905, in which you stated that you desired to have two children, Yamah and Josie West, enrolled as citizens of the Creek Nation.

Applications for Enrollment of Creek Newborn
Act of 1905   Volume XII

You were advised in said letter from the Commissioner that at the date of the writing of said letter this office was without authority to receive or consider applications for enrollment of citizens of the Creek Nation.

The act of Congress approved April 26, 1905, (Public No. 129), makes provision for the enrollment of children living on March 4, 1906, born to duly enrolled citizens of the Creek Nation.

There are inclosed herewith two blank birth affidavits which you are requested to have properly executed, one in the matter of the application for the enrollment of Yamah West and the other in the matter of the application for the enrollment of Josie West, as citizens of the Creek Nation. Each of said affidavits should show the name of the child, the names of its parents, the date of its birth and whether or not said child was living March 4, 1906.

It is further requested that you furnish information which will enable this office to identify you and the mother of said children upon its roll of citizens of the Creek Nation.

Respectfully,

2BA

Commissioner.

HGH

REFER IN REPLY TO THE FOLLOWING:

DEPARTMENT OF THE INTERIOR,
COMMISSIONER TO THE FIVE CIVILIZED TRIBES.

Muskogee, Indian Territory, August 3, 1906.

Thomas West,
    Konawa, Indian Territory.

Dear Sir:

Replying to your letter of July 25, 1906, you are advised that in the matter of the application for the enrollment of Yanah or Yamah and Josie West or Nartake, as citizens of the Creek Nation, this office cannot identify either of the parents, who you state are dead, and you are requested to furnish this office with the names of the parents of the father and the mother of said children, the Creek Indian towns to which each of them belongs, their roll numbers or a description of their lands in the Creek Nation, and any other information that you can secure which would assist in identifying them.

You are further advised that in lieu of the affidavit of the deceased mother, this office requires the affidavits of two disinterested witnesses relative to the birth of said children, and affidavit of the midwife or physician who attended at their birth. Blank forms of birth affidavit are herewith enclosed.

Applications for Enrollment of Creek Newborn
Act of 1905 Volume XII

2 BA
1 Dis. Wit.

Respectfully,
Tams Bixby
Commissioner.

NC 969.

Muskogee, Indian Territory, October 12, 1906.

Thomas West,
    Konawa, Indian Territory.

Dear Sir:

    You are hereby advised that the names of Josie and Yahnah Marpiyecher   are listed on Seminolr Indian card field number 606, and their names are contained in Seminole schedule, opposite numbers 1895 and 1897, respectively, and that they have received their allotments of land in the Seminole Nation.

Respectfully,
Commissioner.

AFFIDAVIT OF DISINTERESTED WITNESS.

UNITED STATES OF AMERICA,
Western DISTRICT,   SS
INDIAN TERRITORY.

    We, the undersigned, on oath state that we are personally acquainted with   Lucy Scott   wife of   Marpiecha Scott   the wife of Marpiecha Scott   ; that there was born to her a   *(blank)*   child on or about the   *(blank)*   day of   *(blank)*   ; that the said child has been named   Josie Scott and Yanah Scott   , and was living March 4, 1906. and are now living

Witnesses: J.P. Johnson
              (Name Illegible)   his
                                John x Wilson
                                mark
                              Harry Tiger

Subscribed and sworn to before me this 27 day of September 1907

Donald Campbell
Notary Public.

Applications for Enrollment of Creek Newborn
Act of 1905   Volume XII

(The Affidavit below typed as given.)

United States of America,)
Western Judicial District) SS.   Affidavitt.
of the Indian Territory.)

    Personally appeared before me a Notary Public for the aforementioned District, Harry Tiger, who is to me know, and who upon being by me duly sworn says my name is Harry Tiger, my age is about 31 years, my Post Office is Sasakwa, Ind Ter. I am a Seminole Indian by blood, I knew Lucy Scott during her lifetime she was a Seminole Indian woman, and was the wife of a Creek Indian named Marpiecha Scott, he was a member of the kessetha Town, they had three children one of whom is now dead, Josie Scott, and Yanah Scott are now living, the Mother Lucy Scott died about nine years ago I do not know when the Father died but I have always understood that the children had been taken off the Seminole Rolls and enrolled with the Father as Creeks, they are now living with (John Wilson that is one of them the Girl, Yanah) and the boy is living with his Grand-Mother Polly Scott.

                                            Harry Tiger

Subscribed and Sworn to before me this 27th day of September 1906 at Wewoka Ind Ter.

                                      Donald Campbell
My Commission expires   Notary Public.
10 day of June 1909.

(The Affidavit below typed as given.)

                                      Affidavit.

United States of America,)
Western Judicial District) SS.
of the Indian Territory.)

    Personally appeared before me a Notary Public for the aforementioned District, John Wilson who is to me known and who upon being by me duly sworn says, my Name is John Wilson, I am a Seminole Indian by blood my Post Office Address is Sasakwa, Ind Ter. I am about 45 years old/I was well acquainted with Lucy Scott, a Seminole woman who was the Mother of Yanah and Josie Scott, their Father was a Creek Indian named Marpukie or Marpiecha Scott he was a member of the Keseetha Town in the Creek Nation, before the allotment of lands in the Indian Territory, he lived near the Little Deep Fork, in the Creek Nation, and had the children taken from the Seminole Rolls, where they rightly blonged with their Mother Lucy (who was my Niece) and said that he intended to have them enrolled with him as Creeks, this was before the allotment of lands, we supposed that he had done so and their names were stricken from the Seminole Rolls, it now appears that he never did have the children enrolled as Creeks and they are without allottments to day, the Father of these Children belonged to the same town in the

Applications for Enrollment of Creek Newborn
Act of 1905   Volume XII

Creek Nation as Eli Hardridge who was the town King. Josie Scott is now about 16 years old and Yanah Scott his Sister is probably about Ten years old, there was another child in between these two who is now dead, the Mother Lucy Scott, died about eight or nine years ago, the Father Marpiecha Scott, died about seven years ago.

                                          his
                                John x Wilson

Witness to mark.   mark
J Coody Johnson
Thomas West

Sworn and Subscribed to before me this 27th day of September, 1906 at Wewoka, Ind Ter.

                                    Donald Campbell
                                    Notary Public.

My Commission expires
10 day of June 1909.

                                                                       BA-121

DEPARTMENT OF THE INTERIOR,
COMMISSION TO THE FIVE CIVILIZED TRIBES.

Muskogee, Indian Territory, March 9, 1905.

In the matter of the application for the enrollment of Arlingee Cowe as a Creek.

Sarty Cowe, being duly sworn, testified as follows:

EXAMINATION BY THE COMMISSION:
Q What is your name? A Sarty Cowe.
Q Have you a child named Arlingee? A I did have one, but it's dead.
Q When was Arlingee born? A December 3, 1901.
Q When did she die? A October 17, 1902.
Q She has been dead now more than two years, has she? A Yes sir.

The witness is identified as Sarty Cowe on Creek Indian card, filed No. 1524, and his name is contained in partial list of Creek citizens by blood approved by the Secretary of the Interior March 28, 1902, Roll No. 4890.

Applications for Enrollment of Creek Newborn
Act of 1905 Volume XII

INDIAN TERRITORY, Western District.

I, J. Y. Miller, a stenographer to the Commission to the Five Civilized Tribes, do hereby certify upon oath that the above and foregoing is a true and complete translation of my notes as same appear in my stenographic report of this case.

JY Miller

Sworn to and subscribed before me this the 19 day of April, 1905.

My Com expires Apr. 11, 1909   Zera E Parrish
                                   Notary Public.

DEPARTMENT OF THE INTERIOR,

COMMISSION TO THE FIVE CIVILIZED TRIBES.
Okmulgee, I. T., April 10, 1905.

In the matter of the application for the enrollment of Pleasant Tobler as a citizen by blood of the Creek Nation.

Mary Adams, being duly sworn, testified as follows:

BY COMMISSION:
Q What is your name? A Mary Adams.
Q How old are you? A Nineteen.
Q What is your post office address? A Okmulgee.
Q Are you a citizen of the Creek Nation? A Yes, sir.
Q To what town do you belong? A Ketchapataka.
Q Do you make application for the enrollment of your minor child, Pleasant Tobler, as a citizen of the Creek Nation? A Yes, sir.
Q What is the name of his father? A Fred Tobler.
Q Is he a citizen of the Creek Nation? A Yes, sir.
Q To what town does he belong? A I don't know, sir.
Q Is he a Creek Freedman or a citizen by blood? A He is a colored geltleman[sic] but I don't know what town he belongs to.
Q Is he your lawful husband? A No, sir.
Q Did you ever live together as man and wife? A No, sir.
Q Does he acknowledge, Pleasant Tobler, as his child? A Yes, sir.

Applications for Enrollment of Creek Newborn
Act of 1905 Volume XII

Q Does he contribute to the support of the child? A No, sir.

---oooOOOooo---

    I, D. C. Skaggs, on oath state that the above and foregoing is a full and true transcript of my stenographic notes as taken in said cause on said date.

                              D. C. Skaggs

Subscribed and sworn to before me this 24 day of July, 1905.

                              J McDermott
                              Notary Public.

NC 973

                        Muskogee, Indian Territory, October 21, 1905.

Mary Adams,
    Okmulgee, Indian Territory.

Dear Madam:

    In the matter of the application for the enrollment of Pleasant Tobler, born April 12, 1903, as a citizen by blood of the Creek Nation, this office desires the affidavits of two disinterested witnesses relative to his birth. Said affidavits must set forth said child's name, the date of his birth, the names of his parents and whether or not he was living on March 4, 1905.

                        Respectfully,
                                      Commissioner.

BIRTH AFFIDAVIT.

                    DEPARTMENT OF THE INTERIOR.
         COMMISSION TO THE FIVE CIVILIZED TRIBES.

    IN RE APPLICATION FOR ENROLLMENT, as a citizen of the Creek Nation, of Pleasant Tobler, born on the 12 day of April, 1903

Name of Father: Fred Tobler	a citizen of the Creek	Nation.
Name of Mother: Mary Adams	a citizen of the Creek	Nation.
Ketchopatcky Town		

                        Postoffice   Okmulgee, Ind. Ter.

Applications for Enrollment of Creek Newborn
Act of 1905   Volume XII

AFFIDAVIT OF MOTHER.

UNITED STATES OF AMERICA, Indian Territory, ⎫
    Western   DISTRICT. ⎭   Child is present

    I, Mary Adams, on oath state that I am 19 years of age and a citizen by blood, of the Creek Nation; that I am not the lawful wife of Fred Tobler, who is a citizen, by adoption of the Creek Nation; that a male child was born to me on 12 day of April, 1903, that said child has been named Pleasant Tobler, and was living March 4, 1905.

                                      Mary Adams

Witnesses To Mark:
  {

    Subscribed and sworn to before me this 10 day of April, 1905.

                                      Drennan C Skaggs
                                      Notary Public.

AFFIDAVIT OF ATTENDING PHYSICIAN OR MID-WIFE.

UNITED STATES OF AMERICA, Indian Territory, ⎫
    Western   DISTRICT. ⎭

    I, Mahaley Adams, a midwife, on oath state that I attended on Miss Mary Adams, ~~wife of   on the   day of   , 190~~ ; that there was born to her on said date a male child; that said child was living March 4, 1905, and is said to have been named Pleasant Tobler   her

                                      Mahaley x Adams

Witnesses To Mark: mark
  { Alex Posey
    DC Skaggs

    Subscribed and sworn to before me 10 day of April, 1905.

                                      Drennan C Skaggs
                                      Notary Public.

Applications for Enrollment of Creek Newborn
Act of 1905   Volume XII

BIRTH AFFIDAVIT.

DEPARTMENT OF THE INTERIOR.
COMMISSION TO THE FIVE CIVILIZED TRIBES.

IN RE APPLICATION FOR ENROLLMENT, as a citizen of the Creek Nation, of Pleasant Tobler, born on the 12th day of April, 1903

Name of Father: Fred Tobler   a citizen of the   Creek   Nation.
Name of Mother: Mary Adams now Tobler   a citizen of the   Creek   Nation.

Postoffice   Okmulgee, I.T.

AFFIDAVIT OF MOTHER.

UNITED STATES OF AMERICA, Indian Territory,
    Western   DISTRICT.

I, Mary Adams, on oath state that I am 19 years of age and a citizen by blood, of the Creek Nation; that I am the lawful wife of Fred Tobler, who is a citizen, by blood of the Creek Nation; that a male child was born to me on 12th day of April, 1903, that said child has been named Pleasant Tobler, and was living March 4, 1905.

nee Adams
Mary Tobler

Witnesses To Mark:

Subscribed and sworn to before me this $3^{\underline{d}}$ day of November, 1905.

Commission expires July 12, 1906.   *(Name Illegible)*
                                              Notary Public.

AFFIDAVIT OF ATTENDING PHYSICIAN OR MID-WIFE.

UNITED STATES OF AMERICA, Indian Territory,
    Western   DISTRICT.

I, Mahala Adams, a Midwife, on oath state that I attended on Miss Mary Adams now Tobler, wife of Fred Tobler on the 12th day of April, 1903; that there was born to her on said date a male child; that said child was living March 4, 1905, and is said to have been named Pleasant Tobler

her
Mahala x Adams
mark

Witnesses To Mark:
  Charles D Rogers
  Wash Adams

Applications for Enrollment of Creek Newborn
Act of 1905   Volume XII

Subscribed and sworn to before me this 3ᵈ day of November, 1905.

Commission expires July 12, 1906.   *(Name Illegible)*
                                       Notary Public.

NC. 975.

Muskogee, Indian Territory, June 22, 1906.

George McIntosh,
    Okmulgee, Indian Territory.

Dear Sirs:

    In the matter of the application for the enrollment of your minor child, Willie McIntosh, as a citizen by blood of the Creek Nation, you are advised that it is required that you furnish this office with the affidavits of the mother of said child, and the midwife, who was in attendance at its birth, said affidavits showing the name of the child, the names of its parents, the date of birth, and whether said child was living March 4, 1906, and for this purpose there is herewith enclosed a blank affidavit. This matter should receive your immediate attention.

                              Respectfully,
1 BA   Commissioner.

NC. 975.

Muskogee, Indian Territory, February 19, 1907.

Betty McIntosh,
    c/o George McIntosh,
        Okmulgee, Indian Territory.

Dear Madam:

    There is herewith enclosed one copy of the statement and order of the Commissioner to the Five Civilized Tribes, dated February 19, 1907, dismissing the application made by you for the enrollment of your minor child, Willie McIntosh, as a citizen by blood of the Creek Nation.

Applications for Enrollment of Creek Newborn
Act of 1905   Volume XII

Register.
LM-2-22-07.

Respectfully,
Commissioner.

REFER IN REPLY TO THE FOLLOWING:
NC. 975.

DEPARTMENT OF THE INTERIOR,
COMMISSIONER TO THE FIVE CIVILIZED TRIBES.

Okmulgee, Ind. Terr.,
Feb. 23, 1907.

Commissioner to the Five Civilized Tribes,
Muskogee, Ind. Terr.

Sir:

According to your instruction directing me to investigate the case of Willie McIntosh, I herewith enclose you the testimony of Lizzie Porter, the mid-wife, and Nancy McCall. I was unable to find Bettie McIntosh the mother of the child and George McIntosh, the father, is living at Eufaula.

I was unable to secure any further testimony in this case.

Respectfully,
Geo. K Davidson
Clerk in Charge of Creek Field Party.

DEPARTMENT OF THE INTERIOR,
COMMISSION TO THE FIVE CIVILIZED TRIBES.
OKMULGEE, I.T., FEB. 23, 1907.

N.C. 975.

In the matter of the application for the enrollment of Willie McIntosh as a citizen of the Creek Nation.

Nancy McCALL, being first duly sworn by Geo. K. Davidson, a Notary Public, testified as follows:

BY THE COMMISSIONER:
Q What is your name? A Nancy McCall.
Q What is your Post Office address? A Okmulgee, I.T.
Q How old are you? A 42 years old.
Q Do you know Bettie McIntosh? A Yes sir, I am acquainted with her.

Applications for Enrollment of Creek Newborn
Act of 1905   Volume XII

Q Do you remember when the child they call Willie McIntosh was born? A In July, latter part. I disremember what day it was.
Q Are you sure it was in July? A Yes sir, I am pretty sure of it. It might have been long about the 12th of July.
Q Do you remember what year it was? A No, I reckon I do not.
Q Do you remember in what month Willie died? A February.
Q The next year? A Yes sir.
Q Do you remember the year that he died? A No sir, I do not.
Q So you are sure that it was born in July and died in February of the next year? A Yes sir, after it was born.
Q Were you at the house when the child died? A Yes sir, I held it in my lap when it died. There wasn't anybody present but her and me.

LIZZIE PORTER, being first duly sworn by Geo. K. Davidson, a Notary Public, testified as follows:

BY THE COMMISSIONER:
Q What is your name? A Lizzie Porter.
Q What is your Post Office address? A Okmulgee, I.T.
Q How old are you? A Twenty-four.
Q Are you a citizen of the Creek Nation? A Yes sir.
Q To what Town do you belong? A Tookpafka.
Q Were you the mid-wife to Bettie McIntosh when Willie was born? A Yes sir.
Q Do you remember the date of his birth? A No sir, I don't.
Q Do you remember the month it was? A It was in August.
Q In what year? A 1904.
Q Were you there when the child died? A Yes sir.
Q What month was it he died in? A February.
Q In what year? A 1905.
Q Were you at the funeral? A Yes sir.
Q So you are sure this child was born in August 1904 and died in February 1905?
A Yes sir.

Geo. K. Davidson, being first duly sworn, states that the above and foregoing is a true and correct transcript of his stenographic notes as taken in said cause on said date.

Geo K Davidson

Subscribed and sworn to before me this 25th day of February, 1907.

(No Signature Given)
Notary Public.

Applications for Enrollment of Creek Newborn
Act of 1905 Volume XII

BIRTH AFFIDAVIT.

DEPARTMENT OF THE INTERIOR.
COMMISSION TO THE FIVE CIVILIZED TRIBES.

IN RE APPLICATION FOR ENROLLMENT, as a citizen of the Creek Nation, of Willie McIntosh, born on the 12th day of July, 1904

Name of Father: George McIntosh   a citizen of the   Creek   Nation.
Name of Mother: Betty McIntosh   a citizen of the   Creek   Nation.

Postoffice   Okmulgee, Ind. Ter.

AFFIDAVIT OF MOTHER.

UNITED STATES OF AMERICA, Indian Territory, }
     Western   DISTRICT. }

I, Betty McIntosh, on oath state that I am 30 years of age and a citizen by Blood, of the Creek Nation; that I am the lawful wife of George McIntosh, who is a citizen, by blood of the Creek Nation; that a male child was born to me on 12th day of July, 1904, that said child has been named Willie McIntosh, and was living March 4, 1905.

                               Betty McIntosh

Witnesses To Mark:
{

Subscribed and sworn to before me this 29th day of November, 1905.

My Com ex Sept. 12. 1906   EH Moore
                                    Notary Public.

AFFIDAVIT OF ATTENDING PHYSICIAN OR MID-WIFE.

UNITED STATES OF AMERICA, Indian Territory, }
     Western   DISTRICT. }

I, Lizzie Porter, a *(blank)*, on oath state that I attended on Mrs. Betty McIntosh, wife of George McIntosh on the 12th day of July, 1904; that there was born to her on said date a male child; that said child was living March 4, 1905, and is said to have been named Willie McIntosh

                               Lizzie Porter

Witnesses To Mark:
{

Applications for Enrollment of Creek Newborn
Act of 1905   Volume XII

Subscribed and sworn to before me this 29th day of November, 1905.

My Com ex Sept. 12. 1906   EH Moore
                                        Notary Public.

NC 975   WSC
                                                             JCL

DEPARTMENT OF THE INTERIOR,
COMMISSIONER TO THE FIVE CIVILIZED TRIBES.

In the matter of the application for the enrollment of Willie McIntosh as a citizen by blood of the Creek Nation.

STATEMENT AND ORDER.

The record in this case shows that on December 6, 1905 application was made, in affidavit form, for the enrollment of Willie McIntosh, as a citizen by blood of the Creek Nation, which action is considered as a continuing application for the the[sic] Creek Nation, under the provisions of the Act of Congress approved April 26, 1906, (34 Stats. 137).

It appears from the evidence that the applicant was born July 12, 1904, but there is nothing whatever to show whether or not he was living on March 4, 1906, although repeated efforts have been made by this office, through field parties, and by correspondence, to obtain such information.

In view of the foregoing, I am of the opinion, that there is no authority of law for the enrollment of said Willie McIntosh as a citizen by blood of the Creek Nation, and the application for his enrollment as such is therefore dismissed.

                                        Tams Bixby   COMMISSIONER.
Muskogee, Indian Territory.
FEB 19 1907

Applications for Enrollment of Creek Newborn
Act of 1905   Volume XII

Gardner & Langston
   Attorneys at Law

P. W. GARDNER
W. P. LANGSTON   HOLDENVILLE, IND. TER.   May 2   1905.

Hon. P. Porter,
Muskogee I.T.

Dear Sir;

We beg to advise you that we have found two families, one with one babie[sic], and the other has two babies, who refuse to have their children enroled[sic]. One of these parties is Ilsey Davis, who has one child, the other is Sissie Coker, who also refuses to have her two children enroled[sic].
Both of these parties are members of Little River Tulsa Town.
Please advise us as to what steps to take in this matter.

                    Yours Very Truly,

                         Ottawa Cain
                         Bunnie McCosar

NC 976

              Muskogee, Indian Territory, September 19, 1905.
              Muskogee, Indian Territory, September 19, 1905.[sic]

Ottawa Cain,
Ottawa Cain,
   and
Bunnie McCosar,
      Holdenville, Indian Territory.

Gentlemen:

   May 4, 1905, there was received by this office through P. Porter, principal chief of the Creek Nation, your communication of May 2, 1905 relative to the child of Ilsey Davis and the two children of Sissie Coter[sic].
   You state in said communication that the parents of these children refuse to have them enrolled.
   You are requested to advise this office as to the given names of the children referred to.
                    Respectfully,
                              Acting Commissioner.

Applications for Enrollment of Creek Newborn
Act of 1905 Volume XII

C 977

DEPARTMENT OF THE INTERIOR,
COMMISSION TO THE FIVE CIVILIZED TRIBES.
Okmulgee, I. T., April 10, 1905.

In the matter of the application for the enrollment of Ned McFarland as a citizen by blood of the Creek Nation.

MELISSA WILEY, being duly sworn, testified as follows:

Through Alex Posey Official Interpreter:

BY COMMISSION:
Q What is your name? A Melissa Wiley.
Q How old are you? A About forty.
Q What is your post office address? A Okmulgee.
Q Are you a citizen of the Creek Nation? A Yes, sir.
Q To what town do you belong? A Cussehta.
Q Do you make application for the enrollment of your minor child, Ned McFarland, as a citizen by blood of the Creek Nation? A Yes, sir.
Q What is the name of the father of this child? A James McFarland.
Q Is he a citizen of the Creek Nation? A No, sir he is a white man.
Q Is he living? A He is dead.
Q Was he your lawful husband? A No, sir.
Q Did he acknowledge the child as his own during his life time? A Yes, sir.
Q Did he contribute to the support of the child? A No, sir.

---oooOOOooo---

I, D. C. Skaggs, on oath state that the above and foregoing is a full and true transcript of my stenographic notes as taken in said cause on said date.

D. C. Skaggs

Subscribed and sworn to before me this 24 dat[sic] of July, 1905.

J. McDermott
Notary Public.

Applications for Enrollment of Creek Newborn
Act of 1905   Volume XII

BIRTH AFFIDAVIT.

DEPARTMENT OF THE INTERIOR.
COMMISSION TO THE FIVE CIVILIZED TRIBES.

IN RE APPLICATION FOR ENROLLMENT, as a citizen of the Creek Nation, of Ned McFarland , born on the 20 day of September , 1901

Name of Father: James McFarland   a citizen of the United States ~~Nation~~.
Name of Mother: Melissa Wiley   a citizen of the   Creek   Nation.
Cussehta Town
                        Postoffice   Okmulgee, I. T.

Child present.

AFFIDAVIT OF MOTHER.

UNITED STATES OF AMERICA, Indian Territory, }
     Western   DISTRICT.

I, Melissa Wiley , on oath state that I am about 40 years of age and a citizen by blood , of the Creek Nation; that I am not the lawful wife of James McFarland , who is a citizen, ~~by~~ *(blank)* of the United States ~~Nation~~; that a male child was born to me on 20 day of September , 1901 , that said child has been named Ned McFarland , and was living March 4, 1905.
                                            her
                                       Melissa x Wiley
Witnesses To Mark: mark
  { DC Skaggs
  { Alex Posey

Subscribed and sworn to before me this 10 day of April , 1905.

                           Drennan C Skaggs
                                Notary Public.

AFFIDAVIT OF ATTENDING PHYSICIAN OR MID-WIFE.

UNITED STATES OF AMERICA, Indian Territory, }
     Western   DISTRICT.

I, Millie Gray , a mid-wife , on oath state that I attended on Mrs. Melissa Wiley, ~~wife of~~ on the 20 day of September , 1901 ; that there was born to her on said date a male child; that said child was living March 4, 1905, and is said to have been named Ned McFarland
                                            her
                                       Millie x Gray
Witnesses To Mark: mark
  { DC Skaggs
  { Alex Posey

Applications for Enrollment of Creek Newborn
Act of 1905   Volume XII

Subscribed and sworn to before me 10 day of April, 1905.

                                        Drennan C Skaggs
                                        Notary Public.

DEPARTMENT OF THE INTERIOR,
COMMISSION TO THE FIVE CIVILIZED TRIBES.
April 29, 1905, Sapulpa, I.T.

In the matter of the application for the enrollment of _____ Brown, _____ Brown, Wisey Long, Suka Long, Martha Conner and Mary Pinehill, as citizens by blood of the Creek Nation.

Ben W. Wadsworth, being duly sworn, testified as follows by E.C. Griesel, a Notary Public, testified as follows:

By Commission:

Q What is your name? A Ben W. Wadsworth.
Q What is your age? A 34.
Q What is your post office? A Bristow.
Q To what town do you belong? A Hickory Ground.
Q You are employed by the Commission under special instructions to secure data relative to children born subsequent to May 25, 1901, and prior to March 4, 1905, and living on said latter date, to citizens of the Creek tribe of Indians whose enrollment has been approved by the Secretary of the Interior prior to the date of the approval of said act, were you? A Yes.
Q You wish to make application for the enrollment of six children the parents of whom are commonly known as Snake Indians? A Yes.
Q How did you obtain this information? A You better take them up one at a time and then I can explain what I had to do in each case.

       Mr. Wadsworth here presents a memorandum upon which appear the names of the children, the names of the parents, the probable age etc., upon which the applications were made.

By Commission:
Q The first one you have here is _____ Brown; who are the parents of this _____ Brown? A Jim and Loda Brown.
Q Are they both living? A Yes
Q To what town do they belong? A Euchee.

Applications for Enrollment of Creek Newborn
Act of 1905   Volume XII

Q How old is this child whose first name is unknown to you? A About two years old.
Q You saw the child, did you? A Yes sir.
Q Did you converse with the parents.[sic] A I tried to but they refused to talk to me.
Q Did they understand the purpose of your visit? A Yes, I suppose they did, for I told them I wanted to enroll their children for them.
Q Did they give you the information you wished? A No sir.
Q How did you get this information? A I got the information from Lewis and Henry Long, brothers-in-law of Jim Brown, they are neighbors of Jim Brown.
Q The neighbors could not give you the names of the children? A Well they knew but they would not give them to me, they said the father ought to give them to me.
Q When did you see this child? A Day before yesterday.
Q Did these parents have another child? A Yes.
Q How old was that child? A About a year old.
Q You saw the child at the same time? A Yes sir. I was able to see them for a little while only, for the mother took them and ran to the woods with them. Shortly afterwards the father left me too, with the remark that he had to work on a house.

Q Who are the parents of Suka Long? A Lewis and Nancy Long.
Q Are they citizens of the Creek Nation? A Yes.
Q Are they living? A Yes sir.
Q Is this child Suka living? A Yes, sir.
Q How old is this child? A It was born April 22, 1903.
Q How did you get the exact date? A I got it from the father.
Q Who gave you the information? A I worried with the father two hours trying to explain the matter and that the child ought to get the allotment and that an application must be made before May the 1st, 1905, and he finally submitted and gave it to me.
Q You saw the child yourself, did you? A Yes sir.

Q Who are the parents of Wisey Beaver? A Wattie and Nancy Beaver.
Q Are they living? A Yes sir.
Q They are citizens of the Creek Nation, are they? A Yes sir.
Q When was this child born? A The child is about two years old.
Q You saw the child? A Yes.
Q How did you get your information? A They would not give me the necessary information.
Q How did you get it? A I got it from one Tom Tiger. He did not know the age of the child but he gave me its name, and the name of the father and mother, but he guessed it was about two years old.
Q You saw the child, did you? A Yes sir.

Q Who are the parents of Martha Conner? A George and Jeannetta Conner.
Q Are they living? A Yes sir.
Q Are they citizens of the Creek Nation? A Yes sir.
Q Did you see this child, Martha Conner? A Yes.
Q When was it born? A They said it was about 30 months old, that was all the information I got. They gave me some information but not sufficient; I got the rest from Hattie Grayson, Indian Territory a neighbor.

Applications for Enrollment of Creek Newborn
Act of 1905   Volume XII

Q Who are the parents of Mary Pinehill? A Lasley and Sallie Pinehill
Q Both are living are they? And are citizens of the Creek Nation? A Yes sir.
Q Did you see the child Mary? A Yes sir.
Q About how old is that child? A I would judge it to be about eight months old.
Q Did you have any difficulty in getting the information? A I worried with them about two hours, they would not give me any information at all, but Hattie Grayson, Indian Territory a neighbor gave me the information.

Q These people are all Snakes are they? A Yes sir.
Q You saw these children and got all the information you have furnished us, last week? A Yes sir.
Q Now Mr. Wadsworth, have you any statements to make to the Commission relative to the enrollment of these children? A Yes sir; Their reason was that that[sic] there would be plenty of time to enroll their children, and they would not be in any hurry at all; that the land belongs to the Creek people and the government could not beat them out of it; as far as the government has already went ahead and enrolled and allotted us Indians without our consent we just let the government finished[sic] them up. That we would not help them finish the matter as the government had gone ahead so far and whatever the end may be we will live and die on it. They claim that as the government has enrolled and allotted them without their consent and now we let the government go ahead and take care of the children; they won't help in any way. Are just sitting back and refuse to give the government any help.
Q You explained the intent and purpose of the Act under which we are now acting, did you? A Yes.
Q You were out among them all week, were you? A Oh yes.

   E.C. Griesel, being duly sworn, on his oath, states that the above and foregoing is a true and correct transcript of his stenographic notes as taken in said cause on said date.

Edw C Griesel

Subscribed and sworn to before me this 5 day of May, 1905.

Zera E Parrish
Notary Public.

N.C. 978.   F.H.W.
DEPARTMENT OF THE INTERIOR,
COMMISSIONER TO THE FIVE CIVILIZED TRIBES.

In the matter of the application for the enrollment of Wisey Beaver as a citizen by blood of the Creek Nation.

DECISION.

The record in this case shows that on April 29, 1905, an affidavit was executed in the matter of the application for the enrollment of Wisey Beaver as a citizen by blood of

Applications for Enrollment of Creek Newborn
Act of 1905 Volume XII

the Creek Nation. Further proceedings were had on the same date before a Creek field party at Sapulpa, Indian Territory. Copy of letter from the Commissioner, bearing date of October 21, 1905, and a letter from the clerk in charge of a Creek enrollment field party on September 12, 1906, are attached to and made part of the record herein.

The evidence shows that the applicant is a member of the Snake faction of Creek Indians and that it was impossible to have the birth affidavit executed by the parents or a relative in the regular form although every endeavor was made by the Commissioner.

The evidence, however, is sufficiently clear to establish the fact that Wisey Beaver is the child of Wattie Beaver, whose name appears in a partial schedule of citizens by blood of the Creek Nation approved by the Secretary of the Interior on March 13, 1902, opposite roll No. 2026. Although the mother, Nancy Beaver, cannot be identified under that name on the records of this office, the fact that she is a member of the Snake faction is sufficient to warrant the conclusion that she is a Creek by blood.

The evidence further shows that the said Wisey Beaver was born in the spring of 1903 and was still living on April 29, 1905.

The Act of Congress approved March 3, 1905, (33 Stats. 1048) provides in part as follows:

> "That the Commission to the Five Civilized Tribes is authorized for sixty days after the date of the approval of this act to receive and consider applications for enrollment, of children, <u>born subsequent to May twenty-fifth, nineteen hundred and one, and prior to March fourth, nineteen hundred and five, and living on said latter date,</u> to citizens of the Creek tribe of Indians whose enrollment has been approved by the Secretary of the Interior prior to the approval of this act; and to enroll and make allotments to such children."

It is, therefore, ordered and adjudged that the said Wisey Beaver is entitled to be enrolled as a citizen by blood of the Creek Nation, in accordance with the provisions of law above quoted, and the application for her enrollment as such is accordingly granted.

                                                Tams Bixby   COMMISSIONER.

Muskogee, Indian Territory,
    January 16, 1907.

BIRTH AFFIDAVIT.

DEPARTMENT OF THE INTERIOR.
COMMISSION TO THE FIVE CIVILIZED TRIBES.

(Snake)

    IN RE APPLICATION FOR ENROLLMENT, as a citizen of the Creek Nation, of Wisey Beaver, born ~~on~~ during the spring of, 1903

Name of Father: Wattie Beaver Lochopoka	a citizen of the Creek Nation.	
Name of Mother: Nancy " Tuskegee	a citizen of the " Nation.	

Applications for Enrollment of Creek Newborn
Act of 1905 Volume XII

Postoffice   Bristow

AFFIDAVIT OF ~~MOTHER~~.   Acquaintance

UNITED STATES OF AMERICA, Indian Territory, }
  Western   DISTRICT. }

I, Ben W. Wadsworth , on oath state that I am 34 years of age and a citizen by blood , of the Creek Nation; that I am ~~the lawful wife of~~ acquaintance of Wattie and Nancy Beaver , who ~~is a~~ are citizens, by blood of the Creek Nation; that a female child was born to ~~me~~ them during the spring of , 1903 , that said child has been named Wisey Beaver, and was living March 4, 1905.

B. W. Wadsworth

Witnesses To Mark:
{

Subscribed and sworn to before me this 29 day of April , 1905.

(Seal)   Edw C Griesel
                              Notary Public.

(The above Birth Affidavit given again.)

                Copy
NC 978

Muskogee, Indian Territory, October 21, 1905.

Nancy Beaver,
  Care Wattie Beaver,
    Bristow, Indian Territory

Dear Madam:

In the matter of the application for the enrollment of your minor child, Wisey Beaver, as a citizen by blood of the Creek Nation and said to have been born in the spring of 1903, this office desires the affidavit of the mother, also of the midwife or physician in attendance at the birth of said child and a blank for that purpose is inclosed herewith.

In the event that there was no physician or midwife in attendance when said child was born, it will be necessary for you to furnish this office with the affidavits of two disinterested witnesses relative to her birth. Said affidavits must set forth said child's name, the date of her birth, the names of her parents and whether or not she was living on March 4, 1905.

Respectfully,

AG 978   Commissioner.

Applications for Enrollment of Creek Newborn
Act of 1905 Volume XII

REFER IN REPLY TO THE FOLLOWING:
N.C. 978

DEPARTMENT OF THE INTERIOR,
COMMISSIONER TO THE FIVE CIVILIZED TRIBES.

Bristow, Indian Territory, September 12, 1906

Commissioner to the Five Civilized Tribes,
    Muskogee, Indian Territory

Dear Sir:

    I have the honor to report that the parents of Wisey Beaver refuse to furnish any proof in the matter of the application for her enrollment as a citizen by blood of the Creek Nation.

                  Respectfully,
                  Jesse McDermott
                      In Charge.

                                                    JWH

N C 978

                Muskogee, Indian Territory, March 1, 1907.

Nancy Beaver,
    % Wattie Beaver,
        Bristow, Indian Territory.

Dear Madam :--

    You are hereby advised that on February 15, 1907, the Secretary of the Interior approved the enrollment of your minor child, Wisey Beaver, as a citizen by blood of the Creek Nation, and that the name of said child appears upon the roll of New Born citizens by blood of the Creek Nation, enrolled under the Act of Congress approved March 3, 1905, as number 1184.

    This child is now entitled to allotment and application therefor should be made without delay at the Creek Land Office, Muskogee, Indian Territory.

                    Respectfully,
                            Commissioner.

Applications for Enrollment of Creek Newborn
Act of 1905   Volume XII

HGH

REFER IN REPLY TO THE FOLLOWING:

N.C. 979

DEPARTMENT OF THE INTERIOR,
COMMISSIONER TO THE FIVE CIVILIZED TRIBES.

Muskogee, Indian Territory, November 20, 1905.

Barney Derrisaw,
    Coweta, Indian Territory.

Dear Sir:

    There is herewith enclosed one copy of the order of the Commissioner to the Five Civilized Tribes, dated November 14, 1905, dismissing the application made by you for the enrollment of Mattie, Adam and Elie Jones (all deceased) as citizens by blood of the Creek Nation.

    The order, with a copy of the proceedings had in the case, is this day transmitted to the Secretary of the Interior for his review and decision. The final decision of the Secretary will be made known to you as soon as this office is informed of the same.

                    Respectfully,

                                Wm O. Beall
                                Acting Commissioner.

AG-979

N.C. 979   I.D.

DEPARTMENT OF THE INTERIOR,
COMMISSIONER TO THE FIVE CIVILIZED TRIBES.

    In the matter of the application for the enrollment of Mattie Jones, deceased, Adam Jones, deceased, and Elie Jones, deceased, as citizens by blood of the Creek Nation.

ORDER

    The record in this case shows that on June 17, 1905, there was filed with the Commission to the Five Civilized Tribes at Muskogee, Indian Territory, the application of Barney Dersaw for the enrollment of Mattie Jones, deceased, Adam Jones, deceased, and Elie Jones, deceased, as citizens by blood of the Creek Nation.

    The evidence shows that said Mattie Jones, deceased, died July 17, 1900, that said Adam Jones, deceased, died June 14, 1901, and that said Elie Jones, deceased, died September 11, 1901.

    It does not appear from the records of this Office that any application was made for the enrollment of said Mattie Jones, deceased, Adam Jones, deceased, and Elie Jones,

Applications for Enrollment of Creek Newborn
Act of 1905   Volume XII

deceased, or any of them, prior to or on September 1, 1904, on which date the rolls of the Creek Nation were closed by order, dated June 13, 1904, of the Secretary of the Interior, under authority in him vested by the act of Congress approved March 3, 1901 (31 Stats., 1058), nor does it appear that application was made for the enrollment of said Mattie Jones, deceased, Adam Jones, deceased, and Elie Jones, deceased, or any of them, prior to June 17, 1905.

The Act of Congress approved March 3, 1905, (Public No. 212) provides:

"That the Commission to the Five Civilized Tribes is authorized for sixty days after the date of the approval of this act to receive and consider applications for enrollment, of children, born subsequent to May twenty-fifth, nineteen hundred and one, and prior to March fourth, nineteen hundred and five, and living on said latter date, to citizens of the Creek tribe of Indians whose enrollment has been approved by the Secretary of the Interior prior to the approval of this act; and to enroll and make allotments to such children."

It is, therefore, ordered that there is no authority of law for the enrollment of said Mattie Jones, deceased, Adam Jones, deceased, and Elie Jones, deceased, or any of them, as citizens by blood of the Creek Nation, and that the application for their enrollment as such should be and the same is hereby dismissed.

Tams Bixby
Commissioner.

Muskogee, Indian Territory,
NOV 14 1905

DEPARTMENT OF THE INTERIOR,
COMMISSION TO THE FIVE CIVILIZED TRIBES.
APRIL 29, 1905, Sapulpa, I.T.

In the matter of the application for the enrollment of _____ Brown, _____ Brown, Wisey Long, Suka Long, Martha Conner and Mary Pinehill, as citizens by blood of the Creek Nation.

Ben W. Wadsworth, being duly sworn, testified as follows by E.C. Griesel, a Notary Public, testified as follows:

By Commission:

Q What is your name? A Ben W. Wadsworth.

Applications for Enrollment of Creek Newborn
Act of 1905   Volume XII

Q What is your age? A 34.
Q What is your post office? A Bristow.
Q To what town do you belong? A Hickory Ground.
Q You are employed by the Commission under special instructions to secure data relative to children born subsequent to May 25, 1901, and prior to March 4, 1905, and living on said latter date, to citizens of the Creek tribe of Indians whose enrollment has been approved by the Secretary of the Interior prior to the date of the approval of said act, were you? A Yes.
Q You wish to make application for the enrollment of six children the parents of whom are commonly known as Snake Indians? A Yes.
Q How did you obtain this information? A You better take them up one at a time and then I can explain what I had to do in each case.

Mr. Wadsworth here presents a memorandum upon which appear the names of the children, the names of the parents, the probable age etc., upon which the applications were made.
By Commission:
Q The first one you have here is _____ Brown; who are the parents of this _____ Brown? A Jim and Loda Brown.
Q Are they both living? A Yes
Q To what town do they belong? A Euchee.
Q How old is this child whose first name is unknown to you? A About two years old.
Q You saw the child, did you? A Yes sir.
Q Did you converse with the parents.[sic] A I tried to but they refused to talk to me.
Q Did they understand the purpose of your visit? A Yes, I suppose they did, for I told them I wanted to enroll their children for them.
Q Did they give you the information you wished? A No sir.
Q How did you get this information? A I got the information from Lewis and Henry Long, brothers-in-law of Jim Brown, they are neighbors of Jim Brown.
Q The neighbors could not give you the names of the children? A Well they knew but they would not give them to me, they said the father ought to give them to me.
Q When did you see this child? A Day before yesterday.
Q Did these parents have another child? A Yes.
Q How old was that child? A About a year old.
Q You saw the child at the same time? A Yes sir. I was able to see them for a little while only, for the mother took them and ran to the woods with them. Shortly afterwards the father left me too, with the remark that he had to work on a house.

Q Who are the parents of Suka Long? A Lewis and Nancy Long.
Q Are they citizens of the Creek Nation? A Yes.
Q Are they living? A Yes sir.
Q Is this child Suka living? A Yes, sir.
Q How old is this child? A It was born April 22, 1903.
Q How did you get the exact date? A I got it from the father.
Q Who gave you the information? A I worried with the father two hours trying to explain the matter and that the child ought to get the allotment and that an application must be made before May the 1st, 1905, and he finally submitted and gave it to me.

Applications for Enrollment of Creek Newborn
Act of 1905   Volume XII

Q You saw the child yourself, did you? A Yes sir.

Q Who are the parents of Wisey Beaver? A Wattie and Nancy Beaver.
Q Are they living? A Yes sir.
Q They are citizens of the Creek Nation, are they? A Yes sir.
Q When was this child born? A The child is about two years old.
Q You saw the child? A Yes.
Q How did you get your information? A They would not give me the necessary information.
Q How did you get it? A I got it from one Tom Tiger. He did not know the age of the child but he gave me its name, and the name of the father and mother, but he guessed it was about two years old.
Q You saw the child, did you? A Yes sir.

Q Who are the parents of Martha Conner? A George and Jeannetta Conner.
Q Are they living? A Yes sir.
Q Are they citizens of the Creek Nation? A Yes sir.
Q Did you see this child, Martha Conner? A Yes.
Q When was it born? A They said it was about 30 months old, that was all the information I got. They gave me some information but not sufficient; I got the rest from Hattie Grayson, Indian Territory a neighbor.

Q Who are the parents of Mary Pinehill? A Lasley and Sallie Pinehill
Q Both are living are they? And are citizens of the Creek Nation? A Yes sir.
Q Did you see the child Mary? A Yes sir.
Q About how old is that child? A I would judge it to be about eight months old.
Q Did you have any difficulty in getting the information? A I worried with them about two hours, they would not give me any information at all, but Hattie Grayson, Indian Territory a neighbor gave me the information.

Q These people are all Snakes are they? A Yes sir.
Q You saw these children and got all the information you have furnished us, last week? A Yes sir.
Q Now Mr. Wadsworth, have you any statements to make to the Commission relative to the enrollment of these children? A Yes sir; Their reason was that that[sic] there would be plenty of time to enroll their children, and they would not be in any hurry at all; that the land belongs to the Creek people and the government could not beat them out of it; as far as the government has already went ahead and enrolled and allotted us Indians without our consent we just let the government finished[sic] them up. That we would not help them finish the matter as the government had gone ahead so far and whatever the end may be we will live and die on it. They claim that as the government has enrolled and allotted them without their consent and now we let the government go ahead and take care of the children; they won't help in any way. Are just sitting back and refuse to give the government any help.
Q You explained the intent and purpose of the Act under which we are now acting, did you? A Yes.
Q You were out among them all week, were you? A Oh yes.

Applications for Enrollment of Creek Newborn
Act of 1905 Volume XII

E.C. Griesel, being duly sworn, on his oath, states that the above and foregoing is a true and correct transcript of his stenographic notes as taken in said cause on said date.

Edw C Griesel

Subscribed and sworn to before me this 5 day of May, 1905.

Drennan C Skaggs
Notary Public.

N.C. 908.   F.H.W.

DEPARTMENT OF THE INTERIOR,
COMMISSIONER TO THE FIVE CIVILIZED TRIBES.

In the matter of the application for the enrollment of Mary Pinehill as a citizen by blood of the Creek Nation.

DECISION.

The record in this case shows that an affidavit was executed on April 29, 1905, in the matter of the application for the enrollment of Mary Pinehill as a citizen by blood of the Creek Nation. Further proceedings were had on the same date before a Creek enrollment field party, at Sapulpa, Indian Territory. Copy of a letter from the Commissioner, bearing date of October 21, 1905, and a letter from the clerk in charge of a Creek field party on September 12, 1906, are attached to and made part of the record herein.

The evidence shows that the applicant is a member of the Snake faction of Creek Indians and that it was impossible to have birth affidavit executed by the parents or a relative in the regular form although every endeavor was made by the Commission. The evidence, however, is sufficiently clear to establish the fact that the said Mary Pinehill is the child of Lasley Pinehill and Sallie Pinehill, whose names appear on a partial schedule of citizens by blood of the Creek Nation approved by the Secretary of the Interior March 13, 1902, opposite roll Nos. 2907 and 2908, respectively.

The evidence further shows that the said Mary Pinehill was born in the summer of 1904, and was still living on April 29, 1905.

The Act of Congress approved March 3, 1905, (33 Stats. 1048) provides in part as follows:

"That the Commission to the Five Civilized Tribes is authorized for sixty days after the date of the approval of this act to receive and consider applications for enrollment, of children, born subsequent to May twenty-fifth, nineteen hundred and one, and prior to March fourth, nineteen hundred and five, and living on said latter date, to citizens of the Creek tribe of Indians whose enrollment has been approved by the Secretary of the Interior prior to the approval of this act; and to enroll and make allotments to such children."

Applications for Enrollment of Creek Newborn
Act of 1905   Volume XII

It is, therefore, ordered and adjudged that the said Mary Pinehill is entitled to be enrolled as a citizen by blood of the Creek Nation, in accordance with the provisions of law above quoted, and the application for his enrollment as such is accordingly granted.

Tams Bixby   COMMISSIONER.

Muskogee, Indian Territory,
January 14, 1907

Copy

BIRTH AFFIDAVIT.

DEPARTMENT OF THE INTERIOR,
COMMISSION TO THE FIVE CIVILIZED TRIBES.

Snake

In Re Application for Enrollment, as a citizen of the Creek Nation, of Mary Pinehill, born during the summer of , 1904

Name of Father: Laslie Pinehill   a citizen of the   Creek   Nation. Lochapoka
Name of Mother: Sallie   "   a citizen of the   "   Nation. Lochapoka

Post-office   Bristow

AFFIDAVIT OF ~~MOTHER~~.   Acquaintance

UNITED STATES OF AMERICA, }
  INDIAN TERRITORY,
  Western   District.

I, Ben W. Wadsworth , on oath state that I am 34 years of age and a citizen by blood , of the Creek Nation; that I am ~~the lawful wife of~~ an acquaintance of Laslie and Sallie Pinehill , who ~~is a~~ are citizens, by blood of the Creek Nation; that a female child was born to ~~me~~ them on during the summer of, 1904 , that said child has been named Mary Pinehill , and ~~is now~~ was living. March 4, 1905

Signed   B. W. Wadsworth

WITNESSES TO MARK:

{

Subscribed and sworn to before me this 29" day of April , 1905.

(Seal)   Signed   Edw C Griesel
                              NOTARY PUBLIC.

Applications for Enrollment of Creek Newborn
Act of 1905   Volume XII

(The above Birth Affidavit given again.)

Copy

NC 980

Muskogee, Indian Territory, October 21, 1905

Sallie Pinehill
    Care Lasley Pinehill,
        Bristow, Indian Territory.

Dear Madam:

    In the matter of the application for the enrollment of your minor child, Mary Pinehill, said to have been born during the summer of 1904, as a citizen by blood of the Creek Nation, this office desires the affidavit of the mother, also of the midwife or physician in attendance at the birth of said child and a blank for that purpose is enclosed herewith.

    In the event that there was no physician or midwife in attendance when said child was born, it will be necessary for you to furnish this office with the affidavits of two disinterested witnesses relative to her birth. Said affidavits must set forth said child's name, the date of her birth, the names of her parents and whether or not she was living on March 4, 1905.

                              Respectfully,
AG 980   Commissioner.

Copy

NC 908

Muskogee, Indian Territory, April 11, 1906

Lasley Pinehill,
    Bristow Indian Territory

Dear Sir:

    Receipt is acknowledged of your letter of April 7, 1906, in which you as when you can come to file for your child, Mary Pinehill.

    There is inclosed herewith copy of letter written to Sallie Pinehill, the mother of said child, October 21, 1905, which was returned to this office unclaimed.

    You are advised to see that the directions in said letter are complied with.

                              Respectfully,
                                                  Acting Commissioner.

HEA 54

Applications for Enrollment of Creek Newborn
Act of 1905 Volume XII

REFER IN REPLY TO THE FOLLOWING:

N.C. 980

DEPARTMENT OF THE INTERIOR,
COMMISSIONER TO THE FIVE CIVILIZED TRIBES.

Bristow, Indian Territory, September 12, 1906

Commissioner to the Five Civilized Tribes,
    Muskogee, Indian Territory

Dear Sir:

    I have the honor to report that the parents of Mary Pinehill refuse to furnish any proof in the matter of the application for her enrollment as a citizen by blood of the Creek Nation.

                  Respectfully,

                            Jesse McDermott
                            In charge.

                                      JWH

N C 980

                Muskogee, Indian Territory, March 1, 1907.

Sallie Pinehill,
    % Lasley Pinehill,
        Bristow, Indian Territory.

Dear Madam :--

    You are hereby advised that on February 15, 1907, the Secretary of the Interior approved the enrollment of your minor child, Mary Pinehill, as a citizen by blood of the Creek Nation, and that the name of said child appears upon the roll of New Born citizens by blood of the Creek Nation, enrolled under the Act of Congress approved March 3, 1905, as number 1185.

    This child is now entitled to allotment and application therefor should be made without delay at the Creek Land Office, Muskogee, Indian Territory.

                    Respectfully,
                              Commissioner.

Applications for Enrollment of Creek Newborn
Act of 1905   Volume XII

DEPARTMENT OF THE INTERIOR,
COMMISSION TO THE FIVE CIVILIZED TRIBES.
DUSTIN, INDIAN TERRITORY, April 22, 1905.

In the matter of the application for the enrollment of certain new borns as citizens of the Creek Nation.

Alex Posey being duly sworn, testified as follows:

By Commission:
Q What is your name, age and post office address? A Alex Posey, 31 and Muskogee.
Q Are you a citizen of the Creek Nation? A Yes sir.
Q Got your land, have you? A Yes sir.
Q You have been engaged recently in the field for the Dawes Commission securing evidence about Creek citizens or new borns? A Yes sir.
Q Have you a list of children for whom application could not be made and about whom you have succeeded in obtaining some information? A Yes sir.
Q You May state the conditions and the names of these children?[sic] You desire to make application for them? A Yes sir.
Q Name them. A Span Hopiye, Tuckabatchee, Jennie Hopiye (or Barnett), Tuckabatchee have a female child about two years old. Post Office, Wetumka, Indian Territory.
Jim Davis, Kialigee, has two new born children--one about two years old (boy); another (a girl) about one year old. Post Office, Dustin, Indian Territory.
Billy Barlow, Quassarte[sic] No. 2 and Lydia Fields, Quassarte[sic] No. 2 have a child about a year old. Post Office, Dustin, Indian Territory.
Q This is the information you received from relatives right around Dustin, Indian Territory on April 22, 1905? A Yes sir.
Q Were you informed that the parents of these children were unwilling to make application for their enrollment? A Yes sir.
Q This was the only way that the rights of these children would be saved? A Yes, sir. I made every effort to obtain direct information from the parents but in every instance they refused to give their testimony.

Lona Merrick, being duly sworn, states that the above and foregoing is a true and correct transcript of her stenographic notes as taken in said cause on said date.

Lona Merrick

Subscribed and sworn to before me this 9 day of May, 1905.

Edw C Griesel
Notary Public.

Applications for Enrollment of Creek Newborn
Act of 1905   Volume XII

Indian Territory, I
                   I ss
Western District   I

   We, the undersigned, on oath state that we are personally acquainted with Jennie Hopiye   wife of   Span Hopiye, deceased   ; and that ~~on or about the~~ sometime in ~~day of~~   June 1902 , a   female   child was born to them and has been named Lucindy Hopiye ; that said child was living March 4, 1905.

   We further state that we have no interest in the above case.

	her
Witnesses to mark:	Louisa x Gray
(Name Illegible)	mark
Alex Posey	Dick Fatt

   Subscribed and sworn to before me this 29 day of March, 1906.

                              Alex Posey
                              Notary Public.

BIRTH AFFIDAVIT.
DEPARTMENT OF THE INTERIOR.
COMMISSION TO THE FIVE CIVILIZED TRIBES.

   IN RE APPLICATION FOR ENROLLMENT, as a citizen of the Creek Nation, of   Lucindy Hopiye , born ~~on the~~ sometime in ~~day of~~ June , 1902

Name of Father: Span Hopiye (deceased)   a citizen of the   Creek   Nation. Tuckabatche
Name of Mother: Jennie Hopiye (nee Fixico)   a citizen of the   Creek   Nation. Tuckabatche
                         Postoffice   Wetumka Ind Ter

AFFIDAVIT OF MOTHER.

UNITED STATES OF AMERICA, Indian Territory, }   Child is present
     Western   DISTRICT.

   I, Jennie Hopiye , on oath state that I am about 30 years of age and a citizen by blood , of the   Creek   Nation; that I am the lawful wife of   Span Hopiye, deceased , who was   a citizen, by blood of the Creek   Nation; that a female   child was born to me

Applications for Enrollment of Creek Newborn
Act of 1905   Volume XII

~~on~~ sometime ~~day of~~ in June , 1902 , that said child has been named Lucindy Hopiye , and was living March 4, 1905.

Witnesses To Mark:
{ *(Name Illegible)*
  Alex Posey

Jennie x Hopiye
her   mark

Subscribed and sworn to before me this 29 day of March , 1906.

Alex Posey
Notary Public.

BIRTH AFFIDAVIT.

DEPARTMENT OF THE INTERIOR.
COMMISSION TO THE FIVE CIVILIZED TRIBES.

IN RE APPLICATION FOR ENROLLMENT, as a citizen of the Creek Nation, of Pearl Amy Boles , born on the 23 day of Dec , 1902

Name of Father: C A Boles   a citizen of the United States Nation.
Name of Mother: Mattie Boles   a citizen of the   Blood[sic] Nation.

Postoffice   Broken Arrow

AFFIDAVIT OF MOTHER.

UNITED STATES OF AMERICA, Indian Territory,
     Western   DISTRICT.

I, Mattie Boles , on oath state that I am 34 years of age and a citizen by Blood , of the Creek   Nation; that I am the lawful wife of   C A Boles   , who is a citizen, by *(blank)* of the United States ~~Nation~~; that a Female   child was born to me on 23   day of December , 1902 , that said child has been named Pearl Amy Boles   , and was living March 4, 1905.

Mattie Boles

Witnesses To Mark:
{

Applications for Enrollment of Creek Newborn
Act of 1905   Volume XII

Subscribed and sworn to before me this 10 day of April, 1905.

Com Exp 1-/25 1906.

W G Cooper
Notary Public.

AFFIDAVIT OF ATTENDING PHYSICIAN OR MID-WIFE.

UNITED STATES OF AMERICA, Indian Territory, ⎫
　Western　　　DISTRICT.　　　　　　　　 ⎬
　　　　　　　　　　　　　　　　　　　　 ⎭

I, Lula M Hall, a Mid-Wife, on oath state that I attended on Mrs. Mattie Boles, wife of C A Boles on the 23 day of December, 1902 ; that there was born to her on said date a Female child; that said child was living March 4, 1905, and is said to have been named Pearl Amy Boles

Lula M Hall

Witnesses To Mark:
{

Subscribed and sworn to before me this 10 day of April, 1905.

Com Exp 1-/25 1906.

W G Cooper
Notary Public.

DEPARTMENT OF THE INTERIOR,
COMMISSION TO THE FIVE CIVILIZED TRIBES.
DUSTIN, INDIAN TERRITORY, April 22, 1905.

In the matter of the application for the enrollment of certain new borns as citizens of the Creek Nation.

Alex Posey being duly sworn, testified as follows:

By Commission:
Q What is your name, age and post office address? A Alex Posey, 31 and Muskogee.
Q Are you a citizen of the Creek Nation? A Yes sir.
Q Got your land, have you? A Yes sir.

Applications for Enrollment of Creek Newborn
Act of 1905   Volume XII

Q You have been engaged recently in the field for the Dawes Commission securing evidence about Creek citizens or new borns? A Yes sir.
Q Have you a list of children for whom application could not be made and about whom you have succeeded in obtaining some information? A Yes sir.
Q You May state the conditions and the names of these children?[sic] You desire to make application for them? A Yes sir.
Q Name them. A   Span Hopiye, Tuckabatchee, Jennie Hopiye (or Barnett), Tuckabatchee have a female child about two years old. Post Office, Wetumka, Indian Territory.
        Jim Davis, Kialigee, has two new born children--one about two years old (boy); another (a girl) about one year old. Post Office, Dustin, Indian Territory.
        Billy Barlow, Quassarte[sic] No. 2 and Lydia Fields, Quassarte[sic] No. 2 have a child about a year old. Post Office, Dustin, Indian Territory.
Q This is the information you received from relatives right around Dustin, Indian Territory on April 22, 1905? A Yes sir.
Q Were you informed that the parents of these children were unwilling to make application for their enrollment? A Yes sir.
Q This was the only way that the rights of these children would be saved? A Yes, sir. I made every effort to obtain direct information from the parents but in every instance they refused to give their testimony.

        Lona Merrick, being duly sworn, states that the above and foregoing is a true and correct transcript of her stenographic notes as taken in said cause on said date.

Lona Merrick

Subscribed and sworn to before me this 9 day of May, 1905.

Edw C Griesel
Notary Public.

DEPARTMENT OF THE INTERIOR,
COMMISSIONER TO THE FIVE CIVILIZED TRIBES.
Dustin, I. T., June 8, 1905.

        In the matter of the application for the enrollment of Sam Butler as a citizen by blood of the Creek Nation.

    LYDIA FIELDS, being duly sworn, testified as follows:

Through Alex Posey Official Interpreter:

BY COMMISSION:
Q What is your name? A Lydia Fields.
Q How old are you? A About twenty-two.
Q What is your post office address? A Dustin.

Applications for Enrollment of Creek Newborn
Act of 1905   Volume XII

Q Are you a citizen of the Creek Nation? A Yes, sir.
Q To what town do you belong? A Quasarte NO. 2.
Q Have you a child named Sam Butler? A No, sir, I have a child named Eddie Butler. I never had a child named Sam.
Q Who is Eddie Butler's father? A A white man by the name of Butler.
Q Was he your lawful husband at the time Eddie was born? A No, sir, I was never married to him. He left our neighborhooood[sic] about the time the child was born and I have never heard of him since.
Q How old is Eddie? A The child is four years old this June.
Q Is Eddie living? A Yes, sir, he is now with his grandfather up at Alabama.
Q Who attended on you at the birth of the child? A Ahne[sic] Davis, who lives in Alabama Town.
Q Have you another child who is about a year old? A I had a young child that died before it was a year old.
Q When did the child die? A He died a day before the Loyal Creek Payment began at Weleetka, Indian Territory and that was last November.
Q What was that child's name? A I died un-named.
Q Who was the child's father? A Billy Barlow.
Q Is Billy Barlow your lawful husband? A No, sir, he is married to another woman.
Q The youngest child then that you have is Eddie Butler? A Yes, sir, I have never had but the two children.

---oooOOOooo---

I, D. C. Skaggs, on oath state that the above and foregoing is a full and true transcript of my stenographic notes as taken in said cause on said date.

Subscribed and sworn to before me this ___ day of _____ 1905.

Notary Public.

BIRTH AFFIDAVIT.
DEPARTMENT OF THE INTERIOR,
COMMISSION TO THE FIVE CIVILIZED TRIBES.

IN RE *Application for Enrollment,* as a citizen of the Creek Nation, of Sammy, born on the 15 day of June , 1901

Name of Father: Butler   a citizen of the   Creek   Nation.
Name of Mother: Liddy Fields   a citizen of the   Creek   Nation.

Post-office: Wetumka I T

Applications for Enrollment of Creek Newborn
Act of 1905   Volume XII

AFFIDAVIT OF MOTHER.

UNITED STATES OF AMERICA, ⎫
    INDIAN TERRITORY.   ⎬
    Western   District. ⎭

I, Liddy Fields , on oath state that I am 25 years of age and a citizen by blood , of the Creek Nation; that I am the un lawful wife of Butler , who is a non citizen, by ~~bl~~ of the Creek Nation; that a male child was born to me on 15 day of June , 1901 , that said child has been named Sammy , and is now living.

                                        her
                                    Liddy x Fields
WITNESSES TO MARK: mark
  { Charles Coachman
    JD Berry

Subscribed and sworn to before me this 9 *day of* September , 1901.

                                    William T. Martin
                                        NOTARY PUBLIC.

AFFIDAVIT OF ATTENDING PHYSICIAN OR MID-WIFE.

UNITED STATES OF AMERICA, ⎫
    INDIAN TERRITORY.   ⎬
    Western   District. ⎭

I, Abram Fields , a Creek citizen by blood 50 years of age , on oath state that I ~~attended on~~ was present when Mrs. Liddy Fields , illegal wife of Butler was confined on the 15 day of June , 1901 ; that there was born to her on said date a male child; that said child is now living and is said to have been named Sammy

                                        his
                                  Abram x Fields
WITNESSES TO MARK: mrk
  { Charles Coachman
    JD Berry

Subscribed and sworn to before me this 9 *day of* September , 1901.

                                    William T. Martin
                                        NOTARY PUBLIC.

Applications for Enrollment of Creek Newborn
Act of 1905 Volume XII

BIRTH AFFIDAVIT.

DEPARTMENT OF THE INTERIOR.
COMMISSION TO THE FIVE CIVILIZED TRIBES.

IN RE APPLICATION FOR ENROLLMENT, as a citizen of the Creek Nation, of Eddie Butler, born ~~on the~~ sometime in ~~day of~~ June, 1901

Name of Father: Myron Butler	a citizen of the US	Nation.
Name of Mother: Lydia Fields	a citizen of the Creek	Nation.

Postoffice   Dustin Ind Ter

AFFIDAVIT OF ATTENDING PHYSICIAN OR MID-WIFE.

UNITED STATES OF AMERICA, Indian Territory,
Western   DISTRICT.

I, Ahne Davis, a midwife, on oath state that I attended on Mrs. Lydia Fields, not the legal wife of Myron Butler ~~on the~~ sometime ~~day of~~ in June, 1901; that there was born to her on said date a male child; that said child was living March 4, 1905, and is said to have been named Eddie Butler

          her
       Ahne x Davis
Witnesses To Mark: mark
 { Alex Posey
   Garret Stone

Subscribed and sworn to before me 3 day of April, 190.

         Alex Posey
         Notary Public.

BIRTH AFFIDAVIT.

DEPARTMENT OF THE INTERIOR.
COMMISSION TO THE FIVE CIVILIZED TRIBES.

IN RE APPLICATION FOR ENROLLMENT, as a citizen of the Creek Nation, of Eddie Butler, born on the 15 day of June, 1901

Name of Father: Myron Butler	a citizen of the US	Nation.
Name of Mother: Lydia Fields	a citizen of the Creek	Nation.

Postoffice   Dustin I T

Applications for Enrollment of Creek Newborn
Act of 1905   Volume XII

AFFIDAVIT OF MOTHER.

UNITED STATES OF AMERICA, Indian Territory,
    Western   DISTRICT.

    I, Lydia Fields , on oath state that I am 23 years of age and a citizen by blood , of the Creek Nation; that I am not the lawful wife of Myron Butler , who is a citizen, by *(blank)* of the U.S. Nation; that a male child was born to me on 15' day of June, 1901 , that said child has been named Eddie butler , and was living March 4, 1905. and is now living

                                   her
                              Lydia x Fields
Witnesses To Mark: mark
  { J McDermott
    (Name Illegible)

    Subscribed and sworn to before me this 19" day of November , 190.

My Commission   J McDermott
Expires July 25' 1907   Notary Public.

NC 984.

                        Muskogee, Indian Territory, November 30, 1906.

Jesse McDermott,
    Creek Enrollment Field Party,
        Dustin, Indian Territory.

Dear Sir:

    On September 9, 1901, there was filed with this office an application in affidavit form for the enrollment of Sammie, minor child of Butler and Liddy Fields, as a citizen of the Creek Nation; on April 22, 1905, further information was received concerning said child. This office requires proof as to whether said child was living March 4, 1905, and the complete record in same is herewith enclosed.

                    Respectfully,
                                     Commissioner.
LM-567.

Applications for Enrollment of Creek Newborn
Act of 1905   Volume XII

JWH

N C 984

Muskogee, Indian Territory, March 1, 1907.

Lydia Field,
    Dustin, Indian Territory.

Dear Madam :--

    You are hereby advised that on February 15, 1907, the Secretary of the Interior approved the enrollment of your minor child, Eddie Butler, as a citizen by blood of the Creek Nation, and that the name of said child appears upon the roll of New Born citizens by blood of the Creek Nation, enrolled under the Act of Congress approved March 3, 1905, as number 1186.

    This child is now entitled to allotment and application therefor should be made without delay at the Creek Land Office, Muskogee, Indian Territory.

                  Respectfully,
                            Commissioner.

NC 985.

Muskogee, Indian Territory, January 16, 1907.

Lydia Fields,
    Dustin, Indian Territory.

Dear Madam:

    There is herewith enclosed one copy of the Statement and Order of the Commissioner to the Five Civilized Tribes, dated January 15, 1907, dismissing the application made by you for the enrollment of your minor child, _____ Barlow, as a citizen by blood of the Creek Nation.

                    Respectfully,
                            Commissioner.

LM-68.

Applications for Enrollment of Creek Newborn
Act of 1905   Volume XII

DEPARTMENT OF THE INTERIOR,
COMMISSION TO THE FIVE CIVILIZED TRIBES.
DUSTIN, INDIAN TERRITORY, April 22, 1905.

In the matter of the application for the enrollment of certain new borns as citizens of the Creek Nation.

Alex Posey being duly sworn, testified as follows:

By Commission:
Q What is your name, age and post office address? A Alex Posey, 31 and Muskogee.
Q Are you a citizen of the Creek Nation? A Yes sir.
Q Got your land, have you? A Yes sir.
Q You have been engaged recently in the field for the Dawes Commission securing evidence about Creek citizens or new borns? A Yes sir.
Q Have you a list of children for whom application could not be made and about whom you have succeeded in obtaining some information? A Yes sir.
Q You May state the conditions and the names of these children?[sic] You desire to make application for them? A Yes sir.
Q Name them.
A Span Hopiye, Tuckabatchee, Jennie Hopiye (or Barnett), Tuckabatchee have a female child about two years old. Post Office, Wetumka, Indian Territory.
   Jim Davis, Kialigee, has two new born children--one about two years old (boy); another (a girl) about one year old. Post Office, Dustin, Indian Territory.
   Billy Barlow, Quassarte[sic] No. 2 and Lydia Fields, Quassarte[sic] No. 2 have a child about a year old. Post Office, Dustin, Indian Territory.
Q This is the information you received from relatives right around Dustin, Indian Territory on April 22, 1905? A Yes sir.
Q Were you informed that the parents of these children were unwilling to make application for their enrollment? A Yes sir.
Q This was the only way that the rights of these children would be saved? A Yes, sir. I made every effort to obtain direct information from the parents but in every instance they refused to give their testimony.

Lona Merrick, being duly sworn, states that the above and foregoing is a true and correct transcript of her stenographic notes as taken in said cause on said date.

Lona Merrick

Subscribed and sworn to before me this 9 day of May, 1905.

Edw C Griesel
Notary Public.

Applications for Enrollment of Creek Newborn
Act of 1905 Volume XII

DEPARTMENT OF THE INTERIOR,
COMMISSIONER TO THE FIVE CIVILIZED TRIBES.
Dustin, I. T., June 8, 1905.

In the matter of the application for the enrollment of Sam Butler as a citizen by blood of the Creek Nation.

LYDIA FIELDS, being duly sworn, testified as follows:

Through Alex Posey Official Interpreter:

BY COMMISSION:
Q What is your name? A Lydia Fields.
Q How old are you? A About twenty-two.
Q What is your post office address? A Dustin.
Q Are you a citizen of the Creek Nation? A Yes, sir.
Q To what town do you belong? A Quasarte NO. 2.
Q Have you a child named Sam Butler? A No, sir, I have a child named Eddie Butler. I never had a child named Sam.
Q Who is Eddie Butler's father? A A white man by the name of Butler.
Q Was he your lawful husband at the time Eddie was born? A No, sir, I was never married to him. He left our neighborhoood[sic] about the time the child was born and I have never heard of him since.
Q How old is Eddie? A The child is four years old this June.
Q Is Eddie living? A Yes, sir, he is now with his grandfather up at Alabama.
Q Who attended on you at the birth of the child? A Ahne[sic] Davis, who lives in Alabama Town.
Q Have you another child who is about a year old? A I had a young child that died before it was a year old.
Q When did the child die? A He died a day before the Loyal Creek Payment began at Weleetka, Indian Territory and that was last November.
Q What was that child's name? A I died un-named.
Q Who was the child's father? A Billy Barlow.
Q Is Billy Barlow your lawful husband? A No, sir, he is married to another woman.
Q The youngest child then that you have is Eddie Butler? A Yes, sir, I have never had but the two children.
(Note beside marked questions above: Died Nov 1904 unnamed)
---oooOOOooo---

I, D. C. Skaggs, on oath state that the above and foregoing is a full and true transcript of my stenographic notes as taken in said cause on said date.

Subscribed and sworn to before me this ___ day of _____ 1905.

Notary Public.

Applications for Enrollment of Creek Newborn
Act of 1905   Volume XII

NC 985   JLD

DEPARTMENT OF THE INTERIOR,
COMMISSIONER TO THE FIVE CIVILIZED TRIBES.

In the matter of the application for the enrollment of _____ Barlow, deceased, as a citizen by blood of the Creek Nation.

....

STATEMENT AND ORDER.

The record in this case shows that on April 22, 1905, application was made by oral testimony, given under oath, supplemented by further testimony given under oath on June 8, 1905, for the enrollment of _____ Barlow, deceased, as a citizen by blood of the Creek Nation, under the provisions of the Act of Congress approved March 3, 1905.

It appears from the evidence filed in this matter that said _____ Barlow, deceased, was born less than one year before the day of its death, which occurred in November 1904.

The Act of Congress approved March 3, 1905, (33 Stats., 1048), provides:

"That the Commission to the Five Civilized Tribes is authorized for sixty days after the date of the approval of this act to receive and consider applications for enrollment, of children, <u>born subsequent to May twenty-fifth, nineteen hundred and one, and prior to March fourth, nineteen hundred and five, and living on said latter date,</u> to citizens of the Creek tribe of Indians whose enrollment has been approved by the Secretary of the Interior prior to the approval of this act; and to enroll and make allotments to such children."

It is, therefore, ordered that the application for the enrollment of said _____ Barlow, deceased, as a citizen by blood of the Creek Nation, be, and the same is, hereby dismissed.

Tams Bixby   Commissioner.

Muskogee, Indian Territory.
JAN 15 1907

Applications for Enrollment of Creek Newborn
Act of 1905   Volume XII

2447   13
C 987

DEPARTMENT OF THE INTERIOR, COMMISSIONER TO THE FIVE CIVILIZED TRIBES.
April 15, 1905, Muskogee, I.T.

In the matter of the application for the enrollment of certain new borns as citizens of the Creek Nation.

Alex Posey, being duly sworn, testified as follows:

By Commission:
Q What is your name, age and post office address? A Alex Posey, 31, Muskogee.
Q Are you a citizen of the Creek Nation? A Yes sir.
Q Got your land, have you? A Yes sir.
Q Have you been engaged recently in the field for the Dawes Commission securing evidence about Creek citizens or new borns? A Yes sir.
Q Have you a list of children for whom application could not be made and about whom you have succeeded in obtaining some information? A Yes sir.
Q You may state the conditions and the names of these children? You desire to make application for them? A Yes sir.
Q Name them.
A Peepsie Manley, born December 22, 1904. Parents: Tom Manley, Eufaula Canadian Town and Katie Scott, Tulsa Canadian Town. PO st[sic] office, Eufaula, Indian Territory.
Setepakee Scott, five years and three months old. Parents: Edward Scott, Eufaula Canadian Town and Tana Scott, Tulsa Canadian Town. Post office, Eufaula, Indian Territory.
Mahlahsee Mitchell, male, born January 1903. Parents: Lewis Mitchell, Eufaula Canadian Town and Bettie Mitchell, Eufaula Canadian Town. Post office, Eufaula, Indian Territory.
Nettie Hill, born March 10, 1904. Parents: John Hill, Okfusky[sic] Canadian and Sarah Deer, Quassarte[sic] No. 1. Post office, Eufaula, Indian Territory.
John Williams, born July 4, 1904. Parents: Thomas Williams, Cussehta Town and Annie Billy, Eufaula, Canadian Town. Post Office, Eufaula, Indian Territory.
Q This is the information you received from relatives right around Eufaula on April 15, 1905? A Yes sir.
Q Were you informed that the parents of these children were unwilling to make application for their enrollment? A Yes sir.
Q This was the only way that the rights of these children could be saved? A Yes sir. I made every effort to obtain direct information from the parents but in every instance they refused to give their testimony.

Lona Merrick, being duly sworn, states that the above and foregoing is a true and correct transcript of her stenographic notes as taken in said cause on said date.

Applications for Enrollment of Creek Newborn
Act of 1905   Volume XII

Lona Merrick

Subscribed and sworn to before me this 18th day of July, 1905.

Edw C Griesel
Notary Public.

BIRTH AFFIDAVIT.

DEPARTMENT OF THE INTERIOR.
COMMISSION TO THE FIVE CIVILIZED TRIBES.

N.C. 987.

IN RE APPLICATION FOR ENROLLMENT, as a citizen of the Creek Nation, of Peepsie Manley, born on or about the 22 day of December, 1904

Name of Father: Tom Manley   a citizen of the   Creek   Nation. Eufaula Canadian
Name of Mother: Katy Manley (nee Scott)   a citizen of the   Creek   Nation. Tulsa Canadian

Postoffice   Eufaula, I.T.

Acquaintances
AFFIDAVIT OF ~~ATTENDING PHYSICIAN OR MID-WIFE~~.

UNITED STATES OF AMERICA, Indian Territory,
Western   DISTRICT.

we are acquainted with
We, the undersigned, ~~a~~ *(blank)*, on oath state that ~~I attended on~~ Mrs. Katy Manley (nee Scott), wife of Tom Manley ~~on the   day of   , 190~~ ; that there was born to her on or about the 22 day of Dec 1904 said date a female child; that said child was living March 4, 1905, and is said to have been named Peepsie Manley

Daniel Lewis
Witnesses To Mark: James Sulphur
{

Subscribed and sworn to before me 11 day of Sept, 1905.

Drennan C Skaggs
Notary Public.

Applications for Enrollment of Creek Newborn
Act of 1905 Volume XII

BIRTH AFFIDAVIT.

DEPARTMENT OF THE INTERIOR.
COMMISSION TO THE FIVE CIVILIZED TRIBES.

IN RE APPLICATION FOR ENROLLMENT, as a citizen of the Creek Nation, of Peepsie Manley, born on the 22 day of December, 1904

Name of Father: Tom Manley   a citizen of the   Creek   Nation.
Eufaula Canadian Town
Name of Mother: Katy Manley (nee Scott)   a citizen of the   Creek   Nation.
Tulsa Canadian Town
                         Postoffice   Eufaula, I.T.

AFFIDAVIT OF MOTHER. Child present.

UNITED STATES OF AMERICA, Indian Territory, }
     Western   DISTRICT.

    I, Katy Manley, on oath state that I am about 18 years of age and a citizen by blood, of the Creek Nation; that I am the lawful wife of Tom Manley, who is a citizen, by blood of the Creek Nation; that a female child was born to me on 22 day of December, 1904, that said child has been named Peepsie Manley, and ~~is now~~ was living. on March 4, 1905.

                                    her
                           Katy x Manley
Witnesses To Mark: mark
   { DC Skaggs
   { Alex Posey

Subscribed and sworn to before me this 17 day of May, 1905.

                         Drennan C Skaggs
                           Notary Public.

AFFIDAVIT OF ATTENDING PHYSICIAN OR MID-WIFE.

UNITED STATES OF AMERICA, Indian Territory, }
     Western   DISTRICT.

                                my daughter
    I, Edward Scott, ~~a~~, on oath state that I attended on ^Mrs. Katy Manley, wife of Tom Manley on the 22 day of December, 1904; that there was born to her on said date a female child; that said child ~~is now~~ was living on March 4, 1905 and is said to have been named Peepsie Manley
                              his
                       Edward x Scott
                           mark

Applications for Enrollment of Creek Newborn
Act of 1905 Volume XII

Witnesses To Mark:
  { DC Skaggs
  { Alex Posey

Subscribed and sworn to before me this 22 day of May, 1905.

Drennan C Skaggs
Notary Public.

(Below is a note that was at the beginning of this file.)

If this is a card case - better make enrollment case of it. If new born affidavit, it is not entitled - born too soon.

DEPARTMENT OF THE INTERIOR,
COMMISSIONER TO THE FIVE CIVILIZED TRIBES.
April 15, 1905, Eufaula, I.T.

In the matter of the application for the enrollment of certain new borns as citizens of the Creek Nation.

Alex Posey, being duly sworn testified as follows:

By Commission:
Q What is your na,e[sic], age and post office address? A Alex Posey, 31, Muskogee.
Q Are you a citizen of the Creek Nation? A Yes sir.
Q Got your land, have you? A Yes sir.
Q Have you been engaged recently in the field for the Dawes Commission securing evidence about Creek citizens or new borns? A Yes sir.
Q Have you a list of children for whom application could not be made and about whom you have succeeded in obtaining some information? A Yes sir.
Q You May state the conditions and the names of these children? You desire to make application for them? A Yes sir.
Q Name them.
(1) Peepsie Manley, born December 22, 1904. Parents: Tom Manley, Eufaula Canadian Town and Katie Scott, Tulsa Canadian Town. Post Office, Eufaula, Indian Territory.

Applications for Enrollment of Creek Newborn
Act of 1905 Volume XII

(2) Setepakee Scott, five years and three months old. Parents: Edward Scott, Eufaula Canadian Town and Tana Scott, Tulsa Canadian Town. Post Office, Eufaula, Indian Territory.
(3) Mahlahsee Mitchell, male, born January 1903. Parents: Lewis Mitchell, Eufaula Canadian Town and Bettie Mitchell, Eufaula Canadian Town. Post Office, Eufaula, Indian Territory.
(4) Nettie Hill, born March 10, 1904. Parents: John Hill, Okfusky[sic] Canadian and Sarah Deere, Quassarte[sic] No. 1. Post Office, Eufaula, Indian Territory.
(5) John Williams, born July 4, 1904. Parents: Thomas Williams, Cussehta Town and Annie Billy, Eufaula, Canadian Town. Post Office, Eufaula, Indian Territory.
Q This is the information you received from relatives right around Eufaula on April 15, 1905? A Yes sir.
Q Were you informed that the parents of these children were unwilling to make application for their enrollment? A Yes sir.
Q This was the only way that the rights of these children could be saved? A Yes sir. I made every effort to obtain direct information from the parents but in every instance they refused to give their testimony.

Lona Merrick, being duly sworn, states that the above and foregoing is a true and correct transcript of her stenographic notes as taken in said cause on said date.

Lona Merrick

Subscribed and sworn to before me this 9 day of May, 1905.

Edw C Griesel
Notary Public.

N C 988

No. 2447.
DEPARTMENT OF THE INTERIOR,
COMMISSION TO THE FIVE CIVILIZED TRIBES.
Eufaula, I. T. May 17, 1905.

In the matter of the application for the enrollment of Setepakee Scott as a citizen by blood of the Creek Nation.

KATY MANLEY, being duly sworn, testified as follows:

Through Alex Posey Official Interpreter:

BY COMMISSION:
Q What is your name? A Katy Manley.
Q What is your age? A About 18.
Q What is your post office address? A Eufaula.
Q Are you a citizen of the Creek Nation? A Yes, sir.

Applications for Enrollment of Creek Newborn
Act of 1905 Volume XII

Q To what town do you belong? A Tulsa Canadian.
Q Do you know Edward and Tana Scott? A Yes, sir, they are my parents.
Q Have you a sister named Setepakee Scott? A Yes, sir.
Q Is Setepakee her proper name? A Millie is her proper name. Setepakee is only a nick-name.
Q Do you know when she was born? A She was born during cotton picking time and will be five years old next autumn.
Q Do you know whether or not application has been made for her enrollment as a citizen by blood of the Creek Nation? A I do not know.
Q She is living is she? A Yes, sir.
Q To what town do the parents of this child belong? A The father belongs to Eufaula Canadian and the mother to Tulsa Canadian Town.

---oooOOOooo---

I, D. C. Skaggs, on oath state that the above and foregoing is a full and true transcript of my stenographic notes as taken in said cause on said date.

D. C. Skaggs

Subscribed and sworn to before me this ___ day of **JUL 27 1905** 1905.

Edw C Griesel
Notary Public.

No. 2447.
DEPARTMENT OF THE INTERIOR,
COMMISSION TO THE FIVE CIVILIZED TRIBES.
Eufaula, I. T., May 22, 1905.

In the matter of the application for the enrollment of Setepakee Scott as a citizen by blood of the Creek Nation.

EDWARD SCOTT, being duly sworn, testified as follows:

Through Alex Posey Official Interpreter:

BY COMMISSION:
Q What is your name? A Edward Scott.
Q How old are you? A 45.
Q What is your post office address? A Eufaula.
Q Are you a citizen of the Creek Nation? A Yes, sir.
Q To what town do you belong? A Eufaula, Canadian.
Q Do you make application for the enrollment of your minor child, Setepakee Scott, as a citizen by blood of the Creek Nation? A Yes, sir.

Applications for Enrollment of Creek Newborn
Act of 1905   Volume XII

Q When was she born? A Five years and four and a half months ago. I think the Town officers of Tulsa Canadian Town made a record of the birth of the child.
Q Who are the town officers? A The child was born during Lewis Deere's term as member of the Creek Council.
Q You are positive are you that the child is that old? A Yes, sir.
Q What is the name of the child's mother? A Tana Scott.
Q To what town does she belong? A Tulsa Canadian.
Q Do you know whether or not the child is enrolled? A I think that Lewis Deere enrolled the child but I do not know whether the child has been enrolled by the Commission or not.
Q Is Setepakee a boy or girl? A Girl.

---oooOOOooo---

I, D. C. Skaggs, on oath state that the above and foregoing is a full and true transcript of my stenographic notes as taken in said cause on said date.

D. C. Skaggs

Subscribed and sworn to before me this ___ day of   JUL 27 1905   1905.

Edw C Griesel
Notary Public.

NC 988   OCH
JCL

DEPARTMENT OF THE INTERIOR,
COMMISSIONER TO THE FIVE CIVILIZED TRIBES.

In the matter of the application for the enrollment of Setepakee Scott as a citizen by blood of the Creek Nation.

DECISION.

The records in the possession of the commissioner show that on April 15, 1905, Alex Posey made application for the enrollment of certain children of citizens by blood of the Creek Nation in order that their rights May be protected, the parents of said children having refused to make application for them, which said application embraced the name of one, Setepakee Scott. Further proceedings were had May 7, 1905, and May 23, 1905.

The evidence shows that said Setepakee Scott is the daughter of Edward Scott and Tana Scott (who is identified as Tena Scott), whose names appear upon a partial schedule of citizens by blood of the Creek Nation approved by the Secretary of the Interior, March 28, 1902, opposite numbers 8535 and 8536 respectively.

The evidence further shows that on May 23, 1905, said child was five years, four and one-half months old, and that said child was living July 1, 1900.

Applications for Enrollment of Creek Newborn
Act of 1905 Volume XII

Although the application herein was not made within the time designated by the Secretary of the Interior under the authority in him vested by the provisions of the Act of Congress approved March 3, 1901 (31 Stats., L. 1010), jurisdiction to consider, the same under the Act of Congress of June 30, 1902; was given to this office and the Department by the provisions of Section 1 of the Act of Congress approved April 26, 1906, (34 Stats. L. 137)

It is, therefore, ordered and adjudged that the said Setepakee Scott is entitled to enrollment under the provisions of the Act of Congress approved June 30, 1902 (32 Stat. 500), and the application for her enrollment as such is accordingly granted.

Tams Bixby   COMMISSIONER.

Muskogee, Indian Territory.
JAN 26 1907

C 988

Dustin, Indian Territory, June 3, 1905.

Commission to the Five Civilized Tribes,
Muskogee, Indian Territory.

Gentlemen:

I return herewith copies of testimony taken in the following cases, as I find it impossible to secure further evidence:

Sarty, Enrollment No. 520.
Chepe and Folle Homahta, Creek Indian Card Field No. 2871.
Katy and Nicey Gano, No. 2465 B.
William Tiger, No. _____ B/
Amy Kelly, No. 2467, B.
Heliswa and Kaska Beaver, No. 2466 B.
Lena Bear, No. ____ B/
Setepake Scott, No. 2447 B.
Mahlahsse Mitchell, No. 2447 B.
Susanna and Onate Johnson, No. 2468 B.

Respectfully,
(Signed) Alex Posey,
Clerk in Charge Creek Field Party.

Applications for Enrollment of Creek Newborn
Act of 1905   Volume XII

NC 988.

Muskogee, Indian Territory, June 21, 1906.

Edward Scott,
    Eufaula, Indian Territory.

Dear Sir:

    In the matter of the application for the enrollment of your minor child, Setepakee Scott, as a citizen by blood of the Creek Nation, you are advised that it is required that you furnish this office with the affidavits of the mother of said child, and the midwife who attended her at its birth, said affidavits showing the name of the child, the names of its parents, the date of birth, and whether said child was living March 4, 1906, and for this purpose there is herewith enclosed a blank affidavit. This matter should receive your immediate attention.

    It appears from the testimony taken in this matter that said child is also called Millie Scott, and in filling out the said affidavit you are requested to insert the correct name of the applicant.

                       Respectfully,

1 BA   Commissioner.

2447 B
#3 C 989

DEPARTMENT OF THE INTERIOR,
COMMISSION TO THE FIVE CIVILIZED TRIBES.
April 15, 1905, Muskogee, Indian Territory I.T.

    In the matter of the application for the enrollment of certain new borns as citizens of the Creek Nation.

    Alex Posey, being duly sworn, testified as follows:

By Commission:
Q What is your name, age and post office address? A Alex Posey, 31, Muskogee.
Q Are you a citizen of the Creek Nation? A Yes sir.
Q Got your land, have you? A Yes sir.

Applications for Enrollment of Creek Newborn
Act of 1905   Volume XII

Q Have you been engaged recently in the field for the Dawes Commission securing evidence about Creek citizens or new borns? A Yes sir.
Q Have you a list of children for whom application could not be made and about whom you have succeeded in obtaining some information? A Yes sir.
Q You may state the conditions and the names of these children? You desire to make application for them? A Yes sir.
Q Name them.
A Peepsie Manley, born December 22, 1904. Parents: Tom Manley, Eufaula Canadian Town and Katie Scott, Tulsa Canadian Town. PO st[sic] office, Eufaula, Indian Territory.
  Setepakee Scott, five years and three months old. Parents: Edward Scott, Eufaula Canadian Town and Tana Scott, Tulsa Canadian Town. Post office, Eufaula, Indian Territory.
✓ Mahlahsee Mitchell, male, born January 1903. Parents: Lewis Mitchell, Eufaula Canadian Town and Bettie Mitchell, Eufaula Canadian Town. Post office, Eufaula, Indian Territory.
  Nettie Hill, born March 10, 1904. Parents: John Hill, Okfusky[sic] Canadian and Sarah Deer, Quassarte[sic] No. 1. Post office, Eufaula, Indian Territory.
  John Williams, born July 4, 1904. Parents: Thomas Williams, Cussehta Town and Annie Billy, Eufaula, Canadian Town. Post Office, Eufaula, Indian Territory.
Q This is the information you received from relatives right around Eufaula on April 15, 1905? A Yes sir.
Q Were you informed that the parents of these children were unwilling to make application for their enrollment? A Yes sir.
Q This was the only way that the rights of these children could be saved? A Yes sir. I made every effort to obtain direct information from the parents but in every instance they refused to give their testimony.

  Lona Merrick, being duly sworn, states that the above and foregoing is a true and correct transcript of her stenographic notes as taken in said cause on said date.

Subscribed and sworn to before me   Signed Lona Merrick
this 9 day of May, 1905.   Signed Edw C Griesel, Notary Public.
  I, Lona Merrick, solemnly swear that I copied the above testimony from the original on the 18th day of July, 1905, and that it is a true copy of same.
                                                                    Lona Merrick
Subscribed and sworn to before me this 18th day of July, 1905.

                                                    Edw C Griesel
                                                        Notary Public.

Applications for Enrollment of Creek Newborn
Act of 1905 Volume XII

No. 2447.
DEPARTMENT OF THE INTERIOR,
COMMISSION TO THE FIVE CIVILIZED TRIBES.
Eufaula, I. T., May 17, 1905.

In the matter of the application for the enrollment of Mahlahsee Mitchell as a citizen by blood of the Creek Nation.

WELAH COCHE, being duly sworn, testified as follows:
Through Alex Posey Official Interpreter:

BY COMMISSION:
Q What is your name? A Welah Coche.
Q How old are you? A I do not know my age.

Witness appears to be about 65 years old.

Q What is your post office address? A Eufaula.
Q Are you a citizen of the Creek Nation? A Yes, sir.
Q To what town do you belong? A Eufaula Canadian Town.
Q Do you know Lewis and Bettie Mitchell? A Yes, sir.
Q What relation are they to you? A Bettie is my grandchild.
Q Do you know a child of theirs named Mahlahsee Mitchell? A Yes, sir, I saw the child a few days after it was born.
Q How old is the child? A The child is going on two years old.
Q When was it born? A It was born in the fall of the year. I remember that the mother, after she was over her sickness, was picking cotton.
Q Is the child living? A Yes, sir.
Q Is it a boy or girl? A Boy.
Q Do you know why the parents have not made application for the enrollment of this child? A Because they are members of the Snake Faction.

BETTIE MITCHELL, being duly sworn, testified as follows:

Through Alex Posey Official Interpreter:

BY COMMISSION:
Q What is your name? Bettie Mitchell.
Q How old are you? A About thirty.
Q What is your post office address? A Eufaula.
Q Are you a citizen of the Creek Nation? A Yes, sir.
Q To what town do you belong? A Eufaula Canadian.
Q Do you make application for the enrollment of your minor child Mahlahsee Mitchell as a citizen by blood of the Creek Nation? A Yes, sir, Mahlahsee means Morris.
Q How old is the child? A The child is over a year old. It was born January 14, 1904.
Q Did you make a record of the birth of the child? A Yes, sir.

Applications for Enrollment of Creek Newborn
Act of 1905   Volume XII

The witness presents a piece of paper upon which is found the following writing: "Morris Mitchell born Jan. 14, in 1904."

Q Who made this record? A The father, Lewis Mitchell.
Q When did he make the record? A At the birth of the child.
Q Welah Coche the grandmother of the child, gave testimony in this case today and she swore that the child was born in the fall of the year? A She was mistaken the child was born in January.
Q Who attended on you at the birth of the child? A No one but the father.

---oooOOOooo---

I, D. C. Skaggs, on oath state that the above and foregoing is a full and true transcript of my stenographic notes as taken in said cause on said date.

Subscribed and sworn to before me this ___ day of _____ 1905.

Notary Public.

BIRTH AFFIDAVIT.

DEPARTMENT OF THE INTERIOR.
COMMISSION TO THE FIVE CIVILIZED TRIBES.

IN RE APPLICATION FOR ENROLLMENT, as a citizen of the Creek Nation, of Morris Mitchell, born on or about the 14 day of January, 1904

Name of Father: Lewis Mitchell   a citizen of the   Creek   Nation.
Eufaula Canadian
Name of Mother: Bettie Mitchell   a citizen of the   Creek   Nation.
Eufaula Canadian

Postoffice   *(blank)*

AFFIDAVIT OF ATTENDING PHYSICIAN OR MID-WIFE.

UNITED STATES OF AMERICA, Indian Territory,
    Western   DISTRICT.

are personally acquainted with We, the undersigned , a—, on oath state that I we attended on Mrs. Bettie Mitchell, wife of Lewis Mitchell on the day of , 190 ; that there was born to her on or about the 14th day of Jan. 1904 said date a male child; that said child was living March 4, 1905, and is said to have been named Morris Mitchell

his
Jimsey x Asbury
mark

Applications for Enrollment of Creek Newborn
Act of 1905 Volume XII

Witnesses To Mark:
{ DC Skaggs
{ Alex Posey

her
Wisey x Asbury
mark

Subscribed and sworn to before me 11 day of September, 1905.

Drennan C Skaggs
Notary Public.

BIRTH AFFIDAVIT.

DEPARTMENT OF THE INTERIOR.
COMMISSION TO THE FIVE CIVILIZED TRIBES.

IN RE APPLICATION FOR ENROLLMENT, as a citizen of the Creek Nation, of Morris Mitchell, born on the 14 day of January, 1904.

Name of Father: Lewis Mitchell   a citizen of the   Creek   Nation.
Eufaula Canadian Town
Name of Mother: Bettie Mitchell   a citizen of the   Creek   Nation.
Eufaula Canadian Town

Postoffice   Eufaula, I. T.

AFFIDAVIT OF MOTHER.

UNITED STATES OF AMERICA, Indian Territory, ⎱
     Western   DISTRICT.   ⎰

I, Bettie Mitchell, on oath state that I am about 30 years of age and a citizen by blood, of the Creek Nation; that I am the lawful wife of ~~Mit~~ Lewis Mitchell, who is a citizen, by blood of the Creek Nation; that a male child was born to me on 14 day of January, 1904, that said child has been named Morris Mitchell, and ~~is now~~ was living. March 4, 1905.

Witnesses To Mark:
{ DC Skaggs
{ Adam Manley

her
Bettie x Mitchell
mark

Subscribed and sworn to before me this 17 day of May, 1905.

Drennan C Skaggs
Notary Public.

Applications for Enrollment of Creek Newborn
Act of 1905 Volume XII

father
AFFIDAVIT OF ~~ATTENDING PHYSICIAN OR MID-WIFE~~.

UNITED STATES OF AMERICA, Indian Territory, ⎫
    Western   DISTRICT. ⎬
                                     ⎭

my wife
      I, Lewis Mitchell , ~~a (blank)~~ , on oath state that I attended on ^ Mrs. Bettie Mitchell , ~~wife of~~ *(blank)* on the 14 day of January , 1904; that there was born to her on said date a male child; that said child ~~is now~~ was living on March 4, 1905 and is said to have been named Morris Mitchell

                                          his
                                  Lewis x Mitchell
                                      mark

Witnesses To Mark:
  { DC Skaggs
    Adam Manley

      Subscribed and sworn to before me this 17 day of May , 1905.

                                  Drennan C Skaggs
                                  Notary Public.

                                                    C 989

                        Dustin, Indian Territory, June 3, 1905.

Commission to the Five Civilized Tribes,
      Muskogee, Indian Territory.

Gentlemen:

      I return herewith copies of testimony taken in the following cases, as I find it impossible to secure further evidence:

    Sarty, Enrollment No. 520.
    Chepe and Folle Homahta, Creek Indian Card Field No. 2871.
    Katy and Nicey Gano, No. 2465 B.
    William Tiger, No. _____B/
    Amy Kelly, No. 2467, B.
    Heliswa and Kaska Beaver, No. 2466 B.
    Lena Bear, No. ____B/
    Setepake Scott, No. 2447 B.
✓Mahlahsse Mitchell, No. 2447 B.
    Susanna and Onate Johnson, No. 2468 B.

                                Respectfully,
                                (Signed) Alex Posey,
                          Clerk in Charge Creek Field Party.

Applications for Enrollment of Creek Newborn
Act of 1905   Volume XII

2447 B
#4 C 990

DEPARTMENT OF THE INTERIOR,
COMMISSION TO THE FIVE CIVILIZED TRIBES.
April 15, 1905, Muskogee, Indian Territory I.T.

In the matter of the application for the enrollment of certain new borns as citizens of the Creek Nation.

Alex Posey, being duly sworn, testified as follows:

By Commission:
Q What is your name, age and post office address? A Alex Posey, 31, Muskogee.
Q Are you a citizen of the Creek Nation? A Yes sir.
Q Got your land, have you? A Yes sir.
Q Have you been engaged recently in the field for the Dawes Commission securing evidence about Creek citizens or new borns? A Yes sir.
Q Have you a list of children for whom application could not be made and about whom you have succeeded in obtaining some information? A Yes sir.
Q You may state the conditions and the names of these children? You desire to make application for them? A Yes sir.
Q Name them.
A Peepsie Manley, born December 22, 1904. Parents: Tom Manley, Eufaula Canadian Town and Katie Scott, Tulsa Canadian Town. PO st[sic] office, Eufaula, Indian Territory.

Setepakee Scott, five years and three months old. Parents: Edward Scott, Eufaula Canadian Town and Tana Scott, Tulsa Canadian Town. Post office, Eufaula, Indian Territory.

Mahlahsee Mitchell, male, born January 1903. Parents: Lewis Mitchell, Eufaula Canadian Town and Bettie Mitchell, Eufaula Canadian Town. Post office, Eufaula, Indian Territory.

✓ Nettie Hill, born March 10, 1904. Parents: John Hill, Okfusky[sic] Canadian and Sarah Deer, Quassarte[sic] No. 1. Post office, Eufaula, Indian Territory.

John Williams, born July 4, 1904. Parents: Thomas Williams, Cussehta Town and Annie Billy, Eufaula, Canadian Town. Post Office, Eufaula, Indian Territory.
Q This is the information you received from relatives right around Eufaula on April 15, 1905? A Yes sir.
Q Were you informed that the parents of these children were unwilling to make application for their enrollment? A Yes sir.
Q This was the only way that the rights of these children could be saved? A Yes sir. I made every effort to obtain direct information from the parents but in every instance they refused to give their testimony.

Applications for Enrollment of Creek Newborn
Act of 1905 Volume XII

Lona Merrick, being duly sworn, states that the above and foregoing is a true and correct transcript of her stenographic notes as taken in said cause on said date.

Subscribed and sworn to before me Signed Lona Merrick
this 9 day of May, 1905. (Signed) Edw C Griesel, Notary Public.

I, Lona Merrick, solemnly swear that I copied the above testimony from the original on the 18th day of July, 1905, and that it is a true copy of same.

Lona Merrick

Subscribed and sworn to before me this 18th day of July, 1905.

Edw C Griesel
Notary Public.

No. 2447.

DEPARTMENT OF THE INTERIOR,
COMMISSION TO THE FIVE CIVILIZED TRIBES.
Eufaula, I. T., May 16, 1905.

In the matter of the application for the enrollment of Nettie Hill as a citizen by blood of the Creek Nation.

SARAH DEERE, being duly sworn, testified as follows:

Through Alex Posey Official Interpreter:

BY COMMISSION:
Q What is your name? A Sarah Deere.
Q How old are you? A About twenty-five.
Q What is your post office address? A Eufaula.
Q Are you a citizen of the Creek Nation? A Yes, sir.
Q To what town do you belong? A Quasarte No. 1.
Q Do you make application for the enrollment of your minor child, Nettie Hill, as a citizen of the Creek Nation? A Yes, sir.
Q Who is the father of the child? A John Hill.
Q Is he a citizen of the Creek Nation? A Yes, sir.
Q To what town does he belong? A Okfuske Canadian.
Q Is he your lawful husband? A No, sir.
Q Were you ever married to him according to Indian Custom? A No?[sic] sir.
Q Does he recognize Nettie as his child? A Yes, sir.
Q Does he contribute towards the support of the child? A He has promised me frequently to help support the child but he has never done so and the burden of supporting the child has fallen to me.
Q When was Nettie born? A March 10, 1904.
Q The child is now living is it? A Yes, sir.
Q Who attended on you at the birth of the child? A No one.
Q Was there any one present at the birth of the child? A No, sir.

Applications for Enrollment of Creek Newborn
Act of 1905   Volume XII

---oooIIIooo---

I, D. C. Skaggs, on oath state that the above and foregoing is a full and true transcript of my stenographic notes as taken in said cause on said date.

D. C. Skaggs

Subscribed and sworn to before me this 17 day of July 1906.

(No Name Given.)
Notary Public.

NC 990

Indian Territory   )
)
Western District) SS

We, the undersigned, on oath state that we are personally acquainted with   Sarah Deere not the lawful wife of   John Hill   ; and that on or about the 10 day of March 1904 , a   female   child was born to them and has been named   Nettie Hill   ; that said child was living March 4, 1905.

We further state that we have no interest in the above case.

Thompson Deere
Daniel Starr

Witnesses to mark:
_____
_____
_____

Subscribed and sworn to before me this 20Th day of February 1906.

J.W. Fowler
Notary Public.

Applications for Enrollment of Creek Newborn
Act of 1905 Volume XII

BIRTH AFFIDAVIT.

DEPARTMENT OF THE INTERIOR.
COMMISSION TO THE FIVE CIVILIZED TRIBES.

IN RE APPLICATION FOR ENROLLMENT, as a citizen of the Creek Nation, of Nettie Hill, born on the 10 day of March, 1904

Name of Father: John Hill   a citizen of the Creek Nation.
Okfuske Canadian Town
Name of Mother: Sarah Deere   a citizen of the Creek Nation.
Quasarte No. 1 Town

Postoffice   Eufaula, Ind. Terr

AFFIDAVIT OF MOTHER. The child is present.

UNITED STATES OF AMERICA, Indian Territory, }
    Western   DISTRICT.

I, Sarah Deere, on oath state that I am about 25 years of age and a citizen by blood, of the Creek Nation; that I am not the lawful wife of John Hill, who is a citizen, by blood of the Creek Nation; that a female child was born to me on 10 day of March, 1904, that said child has been named Nettie Hill, and ~~is now~~ was living. on March 4, 1905.

                 Sarah Deere

Witnesses To Mark:
{

Subscribed and sworn to before me this 16 day of May, 1905.

               Drennan C Skaggs
                  Notary Public.

           relative
AFFIDAVIT OF ~~ATTENDING PHYSICIAN OR MID-WIFE~~.

UNITED STATES OF AMERICA, Indian Territory, }
    Western   DISTRICT.

               am the father of
I, Ben Deere, ~~a——~~, on oath state that I ~~attended on Mrs~~. Sarah Deere, ~~wife of~~ *(blank)* on the *(blank)* day of *(blank)*, 1*(blank)*; that there was born to her on ~~said date~~ or about March 10, 1904, a female child; that said child ~~is now~~ was living on March 4, 1905, and is said to have been named Nettie Hill

                  his
             Ben x Deere
               mark

Applications for Enrollment of Creek Newborn
Act of 1905   Volume XII

Witnesses To Mark:
{ DC Skaggs
{ Alex Posey

Subscribed and sworn to before me this   16 day of May , 1905.

Drennan C Skaggs
Notary Public.

NC-991
DEPARTMENT OF THE INTERIOR,
COMMISSIONER TO THE FIVE CIVILIZED TRIBES.

Muskogee, Indian Territory, November 10, 1905.

In the matter of the application for the enrollment of John Williams as a citizen by blood of the Creek Nation.

Annie Williams, being duly sworn, testified as follows (through Jesse McDermott, Official Interpreter):

EXAMINATION BY THE COMMISSIONER:
Q What is your name? A Annie Williams.
Q How old are you? A Near 30.
Q What is your postoffice? A Eufaula.
Q What is the name of your father? A Lumber Billy?[sic]
Q What is the name of your mother? A Nancy Billy.
Q What Creek Indian Town do you belong to? A Eufaula Canadian.

The witness is identified on Creek Indian card, field No. 3980, opposite Roll No. 9167.

Q Have you a child named John Williams? A Yes sir.
Q Is he living? A Yes sir.
Q When was he born? A He was a year old last Fourth of July.
Q What is the name of the father of this child, Annie? A Thomas Williams.
Q Is he living? A He was sentenced to prison at Leavenworth, Kansas. I don't know whether he is living, but I suppose he is.
Q How long ago was he sent up there? A It has been about two years now.

Applications for Enrollment of Creek Newborn
Act of 1905   Volume XII

Q You know what Creek Indian Town he belonged to? A Cussehta.

Thomas Williams is identified on Creek Indian card, field No. 3980, opposite roll No. 9167.

Q What is the name of his father? A Wilyarme.
Q We have an affidavit here on file, in the body of which your name is given as Annie Billy, and your maiden name and the name signed to the affidavit is given Annie Williams; how do you explain that? A My name is Annie Williams. I signed the first affidavit that way.
Q Is it true, as you state in this affidavit that you are the lawful wife of Thomas Williams? A Yes, I am the lawful wife.
Q Is the child living? A Yes sir.

INDIAN TERRITORY, Western District.
I, J. Y. Miller, a stenographer to the Commissioner to the Five Civilized Tribes, do hereby certify that the above and foregoing is a true and complete translation of my notes as same appear in my stenographic report of this case.

JY Miller

Sworn to and subscribed before me
this the 14th day of November,
1905.

J McDermott
Notary Public.

BIRTH AFFIDAVIT.

DEPARTMENT OF THE INTERIOR.
COMMISSION TO THE FIVE CIVILIZED TRIBES.

IN RE APPLICATION FOR ENROLLMENT, as a citizen of the Creek Nation, of John Williams, born on the 4 day of July , 1904

Name of Father: Thomas Williams   a citizen of the   Creek   Nation.
Cussehta Town
Name of Mother: Annie Billie (Williams)   a citizen of the   *(blank)*   Nation.
Eufaula Canadian
Postoffice   Eufaula, I.T.

Applications for Enrollment of Creek Newborn
Act of 1905 Volume XII

AFFIDAVIT OF MOTHER.

UNITED STATES OF AMERICA, Indian Territory,
Western DISTRICT.

I, Annie Billie , on oath state that I am about 27 years of age and a citizen by blood , of the Creek Nation; that I am the lawful wife of Thomas Williams , who is a citizen, by blood of the Creek Nation; that a male child was born to me on 4 day of July , 1904 , that said child has been named John Williams , and ~~is now~~ was living. on March 4, 1905.

          Annie Williams

Witnesses To Mark:
{

  Subscribed and sworn to before me this 17 day of Y , 1905.

          Drennan C Skaggs
          Notary Public.

AFFIDAVIT OF ATTENDING PHYSICIAN OR MID-WIFE.

UNITED STATES OF AMERICA, Indian Territory,
Western DISTRICT.

                my daughter
I, Nancy Billy , a mid-wife , on oath state that I attended on^ Mrs. Annie Williams , wife of Thomas Williams on the 4 day of July , 1904 ; that there was born to her on said date a male child; that said child ~~is now~~ was living on March 4, 1905 and is said to have been named John Williams

         her
      Nancy x Billy
Witnesses To Mark: mark
{ DC Skaggs
{ Alex Posey

  Subscribed and sworn to before me this 17 day of Y , 1905.

          Drennan C Skaggs
          Notary Public.

Applications for Enrollment of Creek Newborn
Act of 1905 Volume XII

BIRTH AFFIDAVIT.

COPY

DEPARTMENT OF THE INTERIOR.
COMMISSION TO THE FIVE CIVILIZED TRIBES.

IN RE APPLICATION FOR ENROLLMENT, as a citizen of the Creek Nation, of John Williams, born on the 4" day of July, 1904

Name of Father: John Williams	a citizen of the	Creek	Nation.
Name of Mother: Annie Williams (nee Billy)	a citizen of the	Creek	Nation.

Postoffice   Eufaula I.T.

AFFIDAVIT OF MOTHER.

UNITED STATES OF AMERICA, Indian Territory,
  Western   DISTRICT.

I, Annie Williams, on oath state that I am about 27 years of age and a citizen by blood, of the Creek Nation; that I am the lawful wife of Thomas Williams, who is a citizen, by blood of the Creek Nation; that a male child was born to me on 4 day of July, 1904, that said child has been named John Williams, and was living March 4, 1905.

                              Annie Williams

Witnesses To Mark:
{

Subscribed and sworn to before me this 10 day of Nov, 1905.

My Commission   J McDermott
Expires July 25, 1907   Notary Public.

NC 991

                Muskogee, Indian Territory, October 21, 1905.

Annie Williams,
    Care Thomas Williams,
        Eufaula, Indian Territory.

Dear Madam:

In the matter of the application for the enrollment of your minor child, John Williams, born July 4, 1904, as a citizen by blood of the Creek Nation, your name appears in the caption and in the body of the affidavit executed by you, May 17, 1905,

Applications for Enrollment of Creek Newborn
Act of 1905   Volume XII

relative to the birth of said John Williams, as Annie Billie and you sign said affidavit as Annie Williams.

You state that you are the wife of Thomas Williams, a citizen by blood of the Creek Nation, and an examination of the records of this office shows that Williams is the correct surname of your said husband and therefore of you.

There is herewith enclosed form of birth affidavit which has been properly filled out, and if the same correctly states the facts, you are requested to execute it before a notary purlic[sic] and return to this office in the enclosed envelope.

You are advised that this office is unable to identify you on its roll of citizens by blood of the Creek Nation; you are requested to state your maiden name, the names of your parents, the Creek Indian town to which you belong the numbers on your deeds to lands in the Creek Nation.

This matter should receive your prompt attention.

       Respectfully,

            Commissioner.

AG-991

#1   C 993

2448 B.

DEPARTMENT OF THE INTERIOR,
COMMISSION TO THE FIVE CIVILIZED TRIBES.
April 24, 1905.

In the matter of the application for the enrollment of certain new borns as citizens of the Creek Nation.

Alex Posey, being duly sworn, testified as follows:

By Commission:
Q What is your name, age and post office address? A Alex Posey, 31, Muskogee.
Q Are you a citizen of the Creek Nation? A Yes sir
Q Got your land, have you? A Yes sir.
Q You have been engaged recently in the field for the Dawes Commission securing evidence about Creek citizens or new borns? A Yes sir.

Applications for Enrollment of Creek Newborn
Act of 1905   Volume XII

Q Have you a list of children for whom application could not be made and about whom you have succeeded in obtaining some information? A Yes sir.
Q You may state the conditions and the names of these children? You desire to make application for them? A Yes sir.
Q Name them.
A ✓ July Proctor, Weogufky Town, Sukey Proctor, Weogufky Town, have two children --one about three years old and one about six months old. Post office, Hanna, Indian Territory.

    Jacob Bullet, about three years old. Parents: Maxey Bullet, Seminole, and Hannah Bullet, Hillabee. Post Office, Hannah, Indian Territory.

    Connie Hawkins, Hillabee Town, Sabella Hawkins, Okchiye, have two children-- one about three years old and a younger child. Post Office, Hanna, Indian Territory.

    Willie Fisher, Hickory Ground Town, Lussee Fisher, Okfusky[sic] Canadian Town, have two children--one about three years old and a baby. Post Office, Slumpker, Indian Territory.

OK Lizzie Lasley, about three years old, Sam Lasley, born in either August or September, 1904. Parents: Sam Lasley, Okchiye, Wisey Lasley, Weogufky. Post Office, Hanna, Indian Territory.

    Jim Haynes (or Sangee), Okchiye Town, Folotkokee, Weogufky Town have a male child about three years old named Joe. Post Office, Hanna, Indian Territory.

    Taylor Foley, Weogufky, Melinda Foley, Okchiye, have a child about two years old. Post Office, Slumpker, Indian Territory.

    Phillip Lindsey, Tuckabatchee, Cilla Lindsey, Hillabee, have a child about three years old. Post Office, Hanna, Indian Territory.

    Big William (or William Thlocco), Okchiye Town, Cinda Williams, Weogufky Town, have two children -- one about three years old-- one born in February 1905. Post Office Hanna, Indian Territory.

    Freeland Lindsey, Tuckabatchee or Hillabee, Nancy Proctor, Tullahassoche, have a child about two years old. Post Office, Hanna, Indian Territory.

    Timonthluppy George, Weogufky Town, Nellie George, Pukon Tullahassee, have a child about three years old. Post Office, Slumpker, Indian Territory.

    Walter Simmons, Weogufky, Chippie Simmons, Pukon Tullahassee, have a child about one years old. Post Office, Hannah, Indian Territory.

    Jacob Larney (or Green), Arbeka Tulledega Town, Bettie Larney, (or Green), Hillabee Town, have a child. Post Office, Hanna, Indian Territory.

    John Hill, Okchiye, Millie Hill, Weogufky, have a child about three months old. Post Office, Hanna, Indian Territory.

    Jim Pigeon, Okchiye Town, Jennie Pigeon, Okchiye Town, have a child about five months old. Post Office, Hanna, Indian Territory.

    Thomas Deo, Okchiye Town, Nancy Deo, Fish Pond Town, have a child about three months old. Post Office, Hanna, Indian Territory.

    Jack Buckner, born December 17, 1904. Parents: Wiley Buckner, Okchiye, Susie Buckner, Cussehta. Post Office, Hanna, Indian Territory.

Q This is the information you received from relatives right around there on April 24, 1905? A Yes sir.
Q Were you informed that the parents of these children were unwilling to make application for their enrollment? A Yes sir.

Applications for Enrollment of Creek Newborn
Act of 1905   Volume XII

Q This was the only way that the rights of these children would be saved? A Yes sir. I made every effort to obtain direct information from the parents but in every instance they refused to give their testimony.

    Lona Merrick being duly sworn, states that the above and foregoing is a true and correct transcript of his stenographic notes as taken in said cause on said date.

                     (Signed) Lona Merrick

Subscribed and sworn to before me this 9th day of May, 1905.

                     (Signed) Edw C Griesel
                              Notary Public.

    I, Lona Merrick, solemnly swear that I copied the above testimony from the original on the 18th day of July, 1905, and that the same is a true copy of same.

                          Lona Merrick

Subscribed and sworn to before me this 18th day of July, 1905.

                          Edw C Griesel
                             Notary Public.

N.C. 480.

                DEPARTMENT OF THE INTERIOR,
     COMMISSIONER TO THE FIVE CIVILIZED TRIBES.
                NEAR HANNA, INDIAN TERRITORY.
                         December 4, 1906.

    In the matter of the application for the enrollment of two unnamed minor children of Chaeller and Sukey Proctor, as citizens by blood of the Creek Nation.

    ROSE TIGER, being first duly sworn by and examined through Alex Posey, a Notary Public and Official Interpreter, testified as follows:

BY THE COMMISSIONER:

Q What is your name? A Rose Tiger.
Q How old are you? A About 29.
Q What is your postoffice address? A Hanna.
Q Are you a Creek citizen? A Yes sir, I belong to Cussehta town.
Q Are you acquainted with Chaeller and Sukey Proctor? A Yes sir.
Q Are they your neighbors? A Yes sir, they live down just below the Weogufke church house.

Applications for Enrollment of Creek Newborn
Act of 1905 Volume XII

Q Have they some minor children? A Yes sir, they have two.
Q Are these all the children they have? A Yes sir.
Q What are their names? A Sam and Lydia.
Q Are both children living? A Yes sir.
Q Do you know the age of same? A He is about six years old. He is younger than my child Louisa who is about eight years old.
Q Do you know about how old Lydia is? A Between ~~and four~~ three and four years old.
Q Do you know how long Chaeller and Sukey Proctor have been married? A They have been married probably 10 years.
Q Who was Sukey's parents? A Her father was Eseeka or Greenleaf town. Her mother belonged to Weogufke town but I do not know what her name was.
Q What was Sukey's maiden name? A Sukey Seeka.

James B. Myers, being first duly sworn, states, that as stenographer to the Commissioner to the Five Civilized Tribes, he recorded the testimony in the foregoing proceedings, and that the above is a true, and correct transcript of his stenographic notes thereof.

James B Myers

Subscribed and sworn to before me this 10 day of Dec, 1906.

Alex Posey
Notary Public.

N.C. 993.

DEPARTMENT OF THE INTERIOR,
COMMISSIONER TO THE FIVE CIVILIZED TRIBES.
Near Hanna, Indian Territory, December 18, 1906.

In the matter of the application for the enrollment of Sam and Lydia Proctor as citizens by blood of the Creek Nation.

SUKEY PROCTOR, being duly sworn, testified as follows through Jesse McDermott official interpreter.

BY THE COMMISSIONER:

Q What is your name? A Sukey Proctor.
Q What is your age? A About 28.
Q What is your postoffice address? A Hanna.
Q Are you a Creek citizen? A Yes.
Q To which Creek Indian Town do you belong? A Weogufkey[sic].
Q What is the name of your father? A Eseker.
Q What is the name of your mother? A Wetchie.
Q Have you filed on your land? A Yes, the Commission filed for me.
Q Have you the deed to that land? A No, I have no papers of any kind about my land.

Applications for Enrollment of Creek Newborn
Act of 1905   Volume XII

Q Do you know under what name you are enrolled? A No, but when I leased my land, they just called me Sukey, by that, I supposed that I were enrolled as Sukey. Sometimes I am known as Sukey Seker.
Q Are you married? A Yes
Q What s the name of your husband? A Chaeler[sic] Proctor.
Q Have you any children by him? A Yes, I have two.
Q What is the name of the older one? A Sam.
Q When was Sam born? A He was five years old the 9th of this month.
Q What is the name of the next one? A Lydia.
Q When was she born? A She was four years old last October.
Q What date in October? A The 10th.
Q Are both of these children living? A Yes. (The children are present)
Q Wich direction is your allotment from here? A West of here and south of Dustin is what I am told.

---oooOOOooo---

I, Jesse McDermott, on oath state that the above and foregoing is a full and true transcript of my notes as taken in said cause on said date.

Jess McDermott

Subscribed and sworn to before me this 27th day of December, 1906.

My Commission expires   W^{m}FA Gierkes
6-29-1909   Notary Public.

Copy

BIRTH AFFIDAVIT.
DEPARTMENT OF THE INTERIOR.
COMMISSION TO THE FIVE CIVILIZED TRIBES.

IN RE APPLICATION FOR ENROLLMENT, as a citizen of the Creek Nation, of Sam Proctor, born on the 9 day of December, 1901

Name of Father: Jaly Proctor   a citizen of the   Creek   Nation.
Weogufkey
Name of Mother: Suckey Proctor   a citizen of the   Creek   Nation.
Weofugkey
                              Postoffice   Hanna I.T.

Applications for Enrollment of Creek Newborn
Act of 1905   Volume XII

AFFIDAVIT OF MOTHER.

UNITED STATES OF AMERICA, Indian Territory, }   Child present
Western   DISTRICT.

I, Sucky Proctor, on oath state that I am about 28 years of age and a citizen by blood, of the Creek Nation; that I am the lawful wife of Jaly Proctor, who is a citizen, by blood of the Creek Nation; that a male child was born to me on 9" day of December, 1901, that said child has been named Sam Proctor, and was living March 4, 1905.

                                                      her
                                       Suky x Proctor

Witnesses To Mark: mark
{ D C Skaggs
{ Alex Posey

Subscribed and sworn to before me this 29 day of May, 1905.

                                       Drennan C Skaggs
                                       Notary Public.

AFFIDAVIT OF ATTENDING PHYSICIAN OR MID-WIFE.

UNITED STATES OF AMERICA, Indian Territory, }
Western   DISTRICT.

I, Yosta Beaver, a midwife, on oath state that I attended on Mrs. Sucky Proctor, wife of Jaly Proctor on the 9 day of December, 1901 ; that there was born to her on said date a male child; that said child was living March 4, 1905, and is said to have been named Sam Proctor

                                       her
                                     Yosta x Beaver

Witnesses To Mark: mark
{ D C Skaggs
{ Alex Posey

Subscribed and sworn to before me this 29 day of May, 1905.

                                       Drennan C Skaggs
                                       Notary Public.

Applications for Enrollment of Creek Newborn
Act of 1905   Volume XII

BIRTH AFFIDAVIT.

DEPARTMENT OF THE INTERIOR.
COMMISSION TO THE FIVE CIVILIZED TRIBES.

IN RE APPLICATION FOR ENROLLMENT, as a citizen of the Creek Nation, of Lydia Proctor, born on the 10 day of October, 1902

Name of Father: Jaly Proctor   a citizen of the   Creek   Nation.
Weogufke Town
Name of Mother: Sucky Proctor   a citizen of the   Creek   Nation.
Weogufky Town
                           Postoffice   Hanna, I.T.

AFFIDAVIT OF MOTHER.   Child present

UNITED STATES OF AMERICA, Indian Territory, }
      Western   DISTRICT.

I, Sucky Proctor, on oath state that I am about 28 years of age and a citizen by blood, of the Creek Nation; that I am the lawful wife of Jaly Proctor, who is a citizen, by blood of the Creek Nation; that a female child was born to me on 10 day of October, 1902, that said child has been named Lydia Proctor, and is now living. and was living March 4, 1905.

                                        her
                                 Sucky x Proctor
Witnesses To Mark: mark
  { DC Skaggs
  { Alex Posey

Subscribed and sworn to before me this 29 day of May, 1905.

                            Drennan C Skaggs
                            Notary Public.

AFFIDAVIT OF ATTENDING PHYSICIAN OR MID-WIFE.

UNITED STATES OF AMERICA, Indian Territory, }
      Western   DISTRICT.

I, Yosta Beaver, a mid-wife, on oath state that I attended on Mrs. Sucky Proctor, wife of Jaly Proctor on the 10 day of October, 1902; that there was born to her on said date a female child; that said child is now living and was living March 4, 1905, and is said to have been named Lydia Proctor

                                   her
                            Yosta x Beaver
                                  mark

Applications for Enrollment of Creek Newborn
Act of 1905   Volume XII

Witnesses To Mark:
{ DC Skaggs
  Alex Posey

Subscribed and sworn to before me this 29 day of May, 1905.

Drennan C Skaggs
Notary Public.

BIRTH AFFIDAVIT.

DEPARTMENT OF THE INTERIOR.
COMMISSION TO THE FIVE CIVILIZED TRIBES.

IN RE APPLICATION FOR ENROLLMENT, as a citizen of the Creek Nation, of Sam Proctor, born on the 9 day of December, 1901

Name of Father: Jaly Proctor   a citizen of the   Creek   Nation.
Weogufkey[sic] Town
Name of Mother: Suckey Proctor   a citizen of the   Creek   Nation.
Weofugkey Town

Postoffice   Hanna I.T.

AFFIDAVIT OF MOTHER.

UNITED STATES OF AMERICA, Indian Territory, }
    Western   DISTRICT.   Child present

I, Sucky Proctor, on oath state that I am about 28 years of age and a citizen by blood, of the Creek Nation; that I am the lawful wife of Jaly Proctor, who is a citizen, by blood of the Creek Nation; that a male child was born to me on 9" day of December, 1901, that said child has been named Sam Proctor, and was living March 4, 1905.

her
Suky x Proctor
mark

Witnesses To Mark:
{ D C Skaggs
  Alex Posey

Subscribed and sworn to before me this 29 day of May, 1905.

Drennan C Skaggs
Notary Public.

Applications for Enrollment of Creek Newborn
Act of 1905 Volume XII

AFFIDAVIT OF ATTENDING PHYSICIAN OR MID-WIFE.

UNITED STATES OF AMERICA, Indian Territory, ⎱
  Western   DISTRICT.   ⎰

    I, Yosta Beaver , a midwife , on oath state that I attended on Mrs. Sucky Proctor , wife of Jaly Proctor on the 9 day of December , 1901 ; that there was born to her on said date a male child; that said child was living March 4, 1905, and is said to have been named Sam Proctor

                                her
                     Yosta x Beaver
Witnesses To Mark: mark
  { D C Skaggs
    Alex Posey

    Subscribed and sworn to before me this 29 day of May , 1905.

                              Drennan C Skaggs
                              Notary Public.

BIRTH AFFIDAVIT.

                    Copy
             DEPARTMENT OF THE INTERIOR.
COMMISSION TO THE FIVE CIVILIZED TRIBES.

    IN RE APPLICATION FOR ENROLLMENT, as a citizen of the Creek Nation, of Lydia Proctor, born on the 10 day of October, 1902

Name of Father: Jaly Proctor   a citizen of the   Creek   Nation.
Weogufkey
Name of Mother: Sucky Proctor   a citizen of the   Creek   Nation.
Weogufky
                  Postoffice   Hanna, I.T.

              AFFIDAVIT OF MOTHER.   Child present

UNITED STATES OF AMERICA, Indian Territory, ⎱
  Western   DISTRICT.   ⎰

    I, Sucky Proctor , on oath state that I am about 28 years of age and a citizen by blood , of the Creek Nation; that I am the lawful wife of Jaly Proctor , who is a citizen, by blood of the Creek Nation; that a female child was born to me on 10" day of October , 1902 , that said child has been named Lydia Proctor , and was living March 4, 1905.
                                  her
                           Sucky x Proctor
                               mark

Applications for Enrollment of Creek Newborn
Act of 1905 Volume XII

Witnesses To Mark:
  { DC Skaggs
    Alex Posey

    Subscribed and sworn to before me this 29 day of May , 1905.

                                Drennan C Skaggs
                                Notary Public.

AFFIDAVIT OF ATTENDING PHYSICIAN OR MID-WIFE.

UNITED STATES OF AMERICA, Indian Territory,
    Western   DISTRICT.

    I, Yosta Beaver , a mid-wife , on oath state that I attended on Mrs. Sucky Proctor , wife of Jaly Proctor on the 10 day of October , 1902 ; that there was born to her on said date a female child; that said child was living March 4, 1905, and is said to have been named Lydia Proctor

                                  her
                          Yosta x Beaver
Witnesses To Mark: mark
  { DC Skaggs
    Alex Posey

    Subscribed and sworn to before me this 29 day of May , 1905.

                                Drennan C Skaggs
                                Notary Public.

BIRTH AFFIDAVIT.

DEPARTMENT OF THE INTERIOR.
COMMISSION TO THE FIVE CIVILIZED TRIBES.

    IN RE APPLICATION FOR ENROLLMENT, as a citizen of the Creek Nation, of Sam Proctor , born on the 9th day of Dec , 1901

Name of Father: Chaeller Proctor   a citizen of the   Creek   Nation.
Name of Mother: Sukey Proctor   a citizen of the   Creek   Nation.

                        Postoffice   Hanna Ind. Ter.

Applications for Enrollment of Creek Newborn
Act of 1905   Volume XII

AFFIDAVIT OF MOTHER.

UNITED STATES OF AMERICA, Indian Territory, ⎫
    Western   DISTRICT.   ⎭

    I, Sukey Proctor , on oath state that I am about 28 years of age and a citizen by blood , of the Creek Nation; that I am the lawful wife of Chaeller Proctor , who is a citizen, by blood of the Creek Nation; that a male child was born to me on 9th day of December , 1901 , that said child has been named Sam Proctor , and was living March 4, 1905. and is now living

                                                       her
                                          Sukey x Proctor

Witnesses To Mark: mark
  ⎰ J McDermott
  ⎱ Jim Cantrell

    Subscribed and sworn to before me this 18 day of December , 1906.

My Commission   J McDermott
Expires July 25' 1907   Notary Public.

AFFIDAVIT OF ATTENDING PHYSICIAN OR MID-WIFE.

UNITED STATES OF AMERICA, Indian Territory, ⎫
    Western   DISTRICT.   ⎭

    I, Yousta Beaver , a midwife , on oath state that I attended on Mrs. Sukey Proctor , wife of Chaeller Proctor on the 9th day of December , 1901 ; that there was born to her on said date a male child; that said child was living March 4, 1905, and is said to have been named Sam Proctor

                                                       her
                                          Yousta x Beaver

Witnesses To Mark: mark
  ⎰ J McDermott
  ⎱ Jim Cantrell

    Subscribed and sworn to before me this 18 day of December , 1906.

My Commission   J McDermott
Expires July 25' 1907   Notary Public.

Applications for Enrollment of Creek Newborn
Act of 1905   Volume XII

BIRTH AFFIDAVIT.
DEPARTMENT OF THE INTERIOR,
COMMISSIONER TO THE FIVE CIVILIZED TRIBES.
Mch. 4, 1905
ENROLLMENT OF MINORS.   ACT OF CONGRESS, APPROVED APRIL 26, 1906.

IN RE APPLICATION FOR ENROLLMENT, as a citizen of the Creek Nation, of Lydia Proctor, born on the 10 day of Oct, 1902

Name of Father: Chaeller Proctor   a citizen of the   Creek   Nation.
Name of Mother: Sukey Proctor   a citizen of the   Creek   Nation.

Tribal enrollment of father   *(blank)*   Tribal enrollment of mother   *(blank)*

Postoffice   Hanna, Ind Ter

AFFIDAVIT OF MOTHER.

UNITED STATES OF AMERICA, Indian Territory, }
Western   District.   }

I, Sukey Proctor, on oath state that I am about 28 years of age and a citizen by blood, of the Creek Nation; that I am the lawful wife of Chaeller Proctor, who is a citizen, by blood of the Creek Nation; that a female child was born to me on 10th day of October, 1902, that said child has been named Lydia Proctor, and was living March 4, 1906 [1905 struck] and is now living her
                                                            Sukey x Proctor
WITNESSES TO MARK: mark
{ J McDermott
{ Jim Cantrell

Subscribed and sworn to before me this 18 day of Dec, 1906.

My Commission   J McDermott
Expires July 25' 1907   Notary Public.

AFFIDAVIT OF ATTENDING PHYSICIAN OR MID-WIFE.

UNITED STATES OF AMERICA, Indian Territory, }
Western   District.   }

I, Yousta Beaver, a midwife, on oath state that I attended on Sukey Proctor, wife of Chaeller Proctor on the 10th day of Oct, 1902; that there was born to her on said date a female child; that said child was living March 4, 1906, and is said to have been named Lydia Proctor

Applications for Enrollment of Creek Newborn
Act of 1905 Volume XII

WITNESSES TO MARK:
{ J McDermott
{ Jim Cantrell

Yousta x Beaver
her   mark

Subscribed and sworn to before me this 18 day of Dec , 1906.

My Commission
Expires July 25' 1907

J McDermott
Notary Public.

April 24, 1905

In the matter of the application for the enrollment of certain newborns as citizens of the Creek Nation.

Alex Posey testified as follows:

Jaly Proctor, Weogufky town, Sukey Proctor, Weogufky town, have two children, one about three years old and one about six months old. Post office Hanna I T

NC 993

Muskogee I T

October 20, 1905

Sucky Proctor
    Care Jaly Proctor
        Hanna I T

Dear Madam:

    In the matter of the application for the enrollment of your minor children, Sam Proctor, born December 9, 1901 and Lydia Proctor born October 10, 1902 this office is unable to identify you or your husband Jaly Proctor on the final roll of citizens by blood of the Creek Nation.

    You are requested to advise this office as to your maiden name, the names of your parents and of the parents of your said husband, the names of your brothers and sisters, the Creek Indian town to which you belong, your roll number and the roll number of your husband as the same appear on your deeds and allotment certificates, and such other information as will enable this office to identify you on its rolls. You are also requested to state whether or not the correct spelling of the name of your husband Jaly Proctor is Chaeller Proctor.

    This matter should receive your immediate attention.

Applications for Enrollment of Creek Newborn
Act of 1905 Volume XII

Respectfully
C mr

NC 993

JWH

Muskogee, Indian Territory, March 1, 1907.

Sucky Proctor,
% Chaeller Proctor,
Hanna, Indian Territory.

Dear Madam :--

You are hereby advised that on February 15, 1907, the Secretary of the Interior approved the enrollment of your minor children, Sam and Lydia Proctor, as citizens by blood of the Creek Nation, and that the names of said children appear upon the roll of New Born citizens by blood of the Creek Nation, enrolled under the Act of Congress approved March 3, 1905, as numbers 1187 and 1188, respectively.

These children are now entitled to allotment and application therefor should be made without delay at the Creek Land Office, Muskogee, Indian Territory.

Respectfully,
Commissioner.

#2 - C 994

2448 B.

DEPARTMENT OF THE INTERIOR,
COMMISSION TO THE FIVE CIVILIZED TRIBES.
April 24, 1905.

In the matter of the application for the enrollment of certain new borns as citizens of the Creek Nation.

Alex Posey, being duly sworn, testified as follows:

By Commission:
Q What is your name, age and post office address? A Alex Posey, 31, Muskogee.
Q Are you a citizen of the Creek Nation? A Yes sir
Q Got your land, have you? A Yes sir.

Applications for Enrollment of Creek Newborn
Act of 1905 Volume XII

Q You have been engaged recently in the field for the Dawes Commission securing evidence about Creek citizens or new borns? A Yes sir.
Q Have you a list of children for whom application could not be made and about whom you have succeeded in obtaining some information? A Yes sir.
Q You may state the conditions and the names of these children? You desire to make application for them? A Yes sir.
Q Name them.
A July Proctor, Weogufky Town, Sukey Proctor, Weogufky Town, have two children --one about three years old and one about six months old. Post office, Hanna, Indian Territory.
✓ Jacob Bullet, about three years old. Parents: Maxey Bullet, Seminole, and Hannah Bullet, Hillabee. Post Office, Hannah, Indian Territory.
 Connie Hawkins, Hillabee Town, Sabella Hawkins, Okchiye, have two children-- one about three years old and a younger child. Post Office, Hanna, Indian Territory.
 Willie Fisher, Hickory Ground Town, Lussee Fisher, Okfusky[sic] Canadian Town, have two children--one about three years old and a baby. Post Office, Slumpker, Indian Territory.
 Lizzie Lasley, about three years old, Sam Lasley, born in either August or September, 1904. Parents: Sam Lasley, Okchiye, Wisey Lasley, Weogufky. Post Office, Hanna, Indian Territory.
 Jim Haynes (or Sangee), Okchiye Town, Folotkokee, Weogufky Town have a male child about three years old named Joe. Post Office, Hanna, Indian Territory.
 Taylor Foley, Weogufky, Melinda Foley, Okchiye, have a child about two years old. Post Office, Slumpker, Indian Territory.
 Phillip Lindsey, Tuckabatchee, Cilla Lindsey, Hillabee, have a child about three years old. Post Office, Hanna, Indian Territory.
 Big William (or William Thlocco), Okchiye Town, Cinda Williams, Weogufky Town, have two children -- one about three years old-- one born in February 1905. Post Office Hanna, Indian Territory.
 Freeland Lindsey, Tuckabatchee or Hillabee, Nancy Proctor, Tullahassoche, have a child about two years old. Post Office, Hanna, Indian Territory.
 Timonthluppy George, Weogufky Town, Nellie George, Pukon Tullahassee[sic], have a child about three years old. Post Office, Slumpker, Indian Territory.
 Walter Simmons, Weogufky, Chippie Simmons, Pukon Tullahassee, have a child about one years old. Post Office, Hannah, Indian Territory.
 Jacob Larney (or Green), Arbeka Tulledega Town, Bettie Larney, (or Green), Hillabee Town, have a child. Post Office, Hanna, Indian Territory.
 John Hill, Okchiye, Millie Hill, Weogufky, have a child about three months old. Post Office, Hanna, Indian Territory.
 Jim Pigeon, Okchiye Town, Jennie Pigeon, Okchiye Town, have a child about five months old. Post Office, Hanna, Indian Territory.
 Thomas Deo, Okchiye Town, Nancy Deo, Fish Pond Town, have a child about three months old. Post Office, Hanna, Indian Territory.
 Jack Buckner, born December 17, 1904. Parents: Wiley Buckner, Okchiye, Susie Buckner, Cussehta. Post Office, Hanna, Indian Territory.
Q This is the information you received from relatives right around there on April 24, 1905? A Yes sir.

Applications for Enrollment of Creek Newborn
Act of 1905 Volume XII

Q Were you informed that the parents of these children were unwilling to make application for their enrollment? A Yes sir.
Q This was the only way that the rights of these children would be saved? A Yes sir. I made every effort to obtain direct information from the parents but in every instance they refused to give their testimony.

Lona Merrick being duly sworn, states that the above and foregoing is a true and correct transcript of his stenographic notes as taken in said cause on said date.

(Signed) Lona Merrick

Subscribed and sworn to before me this 9th day of May, 1905.

(Signed) Edw C Griesel
Notary Public.

I, Lona Merrick, solemnly swear that I copied the above testimony from the original on the 18th day of July, 1905, and that it is a true copy of same.

Lona Merrick

Subscribed and sworn to before me this 18th day of July, 1905.

Edw C Griesel
Notary Public.

No. 2448.

DEPARTMENT OF THE INTERIOR,
COMMISSION TO THE FIVE CIVILIZED TRIBES.
Hanna, I. T., May 30, 1905.

In the matter of the application for the enrollment of Jacob Bullett as a citizen by blood of the Creek Nation.

MAXEY BULLETT, being duly sworn, testified as follows:

Through Alex Posey Official Interpreter

BY COMMISSION:
Q What is your name? A Maxey Bullett.
Q How old are you? A About twenty-five.
Q What is your post office address? A Hanna.
Q Are you a citizen of the Creek Nation? A No, sir, I am a Seminole.
Q Do you make application for the enrollment of your minor child, Jacob Bullett, as a citizen by blood of the Creek Nation? A Yes, sir.
Q What is the name of the child's mother? A Hannah Bullett.

Applications for Enrollment of Creek Newborn
Act of 1905   Volume XII

Q Is she your lawful wife? A Yes, sir.
Q Do you know whether or not shw would be willing to execute an affidavit relative to the birth of this child? A She will not make an affidavit. Her father, William Thlocco, is very much opposed to allotment and is opposed to her making application for the child. She is living with her father, (William Thlocco, on the above date, stated to the Commission that he would rather kill his children than make application for their enrollment)
Q Is she a citizen of the Creek Nation? A Yes, sir.
Q to[sic] what town does she belong? A Hillabee.
Q If it should be found that your child, Jacob Bullett, is entitled enrollment in either the Creek or Seminole Nation, in which nation do you desire him enrolled? A In the Creek Nation.
Q Who attended on your wife at the birth of Jacob? A I attended upon her.

---oooOOOooo---

I, D. C. Skaggs, on oath state that the above and foregoing is a full and true transcript of my stenographic notes as taken in said cause on said date.

D. C. Skaggs

Subscribed and sworn to before me this 18 day of July 1905.

Edw C Griesel
Notary Public.

NC. 994   JCL.
          OCH.

DEPARTMENT OF THE INTERIOR,
COMMISSIONER TO THE FIVE CIVILIZED TRIBES.

In the matter of the application for the enrollment of Jacob Bullett as a citizen by blood of the Creek Nation.

DECISION.

The record in this case shows that on April 24, 1905, application was made for the enrollment of certain new borns as citizens by blood of the Creek Nation, which said application embraced the name of Jacob Bullett. On May 30, 1905, an affidavit was filed in the matter of the application for the enrollment of said Jacob Bullett and further proceedings were had on said date. Supplemental affidavit was filed October 16, 1905.

The evidence and the records in the possession of the Commissioner show that said Jacob Bullett is the child of Hannah Bullett, who is identified as Hannah Big William on a schedule of citizens by blood of the Creek Nation approved by the Secretary of the Interior March 25, 1902, opposite number 8429; and that his father is Maxey Bullett, a citizen of the Seminole Nation.

Applications for Enrollment of Creek Newborn
Act of 1905 Volume XII

The records of the commissioner show that said Jacob Bullett is not enrolled as a citizen of the Seminole Nation, and that no application has been made for his enrollment as such.

The evidence shows that the father of said child elects to have him enrolled as a citizen by blood of the Creek Nation.

The evidence further shows that said Jacob Bullett was born March 16, 1902 and was living March 4, 1905.

The Act of Congress approved March 3, 1905, (33 Stats. 1048) provides in part as follows:

"That the Commission to the Five Civilized Tribes is authorized for sixty days after the date of the approval of this act to receive and consider applications for enrollment, of children, born subsequent to May twenty-fifth, nineteen hundred and one, and prior to March fourth, nineteen hundred and five, and living on said latter date, to citizens of the Creek tribe of Indians whose enrollment has been approved by the Secretary of the Interior prior to the approval of this act; and to enroll and make allotments to such children."

It is, therefore, ordered and adjudged that the said Jacob Bullett is entitled to be enrolled as a citizen by blood of the Creek Nation, in accordance with the provisions of the Act of Congress above quoted, and the application for his enrollment as such is accordingly granted.

Muskogee, Indian Territory   Tams Bixby   Commissioner.
FEB 2- 1907

BIRTH AFFIDAVIT.

DEPARTMENT OF THE INTERIOR.
COMMISSION TO THE FIVE CIVILIZED TRIBES.

IN RE APPLICATION FOR ENROLLMENT, as a citizen of the Creek Nation, of Jacob Bullett, born on the 16 day of March, 1902

Name of Father: Maxey Bullett   a citizen of the Seminole Nation.
Name of Mother: Hanna Bullett   a citizen of the Creek Nation.
Hillabee

                Postoffice   Hanna I T

Applications for Enrollment of Creek Newborn
Act of 1905 Volume XII

AFFIDAVIT OF ATTENDING PHYSICIAN OR MID-WIFE.

UNITED STATES OF AMERICA, Indian Territory,
Western DISTRICT.

my wife
I, Maxey Bullett , a~~ (blank)~~ , on oath state that I attended on ^ Mrs. Hanna , ~~wife of~~ *(blank)* on the 16 day of March , 1902 ; that there was born to her on said date a male child; that said child was living March 4, 1905, and is said to have been named Jacob Bullett

           Maxey Bullett

Witnesses To Mark:
{

Subscribed and sworn to before me this 30 day of May, 1905.

           Drennan C Skaggs
           Notary Public.

BIRTH AFFIDAVIT.

DEPARTMENT OF THE INTERIOR.
COMMISSION TO THE FIVE CIVILIZED TRIBES.

IN RE APPLICATION FOR ENROLLMENT, as a citizen of the Creek Nation, of Jacob Bullett, born on the 16 day of March , 1902

Name of Father: Maxey Bullett   a citizen of the Seminole Nation.
Name of Mother: Hannah Bullett   a citizen of the Creek Nation.

      Postoffice   Hannah IT

AFFIDAVIT OF ATTENDING PHYSICIAN OR MID-WIFE.

UNITED STATES OF AMERICA, Indian Territory,
Western DISTRICT.

        we are personally acquainted with
We, the undersigned , a~~——~~, on oath state that ~~I attended on~~ Mrs. Hannah Bullett, wife of Maxey Bullett ~~on the day of , 190~~ ; that there was born to her on March 16, 1902 ~~said date~~ a male child; that said child was living March 4, 1905, and is said to have been named Jacob Bullett

         her
      Susie x Buckner
Witnesses To Mark: mark
 { DC Skaggs   her
   Alex Posey   Sallie x Bruner
         mark

Applications for Enrollment of Creek Newborn
Act of 1905   Volume XII

Subscribed and sworn to before me 7 day of October, 1905.

Drennan C Skaggs
Notary Public.

(The above Birth Affidavit given again.)

(The affidavit of the father, above, given again.)

April 24, 1905

In the matter of the application for the enrollment of certain new borns as citizens of the Creek Nation.

Alex Posey testified as follows

Jacob Bullet, about 3 years old. Parents Maxey Bullet, Seminole and Hannah Bullet, Hillabee. Postoffice Hanna, Indian Territory IT

NC 994

Muskogee I T July 15, 1905

Chief Clerk
    Seminole En Div
Dear Sir

    May 30 1905 application was made to the Commission to the Five Civilized Tribes for the enrollment of Jacob Bullett, born March 16, 1902 as a citizen by blood of the Creek Nation. It is stated in said application that the father of said child is Maxey Bullett, a citizen of the Seminole Nation, and that the mother is Hannah Bullett, a citizen of the Creek Nation.

    You are requested to inform the Creek En Div as to whether application has been made for the enrollment of said Jacob Bullett as a citizen of the Seminole Nation and if so what disposition has been made of the same

Respectfully
Comr

Applications for Enrollment of Creek Newborn
Act of 1905   Volume XII

W.F.
DEPARTMENT OF THE INTERIOR,
COMMISSIONER TO THE FIVE CIVILIZED TRIBES.

Muskogee, Indian Territory July 19, 1905.

Chief Clerk,
    Creek Enrollment Division.

Dear Sir:

Receipt is acknowledged of your letter of July 15, 1905, (NC-994) stating that application was made to the Commission to the Five Civilized Tribes for the enrollment of Jacob Bullett, born March 16, 1902, child of Maxey Bullett, a citizen of the Seminole Nation, and Hannah Bullett, a citizen of the Creek Nation, as a citizen by blood of the Creek Nation and requesting to be informed as to whether application was made for the enrollment of said child as a citizen of the Seminole Nation.

In reply to your letter you are informed that it does not appear from an examination of the records of this office that any application was made for the enrollment of said Jacob Bullet as a citizen of the Seminole Nation.

Respectfully,
Tams Bixby   Commissioner.

NC 944

Muskogee I T Oct 21 05

Maxey Bullett
    Hanna I T

Dear Sir

In the matter of the application for the enrollment of your minor child, Jacob Bullett, born March 16, 1902, as a citizen by blood of the Creek Nation, this office is unable to identify your wife, Hannah Bullett, the mother of said child, on its final roll of citizens by blood of the Creek Nation, you are requested to state ~~your~~ her maiden name, the names of her parents, the Creek Indian Town to which she belongs and the numbers which appear on her deeds to land in the Creek Nation.

Respectfully

Comr

Applications for Enrollment of Creek Newborn
Act of 1905 Volume XII

DEPARTMENT OF THE INTERIOR,
COMMISSION TO THE FIVE CIVILIZED TRIBES.
EUFAULA, I.T. April 19, 1905.

In the matter of the application for the enrollment of certain new born children concerning whom no application could be obtained except through testimony.

Jimsey Fish and William Givens, being duly sworn, testified as follows, through Official Interpreter, Alex Posey.

Examination by the Commission:
Q What is your name? A Jimsey Fish.
Q How old are you? A I have never been able to determine my age. (Witness appears to be about 48).
Q What is your post office? A Mellette, I.T.
Q Do you know of some new born children whose parents are unwilling to have them enrolled? A Yes sir.
Q These about whom you and Mr. Givens are testifying are children all born since May 25, 1901? And for whom application could only be made in this way? A Yes sir.

Q What is your name? A William Givens.
Q How old are you? A I am 25.
Q What is your post office address? A Mellette.

Statement: Nocus Ela has two children--his white name is Jim Davis--he belongs to Kialigee Town--I don't know the name of his wife, but she belongs to Kialigee town; one of them is walking and the other is younger. The one that is walking is a boy, don't know the sex of the other. The oldest is named Johnny, don't know the other's name. Both are living. They are both new born children and Nocus said the other day that he had never enrolled them--the post office is Hanna.

Bob and Mahala Bender have two children--these people belong to Tuckabatchee and Hillabee Towns respectively--one of the children is Thomas and the other is Easma--Thomas is just beginning to talk and Easma is older than Thomas. Their post office is Mellette. These children are new borns also.

Josie and Mahala Roberts have two children--the parents belong to Hutchechuppa and Kialigee respectively-- I don't [sic] the names of the children-- one is walking and the other is a baby yet a small child.
Q Were both of them born since May 25, 1901? A Yes sir. The oldest is a girl and I don't know the sex of the youngest. Both are living. Their post office is Indianola.

Thompson Fields and Susie Fields--he is of Okchiye or Fish Pond, I don't know which, and Susie belongs to Hutchechuppa; they have one child born since May 25, 1901, I don't know but I think the gi child is a girl. It is living, the child is not able to crawl but can sit up.

Applications for Enrollment of Creek Newborn
Act of 1905   Volume XII

    Earnest and Nicey Gouge, of Hickory Ground and Hillabee Towns respectively--- had two children the last time I was at their house--both were born since May 25, don't know the names, both boys I think, both living, post office, Hanna.

    ✓ Connie Hawkins of Hillabee Town and Sybilla Hawkins of Fish Pond (?) I don't know her town; they had one child at the time I was at their house; I was at their house last summer 1904, don't know whether a boy or girl, born after May 25, 1901, it was a small child at that time, it is living. Post Office, Hanna.

    Micco Emarthla, his white name if Noodle Walker, and Sallie Emarthla, both parents belong to Kialigee, have one child named Walter born since May 25, 1901, and living. Post Office, Indianola.

    Wiley Fish of Tuckabatchee and Hettie Fish of Kialigee, post office, Mellette, have two children, but one is probably too old being about seven years old, but the field party last year failed to get that old one. The youngest was probably born since May 25, 1901. It is a boy and living. The oldest one is name John I don't know the other.

    Noah Roberts of Kialigee and Hannah Roberts of Hillabee post office, Mellette, have one child name not known, born since May 25, 1901. Don't know the sex, it is living. Noah also has a step-son about seven years old that has never been enrolled named Walter Starr.

Questions addressed to both witnesses:
Q These statements which you have made are for the purpose of getting enrolled the new born children of parents belonging to the Snake Faction? A Yes sir.
Q Neither of you are related to them? A I Jimsey am related to Wiley Fish, who is the son of my brother and that's all.

    Henry G. Hains, being duly sworn, on his oath, states that the above and foregoing is a true and correct transcript of his stenographic notes as taken in said cause on said date.

                                                  Henry G. Hains

Subscribed and sworn to before me this 11th day of May, 1905.

                                            Drennan C Skaggs
                                            Notary Public.

Applications for Enrollment of Creek Newborn
Act of 1905 Volume XII

#2 - C 994

2448 B.

DEPARTMENT OF THE INTERIOR,
COMMISSION TO THE FIVE CIVILIZED TRIBES.
April 24, 1905.

In the matter of the application for the enrollment of certain new borns as citizens of the Creek Nation.

Alex Posey, being duly sworn, testified as follows:

By Commission:
Q What is your name, age and post office address? A Alex Posey, 31, Muskogee.
Q Are you a citizen of the Creek Nation? A Yes sir
Q Got your land, have you? A Yes sir.
Q You have been engaged recently in the field for the Dawes Commission securing evidence about Creek citizens or new borns? A Yes sir.
Q Have you a list of children for whom application could not be made and about whom you have succeeded in obtaining some information? A Yes sir.
Q You may state the conditions and the names of these children? You desire to make application for them? A Yes sir.
Q Name them.
A July Proctor, Weogufky Town, Sukey Proctor, Weogufky Town, have two children --one about three years old and one about six months old. Post office, Hanna, Indian Territory.
Jacob Bullet, about three years old. Parents: Maxey Bullet, Seminole, and Hannah Bullet, Hillabee. Post Office, Hannah, Indian Territory.
✓ Connie Hawkins, Hillabee Town, Sabella Hawkins, Okchiye, have two children-- one about three years old and a younger child. Post Office, Hanna, Indian Territory.
Willie Fisher, Hickory Ground Town, Lussee Fisher, Okfusky[sic] Canadian Town, have two children--one about three years old and a baby. Post Office, Slumpker, Indian Territory.
Lizzie Lasley, about three years old, Sam Lasley, born in either August or September, 1904. Parents: Sam Lasley, Okchiye, Wisey Lasley, Weogufky. Post Office, Hanna, Indian Territory.
Jim Haynes (or Sangee), Okchiye Town, Folotkokee, Weogufky Town have a male child about three years old named Joe. Post Office, Hanna, Indian Territory.
Taylor Foley, Weogufky, Melinda Foley, Okchiye, have a child about two years old. Post Office, Slumpker, Indian Territory.
Phillip Lindsey, Tuckabatchee, Cilla Lindsey, Hillabee, have a child about three years old. Post Office, Hanna, Indian Territory.
Big William (or William Thlocco), Okchiye Town, Cinda Williams, Weogufky Town, have two children -- one about three years old-- one born in February 1905. Post Office Hanna, Indian Territory.
Freeland Lindsey, Tuckabatchee or Hillabee, Nancy Proctor, Tullahassoche, have a child about two years old. Post Office, Hanna, Indian Territory.

Applications for Enrollment of Creek Newborn
Act of 1905   Volume XII

Timonthluppy George, Weogufky Town, Nellie George, Pukon Tullahassee[sic], have a child about three years old. Post Office, Slumpker, Indian Territory.

Walter Simmons, Weogufky, Chippie Simmons, Pukon Tullahassee, have a child about one years old. Post Office, Hannah, Indian Territory.

Jacob Larney (or Green), Arbeka Tulledega Town, Bettie Larney, (or Green), Hillabee Town, have a child. Post Office, Hanna, Indian Territory.

John Hill, Okchiye, Millie Hill, Weogufky, have a child about three months old. Post Office, Hanna, Indian Territory.

Jim Pigeon, Okchiye Town, Jennie Pigeon, Okchiye Town, have a child about five months old. Post Office, Hanna, Indian Territory.

Thomas Deo, Okchiye Town, Nancy Deo, Fish Pond Town, have a child about three months old. Post Office, Hanna, Indian Territory.

Jack Buckner, born December 17, 1904. Parents: Wiley Buckner, Okchiye, Susie Buckner, Cussehta. Post Office, Hanna, Indian Territory.

Q This is the information you received from relatives right around there on April 24, 1905? A Yes sir.

Q Were you informed that the parents of these children were unwilling to make application for their enrollment? A Yes sir.

Q This was the only way that the rights of these children would be saved? A Yes sir. I made every effort to obtain direct information from the parents but in every instance they refused to give their testimony.

Lona Merrick being duly sworn, states that the above and foregoing is a true and correct transcript of his stenographic notes as taken in said cause on said date.

(Signed) Lona Merrick

Subscribed and sworn to before me this 9th day of May, 1905.

(Signed) Edw C Griesel
Notary Public.

I, Lona Merrick, solemnly swear that I copied the above testimony from the original on the 18th day of July, 1905, and that it is a true copy of same.

Lona Merrick

Subscribed and sworn to before me this 18th day of July, 1905.

Edw C Griesel
Notary Public.

Applications for Enrollment of Creek Newborn
Act of 1905   Volume XII

BIRTH AFFIDAVIT.

DEPARTMENT OF THE INTERIOR.
COMMISSION TO THE FIVE CIVILIZED TRIBES.

IN RE APPLICATION FOR ENROLLMENT, as a citizen of the Creek Nation, of Pink Hawkins, born on the 4 day of July, 1902

Name of Father: Conner[sic] Hawkins   a citizen of the   Creek   Nation.
Hillabee Town
Name of Mother: Sabella Hawkins   a citizen of the   Creek   Nation.
Okchiye Town

Postoffice   Hanna, Ind. Terr.

AFFIDAVIT OF ATTENDING PHYSICIAN OR MID-WIFE.

UNITED STATES OF AMERICA, Indian Territory,
    Western   DISTRICT.

we are personally acquainted with We, *(blank)* , a—, on oath state that I attended on Mrs. Sabella Hawkins, wife of Conner Hawkins on the day of , 1 ; that there was born to her on or about the fourth (4) day of July, 1902 said date a male child; that said child was living March 4, 1905, and is said to have been named Pink Hawkins

                             David Cummings
Witnesses To Mark: her
   { DC Skaggs   Louisa x Cummings
     Alex Posey   mark

Subscribed and sworn to before me 6 day of Oct, 1905.

                             Drennan C Skaggs
                                 Notary Public.

BIRTH AFFIDAVIT.

DEPARTMENT OF THE INTERIOR.
COMMISSION TO THE FIVE CIVILIZED TRIBES.

IN RE APPLICATION FOR ENROLLMENT, as a citizen of the Creek Nation, of Nellie Hawkins, born on the 9 day of Nov, 1904

Name of Father: Conner[sic] Hawkins   a citizen of the   Creek   Nation.
Hillabee Town
Name of Mother: Sabella Hawkins   a citizen of the   Creek   Nation.

Applications for Enrollment of Creek Newborn
Act of 1905 Volume XII

Postoffice   Hanna, Ind. Terr.

AFFIDAVIT OF ATTENDING PHYSICIAN OR MID-WIFE.

UNITED STATES OF AMERICA, Indian Territory,
Western   DISTRICT.

we are personally acquainted with We, *(blank)* , a—, on oath state that I attended on Mrs. Sabella Hawkins , wife of Connie Hawkins on the day of , 1 ; that there was born to her on or about the 9th day of Nov., 1904 said date a female child; that said child was living March 4, 1905, and is said to have been named Nellie Hawkins

Witnesses To Mark:
{ DC Skaggs
  Alex Posey

David Cummings
her
Louisa x Cummings
mark

Subscribed and sworn to before me 6 day of Oct, 1905.

Drennan C Skaggs
Notary Public.

BIRTH AFFIDAVIT.

DEPARTMENT OF THE INTERIOR.
COMMISSION TO THE FIVE CIVILIZED TRIBES.

IN RE APPLICATION FOR ENROLLMENT, as a citizen of the Creek Nation, of Nellie Hawkins , born on the 9 day of November , 1904

Name of Father: Conner Hawkins   a citizen of the   Creek   Nation.
Hillabee Town
Name of Mother: Subella[sic] Hawkins   a citizen of the   Creek   Nation.
Okchiye Town

Postoffice   Hanna, Ind. Terr.

AFFIDAVIT OF MOTHER.

UNITED STATES OF AMERICA, Indian Territory,
Western   DISTRICT.

I, Subella Hawkins , on oath state that I am 28 years of age and a citizen by blood , of the Creek Nation; that I am the lawful wife of Conner Hawkins , who is a citizen, by blood of the Creek Nation; that a female child was born to me on 9 day

Applications for Enrollment of Creek Newborn
Act of 1905   Volume XII

of November, 1904, that said child has been named Nellie Hawkins, and ~~is now~~ was living. on March 4, 1905.

Subella Hawkins

Witnesses To Mark:
{

Subscribed and sworn to before me this 23 day of May, 1905.

Drennan C Skaggs
Notary Public.

AFFIDAVIT OF ATTENDING PHYSICIAN OR MID-WIFE.

UNITED STATES OF AMERICA, Indian Territory,
Western   DISTRICT.

Amelia
I, ~~Mary Ann~~ Hutton, a mid-wife, on oath state that I attended on Mrs. Subella Hawkins, wife of Conner Hawkins ~~on the   day of   , 1 ~~; about seven months ago that there was born to her on said date a female child; that said child ~~is now~~ was living on March 4, 1905, and is said to have been named Nellie Hawkins

her
Amelia x Hutton
mark

Witnesses To Mark:
{ DC Skaggs
  Alex Posey

Subscribed and sworn to before me this 24 day of May, 1905.

Drennan C Skaggs
Notary Public.

BIRTH AFFIDAVIT.

DEPARTMENT OF THE INTERIOR.
COMMISSION TO THE FIVE CIVILIZED TRIBES.

IN RE APPLICATION FOR ENROLLMENT, as a citizen of the Creek Nation, of Pink Hawkins, born on the 4 day of July, 1902

Name of Father: Conner Hawkins   a citizen of the   Creek   Nation.
Hillabee Town
Name of Mother: Subella[sic] Hawkins   a citizen of the   Creek   Nation.
Okchiye Town

Postoffice   Hanna, I. T.

Applications for Enrollment of Creek Newborn
Act of 1905   Volume XII

AFFIDAVIT OF MOTHER.

Child present.

UNITED STATES OF AMERICA, Indian Territory,
   Western   DISTRICT.

    I, Subella Hawkins , on oath state that I am 28 years of age and a citizen by blood , of the Creek Nation; that I am the lawful wife of Conner Hawkins , who is a citizen, by blood of the Creek Nation; that a male child was born to me on 4 day of July , 1902 , that said child has been named Pink Hawkins , and ~~is now~~ was living.on March 4, 1905.

                                Subella Hawkins

Witnesses To Mark:
{

    Subscribed and sworn to before me this 23 day of May , 1905.

                                  Drennan C Skaggs
                                  Notary Public.

AFFIDAVIT OF ATTENDING PHYSICIAN OR MID-WIFE.

UNITED STATES OF AMERICA, Indian Territory,
   Western   DISTRICT.

    I, Chiye Hope , a mid-wife , on oath state that I attended on Mrs. Subella Hawkins , wife of Conner Hawkins ~~on the day of , 1~~ ; that there was born to her on said date a male child; that said child ~~is now~~ was living on March 4, 1905, and is said to have been named Pink Hawkins

                                      her
                            Chiye x Hope

Witnesses To Mark: mark
{ DC Skaggs
  Alex Posey

    Subscribed and sworn to before me this 24 day of May, 1905.

                                  Drennan C Skaggs
                                  Notary Public.

Applications for Enrollment of Creek Newborn
Act of 1905   Volume XII

NC-995.

Muskogee, Indian Territory, November 10, 1905

Subella Hawkins,
    c/o Conner Hawkins,
        Hannah, Indian Territory.

Dear Madam:

In the matter of the application for the enrollment of your minor children, Pink Hawkins and Nellie Hawkins, as citizens by blood of the Creek Nation, you are advised that this office has been unable to identify you upon the final roll of citizens by blood of the Creek Nation. It is necessary that you be so identified before the rights of your said children can be finally determined.

You are therefore requested to state the name under which you are finally enrolled, your age, the names of your parents and other members of your family, the Creek Indian town to which you belong and your final roll number as the same appears upon your allotment certificate and deeds.

You are also requested to state whether you were ever known by the name of Sepile Hawkins.

                Respectfully,

                          Commissioner.

N.C. 995

Muskogee, Indian Territory, December 18, 1905.

Subella Hawkins,
    Care Conner Hawkins,
        Hanna, Indian Territory.

Dear Madam:

In the matter of the application for the enrollment of your minor children, Pink Hawkins, born July 4, 1902, and Nellie Hawkins, born November 9, 1904, as citizens by blood of the Creek Nation, you are again advised that this office is unable to identify you on its final roll of citizens by blood of the Creek Nation. It is necessary that you be so identified before the rights of said child can be finally determined; you are requested to state your maiden name, the names of your parents, the Creek Indian town to which you belong and your roll number as the same appears on your deeds to land in the Creek Nation.

You are also requested to state whether your correct name is not in fact Sepile Hawkins. If your correct name is other than Subella Hawkins, it will be necessary for

Applications for Enrollment of Creek Newborn
Act of 1905   Volume XII

you to execute a new affidavit in the case of each of said children, being careful to sign thereto your name as the same appears in the body of the affidavit.

Blank forms of birth affidavit are enclosed herewith.

Respectfully,
Commissioner.

2 BA

NC-996
DEPARTMENT OF THE INTERIOR,
COMMISSIONER TO THE FIVE CIVILIZED TRIBES.,

Muskogee, Indian Territory, October 26, 1905.

In the matter of the application for the enrollment of Alma Dee Granberry as a citizen of the Creek Nation.

Mattie Granberry, being duly sworn, testified as follows:

EXAMINATION BY THE COMMISSIONER:
Q What is your name? A Mattie Granberry.
Q How old are you? A 29 years old.
Q What is your postoffice address? A Boynton.
Q What is the name of your father? A Enoch Flack.
Q Was he a citizen of the Creek Nation? A Citizen of the Choctaw Nation.
Q Choctaw Freedman? A Yes sir.
Q What is the name of your mother? A Cornelia Flack.
Q Is Cornelia living? A Yes sir.
Q Have you a brother? A Yes sir.
Q What is his name? A John Flack.
Q Is he living? A Yes sir.
Q Have you a child that was born in the last three or four years? A One.
Q What is the name of that child? A Alma Dee Granberry.
Q Is that child living? A Yes, it is here.
Q When was this little girl here born? A December 13, 1903.
Q How old will it be this--? A Two years old yes December.
Q Did you have a doctor when it was born? A Yes sir.

Applications for Enrollment of Creek Newborn
Act of 1905   Volume XII

Q What is his name? A Alston.

INDIAN TERRITORY, Western District.

I, J. Y. Miller, a stenographer to the Commissioner to the Five Civilized Tribes, do hereby certify that the above and foregoing is a true and complete translation of my notes as same appear in my stenographic report of this case.

JY Miller

Sworn to and subscribed before me
this the 27th day of October,
1905.

Edw C Griesel
Notary Public.

BIRTH AFFIDAVIT.

Department of the Interior,
COMMISSION TO THE FIVE CIVILIZED TRIBES.

IN RE APPLICATION FOR ENROLLMENT, as a citizen of the Creek Nation, of Alma Dee Granberry, born on the 13 day of December , 1903

Name of Father: James Granberry   a citizen of the United StatesNation.
Name of Mother: Mattie Granberry   a citizen of the   Creek   Nation.
 Tuckegee Town

Post-Office: Boynton, I.T.

AFFIDAVIT OF MOTHER.

UNITED STATES OF AMERICA,
   INDIAN TERRITORY,
   Western   District.

I, Mattie Granberry , on oath state that I am 28 years of age and a citizen by blood , of the Creek Nation; that I am the lawful wife of James Granberry , who is a citizen, by *(blank)* of the United States Nation; that a female child was born to me on 13 day of December , 1903 , that said child has been named Alma Dee Granberry , and ~~is now~~ was living. on March 4, 1905.

Mattie Granberry

WITNESSES TO MARK:
{

Subscribed and sworn to before me this 3 day of April, 1905.

Drennan C Skaggs
Notary Public.

Applications for Enrollment of Creek Newborn
Act of 1905 Volume XII

AFFIDAVIT OF ATTENDING PHYSICIAN OR MID-WIFE.

UNITED STATES OF AMERICA,
INDIAN TERRITORY,
Western District.

I, A. J. Alston , a Physician , on oath state that I attended on Mrs. Mattie Granberry , wife of James Granberry on the 13 day of Dec , 1903 ; that there was born to her on said date a female child; that said child is now was living on March 4, 1905, and is said to have been named Alma Dee Granberry

A. J. Alston

WITNESSES TO MARK:

Subscribed and sworn to before me this 11 day of April, 1905.

my term expires Oct 1, 1908.   Geo L Robinson
                                       Notary Public.

Nc[sic] 996

Muskogee, Indian Territory, October 21, 1905.

Mattie Granberry,
    Care James Granberry,
        Boynton, Indian Territory.

Dear Madam:

In the matter of the application for the enrollment of your minor child, Alma Dee Granberry, born December 13, 1903, as a citizen by blood of the Creek Nation, this office is unable to identify you on its roll of citizens by blood of the Creek Nation; you are requested to state your maiden name, the names of your parents, the Creek Indian town to which you belong, your roll number as the same appears on your deeds and allotment certificate.

This matter should receive your prompt attention.

Respectfully,

Commissioner.

Applications for Enrollment of Creek Newborn
Act of 1905   Volume XII

NC 997

Muskogee, Indian Territory, October 21, 1905.

Jude Gilbert,
    Care Louis W. Gilbert,
        Henryetta, Indian Territory.

Dear Madam:

    In the matter of the application for the enrollment of your minor child, Jeniry Gilbert, born August 16, 1903, as a citizen by blood of the Creek Nation, you are advised that it will be necessary for you to again file in this case the affidavit of the midwife who attended at the birth of said child, for the reason that the affidavit heretofore filed is written with such poor quality of ink that the same is now illegible.

    You are further advised that this office is unable to identify you on its roll of citizens of the Creek Nation; you are requested to state your maiden name, the names of your parents, the Creek Indian town to which you belong your roll number as same appears on your deeds and allotment certificate.

                      Respectfully,

                                        Commissioner.

AG-997

(The letter below typed as given.)

                                        Copy

N.C. 997
Henryetta, I.T. 11/20 1905
Comissioner to 5 Civilized Tribes

Dear Sir:

    Yours of Oct 21 at hand   enclosed will find new affidavit of midwife   My maiden name was Jude Whetstone Creek Ind Roll #3522 I was alloted as Jude Furr My deed No is 2193 File #2328 My mother s name was Nancy Caroline Whetstone my father s name Anderson Whetstone

                            Yours Truly
                            Jude Gilbert

Applications for Enrollment of Creek Newborn
Act of 1905 Volume XII

BIRTH AFFIDAVIT.

DEPARTMENT OF THE INTERIOR.
COMMISSION TO THE FIVE CIVILIZED TRIBES.

IN RE APPLICATION FOR ENROLLMENT, as a citizen of the Creek Nation, of Jeniry Gilbert, born on the 16th day of August, 1903

Name of Father: Louis W Gilbert   a citizen of the United States Nation.
Name of Mother: Jude Gilbert Nee Furr   a citizen of the   Creek   Nation.

Postoffice   *(blank)*

AFFIDAVIT OF MOTHER.

UNITED STATES OF AMERICA, Indian Territory,
    Western Judicial   DISTRICT.

    I, Jude Gilbert Nee Furr, on oath state that I am *(blank)* years of age and a citizen by blood, of the Creek Nation; that I am the lawful wife of Louis W Gilbert, who is a citizen, by *(blank)* of the United States ~~Nation~~; that a Female child was born to me on 16th day of August, 1903, that said child has been named Jeniry Gilbert, and was living March 4, 1905.

                                           Jude Gilbert nee Furr

Witnesses To Mark:
{

    Subscribed and sworn to before me this 24th day of October, 1905.

                                  E E Schock
                                  Notary Public.
                              My Commission Expires
                                  Jan 18th 1908

AFFIDAVIT OF ATTENDING PHYSICIAN OR MID-WIFE.

UNITED STATES OF AMERICA, Indian Territory,
    Western Judicial   DISTRICT.

    I, Mary J Miller, a midwife, on oath state that I attended on Mrs. Jude Gilbert, wife of Louis W Gilbert on the 16th day of August, 1903; that there was born to her on said date a Female child; that said child was living March 4, 1905, and is said to have been named Jeniry Gilbert

                                        Mary J Miller

Witnesses To Mark:
{

Applications for Enrollment of Creek Newborn
Act of 1905   Volume XII

Subscribed and sworn to before me this 24th day of October, 1905.

E E Schock
Notary Public.
My Commission Expires
Jan 18th 1908

BIRTH AFFIDAVIT.

DEPARTMENT OF THE INTERIOR.
COMMISSION TO THE FIVE CIVILIZED TRIBES.

IN RE APPLICATION FOR ENROLLMENT, as a citizen of the Creek Nation, of Jeniry Gilbert, born on the 16 day of August, 1903

Name of Father: Louis W Gilbert   a citizen of the United States Nation.
Name of Mother: Jude Gilbert   a citizen of the   Creek   Nation.
Ketchopatcky Town

Postoffice   Henryetta, Ind. Ter.

AFFIDAVIT OF MOTHER.

UNITED STATES OF AMERICA, Indian Territory,
Western   DISTRICT.   Child is present

I, Jude Gilbert, on oath state that I am 40 years of age and a citizen by blood, of the Creek Nation; that I am the lawful wife of Louis W Gilbert, who is a citizen, by *(blank)* of the United States Nation; that a female child was born to me on 16 day of August, 1903, that said child has been named Jeniry Gilbert, and was living March 4, 1905.

Jude Gilbert

Witnesses To Mark:

Subscribed and sworn to before me this 10 day of April, 1905.

Drennan C Skaggs
Notary Public.

Applications for Enrollment of Creek Newborn
Act of 1905   Volume XII

NC. 998.
DEPARTMENT OF THE INTERIOR,
COMMISSIONER TO THE FIVE CIVILIZED TRIBES.
MUSKOGEE, INDIAN TERRITORY.
JUNE 2, 1906.

In the matter of the application for the enrollment of Bettie Fisher, deceased, as a citizen by blood of the Creek Nation.
Q[sic]
Willie Fisher, being duly sworn, testified as follows, through Official Interpreter, Lona Merrick.

Q What is your name? A Willie Fisher.
Q What is your age? A 39.
Q What is your post office address? A Trenton.
Q What Creek Indian town do you belong to? A Hickory Ground.
Q What was the name of your mother? A Bettie Fisher.
Q What was the name of your father? A William Fisher.
Q Is he living? A No sir, he is dead, he died about two years ago.
Q Is your mother living? A No sir, she died when I was about a year old.
Q Was your mother part Cherokee? A Yes sir.

Witness is identified as Willie Fisher, opposite Creek Indian Roll No. 9933.

Q Did you have a child by the name of Bettie? A Yes sir, she is dead.
Q What was the name of her mother? A Lucy Fisher.
Q What Creek Indian town does she belong to? A Okfuskee Canadian.
Q What was Lucy's fathers[sic] name? A Billy James
Q Was he ever called Captain Billy? A Yes sir, he was captain of the lighthorse.
Q Do you know Lucy's mother's name? A No sir, I have forgotten her name.
Q Did you have another child by Lucy? A Yes sir, Billy.
Q Is Billy living? A Yes sir.
Q Why did Lucy testify then that this child Bettie, who died in September, 1899, that was the only child she ever had, do you know? A I guess she was mistaken. Maybe she didn't understand what they were asking her.
Q Did she have another child by another man? A Yes sir, Emma Dorsey.
Q Is Emma Dorsey living? A No sir, she has been dead nearly three years.
Q Lucy and Billy living with you at Trenton? A Yes sir.
Q That is their post office address? A Yes sir.

Lona Merrick, being duly sworn, states that the above and foregoing is a fulle[sic] and correct transcript of her stenographic notes as taken in said cause on said date.

Lona Merrick

Subscribed and sworn to before me this 4th day of June, 1906.

Applications for Enrollment of Creek Newborn
Act of 1905 Volume XII

HGHains
Notary Public.

#4 - C 998

2448 B.

DEPARTMENT OF THE INTERIOR,
COMMISSION TO THE FIVE CIVILIZED TRIBES.
April 24, 1905.

In the matter of the application for the enrollment of certain new borns as citizens of the Creek Nation.

Alex Posey, being duly sworn, testified as follows:

By Commission:
Q What is your name, age and post office address? A Alex Posey, 31, Muskogee.
Q Are you a citizen of the Creek Nation? A Yes sir
Q Got your land, have you? A Yes sir.
Q You have been engaged recently in the field for the Dawes Commission securing evidence about Creek citizens or new borns? A Yes sir.
Q Have you a list of children for whom application could not be made and about whom you have succeeded in obtaining some information? A Yes sir.
Q You may state the conditions and the names of these children? You desire to make application for them? A Yes sir.
Q Name them.
A   July Proctor, Weogufky Town, Sukey Proctor, Weogufky Town, have two children --one about three years old and one about six months old. Post office, Hanna, Indian Territory.
     Jacob Bullet, about three years old. Parents: Maxey Bullet, Seminole, and Hannah Bullet, Hillabee. Post Office, Hannah, Indian Territory.
     Connie Hawkins, Hillabee Town, Sabella Hawkins, Okchiye, have two children--one about three years old and a younger child. Post Office, Hanna, Indian Territory.
✓   Willie Fisher, Hickory Ground Town, Lussee Fisher, Okfusky[sic] Canadian Town, have two children--one about three years old and a baby. Post Office, Slumpker, Indian Territory.
     Lizzie Lasley, about three years old, Sam Lasley, born in either August or September, 1904. Parents: Sam Lasley, Okchiye, Wisey Lasley, Weogufky. Post Office, Hanna, Indian Territory.
     Jim Haynes (or Sangee), Okchiye Town, Folotkokee, Weogufky Town have a male child about three years old named Joe. Post Office, Hanna, Indian Territory.
     Taylor Foley, Weogufky, Melinda Foley, Okchiye, have a child about two years old. Post Office, Slumpker, Indian Territory.
     Phillip Lindsey, Tuckabatchee, Cilla Lindsey, Hillabee, have a child about three years old. Post Office, Hanna, Indian Territory.

Applications for Enrollment of Creek Newborn
Act of 1905 Volume XII

Big William (or William Thlocco), Okchiye Town, Cinda Williams, Weogufky Town, have two children -- one about three years old-- one born in February 1905. Post Office Hanna, Indian Territory.

Freeland Lindsey, Tuckabatchee or Hillabee, Nancy Proctor, Tullahassoche, have a child about two years old. Post Office, Hanna, Indian Territory.

Timonthluppy George, Weogufky Town, Nellie George, Pukon Tullahassee[sic], have a child about three years old. Post Office, Slumpker, Indian Territory.

Walter Simmons, Weogufky, Chippie Simmons, Pukon Tullahassee, have a child about one years old. Post Office, Hannah, Indian Territory.

Jacob Larney (or Green), Arbeka Tulledega Town, Bettie Larney, (or Green), Hillabee Town, have a child. Post Office, Hanna, Indian Territory.

John Hill, Okchiye, Millie Hill, Weogufky, have a child about three months old. Post Office, Hanna, Indian Territory.

Jim Pigeon, Okchiye Town, Jennie Pigeon, Okchiye Town, have a child about five months old. Post Office, Hanna, Indian Territory.

Thomas Deo, Okchiye Town, Nancy Deo, Fish Pond Town, have a child about three months old. Post Office, Hanna, Indian Territory.

Jack Buckner, born December 17, 1904. Parents: Wiley Buckner, Okchiye, Susie Buckner, Cussehta. Post Office, Hanna, Indian Territory.

Q This is the information you received from relatives right around there on April 24, 1905? A Yes sir.

Q Were you informed that the parents of these children were unwilling to make application for their enrollment? A Yes sir.

Q This was the only way that the rights of these children would be saved? A Yes sir. I made every effort to obtain direct information from the parents but in every instance they refused to give their testimony.

Lona Merrick being duly sworn, states that the above and foregoing is a true and correct transcript of his stenographic notes as taken in said cause on said date.

(Signed) Lona Merrick

Subscribed and sworn to before me this 9th day of May, 1905.

(Signed) Edw C Griesel
Notary Public.

I, Lona Merrick, solemnly swear that I copied the above testimony from the original on the 18th day of July, 1905, and that it is a true copy of same.

Lona Merrick

Subscribed and sworn to before me this 18th day of July, 1905.

Edw C Griesel
Notary Public.

Applications for Enrollment of Creek Newborn
Act of 1905   Volume XII

N. C. 998.

DEPARTMENT OF THE INTERIOR,
COMMISSIONER TO THE FIVE CIVILIZED TRIBES.
Trenton, I. T., October 7, 1905.

In the matter of the application for the enrollment of Bettie Fisher, deceased, as a citizen by blood of the Creek Nation.

LUCY FISHER, being duly sworn, testified as follows:

Through Alex Posey Official Interpreter:

BY THE COMMISSIONER:
Q What is your name? A Lucy Fisher.
Q How old are you? A I do not know.

Witness appears to be about thirty-eight years of age.

Q What is your post office address? A Trenton.
Q Are you a citizen of the Creek Nation? A Yes, sir.
Q To what town do you belong? A Okfuske Canadian.
Q You have heretofore given information about your child, Bettie, have you not? A Yes, sir.
Q Have you a younger child than Bettie? A No, sir, Bettie is the only child I have and she is now dead.
Q When did Bettie die? A Three weeks ago, on Tuesday.

---oooOOOooo---

I, D. C. Skaggs, on oath state that the above and foregoing is a full and true transcript of my stenographic notes as taken in said cause on said date.

D. C. Skaggs

Subscribed and sworn to before me this 16 day of Oct 1905.

Edw C Griesel
Notary Public.

_____

(The above testimony given again.)

_____

Applications for Enrollment of Creek Newborn
Act of 1905 Volume XII

BIRTH AFFIDAVIT.

DEPARTMENT OF THE INTERIOR.
COMMISSION TO THE FIVE CIVILIZED TRIBES.

IN RE APPLICATION FOR ENROLLMENT, as a citizen of the Creek Nation, of Bettie Fisher, born on the 2 day of July , 1902

Name of Father: Willie Fisher	a citizen of the Creek	Nation.
Name of Mother: Lucy Fisher	a citizen of the Creek	Nation.

Postoffice   Trenton, I.T.

AFFIDAVIT OF ATTENDING PHYSICIAN OR MID-WIFE.

UNITED STATES OF AMERICA, Indian Territory,
    Western   DISTRICT.

personally acquainted with
We, the undersigned   , a—, on oath state that I we are ^ attended on Mrs. Lucy Fisher , wife of Willie Fisher on the   day of   , 1 ; that there was born to her on July 2, 1901 said date a female   child; that said child was living March 4, 1905, and is said to have been named Bettie Fisher   her
                                                         Nellie x Timonthlubby
Witnesses To Mark: mark
 { DC Skaggs   his
   Alex Posey   Hullie x Proctor
                                                         mark
Subscribed and sworn to before me 7 day of October, 1905.

Drennan C Skaggs
Notary Public.

Applications for Enrollment of Creek Newborn
Act of 1905 Volume XII

DEPARTMENT OF THE INTERIOR.
COMMISSION TO THE FIVE CIVILIZED TRIBES.

In the matter of the death of Bettie Fisher a citizen of the Creek Nation, who formerly resided at or near Trenton , Ind. Ter., and died on the 19th day of September , 1905

AFFIDAVIT OF RELATIVE.

UNITED STATES OF AMERICA, Indian Territory,
Western DISTRICT.

I, Lucy Fisher , on oath state that I am about 38 years of age and a citizen by blood , of the Creek Nation; that my postoffice address is Trenton , Ind. Ter.; that I am the mother of Bettie Fisher who was a citizen, by blood , of the Creek Nation and that said Bettie Fisher died on the 19th day of September, 1905

                                                  her
                                        Lucy x Fisher
Witnesses To Mark: mark
   { DC Skaggs
     Alex Posey

Subscribed and sworn to before me this 7" day of October , 1905.

                                Drennan C Skaggs
                                Notary Public.

BIRTH AFFIDAVIT.
DEPARTMENT OF THE INTERIOR.
COMMISSION TO THE FIVE CIVILIZED TRIBES.

IN RE APPLICATION FOR ENROLLMENT, as a citizen of the Creek Nation, of Bettie Fisher , born on the 2 day of July , 1902

Name of Father: Willie Fisher   a citizen of the Creek Nation.
Hickory Ground
Name of Mother: Lucy Fisher   a citizen of the Creek Nation.
Okfuskee Canadian
                      Postoffice   Selumker[sic], I.T.

Applications for Enrollment of Creek Newborn
Act of 1905 Volume XII

AFFIDAVIT OF MOTHER.
Child present

UNITED STATES OF AMERICA, Indian Territory,
Western DISTRICT.

I, Lucy Fisher , on oath state that I am about 39 years of age and a citizen by blood , of the Creek Nation; that I am the lawful wife of Willie Fisher , who is a citizen, by blood of the Creek Nation; that a female child was born to me on 2 day of July , 1902 , that said child has been named Bettie Fisher , and is now living. and was living on March 4, 1905

             her
           Lucy x Fisher
Witnesses To Mark: mark
 DC Skaggs
 Alex Posey

Subscribed and sworn to before me this 29 day of May , 1905.

         Drennan C Skaggs
         Notary Public.

AFFIDAVIT OF ATTENDING PHYSICIAN OR MID-WIFE.

UNITED STATES OF AMERICA, Indian Territory,
Western DISTRICT.

                    my wife
I, Willie Fisher , a ~~(blank)~~ , on oath state that I attended on ^ Mrs. Lucy Fisher, ~~wife of~~ *(blank)* on the 2 day of July , 1902 ; that there was born to her on said date a female child; that said child is now living and was living on March 4, 1905 and is said to have been named Bettie Fisher

           Willie Fisher
Witnesses To Mark:
 {

Subscribed and sworn to before me this 29 day of May , 1905.

         Drennan C Skaggs
         Notary Public.

Applications for Enrollment of Creek Newborn
Act of 1905   Volume XII

NC 998

Muskogee, Indian Territory, October 23, 1905.

Lucy Fisher,
    Care Willie Fisher,
        Trenton,.

Dear Madam:

    In the matter of the application for the enrollment of your minor child, Bettie Fisher, born July 2, 1902, as a citizen by blood of the Creek Nation, this office is unable to identify you or your husband, Willie Fisher, on its final roll of citizens by blood of the Creek Nation; you are requested to state the names of the parents of both yourself and husband, the Creek Indian town to which you belong and your roll numbers as the same appear on your deeds and allotment certificates, also state your maiden name.

                Respectfully,
                          Commissioner.

NC-998

Muskogee, Indian Territory, December 16, 1905.

Lucy Fisher,
    Care of Willie Fisher,
        Trenton, Indian Territory.

Dear Madam:

    In the matter of the application for the enrollment of your minor child, Bettie Fisher, born July 2, 1902, as a citizen by blood of the Creek Nation, this Office is unable to identify you or your husband, Willie Fisher, on its final roll of citizens by blood of the Creek Nation. It is necessary that you be so identified before the right to enrollment of said child can be determined.

    You are requested to write this Office at an early date, giving your maiden name, the names of your parents and those of said Willie Fisher, the Creek Indian Town to which each of you belongs, and, if possible, your names and roll numbers as same appear on your respective allotment certificates or deeds to land in the Creek Nation.

                Respectfully,
                          Commissioner.

Applications for Enrollment of Creek Newborn
Act of 1905 Volume XII

#5 - C 1000

2448 B.

DEPARTMENT OF THE INTERIOR,
COMMISSION TO THE FIVE CIVILIZED TRIBES.
April 24, 1905.

In the matter of the application for the enrollment of certain new borns as citizens of the Creek Nation.

Alex Posey, being duly sworn, testified as follows:

By Commission:
Q What is your name, age and post office address? A Alex Posey, 31, Muskogee.
Q Are you a citizen of the Creek Nation? A Yes sir
Q Got your land, have you? A Yes sir.
Q You have been engaged recently in the field for the Dawes Commission securing evidence about Creek citizens or new borns? A Yes sir.
Q Have you a list of children for whom application could not be made and about whom you have succeeded in obtaining some information? A Yes sir.
Q You may state the conditions and the names of these children? You desire to make application for them? A Yes sir.
Q Name them.
A   July Proctor, Weogufky Town, Sukey Proctor, Weogufky Town, have two children --one about three years old and one about six months old. Post office, Hanna, Indian Territory.
        Jacob Bullet, about three years old. Parents: Maxey Bullet, Seminole, and Hannah Bullet, Hillabee. Post Office, Hannah, Indian Territory.
        Connie Hawkins, Hillabee Town, Sabella Hawkins, Okchiye, have two children-- one about three years old and a younger child. Post Office, Hanna, Indian Territory.
        Willie Fisher, Hickory Ground Town, Lussee Fisher, Okfusky[sic] Canadian Town, have two children--one about three years old and a baby. Post Office, Slumpker, Indian Territory.
        ✓ Lizzie Lasley, about three years old, Sam Lasley, born in either August or September, 1904. Parents: Sam Lasley, Okchiye, Wisey Lasley, Weogufky. Post Office, Hanna, Indian Territory.
        Jim Haynes (or Sangee), Okchiye Town, Folotkokee, Weogufky Town have a male child about three years old named Joe. Post Office, Hanna, Indian Territory.
        Taylor Foley, Weogufky, Melinda Foley, Okchiye, have a child about two years old. Post Office, Slumpker, Indian Territory.
        Phillip Lindsey, Tuckabatchee, Cilla Lindsey, Hillabee, have a child about three years old. Post Office, Hanna, Indian Territory.
        Big William (or William Thlocco), Okchiye Town, Cinda Williams, Weogufky Town, have two children -- one about three years old-- one born in February 1905. Post Office Hanna, Indian Territory.
        Freeland Lindsey, Tuckabatchee or Hillabee, Nancy Proctor, Tullahassoche, have a child about two years old. Post Office, Hanna, Indian Territory.

Applications for Enrollment of Creek Newborn
Act of 1905 Volume XII

Timonthluppy George, Weogufky Town, Nellie George, Pukon Tullahassee[sic], have a child about three years old. Post Office, Slumpker, Indian Territory.

Walter Simmons, Weogufky, Chippie Simmons, Pukon Tullahassee, have a child about one years old. Post Office, Hannah, Indian Territory.

Jacob Larney (or Green), Arbeka Tulledega Town, Bettie Larney, (or Green), Hillabee Town, have a child. Post Office, Hanna, Indian Territory.

John Hill, Okchiye, Millie Hill, Weogufky, have a child about three months old. Post Office, Hanna, Indian Territory.

Jim Pigeon, Okchiye Town, Jennie Pigeon, Okchiye Town, have a child about five months old. Post Office, Hanna, Indian Territory.

Thomas Deo, Okchiye Town, Nancy Deo, Fish Pond Town, have a child about three months old. Post Office, Hanna, Indian Territory.

Jack Buckner, born December 17, 1904. Parents: Wiley Buckner, Okchiye, Susie Buckner, Cussehta. Post Office, Hanna, Indian Territory.

Q This is the information you received from relatives right around there on April 24, 1905? A Yes sir.

Q Were you informed that the parents of these children were unwilling to make application for their enrollment? A Yes sir.

Q This was the only way that the rights of these children would be saved? A Yes sir. I made every effort to obtain direct information from the parents but in every instance they refused to give their testimony.

Lona Merrick being duly sworn, states that the above and foregoing is a true and correct transcript of his stenographic notes as taken in said cause on said date.

(Signed) Lona Merrick

Subscribed and sworn to before me this 9th day of May, 1905.

(Signed) Edw C Griesel
Notary Public.

I, Lona Merrick, solemnly swear that I copied the above testimony from the original on the 18th day of July, 1905, and that it is a true copy of same.

Lona Merrick

Subscribed and sworn to before me this 18th day of July, 1905.

Edw C Griesel
Notary Public.

Applications for Enrollment of Creek Newborn
Act of 1905   Volume XII

2448-B.

C 1000

DEPARTMENT OF THE INTERIOR,
COMMISSION TO THE FIVE CIVILIZED TRIBES.
Trenton, I. T., June 7, 1905.

In the matter of the application for the enrollment of Lizzie and Daniel Lasley as citizens by blood of the Creek Nation.

BARNEY GREEN, being duly sworn, testified as follows:

Through Alex Posey Official Interpreter:

BY COMMISSION:
Q What is your name? A Barney Green.
Q How old are you? A Forty-four.
Q What is your post office address? A Trenton.
Q Are you a citizen of the Creek Nation? A Yes, sir.
Q To what town do you belong? A Weogufke.
Q Do you know Sam and Wicey Lasley? A Yes, sir.
Q Are they members of your town? A Wicey is a member of my town but sam belongs to Okchiye.
Q Do you know their children, Lizzie and Daniel Lasley? A Yes, sir.
Q Do you know when Lizzie was born? A I do not know when the child was born but she is about three years old or a little over. She is not yet old enough to speak distinctly.
Q Are you positive that she is not four years old? A Yes, sir.
Q Do you know when Daniel was born? A He was born in either August or September, 1904.
Q Are both of these children living? A Yes, sir. They have two other children Minnie and Lula who have never been enrolled by the Commission. The parents were opposed to taking allotment. I appeared before the Commission at Muskogee and gave information about them but was advised that the parents would have to make the application and I let the matter drop. Minnie is about eleven years old and Lula is between six and seven years old.
Q When did you appear before the Commission? A I think it was sojetime[sic] in 1901. Wash Grayson, Indian Territory of Eufaula, Indian Territory interpreted for me. At that time I owned improvements on land in eccess[sic] of my allotment and wished to allot some of my kinsmen and town people on the improvements but when the commission informed me that it would be necessary for the parents to make the application I gave myself no further concern about the matter and the children have never been enrolled.

---oooOOOooo---

I, D. C. Skaggs, on oath state that the above and foregoing is a full and true transcript of my stenographic notes as taken in said cause on said date.

D. C. Skaggs

Applications for Enrollment of Creek Newborn
Act of 1905   Volume XII

Subscribed and sworn to before me this ___ day of JUL 17 1905 1905.

Edw C Griesel
Notary Public.

N.C. 1000   F.H.W.
DEPARTMENT OF THE INTERIOR,
COMMISSIONER TO THE FIVE CIVILIZED TRIBES.

In the matter of the application for the enrollment of Lizzie Lasley and Sam Lasley as citizens by blood of the Creek Nation.

DECISION.

The record in this case shows that on April 24, 1905, Alex Posey appeared before the Commission to the Five Civilized Tribes, at Muskogee, Indian Territory, and testifies in the matter of the application for the enrollment of certain new borns as citizens of the Creek Nation"[sic], in which testimony appears the following statement:

"Lizzie Lasley, about three years old, Sam Lasley, born in either August or September, 1904. Parents: Sam Lasley, Okchiye, Wisey Lasley, Weogufky. Post office, Hanna, Indian Territory."

Said statement is herein considered an original application for the enrollment of Lizzie and Sam Lasley as citizens by blood of the Creek Nation in order that the rights of the applicants be protected; their parents being affiliated with the Snake or disaffected faction of Creek Indians. Further proceedings were had on June 7, 1905, before a Creek enrollment field party at Trenton, Indian Territory.

The records of this office and the evidence in this case show that the applicants, Lizzie Lasley and Sam Lasley, are the children of Sam and Wisey Lasley; whose names appear on a partial schedule of citizens by blood of the Creek approved by the Secretary of the Interior March 28, 1902, opposite roll Nos. 8221 and 8222 respectively.

It further appears that the said Lizzie Lasley was born some time during the year 1902, that the applicant, Sam Lasley, was born in August or September, 1904, and that both were still living on the date of the last proceedings herein.

The Act of Congress approved March 3, 1905, (33 Stats. 1048) provides in part as follows:

"That the Commission to the Five Civilized Tribes is authorized for sixty days after the date of the approval of this act to receive and consider applications for enrollment, of children, born subsequent to May twenty-fifth, nineteen hundred and one, and prior to March fourth, nineteen hundred and five, and living on said latter date, to citizens of the Creek tribe of Indians whose enrollment has been approved by the Secretary of the Interior prior to the approval of this act; and to enroll and make allotments to such children."

Applications for Enrollment of Creek Newborn
Act of 1905 Volume XII

It is, therefore, ordered and adjudged that the said Lizzie Lasley and Sam Lasley are entitled to be enrolled as a citizens by blood of the Creek Nation, in accordance with the provisions of law above quoted, and the application for their enrollment as such is accordingly granted.

Tams Bixby COMMISSIONER.

Muskogee, Indian Territory,
[JAN 18 1907

N C 1000

Muskogee, Indian Territory, March 2, 1907.

Wisey Lasley,
    Care of Sam Lasley,
        Hanna, Indian Territory.

Dear Madam:

You are hereby advised that on March 2, 1907 the Secretary of the Interior approved the enrollment of your minor children, Lizzie and Sam Lasley, as citizens by blood of the Creek Nation, and that the names of said children appear upon the roll of new born citizens by blood of the Creek Nation enrolled under the Act of Congress approved March 3, 1905, as numbers 1241 and 2142[sic] respectively.

These children are now entitled to allotments and application therefor should be made without delay at the Creek Land Office, Muskogee, Indian Territory.

Respectfully,
Commissioner.

#6 - C 1002

2448 B.

DEPARTMENT OF THE INTERIOR,
COMMISSION TO THE FIVE CIVILIZED TRIBES.
April 24, 1905.

In the matter of the application for the enrollment of certain new borns as citizens of the Creek Nation.

Applications for Enrollment of Creek Newborn
Act of 1905 Volume XII

Alex Posey, being duly sworn, testified as follows:

By Commission:
Q What is your name, age and post office address? A Alex Posey, 31, Muskogee.
Q Are you a citizen of the Creek Nation? A Yes sir
Q Got your land, have you? A Yes sir.
Q You have been engaged recently in the field for the Dawes Commission securing evidence about Creek citizens or new borns? A Yes sir.
Q Have you a list of children for whom application could not be made and about whom you have succeeded in obtaining some information? A Yes sir.
Q You may state the conditions and the names of these children? You desire to make application for them? A Yes sir.
Q Name them.
A   July Proctor, Weogufky Town, Sukey Proctor, Weogufky Town, have two children --one about three years old and one about six months old. Post office, Hanna, Indian Territory.

Jacob Bullet, about three years old. Parents: Maxey Bullet, Seminole, and Hannah Bullet, Hillabee. Post Office, Hannah, Indian Territory.

Connie Hawkins, Hillabee Town, Sabella Hawkins, Okchiye, have two children-- one about three years old and a younger child. Post Office, Hanna, Indian Territory.

Willie Fisher, Hickory Ground Town, Lussee Fisher, Okfusky[sic] Canadian Town, have two children--one about three years old and a baby. Post Office, Slumpker, Indian Territory.

Lizzie Lasley, about three years old, Sam Lasley, born in either August or September, 1904. Parents: Sam Lasley, Okchiye, Wisey Lasley, Weogufky. Post Office, Hanna, Indian Territory.

✓ Jim Haynes (or Sangee), Okchiye Town, Folotkokee, Weogufky Town have a male child about three years old named Joe. Post Office, Hanna, Indian Territory.

Taylor Foley, Weogufky, Melinda Foley, Okchiye, have a child about two years old. Post Office, Slumpker, Indian Territory.

Phillip Lindsey, Tuckabatchee, Cilla Lindsey, Hillabee, have a child about three years old. Post Office, Hanna, Indian Territory.

Big William (or William Thlocco), Okchiye Town, Cinda Williams, Weogufky Town, have two children -- one about three years old-- one born in February 1905. Post Office Hanna, Indian Territory.

Freeland Lindsey, Tuckabatchee or Hillabee, Nancy Proctor, Tullahassoche, have a child about two years old. Post Office, Hanna, Indian Territory.

Timonthluppy George, Weogufky Town, Nellie George, Pukon Tullahassee[sic], have a child about three years old. Post Office, Slumpker, Indian Territory.

Walter Simmons, Weogufky, Chippie Simmons, Pukon Tullahassee, have a child about one years old. Post Office, Hannah, Indian Territory.

Jacob Larney (or Green), Arbeka Tulledega Town, Bettie Larney, (or Green), Hillabee Town, have a child. Post Office, Hanna, Indian Territory.

John Hill, Okchiye, Millie Hill, Weogufky, have a child about three months old. Post Office, Hanna, Indian Territory.

Jim Pigeon, Okchiye Town, Jennie Pigeon, Okchiye Town, have a child about five months old. Post Office, Hanna, Indian Territory.

Applications for Enrollment of Creek Newborn
Act of 1905   Volume XII

     Thomas Deo, Okchiye Town, Nancy Deo, Fish Pond Town, have a child about three months old. Post Office, Hanna, Indian Territory.
     Jack Buckner, born December 17, 1904. Parents: Wiley Buckner, Okchiye, Susie Buckner, Cussehta. Post Office, Hanna, Indian Territory.
Q This is the information you received from relatives right around there on April 24, 1905? A Yes sir.
Q Were you informed that the parents of these children were unwilling to make application for their enrollment? A Yes sir.
Q This was the only way that the rights of these children would be saved? A Yes sir. I made every effort to obtain direct information from the parents but in every instance they refused to give their testimony.

     Lona Merrick being duly sworn, states that the above and foregoing is a true and correct transcript of his stenographic notes as taken in said cause on said date.

                         (Signed) Lona Merrick

Subscribed and sworn to before me this 9th day of May, 1905.

                         (Signed) Edw C Griesel
                                  Notary Public.

     I, Lona Merrick, solemnly swear that I copied the above testimony from the original on the 18th day of July, 1905, and that it is a true copy of same.

                              Lona Merrick

Subscribed and sworn to before me this 18th day of July, 1905.

                             Edw C Griesel
                                  Notary Public.

BIRTH AFFIDAVIT.

DEPARTMENT OF THE INTERIOR.
COMMISSION TO THE FIVE CIVILIZED TRIBES.

     IN RE APPLICATION FOR ENROLLMENT, as a citizen of the Creek Nation, of Joseph Haines, born on the 30 day of November , 1904

Name of Father: Jim Haines (or Yahola Fixico)   a citizen of the   Creek   Nation.
Okchiye Town
Name of Mother: Folothoka Haines   a citizen of the   Creek   Nation.
Weogufke Town
                        Postoffice   Hanna, I.T.

Applications for Enrollment of Creek Newborn
Act of 1905   Volume XII

Child present
AFFIDAVIT OF MOTHER.

UNITED STATES OF AMERICA, Indian Territory, }
   Western   DISTRICT.

    I, Folothoka Haines , on oath state that I am about 28 years of age and a citizen by blood , of the Creek Nation; that I am the lawful wife of Jim Haines , who is a citizen, by blood of the Creek Nation; that a male child was born to me on 30 day of November , 1904 , that said child has been named Joseph Haines , and is now living. and was living March 4, 1905

                                          her
Witnesses To Mark: Folothoka x Haines
  { DC Skaggs   mark
  { Alex Posey

    Subscribed and sworn to before me this 31 day of May , 1905.

                         Drennan C Skaggs
                         Notary Public.

AFFIDAVIT OF ATTENDING PHYSICIAN OR MID-WIFE.

UNITED STATES OF AMERICA, Indian Territory, }
   Western   DISTRICT.

                                                              my wife
    I, Jim Haines (or Yahola Fixico) , ~~a (blank)~~ , on oath state that I attended on ^ Mrs. Folothoka Haines , ~~wife of~~ (blank) on the 30 day of November , 1904 ; that there was born to her on said date a male child; that said child is now living and was living March 4, 1905 and is said to have been named Joseph Haines

                                       his
Witnesses To Mark: Jim x Haines
  { DC Skaggs   mark
  { Alex Posey

    Subscribed and sworn to before me this 31 day of May , 1905.

                         Drennan C Skaggs
                         Notary Public.

Applications for Enrollment of Creek Newborn
Act of 1905 Volume XII

Western District
Indian Territory   SS

    We, the undersigned, on oath state that we are personally acquainted with Folothoker[sic] Fixico   wife of   Yarhola Fixico   ; and that on or about the 30 day of Nov 1903 , a   male   child was born to them and has been named   Joseph Fixico   ; that said child was living March 4, 1905.

    We further state that we have no interest in the above case.

                                    Geo Simmons

Witness to mark: Jackson Bruner

_____
_____
_____
_____

Subscribed and sworn to before
me this 28 day of Nov 1906.
                                    J McDermott
My Com Exp
July 25" 1907

_____

BIRTH AFFIDAVIT.
DEPARTMENT OF THE INTERIOR.
COMMISSION TO THE FIVE CIVILIZED TRIBES.

_____

    IN RE APPLICATION FOR ENROLLMENT, as a citizen of the Creek Nation, of Joseph Fixico, born on the 30 day of Nov , 1903

Name of Father: Yarholar Fixico   a citizen of the   Creek   Nation.
Name of Mother: Folothoka Fixico   a citizen of the   Creek   Nation.

                        Postoffice   Trenton I.T.

_____

                    AFFIDAVIT OF MOTHER.

UNITED STATES OF AMERICA, Indian Territory,
    Western   DISTRICT.

    I, Folothoka Fixico , on oath state that I am   about 29   years of age and a citizen by blood , of the Creek Nation; that I am the lawful wife of Yarholar Fixico , who is a citizen, by blood of the Creek Nation; that a male child was born to me on

Applications for Enrollment of Creek Newborn
Act of 1905 Volume XII

30 day of November, 1903, that said child has been named Joseph Fixico, and was living March 4, 1905 and is now living her

                                       Folothoka x Fixico

Witnesses To Mark: mark
  { J McDermott
    Jim Cantrell

    Subscribed and sworn to before me this 28" day of November, 1906.

My Com Exp   J McDermott
July 25" 1907   Notary Public.

REFER IN REPLY TO THE FOLLOWING:
N. C. 1002.

DEPARTMENT OF THE INTERIOR,
COMMISSIONER TO THE FIVE CIVILIZED TRIBES.

                          Dustin, Indian Territory, November 28, 1906.

Commissioner to the Five Civilized Tribes,
    Muskogee, Indian Territory.

Dear Sir:

    There are herewith enclosed copies of record in the matter of the application for the enrollment of Joseph Fixeco[sic] as a citizen by blood of the Creek Nation together with an affidavit of the mother corroborated by the affidavits of two disinterested witnesses that the said child was born November 30, 1903. The original affidavit on file shows the date of birth November 30, 1904.

                              Respectfully,
                              Jesse McDermott

N. C. 1002.   F.H.W.
                                                                                A.G.

                    DEPARTMENT OF THE INTERIOR,
        COMMISSIONER TO THE FIVE CIVILIZED TRIBES.

    In the matter of the application for the enrollment of Joseph Fixeco as a citizen by blood of the Creek Nation.

                                    D E C I S I O N.

    The record in this case shows that on April 24, 1905, Alex Posey appeared before the Commission to the Five Civilized Tribes and gave testimony "in the matter of the

Applications for Enrollment of Creek Newborn
Act of 1905   Volume XII

application for the enrollment of certain new borns as citizens of the Creek Nation", in which testimony appears the following statement:

> "Jim Haynes (or Sangee), Okchiye, Folothokee, Weogufky Town have a male child about three years old named Joe. Post office, Hanna, Indian Territory."

The said statement is herein considered an original application for the enrollment of Joseph Fixeco as a citizen by blood of the Creek Nation; the father (Jim Haynes) being subsequently identified on the Creek Indian roll as Yarhola Fixeco.

Supplemental affidavits as to the birth of the applicant filed May 30, 1905 and November 30, 1906, are attached to and made a part of the record herein.

The evidence and the records of this office show that the applicant, Joseph Fixeco and Joe Haynes are one and the same and that the said Joseph Fixeco is the child of Yarhola Fixeco and "Foluthoker", whose names appear on a partial schedule of citizens by blood of the Creek Nation approved by the Secretary of the Interior March 28, 1902, opposite roll Nos. 8209 and 7881 respectively.

It further appears from the weight of the evidence that the said Joseph Fixeco was born November 30, 1903, and was still living November 28, 1906.

The Act of Congress approved March 3, 1905, (33 Stats. 1048) provides in part as follows:

> "That the Commission to the Five Civilized Tribes is authorized for sixty days after the date of the approval of this act to receive and consider applications for enrollment, of children, born subsequent to May twenty-fifth, nineteen hundred and one, and prior to March fourth, nineteen hundred and five, and living on said latter date, to citizens of the Creek tribe of Indians whose enrollment has been approved by the Secretary of the Interior prior to the approval of this act; and to enroll and make allotments to such children."

It is, therefore, ordered and adjudged that the said Joseph Fixeco is entitled to be enrolled as a citizen by blood of the Creek Nation, in accordance with the provisions of law above quoted, and the application for his enrollment as such is accordingly granted.

Tams Bixby   Commissioner.

Muskogee, Indian Territory,
JAN 24 1907

Applications for Enrollment of Creek Newborn
Act of 1905   Volume XII

BIRTH AFFIDAVIT.

DEPARTMENT OF THE INTERIOR.
COMMISSION TO THE FIVE CIVILIZED TRIBES.

IN RE APPLICATION FOR ENROLLMENT, as a citizen of the Creek Nation, of Joseph Haines, born on the 30 day of November, 1904

Name of Father: Jim Haines Okchiye   a citizen of the Creek Nation.
Name of Mother: Folothoka Haines Weogufke   a citizen of the Creek Nation.

Postoffice   Hanna, I.T.

AFFIDAVIT OF MOTHER.

UNITED STATES OF AMERICA, Indian Territory, } Child present
Western   DISTRICT.

I, Folothoka Haines, on oath state that I am about 28 years of age and a citizen by blood, of the Creek Nation; that I am the lawful wife of Jim Haines, who is a citizen, by blood of the Creek Nation; that a male child was born to me on 30 day of November, 1904, that said child has been named Joseph Haines, and is now living. and was living March 4, 1905

                         her
              Folothoka x Haines

Witnesses To Mark: mark
{ DC Skaggs
   Alex Posey

Subscribed and sworn to before me this 31 day of May, 1905.

                 Drennan C Skaggs
                 Notary Public.

AFFIDAVIT OF ATTENDING PHYSICIAN OR MID-WIFE.

UNITED STATES OF AMERICA, Indian Territory, }
Western   DISTRICT.

                                                             my wife

I, Jim Haines (or Yahola Fixico), a *(blank)*, on oath state that I attended on ^ Mrs. Folothoka Haines, ~~wife of~~ *(blank)* on the 30 day of November, 1904; that there was born to her on said date a male child; that said child is now living and was living March 4, 1905 and is said to have been named Joseph Haines

                      his
             Jim x Haines
                mark

Applications for Enrollment of Creek Newborn
Act of 1905   Volume XII

Witnesses To Mark:
   { DC Skaggs
     Alex Posey

    Subscribed and sworn to before me this 31 day of May, 1905.

                                Drennan C Skaggs
                                Notary Public.

NC 1002.

                          Muskogee, Indian Territory, October 23, 1905.

Foluthoker Fixeco (or Jim Haines),
    Hanna, Indian Territory.

Dear Madam:

    In the matter pf[sic] the application for the enrollment of your minor child, Joseph Haines, born November 30, 1904, you state in your affidavit executed May 31, 1905, that the father of said child is name[sic] Jim Haines or Yahola Fixico, that you are the lawful wife of said Jim Haines or Yahola Fixico; and your name is signed to the Affidavit Folothoka Haines.

    Your said husband has been identified on the final roll of citizens by blood of the Creek Nation as Yarhola Fixico and you have been identified on said roll as Foluthoker Fixeco.

    If you are, as stated, the lawful wife of said Yarhola Fixeco it necessarily follows that the correct surname of yourself and of said child is also Fixeco.

    There is herewith enclosed a borm[sic] of birth affidavit properly filled out and you are requested to execute same before a notary public, being careful that he affixes his name and notarial seal and return to this office in the enclosed envelope.

    This office desires affidavit of the midwife or physician in attendance at the birth of said child.

    In the event that there was no physician or midwife in attendance when said child was born, it will be necessary for you to furnish this office with the affidavits of two disinterested witnesses relative to his birth. Said affidavits must set forth said child's name, the date of his birth, the names of his parents and whether or not he was living on March 4, 1905.

                      Respectfully,
                                    Commissioner.

Applications for Enrollment of Creek Newborn
Act of 1905   Volume XII

N C 1002.

Muskogee, Indian Territory, March 7, 1907.

Foluthoker Fixeco,
  Care of Yarhola Fixeco,
    Hanna, Indian Territory.

Dear Madam:

You are hereby advised that on March 2, 1907 the Secretary of the Interior approved the enrollment of your minor child, Joseph Fixeco, as a citizen by blood of the Creek Nation, and that the name of said child appears upon the roll of citizens by blood of the Creek Nation enrolled under the Act of Congress approved March 3, 1905, as number 1243.

This child is now entitled to allotment and application therefor should be made without delay at the Creek Land Office, Muskogee, Indian Territory.

Respectfully,
Commissioner.

#7 - C 1003

2448 B.

DEPARTMENT OF THE INTERIOR,
COMMISSION TO THE FIVE CIVILIZED TRIBES.
April 24, 1905.

In the matter of the application for the enrollment of certain new borns as citizens of the Creek Nation.

Alex Posey, being duly sworn, testified as follows:

By Commission:
Q What is your name, age and post office address? A Alex Posey, 31, Muskogee.
Q Are you a citizen of the Creek Nation? A Yes sir
Q Got your land, have you? A Yes sir.
Q You have been engaged recently in the field for the Dawes Commission securing evidence about Creek citizens or new borns? A Yes sir.

Applications for Enrollment of Creek Newborn
Act of 1905   Volume XII

Q Have you a list of children for whom application could not be made and about whom you have succeeded in obtaining some information? A Yes sir.
Q You may state the conditions and the names of these children? You desire to make application for them? A Yes sir.
Q Name them.
A   July Proctor, Weogufky Town, Sukey Proctor, Weogufky Town, have two children --one about three years old and one about six months old. Post office, Hanna, Indian Territory.
    Jacob Bullet, about three years old. Parents: Maxey Bullet, Seminole, and Hannah Bullet, Hillabee. Post Office, Hannah, Indian Territory.
    Connie Hawkins, Hillabee Town, Sabella Hawkins, Okchiye, have two children--one about three years old and a younger child. Post Office, Hanna, Indian Territory.
    Willie Fisher, Hickory Ground Town, Lussee Fisher, Okfusky[sic] Canadian Town, have two children--one about three years old and a baby. Post Office, Slumpker, Indian Territory.
    Lizzie Lasley, about three years old, Sam Lasley, born in either August or September, 1904. Parents: Sam Lasley, Okchiye, Wisey Lasley, Weogufky. Post Office, Hanna, Indian Territory.
    Jim Haynes (or Sangee), Okchiye Town, Folotkokee, Weogufky Town have a male child about three years old named Joe. Post Office, Hanna, Indian Territory.
    ✓Taylor Foley, Weogufky, Melinda Foley, Okchiye, have a child about two years old. Post Office, Slumpker, Indian Territory.
    Phillip Lindsey, Tuckabatchee, Cilla Lindsey, Hillabee, have a child about three years old. Post Office, Hanna, Indian Territory.
    Big William (or William Thlocco), Okchiye Town, Cinda Williams, Weogufky Town, have two children -- one about three years old-- one born in February 1905. Post Office Hanna, Indian Territory.
    Freeland Lindsey, Tuckabatchee or Hillabee, Nancy Proctor, Tullahassoche, have a child about two years old. Post Office, Hanna, Indian Territory.
    Timonthluppy George, Weogufky Town, Nellie George, Pukon Tullahassee[sic], have a child about three years old. Post Office, Slumpker, Indian Territory.
    Walter Simmons, Weogufky, Chippie Simmons, Pukon Tullahassee, have a child about one years old. Post Office, Hannah, Indian Territory.
    Jacob Larney (or Green), Arbeka Tulledega Town, Bettie Larney, (or Green), Hillabee Town, have a child. Post Office, Hanna, Indian Territory.
    John Hill, Okchiye, Millie Hill, Weogufky, have a child about three months old. Post Office, Hanna, Indian Territory.
    Jim Pigeon, Okchiye Town, Jennie Pigeon, Okchiye Town, have a child about five months old. Post Office, Hanna, Indian Territory.
    Thomas Deo, Okchiye Town, Nancy Deo, Fish Pond Town, have a child about three months old. Post Office, Hanna, Indian Territory.
    Jack Buckner, born December 17, 1904. Parents: Wiley Buckner, Okchiye, Susie Buckner, Cussehta. Post Office, Hanna, Indian Territory.
Q This is the information you received from relatives right around there on April 24, 1905? A Yes sir.
Q Were you informed that the parents of these children were unwilling to make application for their enrollment? A Yes sir.

Applications for Enrollment of Creek Newborn
Act of 1905 Volume XII

Q This was the only way that the rights of these children would be saved? A Yes sir. I made every effort to obtain direct information from the parents but in every instance they refused to give their testimony.

    Lona Merrick being duly sworn, states that the above and foregoing is a true and correct transcript of his stenographic notes as taken in said cause on said date.

                             (Signed) Lona Merrick

Subscribed and sworn to before me this 9th day of May, 1905.

                             (Signed) Edw C Griesel
                                         Notary Public.

    I, Lona Merrick, solemnly swear that I copied the above testimony from the original on the 18th day of July, 1905, and that it is a true copy of same.

                                     Lona Merrick

Subscribed and sworn to before me this 18th day of July, 1905.

                                    Edw C Griesel
                                         Notary Public.

N.C. 1003.

                    DEPARTMENT OF THE INTERIOR,
            COMMISSIONER TO THE FIVE CIVILIZED TRIBES.
              Near Hanna, Indian Territory, January 24, 1907.

    In the matter of the application for the enrollment of Arney Foley, as a citizen by blood of the Creek Nation.
    JOHN W. MOORS, being duly sworn, by J. McDermott, a notary public, testified as follows:

BY THE COMMISSIONER:

Q What is your name? A John W. Moore.
Q What is your age? A About 40.
Q What is your postoffice address? A Trenton, Indian Territory.
Q Are you a Creek citizen? A No sir, my family is.
Q Do you know Taylor Foley? A Yes sir.
Q Do you know his wife Melinda Foley? A Yes sir, when she is at home, she stays at that little house right down there. (Indicating a log house near by)

Applications for Enrollment of Creek Newborn
Act of 1905   Volume XII

Q The Field Party has just made a visit to the house and no one there; where do you suppose the family has gone? A If they are not at home, I can't tell you where they are.
Q Do you know Melinda's maiden name? A No sir, I do not.
Q Do you know the name of her mother? A No sir, her mother died when she small child I am told.
Q Do you know the name of her father? A Metup Heneha is what they call him round here.
Q What Creek Indian Town is Melinda a member of? A Okchiye.
Q Do you know a child of hers named Arney? A Yes, she has a child that appears to be about four or five years old. I do not know anything about when it was born but it is the same child that she had when she and Taylor were living together.
Q Are you any relations of theirs? A no sir, just my neighbors.

I, Jesse McDermott, on oath state that the above and foregoing is a full and true transcript of my notes as taken in said cause on said date.

Jesse McDermott

Subscribed and sworn to before me, this 25 day of January, 1907.

W.R. Blake
Notary Public.

NC 1003.   OCH

DEPARTMENT OF THE INTERIOR,
COMMISSIONER TO THE FIVE CIVILIZED TRIBES.

In the matter of the application for the enrollment of Arney Foley, as a citizen by blood of the Creek Nation.

DECISION.

The record in this case shows that on April 24, 1905, application was made for the enrollment of "certain new borns as citizens of the Creek Nation", embracing "a child about two years old" of Taylor Foley and Melinda Foley.
The record further shows that on May 31, 1905, application was made, in affidavit form, for the enrollment of Arney Foley, as a citizen by blood of the Creek Nation, the minor child of Taylor Foley and Melindy Foley.
It appearing that the child first above referred to and Arney Foley is the same person, the proceeding had on April 24, 1905, is herein considered an original application for the enrollment of said Arney Foley, as a citizen by blood of the Creek Nation. Supplemental affidavit as to the date of birth of said child was filed January 24, 1907. Further proceedings were had on the date last mentioned.
The evidence in this case shows that said Arney Foley is the minor child of Melinda Foley and Taylor Foley, whose names appear as "Melinda" and "Taylor Foley"

Applications for Enrollment of Creek Newborn
Act of 1905   Volume XII

respectively, upon a schedule of citizens by blood of the Creek Nation, approved by the Secretary of the Interior March 28, 1902, opposite numbers 8210 and 7836, respectively.

The evidence further shows that said Arney Foley was born July 9, 1902, and was living March 4, 1905.

It is, therefore, ordered and adjudged that the said Arney Foley is entitled to be enrolled as a citizen by blood of the Creek Nation, in accordance with the provisions of law above quoted, and the application for her enrollment as such is accordingly granted.

Tams Bixby   COMMISSIONER.

Muskogee, Indian Territory,
FEB 5- 1907

2448 B.
DEPARTMENT OF THE INTERIOR,
COMMISSION TO THE FIVE CIVILIZED TRIBES.
APRIL 24, 1905.

In the matter of the application for the enrollment of certain new borns as citizens of the Creek Nation.

Alex Posey, being duly sworn, testified as follows:

Statement: Taylor Foley, Weogufky, Melinda Foley, Okchiye, have a child about two years old. Post Office, Slumpker, Indian Territory.

Phillip Lindsey, Tuckabctehee[sic], Cilla Lindsey, Hillabee, have a child about three years old. Post Office, Hanna, Indian Territory.

BIRTH AFFIDAVIT.
DEPARTMENT OF THE INTERIOR.
COMMISSION TO THE FIVE CIVILIZED TRIBES.

IN RE APPLICATION FOR ENROLLMENT, as a citizen of the Creek Nation, of Arney Foley, born on the 9 day of July , 1902

Name of Father: Taylor Foley Weog[sic]   a citizen of the   Creek   Nation.
Name of Mother: Melinda Proctor (nee Foley) Okchiye   a citizen of the   "   Nation.

Postoffice   Hanna IT

Applications for Enrollment of Creek Newborn
Act of 1905   Volume XII

AFFIDAVIT OF MOTHER.

UNITED STATES OF AMERICA, Indian Territory, ⎫
    Western   DISTRICT.   ⎬   Child present

I, Melindy Proctor , on oath state that I am about 22 years of age and a citizen by blood , of the Creek Nation; that I ~~am~~ was formerly the lawful wife of Taylor Foley , who is a citizen, by blood of the Creek Nation; that a female child was born to me on 9 day of July , 1902 , that said child has been named Arney Foley , and was living March 4, 1905.

                                    her
                            Melindy x Proctor
Witnesses To Mark: mark
  { DC Skaggs
    Alex Posey

Subscribed and sworn to before me this 31 day of May , 1905.

                              Drennan C Skaggs
                              Notary Public.

AFFIDAVIT OF ATTENDING PHYSICIAN OR MID-WIFE.

UNITED STATES OF AMERICA, Indian Territory, ⎫
    Western   DISTRICT.   ⎬

                              was present with
I, Matup Heneha , ~~a—~~, on oath state that I ~~attended on~~ Mrs. Melindy Proctor , former wife of Taylor Foley on the 9 day of July , 1902 ; that there was born to her on said date a female child; that said child was living March 4, 1905, and is said to have been named Arney Foley   his
                            Matup x Heneha
Witnesses To Mark: mark
  { DC Skaggs
    Alex Posey

Subscribed and sworn to before me 31 day of May, 1905.

                              Drennan C Skaggs
                              Notary Public.

(The above Birth Affidavit given again.)

Applications for Enrollment of Creek Newborn
Act of 1905   Volume XII

AFFIDAVIT OF DISINTERESTED WITNESS.

UNITED STATES OF AMERICA,
Western DISTRICT,   SS
INDIAN TERRITORY.

We, the undersigned, on oath state that we are personally acquainted with Melinda Foley the wife of Taylor Foley ; that there was born to her a female child on or about the 9" day of July 1902 ; that the said child has been named Arney Foley , and was living March 4, 1906.

We further state that we have no interest in the above case.

Witnesses: Jesse McDermott
              Jesse McDermott
              R.B. Selvidge
              R.B. Selvidge   her
                                       Sallie x Bruner
                                            mark
                                             her
                                       Millie x Bullett
                                            mark

Subscribed and sworn to before me this 24 day of January, 1907.

My Commission   J McDermott
Expires July 25" 1907   Notary Public.

NC 1003.

Muskogee, Indian Territory, October 23, 1905.

Melindy Proctor,
      Hanna, Indian Territory.

Dear Madam:

In the matter of the application for the enrollment of your minor child, Arney Foley, born July 9, 1902, as a citizen by blood of the Creek Nation, this office is unable to identify you on its final roll of citizens by blood of the Creek Nation under the name of Melindy Proctor or Melindy Foley.

You are requested to state your maiden name, the names of your parents, the Creek Indian town to which you belong and your roll number as same appears on your deeds and allotment certificate.

Respectfully,
                                           Commissioner.

Applications for Enrollment of Creek Newborn
Act of 1905   Volume XII

N C 1003.

Muskogee, Indian Territory, March 7, 1907.

Melindy Foley,
    Care of Thomas Red,
        Hanna, Indian Territory.

Dear Madam:

    You are hereby advised that on March 2, 1907 the Secretary of the Interior approved the enrollment of your minor child, Arney Foley, as a citizen by blood of the Creek Nation, and that the name of said child appears upon the roll of citizens by blood of the Creek Nation enrolled under the Act of Congress approved March 3, 1905, as number 1244.

    This child is now entitled to allotment and application therefor should be made without delay at the Creek Land Office, Muskogee, Indian Territory.

                Respectfully,

                                  Commissioner.

                                2448. B

                COPY.   #8 - C 1004

DEPARTMENT OF THE INTERIOR,
COMMISSION TO THE FIVE CIVILIZED TRIBES.
April 24, 1905.

    In the matter of the application for the enrollment of certain new borns as citizens of the Creek Nation.

    Alex Posey, being duly sworn, testified as follows:

By Commission:
Q What is your name, age and post office address? A Alex Posey, 31, Muskogee.
Q Are you a citizen of the Creek Nation? A Yes sir
Q Got your land, have you? A Yes sir.
Q You have been engaged recently in the field for the Dawes Commission securing evidence about Creek citizens or new borns? A Yes sir.

Applications for Enrollment of Creek Newborn
Act of 1905   Volume XII

Q Have you a list of children for whom application could not be made and about whom you have succeeded in obtaining some information? A Yes sir.
Q You may state the conditions and the names of these children? You desire to make application for them? A Yes sir.
Q Name them.
A   July Proctor, Weogufky Town, Sukey Proctor, Weogufky Town, have two children --one about three years old and one about six months old. Post office, Hanna, Indian Territory.

Jacob Bullet, about three years old. Parents: Maxey Bullet, Seminole, and Hannah Bullet, Hillabee. Post Office, Hannah, Indian Territory.

Connie Hawkins, Hillabee Town, Sabella Hawkins, Okchiye, have two children-- one about three years old and a younger child. Post Office, Hanna, Indian Territory.

Willie Fisher, Hickory Ground Town, Lussee Fisher, Okfusky[sic] Canadian Town, have two children--one about three years old and a baby. Post Office, Slumpker, Indian Territory.

Lizzie Lasley, about three years old, Sam Lasley, born in either August or September, 1904. Parents: Sam Lasley, Okchiye, Wisey Lasley, Weogufky. Post Office, Hanna, Indian Territory.

Jim Haynes (or Sangee), Okchiye Town, Folotkokee, Weogufky Town have a male child about three years old named Joe. Post Office, Hanna, Indian Territory.

Taylor Foley, Weogufky, Melinda Foley, Okchiye, have a child about two years old. Post Office, Slumpker, Indian Territory.

✓ Phillip Lindsey, Tuckabatchee, Cilla Lindsey, Hillabee, have a child about three years old. Post Office, Hanna, Indian Territory.

Big William (or William Thlocco), Okchiye Town, Cinda Williams, Weogufky Town, have two children -- one about three years old-- one born in February 1905. Post Office Hanna, Indian Territory.

Freeland Lindsey, Tuckabatchee or Hillabee, Nancy Proctor, Tullahassoche, have a child about two years old. Post Office, Hanna, Indian Territory.

Timonthluppy George, Weogufky Town, Nellie George, Pukon Tullahassee[sic], have a child about three years old. Post Office, Slumpker, Indian Territory.

Walter Simmons, Weogufky, Chippie Simmons, Pukon Tullahassee, have a child about one years old. Post Office, Hannah, Indian Territory.

Jacob Larney (or Green), Arbeka Tulledega Town, Bettie Larney, (or Green), Hillabee Town, have a child. Post Office, Hanna, Indian Territory.

John Hill, Okchiye, Millie Hill, Weogufky, have a child about three months old. Post Office, Hanna, Indian Territory.

Jim Pigeon, Okchiye Town, Jennie Pigeon, Okchiye Town, have a child about five months old. Post Office, Hanna, Indian Territory.

Thomas Deo, Okchiye Town, Nancy Deo, Fish Pond Town, have a child about three months old. Post Office, Hanna, Indian Territory.

Jack Buckner, born December 17, 1904. Parents: Wiley Buckner, Okchiye, Susie Buckner, Cussehta. Post Office, Hanna, Indian Territory.
Q This is the information you received from relatives right around there on April 24, 1905? A Yes sir.
Q Were you informed that the parents of these children were unwilling to make application for their enrollment? A Yes sir.

Applications for Enrollment of Creek Newborn
Act of 1905   Volume XII

Q This was the only way that the rights of these children would be saved? A Yes sir. I made every effort to obtain direct information from the parents but in every instance they refused to give their testimony.

  Lona Merrick being duly sworn, states that the above and foregoing is a true and correct transcript of his stenographic notes as taken in said cause on said date.

            (Signed) Lona Merrick

Subscribed and sworn to before me this 9th day of May, 1905.

            (Signed) Edw C Griesel
Seal.   Notary Public.

  I, Lona Merrick, solemnly swear that I copied the above testimony from the original on the 18th day of July, 1905, and that it is a true copy of same.

              Lona Merrick

Subscribed and sworn to before me this 18th day of July, 1905.

            Edw C Griesel
            Notary Public.

                N C 1004
No. 2448.
      DEPARTMENT OF THE INTERIOR,
    COMMISSION TO THE FIVE CIVILIZED TRIBES.
        Hanna, I. T., May 31, 1905.

  In the matter of the application for the enrollment of a minor child of Phillip and Cilla Lindsey as a citizen by blood of the Creek Nation.

    LEWIS LINDSEY, being duly sworn, testified as follows

  Through Alex Posey Official Interpreter:

  BY COMMISSION:
Q What is your name? A Lewis Lindsey.
Q How old are you? A About eighteen.
Q What is your post office address? A Hanna.
Q Are you a citizen of the Creek Nation? A Yes, sir.
Q to[sic] what town do you belong? A Tuckabatche.
Q Do you know Phillip and Cilla Lindsey? A Yes, sir.
Q What relation are they to you? A Phillip is my father and Cilla is my step-mother.
Q Have they a child born since May 25, 1901? A They have a girl na[sic] named Tosa.

Applications for Enrollment of Creek Newborn
Act of 1905   Volume XII

Q When was Tosa born? A I do not know.
Q How old is the child? A About seven years old.
Q Have they a younger child than Tosa? A No, sir, she is the youngest child they have.
Q Are you positive that Tosa is seen years old? A Yes, sir.

---oooOOOooo---

I, D. C. Skaggs, on oath state that the above and foregoing is a full and true transcript of my stenographic notes as taken in said cause on said date.

D. C. Skaggs

Subscribed and sworn to before me this ___ day of JUL 17 1905 1905.

Edw C Griesel
Notary Public.

NC 1004

WSC
JCL

DEPARTMENT OF THE INTERIOR,
COMMISSIONER TO THE FIVE CIVILIZED TRIBES.

In the matter of the application for the enrollment of Tosa Lindsey as a citizen by blood of the Creek Nation.

DECISION.

The record in this case shows that on April 24, 1905, the testimony of Alex Posey was taken by this office, "in the matter of the application for the enrollment of certain new borns as citizens of the Creek Nation" and that in said proceeding the said Alex Posey testified that Phillip Lindsey and Cilla Lindsey had a child about three years old. Said action is considered as an original application for the enrollment of said child. Further proceedings were had on May 31, 1905.

In the proceedings had on May 31, 1905, Lewis Lindsey a son of the aforesaid Phillip Lindsey, testified that his father and his step-mother, Cilla Lindsey had a girl child named Tosa, who was about seven years old on the date of said proceeding, and that it was the youngest child that the said Phillip Lindsey and Cilla Lindsey had.

As it appears from the evidence that the child to which Alex Posey referred is the same child as the one to which Lewis Lindsey referred, further reference will be made tos aid child as Tosa Lindsey.

It further appears from the evidence and the records in the possession of this office that the applicant, Tosa Lindsey is the child of Phillip Lindsey and Cilla Lindsey, whose names appear on a partial schedule of citizens by blood of the Creek Nation, approved by the Secretary of the Interior, March 28, 1902, opposite numbers 8058 and 8386, respectively.

Applications for Enrollment of Creek Newborn
Act of 1905   Volume XII

Diligent efforts have been made by this office, through field parties, to secure further information relative to the age of this child, but without success, for the reason that the parents are members of the so called Snake faction, and refuse to give any information whatever in regard to enrollment matters.

Although the testimony of the only two witnesses who testified in this matter is conflicting as to when the child was born, the better opinion would seem to be that it was born prior to July 1, 1900, and that it was living at the time of the last proceedings had herein.

It is, therefore, ordered and adjudged that the applicant Tosa Lindsey is entitled to be enrolled as a citizen by blood of the Creek Nation, under the provisions of the Act of Congress approved March 1, 1901 (31 Stats L. 861) and the application for her enrollment as such is accordingly granted.

Tams Bixby   COMMISSIONER.

Muskogee, Indian Territory,
   FEB 20 1907

N.C. 1004.

Muskogee, Indian Territory January 9, 1907.

Silla[sic] Lindsey,
   Care Phillip Lindsey,
      Hanna, Indian Territory.

Dear Madam:

In the matter of the application for the enrollment of your minor child said to have been born on or about the year 1902, as a citizen by blood of the Creek Nation, this office desires the affidavit of the mother, also of the midwife or physician in attendance at the birth of said child and a blank for that purpose is herewith enclosed. You will be allowed ten days in which to properly execute same.

In the event that there was no midwife or physician in attendance when said child was born, it will be necessary for you to furnish this office with the affidavit of two disinterested witnesses. Said affidavits must set forth the name of said child, the names of its parents, the date of its birth and whether or not it was living March 4, 1905.

Respectfully,

BA Commissioner.

Applications for Enrollment of Creek Newborn
Act of 1905 Volume XII

COPY. 2448 B.

DEPARTMENT OF THE INTERIOR,
COMMISSION TO THE FIVE CIVILIZED TRIBES.
April 24, 1905.

In the matter of the application for the enrollment of certain new borns as citizens of the Creek Nation.

Alex Posey, being duly sworn, testified as follows:

By Commission:
Q What is your name, age and post office address? A Alex Posey, 31, Muskogee.
Q Are you a citizen of the Creek Nation? A Yes sir
Q Got your land, have you? A Yes sir.
Q You have been engaged recently in the field for the Dawes Commission securing evidence about Creek citizens or new borns? A Yes sir.
Q Have you a list of children for whom application could not be made and about whom you have succeeded in obtaining some information? A Yes sir.
Q You may state the conditions and the names of these children? You desire to make application for them? A Yes sir.
Q Name them.
A   July Proctor, Weogufky Town, Sukey Proctor, Weogufky Town, have two children --one about three years old and one about six months old. Post office, Hanna, Indian Territory.

Jacob Bullet, about three years old. Parents: Maxey Bullet, Seminole, and Hannah Bullet, Hillabee. Post Office, Hannah, Indian Territory.

Connie Hawkins, Hillabee Town, Sabella Hawkins, Okchiye, have two children-- one about three years old and a younger child. Post Office, Hanna, Indian Territory.

Willie Fisher, Hickory Ground Town, Lussee Fisher, Okfusky[sic] Canadian Town, have two children--one about three years old and a baby. Post Office, Slumpker, Indian Territory.

Lizzie Lasley, about three years old, Sam Lasley, born in either August or September, 1904. Parents: Sam Lasley, Okchiye, Wisey Lasley, Weogufky. Post Office, Hanna, Indian Territory.

Jim Haynes (or Sangee), Okchiye Town, Folotkokee, Weogufky Town have a male child about three years old named Joe. Post Office, Hanna, Indian Territory.

Taylor Foley, Weogufky, Melinda Foley, Okchiye, have a child about two years old. Post Office, Slumpker, Indian Territory.

Phillip Lindsey, Tuckabatchee, Cilla Lindsey, Hillabee, have a child about three years old. Post Office, Hanna, Indian Territory.

✓Big William (or William Thlocco), Okchiye Town, Cinda Williams, Weogufky Town, have two children -- one about three years old-- one born in February 1905. Post Office Hanna, Indian Territory.

Freeland Lindsey, Tuckabatchee or Hillabee, Nancy Proctor, Tullahassoche, have a child about two years old. Post Office, Hanna, Indian Territory.

Timonthluppy George, Weogufky Town, Nellie George, Pukon Tullahassee[sic], have a child about three years old. Post Office, Slumpker, Indian Territory.

Applications for Enrollment of Creek Newborn
Act of 1905 Volume XII

Walter Simmons, Weogufky, Chippie Simmons, Pukon Tullahassee, have a child about one years old. Post Office, Hannah, Indian Territory.

Jacob Larney (or Green), Arbeka Tulledega Town, Bettie Larney, (or Green), Hillabee Town, have a child. Post Office, Hanna, Indian Territory.

John Hill, Okchiye, Millie Hill, Weogufky, have a child about three months old. Post Office, Hanna, Indian Territory.

Jim Pigeon, Okchiye Town, Jennie Pigeon, Okchiye Town, have a child about five months old. Post Office, Hanna, Indian Territory.

Thomas Deo, Okchiye Town, Nancy Deo, Fish Pond Town, have a child about three months old. Post Office, Hanna, Indian Territory.

Jack Buckner, born December 17, 1904. Parents: Wiley Buckner, Okchiye, Susie Buckner, Cussehta. Post Office, Hanna, Indian Territory.

Q This is the information you received from relatives right around there on April 24, 1905? A Yes sir.

Q Were you informed that the parents of these children were unwilling to make application for their enrollment? A Yes sir.

Q This was the only way that the rights of these children would be saved? A Yes sir. I made every effort to obtain direct information from the parents but in every instance they refused to give their testimony.

Lona Merrick being duly sworn, states that the above and foregoing is a true and correct transcript of his stenographic notes as taken in said cause on said date.

(Signed) Lona Merrick

Subscribed and sworn to before me this 9th day of May, 1905.

(Signed) Edw C Griesel
Notary Public.

I, Lona Merrick, solemnly swear that I copied the above testimony from the original on the 18th day of July, 1905, and that it is a true copy of same.

Lona Merrick

Subscribed and sworn to before me this 18th day of July, 1905.

Edw C Griesel
Notary Public.

Applications for Enrollment of Creek Newborn
Act of 1905 Volume XII

Supplemental-

DEPARTMENT OF THE INTERIOR,
COMMISSION TO THE FIVE CIVILIZED TRIBES.
Hanna, I. T., June 6, 1905.

In the matter of the application for the enrollment of children of William Thlocco or Big William and Cinda William as citizens by blood of the Creek Nation.

JOHN BRUNER, being duly sworn, testified as follows

Through Alex Posey Official Interpreter:

BY COMMISSION:
Q What is your name? A John Bruner.
Q How old are you? A Between fifty-three and fifty-four years old.
Q What is your post office address? A Hanna.
Q To what town do you belong? A Wewgufke[sic].
Q Do you know Gib[sic] William or William Thlocco and his wife Cinda? A Yes, sir, Cinda is a member of my town.
Q Have they any children born since May 25, 1901? A They have a daughter named Tana who is something like five years old. I do not know the year in which she was born. Wiley Buckner has a son named Andy about the same age. Tana, however, I think is a little older than Andy.
Q Do you know whether or not the parents have ever made application for the enrollment of Tana? A I do not know as to that. Probably they have not as the father is a member of the Snake Faction.
Q Have they a younger child than Tana? A Yes, sir.
Q Do you know what the name of the child is? A I do not know, but Maxey Bullett would know.
Q Do you know when the child was born? A I am unable to fix the date of its birth but it was born yes Spring; perhaps in February.
Q Was the child born before the Commission was a Dustin receiving application for the enrollment of new-born Creeks? A Yes, sir.

SUSIE BUCKNER, being duly sworn, testified as follows

Through Alex Posey Official Interpreter:

BY COMMISSION:
Q What is your name? A Susie Buckner.
Q How old are you? A I do not know my age.

Mother of the witness states that she is forty years of age.

Q What is your post office address? A Hanna.
Q To what town do you belong? A Cussehta.

Applications for Enrollment of Creek Newborn
Act of 1905 Volume XII

Q Do you know Big William or William Thlocco and his wife Cinda? A Yes, sir.
Q Have they any children born since May 25, 1901? A I do not know. They have a baby.
Q Have they other children? A They have three other children.
Q Do you know their names? A The oldest is named Lucy and another named Tana. I do not know the name of the other one.
Q How old is Tana? A I do not know.
Q Have you a child named Andy? A Yes, sir.
Q How much older is Tana than Andy? A I do not know; perhaps over a year.
Q When was your child, Andy, born? A

Witness presents a day-book containing various records and accounts, among which the following entry, written in the Creek Language, is found:
"Many B. was born March 8, 1901."

Q Does Many B. refer to your child, Andy? A Yes, sir, Many is nick-named Andy.
Q Who made this record? A My husband, Wiley Buckner.

---oooOooo---

I, D. C. Skaggs, on oath state that the above and foregoing is a full and true transcript of my stenographic notes as taken in said cause on said date.

D. C. Skaggs

Subscribed and sworn to before me this ___ day of JUL 17 1905 1905.

Edw C Griesel
Notary Public.

Supplemental-   C 1005

DEPARTMENT OF THE INTERIOR,
COMMISSIONER TO THE FIVE CIVILIZED TRIBES.
Trenton, I. T., June 7, 1905.

In the matter of the application for the enrollment of children of William Thlocco or Big William and Cinda William as citizens by blood of the Creek Nation.

GEORGE SIMMONS, being duly sworn, testified as follows

Through Alex Posey Official Interpreter:

BY COMMISSION:
Q What is your name? A George Simmons.
Q How old are you? A About thirty9eight[sic].

Applications for Enrollment of Creek Newborn
Act of 1905   Volume XII

Q What is your post office address? A Trenton.
Q Are you a citizen of the Creek Nation? A Yes, sir.
Q To what town do you belong? A Hillabee.
Q Are you acquainted with William Thlocco or Big William and his wife Cinda? A Yes, sir, Big William's daughter is my wife.
Q Have they any children born since May 25, 1901, and for whom they have made no application. A Yes, sir, they have three children.
Q What are their names? A One is named Tana, she is about six years old.
Q Do you know in what year and month she was born? A I think she was born in 1903, and is going on three years old. I do not know what month she was born in.
Q Are you positive that she was born since May 25, 1901? A Yes, sir.
Q She is living is she? A Yes, sir.
Q What is the name of the next child? A The youngest child is a baby an is not yet named.
Q Is it a boy or girl? A A boy.
Q When was it born? A The child was born in February of this year but I do not know on what day.
Q Are you positive the child was born in February of this year? A Yes, sir.
Q Is that child living? A Yes, sir.
Q To what towns do the parents belong? A The father belongs to Okchiye and the mother belongs to Weogufke.

---oooOOOooo---

I, D. C. Skaggs, on oath state that the above and foregoing is a full and true transcript of my stenographic notes as taken in said cause on said date.

D. C. Skaggs

Subscribed and sworn to before me this ___ day of   JUL 17 1905   1905.

Edw C Griesel
Notary Public.

N.C. 1005.   F.H.W.
DEPARTMENT OF THE INTERIOR,
COMMISSIONER TO THE FIVE CIVILIZED TRIBES.

In the matter of the application for the enrollment of Bettie Williams[sic] and (Baby) Williams as citizens by blood of the Creek Nation.

DECISION.

The record in this case shows that on April 24, 1905, Alex Posey testified under oath before the Commission to the Five Civilized Tribes, at Muskogee, Indian Territory,

Applications for Enrollment of Creek Newborn
Act of 1905   Volume XII

in the matter of the applications for the enrollment of certain new borns as citizens of the Creek Nation. In this testimony among other statements appears the following:

"Big William (or William Thlocco), Okchiye Town, Cinda Williams, Weogufky Town, have two children--one about three years old--one born in February 1905. Post office, Hanna, Indian Territory."

This statement is herein considered an application for the enrollment of the said Bettie Williams and the unnamed baby of the said Big and Cinda Williams, in order that the rights of the said applicants be protected. The said unnamed child in the future consideration of this case will be known as Baby Williams. Further proceedings were had on June 6 and 7, 1905, before Creek enrollment parties at Hanna and Trenton, Indian Territory.

It is shown in evidence and by the records of this office that the Commission in April 1905 made every effort to secure birth affidavits executed in regular form by the parents or near relatives of the said applicants but were unable to do so.

It is further shown in evidence that at this time, April 1905, the said Alex Posey was actively engaged in attempting to locate and identify minor children of the Snake or disaffected faction of Creek Indians.

The evidence is however under the circumstances clear enough to warrant the following conclusions, viz: that the said Bettie Williams was born some time in 1902 or 1903, that Baby Williams was born in February, 1905 and that both of said applicants were living on the date of the last proceedings herein.

The evidence further shows that the said Bettie and Baby Williams are the children of Wilumpka and Sinthe Williams, whose names appear in a partial schedule of citizens by blood of the Creek Nation approved by the Secretary of the Interior March 28, 1902, opposite roll Nos. 7795 and 7796, respectively.

It is further shown in evidence that the identity of Wilumpka is the same as Big Williams or William Thlocco referred to in the application and it is further shown that Sinthe and Cinda Williams is the same.

The Act of Congress approved March 3, 1905, (33 Stats. 1048) provides in part as follows:

"That the Commission to the Five Civilized Tribes is authorized for sixty days after the date of the approval of this act to receive and consider applications for enrollment, of children, born subsequent to May twenty-fifth, nineteen hundred and one, and prior to March fourth, nineteen hundred and five, and living on said latter date, to citizens of the Creek tribe of Indians whose enrollment has been approved by the Secretary of the Interior prior to the approval of this act; and to enroll and make allotments to such children."

It is, therefore, ordered and adjudged that the said Bettie Williams and Baby Williams are entitled to be enrolled as citizens by blood of the Creek Nation, in accordance with the provisions of law above quoted, and the application for their enrollment as such is accordingly granted.

Applications for Enrollment of Creek Newborn
Act of 1905   Volume XII

Muskogee, Indian Territory,
January 14- 1907

Tams Bixby   Commissioner.

Dustin, Indian Territory, June 8, 1905.

Commission to the Five Civilized Tribes,
  Muskogee, Indian Territory.

Gentlemen:

There is enclosed herewith testimony in the matter of the application for enrollment of the children is San and Wisey Lasley, No. 2448)B, also the children of William Thlocco (or Big William) and Cinda William, No. 2449-B, as citizens by blood of the Creek Nation. I find it impossible to secure further evidence about these children.

Respectfully,
Signed   Alex Posey
Clerk in Charge Creek Field Party.

N C 1005

JWH

Muskogee, Indian Territory, March 1, 1907.

Cinda Williams
  % Big Williams,
    Hanna, Indian Territory.

Dear Madam :--

You are hereby advised that on February 15, 1907, the Secretary of the Interior approved the enrollment of your minor children, Bettie and Baby Williams, as citizens by blood of the Creek Nation, and that the names of said children appear upon the roll of New Born citizens by blood of the Creek Nation, enrolled under the Act of Congress approved March 3, 1905, as numbers 1189 and 1190, respectively.

These children are now entitled to allotment and application therefor should be made without delay at the Creek Land Office, Muskogee, Indian Territory.

Respectfully,
Commissioner.

Index

ADAMS
  Mahala 190
  Mahaley 189
  Mary 187,188,189,190
  Wash 190
AH LA CO CON THLA MY 124
AH-LA-CON-TAY 85
ALFORD
  Viola 169
ALLEN
  George 155
  Jesse 58
ALSTON
  A J 280
ANDERSON
  Martha 14,15,16,17,18
  Millie 11
  Sissy 14
  Willie 14,15,16,17,18
ANINE
  W H 147
ARMSTEAD
  Sam 176
ASBURY
  Jimsey 237
  Wisey 238

BARLOE
  Billy 223
BARLOW 222,225
  Billy 213,217,218,224
BARNETT
  D A 15
  David 14
  David A 14
  Herford 156
  Jennie 213,217,223
  Linda 86
  Lydia 64
  Miller 86
BEALL
  Wm O 112,124,205
BEALLS
  W O 124
BEAR
  Lena 233,239
BEAVER
  Earnest 137
  Ella.. 126,128,129,130,131,132,
133,134,135,136,137
  Hecton 128
  Heliswa 233,239
  John 126,127,128,129,130,
131,132,133,134,135,136,137
  John Charles 127
  Joseph Charles.126,128,129,130,131,
132,133,134,135,136
  Joseph Charlie 137
  Kaska 233,239
  Nancy 25,46,52,200,202,203,204,208
  Suka 23
  Wattie 25,46,52,200,202,203,204,208
  Wisey 25,46,52,200,201,202,
203,204,208
  Yosta 253,254,256,257
  Yousta 258,259,260
BEIDLEMAN
  George C 175
BENDER
  Bob 269
  Easma 269
  Mahala 269
  Thomas 269
BENSON
  Robert 15
BERRY
  J D 219
BIG WILLIAM 90,262,271,286,292,
297,313,317,319,320,321,322,323
  Hannah 264
BIGGS
  George C 49,50
  Jeannetta 49,50
  Martha 49,50
BIL WILLIAM 249
BILLIE
  Annie 245,246,248
BILLY
  Annie 226,230,235,240,245,247
  Lumber 244
  Nancy 244,246
BIT WILLIAM 306
BIXBY
  Tams 4,5,6,8,28,29,34,50,59,62,

325

70,72,76,77,78,94,104,107,109,114,
121,122,129,136,137,138,143,152,153,
184,195,202,206,210,225,233,265,
268,296,302,309,316,323
BIXBY, ... 157
BLAKE
   W R 308
BLAKEMORE
   Elijah P 178
BOLES
   C A 215,216
   Mattie 215,216
   Pearl Amy 215,216
BOWLEGS
   Gussie 1,2,3,4,5,6,7
   Lula 1,3,5,6,7
   Robert 1,2,3,5,6,7
BRIDLEMAN
   George C 176
BRIGHT
   Samuel 148
BROWN 206
   Com-pe-cin-ny 56,57
   Com-pe-sen-ney 54,55
   Con-pe-sin-ney 57,58
   Jim 24,45,51,52,56,57,59,
199,200,207
   John 54,57,58,59
   Julia 83
   Loda 24,45,51,54,55,56,57,58,
59,199,207
   Mahala 97
   Nancy Davis 85
   S W 71,73,74,151
   Saml W 124
   Samson 83
   Samuel W 125
   Timmie 101,102
   Willie 55,56,57,58,59
BRUNER
   Georgia 59,60,61
   Ilsey 62
   Jackson 300
   Paul 155
   Pauline 155
   Pinkey 60,61
   R R 59

   Ruby 59,60,61
   Sallie 266,311
   Sissie 145
   Taylor 62,63
   Turner 62,63
BUCK
   Sarah 155
BUCKNER
   Andy 320
   Jack 91,249,262,272,286,293,
298,306,313,318
   Many B 320
   Susie 91,249,262,266,272,286,
293,298,306,313,318,319
   Wiley 91,249,262,272,286,293,
298,306,313,318,320
BUCKTROT
   Con-char-char 29,30
   Mattie 29,30
   Sagie 29,30
BULLET
   Hannah 90,249,262,267,271,285,
292,297,306,313,317
   Jacob 90,249,262,267,271,285,
292,297,306,313,317
   Maxey 90,249,262,267,271,285,
292,297,306,313,317
BULLETT
   Hanna 265,266
   Hannah 263,264,266,267,268
   Jacob 263,264,265,266,267,268
   Maxey. 263,264,265,266,267,268,319
   Millie 311
BUTLER 218,219,221
   Eddie 218,220,221,222,224
   Myron 220,221
   Sam 217,218,224
BUTTS AND BLISS 44

CAIN
   Ottawa 196
CALLOWAY
   L M 54,55,56
CAMPBELL
   Donald 184,185,186
   Harry 99,102,103
CANTRELL

Index

Jim 15,17,258,259,260,301
CAPTAIN BILLY 284
CATES
   Governor 63,64,65
   Joseph 63,65
   Lydia 63,64,65
CEASAR
   Calley 155
CHAR CO TE TEN NA
   Polly 71
CHAR CO-TE-TEN-NA
   Ella 71
CHARCOTE TENNA
   Katie 77
CHAR-CO-TE-TEN-NA
   Ella 72,73,74,75,76,77
   Ellen 72,73,74,76,77
   Katie 71,72,73,74,75,76,77
   Polly 74,75,77
CHEATHAM
   Frank 8,9,10
   W L 54,55,56
   Wm L 54,55,56
CHIEF
   Louvena 9,10
   Millie 11
CHISHOLM
   Jennie 138,139,140,141,143
   Mamie 138,139,140,141,143,144
   Susan Tomahawk 138
CLAYTON
   J P 162
CLOWRY
   Robert C 142
COACHMAN
   Charles 219
CO-AH 27
COCHE
   Welah 236,237
COHONEY
   Arleka 151
COKER
   Sissie 196
COMIE
   Larley 20,21,22
   Martha 20,21,22
   Thomas 21,22

CONE
   Mamie 141
   Manie 141
CONNER
   Geoge 200
   George 25,46,47,48,52,208
   Jeannetta 25,46,52,200,208
   Jennetta 47,48
   Martha 23,25,45,46,47,48,49,50,
   51,52,199,200,206,208
COON
   George 143
COONE
   He memie 141
COOPER
   W G 216
COSAR
   Lizzie 79
COTER
   Sissie 196
COTT
   W M 171
COWE
   Arlingee 186
   Sarty 186
CROWELL 117
   Benn 116
   Bob 116
   Edward J 117
   Edward L 118,119,120,121
   Edward L, Jr 116,121
   Frances Willard 116,117,120,121
   Francis Willard 119,120,121
   Francis Willion 119
   Ida 118
   Ida May 116,117,119,120,121
   J A 118
   Joe 116
   Martha 118
   Robert 117
   Robert A 116,117
   Tom 116
CUMMINGS
   David 273,274
   Larley 19,22,23
   Louisa 273,274
   Martha 22

Thomas 19,22
DAVIDSON
  Charles A 170
  Chas A 170,171
  Geo K 192,193
DAVIS
  Addie 85,87,88
  Ahne 218,220
  Bill 106
  Eddie 85,86
  Georgia 155
  Ilsey 196
  Jim 213,217,223,269
  Johnny 269
  Lewis 155
  Tom 85,86,87,88
DE-CON-SAC 85,86
DEER
  Israel 14
  Sarah 226,235,240
DEERE
  Ben 243
  Lewis 232
  Sarah 230,241,242,243
  Thompson 242
DEO
  Nancy 91,249,262,272,286,293, 298,306,313,318
  Thomas 91,249,262,272,286,293, 298,306,313,318
DERRISAW
  Barney 205
DICKSON
  Lottie 155
DILLEY
  W Y 138,139
DODGE
  Emma 155
DONCARLOS
  C C 65,66
DORSEY
  Emma 284
DOWNING
  Anday 101
  Andy .. 96,97,98,100,101,102,103,104
  James 96,97,100,101,102,103
  Mahala 96,97,98,100
  Mahale 101,102,103,104
  Mahele 103
DYSON
  Wesley M 171,172
EDWARDS
  Henry 155
  Ida 116
  Ida May 117,119
ELA
  Nocus 269
ELLIOTT
  J J 133,134
EMARTHLA
  Micco 270
  Sallie 270
  Walter 270
ESEEKA 251
ESEKER 251
EUCONGODALIE 122,123,124, 125,126
EWING
  P B 113
FATT
  Dick 214
FIELD
  Lydia 222
FIELDS
  Abram 219
  Liddy 218,219,221
  Lydia .. 213,217,220,221,222,223,224
  Susie 269
  Thompson 269
FIFE
  Elijah 12,13
  Exie 12,13
  Millie 12,13
FISH
  Hettie 270
  Jimsey 269
  Wiley 270
FISHER
  Bettie 284,287,288,289,290,291
  Lucy 284,287,288,289,290,291
  Lussee 90,249,262,271,285,292,

297,306,313,317
William.. 284
Willie.......... 90,249,262,271,284,285,
288,289,290,291,292,297,306,313,317
FIXECO
   Foluthoker 304,305
   Joseph............................ 301,302,305
   Yarhola.......................... 302,304,305
FIXICO
   Folothoka.............................. 300,301
   Folothoker 300
   Jennie.. 214
   Joseph................................. 300,301
   Yahola 298,299,303,304
   Yarhola...................................... 300
   Yarholar..................................... 300
FLACK
   Cornelia..................................... 278
   Enoch... 278
   John... 278
FLESHER
   M Z.. 32
FLINN
   B W, MD............................ 32,37,42
FLOURNAY
   M C... 66
FLYNN
   B W 37,39
   B W, MD...................................... 39
   Dr.. 32,42
   T W................................ 132,133,134
FOE
   Magie Nola................................. 155
FOLEY
   Arney 307,308,309,310,311,312
   Melinda....... 90,249,262,271,285,292,
   297,306,307,308,309,311,313,317
   Melindy 308,312
   Taylor 90,249,262,271,285,292,
   297,306,307,308,309,310,311,313,317
FOLOTKOKEE..... 90,249,262,271,285,
292,297,306,313,317
FOLUTHOKER 302
FOWLER
   J W 242
FRICK
   J L 31,32,33,34,35,36,

37,38,39,40,42
   Jay 31,32,33,34,36,37,
38,39,40,41,42
   Mamie 33,39,41
   Mayme 33,34,35,36,37,38,
39,40,41,42
   Mayme Perryman 32,42
   Mrs J L 35,40
   William... 31,32,33,34,35,39,40,41,42
   Willie.. 41,42
FRIDAY
   Berry................. 144,145,146,147,148
   Jennie 89,144,145,146,147,148
   Willie.... 89,144,145,146,147,148,149
FULLER
   Mrs 128
FURR
   Jude 282

GALLAHER
   Dr J W 116
   J W 120
GANA
   Katy... 233
   Nicey.. 233
GANO
   Katy... 239
   Nicey.. 239
GARDNER
   P W.. 196
GARDNER & LANGSTON 196
GARRIGUES
   Anna...................................... 14,127
GENTRY
   Joshua... 155
GEORGE
   Nellie.......... 90,249,262,272,286,293,
297,306,313,318
   Timonthluppy 90,249,262,272,286,
293,297,306,313,318
GHANT
   Mr.. 60
GIBSON
   Thelma Maud 155
GIERKES
   Wm F A 146,148,252
GIERKEY

William F A 89
GILBERT
   Jeniry 281,282,283
   Jude................................ 281,282,283
   Louis W 281,282,283
GIVENS
   William.. 269
GOODWIN
   F M.. 95
GOUGE
   Earnest... 270
   Nicey 270
GRAHAM
   Lewis 10,11,12
   Louis....................................... 8,9
   Millie 8,9,11
   Selie 7,8,9,10
   Sissie 10,11,12
GRANBERRY
   Alma Dee............................. 278,280
   James 280
   Mattie 278,280
GRANSBERRY
   Alma Dee................................... 279
   James 279
   Mattie 279
GRAY
   Louisa... 214
   Millie 198
GRAYSON
   Aaron 20,22
   Frank............................... 113,114,115
   Hattie 25,46,53,200,201,208
   Lizzie.............................. 113,114,115
   Patience 148
   Patient.. 147
   Tom 113,114
   Wash.. 294
GREEN
   Barney 294
   Bettie 91,249,262,272,293,
   297,306,313,318
   Jacob...........91,249,262,272,286,293,
   297,306,313,318
GRIESEL
   E C..............23,26,45,47,51,53,84,96,
   98,134,136,199,201,206,209

Edw C.........26,28,30,47,48,49,53,56,
57,67,68,69,71,75,80,81,82,84,87,91,
93,98,100,107,129,134,135,136,145,
151,160,174,201,203,209,210,213,217,
223,227,230,231,232,235,241,250,
263,264,272,279,286,287,293,295,298,
307,314,315,318,320,321
GRISEL
   E C 97
GULLAHER
   J W 117
HAINES
   Folothoka.................298,299,303,304
   Jim 298,299,303,304
   Joseph.....................298,299,303,304
HAINS
   G H... 16,86
   H G..................118,119,130,131,285
   Henry G.......................14,19,20,270
HARDRIDGE
   Eli.. 186
HARJO
   Alex..................................... 19,22,23
   Martha................................ 19,22,23
   Silby 22
HARLINGS
   Tony 155
HARPER
   Shawnee 91
HARRIS
   Mahala... 97
HARRISON
   R P.. 97
HARRY
   Lizzie....................................... 65,66
HARVISON
   Geo A 20,21,22
HASON
   Flutcher 176
HAWKINS
   Conner.............273,274,275,276,277
   Connie 90,249,262,270,271,
   274,285,292,297,306,313,317
   Gabriel... 155
   Nellie.......................273,274,275,277
   Pink 273,275,276,277

Index

Sabella 90,249,262,271,273, 274,285,292,297,306,313,317
Sepile 277
Subella 274,275,276,277
Sybilla 270
HAY
  Eggie 70,71
  John 70,71,72,73,74,75,76
  Modie 70,71
HAYNES
  Jim 90,249,262,271,285,292, 297,302,306,313,317
  Joe 90,262,271,285,297,302, 306,313,317
HE-CA-TAH 72,73,76,77
HELTON
  J A 65
HENEHA
  Matup 310
  Metup 308
HENSHAW
  Dr 127
  F A 127,128,132,133,135,137
  F A, MD 133
HE-TAH-OO-OO-TAN 76
HILL
  John 91,226,230,235,240,241, 242,243,249,262,272,286,293,297,306, 313,318
  Millie 91,249,262,272,286,293, 297,306,313,318
  Nettie ..226,230,235,240,241,242,243
  Pearl 116
  Richard J 61
  Richard Joseph 83
HILLS
  Pearl 119
HLL
  LUL M 216
HOGAN
  Julia 82,83,84
  Robert 82,83,84
  Robt 83
  Willie D 82,83,84
HOGANS
  Julia A 82,84
HOLMES

C W 8,9,10
  Redman 105
HOLT
  Ceborn 156
HOMAHTA
  Chepe 233,239
  Folle 233,239
HOPE
  Chiye 276
HOPIYE
  Jennie 213,214,215,217,223
  Lucindy 214,215
  Span 213,214,217,223
HOYT
  W R 166,167
HUFFINGTON BROS 150
HUTKE
  Mary 81
HUTTON
  Amelia 275

IRELAN
  O M 97
ISLAND
  Callie 48,49
  George 48,49
ISPOGEE
  Jennie 81
ISPOKOGEE
  Belcher 81
  Jennie 81
  Noah 81

JACOB
  Eli 145
JAMES
  Billy 284
  Jane 108
  Katie 107,111
  Kattie 107
JA-TAH-KE-CON-CAH-NEY 85
JA-TAH-KO-CO-CAH-NEY 85
JA-TAH-KO-CON-CAH-NEY 86,87
JEFFRIES
  Mattie 155
  Tom 155
JESSE

Massey.. 15
JESSIE
   Sissie.. 15
   Sissy 16,17
JIM
   Sissy 14,17,18
JIMMIE 124
JOHNSON
   Anderson 72,77
   Andres 77
   J C... 3,4
   J Coody... 186
   J P... 184
   John 107,111,112
   Johnnie 104,105,106,107,108,
   109,110
   Nora..........104,106,107,108,109,110,
   111,112
   Onate 233,239
   Sandy.. 79
   Susanna..................................... 233,239
JONES
   Adam 205,206
   Elie 205,206
   M C... 22
   Mattie 205,206

KAKANA.. 150
KAKANEY 151
KARY
   Hanah 176
KELLY
   Amy.. 233,239
KEPLEY
   James K 146
KING... 124

LANDMAN
   J M.. 35,40
LANGSTON
   W P... 196
LARNEY
   Bettie 91,249,262,272,286,293,
   297,306,313,318
   Jacob............91,249,262,272,286,293,
   297,306,313,318
LARRABEE

   C F.. 154
LASLEY
   Daniel... 294
   Lizzie..........90,249,262,271,285,292,
   294,295,296,297,306,313,317
   Lula 294
   Minnie 294
   Sam.............90,249,262,271,285,292,
   294,295,296,297,306,313,317
   San.. 323
   Wicey 294
   Wisey 90,249,262,271,285,292,
   295,296,297,306,313,317,323
LEE
   Gano 66,67,68,69
   John 66
   Johnson....................................... 67,69
   Joseph...................................... 66,68,69
   Sissie 66,67,68,69
LEVI
   Eddie 155
LEWIS
   Daniel... 227
   Millie 12
LINDSEY
   Cilla..................90,249,262,271,285,
   292,297,306,309,313,314,315,317
   Columbia........................92,93,94,95
   Freeland........90,91,92,93,94,249,262,
   271,286,292,297,306,313,317
   Lewis.. 314
   Nancy 271
   Philip 314
   Phillip 90,249,262,271,285,292,
   297,306,309,313,315,316,317
   Silla 316
   Tosa..................................314,315,316
LISTON
   Joseph...................................... 133,134
LITTLEHEAD
   Nannie 30
LONG
   Henry......................24,45,52,200,207
   Lannie.............................26,27,54,55,56
   Lewis 24,26,27,28,29,45,46,
   -52,200,207
   Louis.. 27

Nancy 27,28,29,46,52,200,207
Sa-ke.. 26,27
Suka............23,24,27,28,45,46,51,52,
199,200,206,207
Suke.. 29
Wisey..................... 23,45,51,199,206
LOWERY
Dr... 32
LOWRY
Sydney A, MD......................... 35,40
Sydney A, Phy, MD....................... 35
LUCY 13
LUSK
A M 170
LYNCH
R E... 42
Robert E..................... 35,37,38,40,41

MCCALL
Nancy 192
MCCOSAR
Bunnie 196
MCDERMOTT
J 15,16,17,36,72,86,96,127,177,
188,197,221,245,247,258,259,260,300,
301,307,311
Jesse............30,32,33,49,50,67,68,69,
71,75,80,81,84,87,130,131,134,136,20
4,212,221,244,251,252,301,308,311
MCFARLAND
James 198
Ned 197,198
MCGIRT
Hettie 15
MCINTOSH
Bettie 192,193
Betty 191,194
George 191,192,194
Josiah 155
Nelson 155
Willie............... 191,192,193,194,195
MACKIN
Joe 132
MCQUEEN
Ann... 84
MANLEY
Adam 238,239

Katie 229
Katy 227,228,230
Peepsie 226,227,228,229,235,240
Tom 226,227,228,229,235,240
MARLOW
Ellen 160
MARPIYECHER
Josie.. 184
Yahnah 184
MARS
F L 73,74,79
James J 73,74
MARTIN
William T 219
MELAR... 14
MERITT
E B 95
MERRICK
Lona 91,118,119,213,217,223,
226,227,230,235,241,250,263,272,284,
286,293,298,307,314
Mona 318
MILLER
J Y 151,160,173,176,177,
187,245,279
Mary J 282
MITCHELL
Bettie 226,230,235,236,237,
238,239,240
Lewis...............226,230,235,236,237,
238,239,240
Mahlahsee .226,230,233,235,236,240
Mahlahsse.................................... 239
Morris......................236,237,238,239
MITCHENER
W C 181
W C, MD..................................... 181
MONROE
Lum 161
Millie 161
MOORE
E H 194,195
John W 307
MORGAN
W B 166,167
William B 165,166,167
MORRIS

Index

(Illegible) 120
F B 115
Fannie 115
MOTT
M L 153
MYERS
James B 251

NARTAKE 183
NASH
Frank 148
Jennie 144,147,148,149
NEVINS
Katie 110
Katy 111

O'REILLY
E I 115
OWEN
Elva 44
Nellie 43,44

PARRISH
Zera E 98,187,201
Zera Ellen 129,145
PAYNE
R O 120
PERRYMAN
Ed 158
Eddie 157
Leah 157,158
Mamie 31,33,36,41
Sarah 157,158,159
Willie 155
PETERS
Lucindia 147
PHILIPS
Rina 3,6
PIGEON
Jennie 91,249,262,272,286,293,
297,306,313,318
Jim 91,249,262,272,286,293,
297,306,313,318
PINEHILL
Lasley 25,46,53,201,208,
209,211,212
Laslie 210

Mary 23,25,45,46,51,53,199,
201,206,208,209,210,211,212
Sallie 25,46,53,201,208,209,
210,211,212
PO-CON-WE-NEY 85
PO-KO-CON-WE-NEY 85
PORTER
Lizzie 192,193,194
P 196
POSEY
Alex 13,16,26,27,86,90,91,92,93,
108,141,159,189,197,198,213,214,215,
216,217,220,223,226,228,229,230,
232,233,234,236,238,239,240,241,244,
246,248,250,251,253,254,255,256,
260,261,263,266,267,269,271,273,274,
275,276,285,287,288,289,290,292,
294,295,297,299,301,303,304,305,309,
310,312,315,317,319,320,321,322,
323
PRICE
James Lawrence 159
M B 159,161,162
Minnie May 159,160,161,162,163
Mose B 160,161,163
Moses B 163
Sallie 159,160,161,162,163
PROCTOR
Chaeler 252
Chaeller 250,251,257,258,259,
260,261
Hullie 92,288
Jaly 252,253,254,255,256,257,260
July 90,249,262,271,285,292,297,
306,313,317
Lumber 92
Lydia 251,252,254,256,257,259,
260,261
Melinda 309
Melindy 310,311
Nancy 90,91,92,93,94,249,262,
286,292,297,306,313,317
Sam 251,252,253,255,256,257,
258,260,261
Suckey 255
Sucky .. 252,253,254,255,256,257,261
Sukey 90,249,250,251,257,258,

259,260,262,271,285,292,297,306,313, 317
Suky 253

QWLAH
P M 176

RANKIN
R A 158
RED
Thomas 312
RENTIE
Douglas 2
RIEGLE
J F 37
ROBERTS
Hannah 270
Josie 269
Mahala 269
Noah 270
ROBINSON
Geo L 280
ROGERS
Charles D 190
Chepon 78,79,80
Jemima 78,79,80
Lucy 78,79,80
ROLAND
Amos 85
ROSS 117
Mr T E 116
T E 117,119
Tom 118

SABOURIS
Frank C 1
SAL-CON-CAH-NEY 85
SAMMIE 221
SAMMY 218,219
SANDERS
Gennie 155
R B 40
SANGEE
Jim 90,249,262,271,285,292, 297,302,306,313,317
Joe 90,262,271,285,297,302, 306,313,317

SANGER
Jaunitta 171,172
Stephen 171,172
Stephen C 169
Viola 171,172
SANGO
Delila 104,106,107,108,109, 110,111,112
Delilah 112
Jackson 105,106
Leah 105
Lucinda 105
SAN-GO
Millie 83
SANGO
Timmie 105
SARTY 233,239
SAT-AH-CO-CON-COH-NY 87
SCHOCK
E E 282,283
SCOTT
Edward 226,228,230,231,232, 234,235,240
Josie 184,185,186
Katie 226,235,240
Katy 227,228
Lucy 184,185,186
Marguerite 156
Marpiecha 184,185,186
Marpiyecher 182
Marpukie 185
Millie 231,234
Polly 185
Robert 155
Setepake 233,239
Setepakee 226,230,231,232,233, 234,235,240
Tana 226,230,231,232,235,240
Tena 232
Yanah 184,185,186
SEEKA
Sukey 251
SEKER
Sukey 252
SELVIDGE
R B 311
SHELBY

David .30,49,67,68,69,71,75,80,81,87
SHELTON
   Julia 176
SHIELDS
   Charles J 180,181
   Charles Jackson, Jr 180,181
   Clara Williams...................... 180,181
SHOENFELT
   J Blair 42
SIMMONS
   Chi[[le 313
   Chippie 91,249,262,272,286,293,
297,306,318
   Geo 300
   George 320
   Walter 91,249,262,272,286,293,
297,306,313,318
SIMS
   E W.. 65,66
SKAGGS
   D C 26,27,72,86,93,107,108,
139,159,188,189,197,198,218,224,228,
229,231,232,237,238,239,242,244,
246,253,254,255,256,257,264,266,273,
274,275,276,287,288,289,290,294,
299,303,304,310,315,320,321
   Drennan C.......26,47,53,108,159,164,
165,174,175,177,181,182,189,198,199,
209,227,228,229,238,239,243,244,
246,253,254,255,256,257,266,267,270,
273,274,275,276,279,283,288,289,
290,299,303,304,310
SKAHAKAH
   Susan 139
SKAHKAH
   Susan 138,139
SKAH-KAH
   Susan 140,143,144
SKAHKAH
   Susie 141
SLATTERY
   John F 176
SMOOT
   E A 166,167,169
   G W 166,167,169
SNAKE...........45,49,51,93,199,201,202,
207,208,209,236,270,295,316,319,322

SNAKES 46,53
SNAP
   Andy.........................99,102,103,104
   James..................99,100,101,102,103
   Mahale.............................101,102,104
   Mahele............................. 99,100,103
SNEED
   Charlie.. 173
   George 172,173,176,177,178,179
   George Everett............................ 173
   George W ..173,174,175,176,178,179
   George Washington..................... 173
   Hanah 177
   Hannah 173,174,175,176,178
   John.. 176
   Larzar 173,177,178,179
   Leonard 173
   Maron.. 173
   Martha 173
   Rose.. 178
   Susie Rose .172,173,174,175,176,179
STAMPS
   Will..................................... 116,119
STARR
   Daniel.. 242
   Walter 270
STEWART
   A I 138
STONE
   Garret 220
SULLIVAN
   Jay.. 31,33
   Mamie 31,33,35,36
   P P 31,32,35,36
   William..............................31,33,35,36
SULPHUR
   James.. 227

TA-SAN-KAY-NAY 85
TAYLOR
   Dennis 155
THLOCCO
   Cinda..............................306,320,321
   Lucy 320
   Tana................................319,320,321
   William.......90,249,262,264,271,286,
292,297,306,313,317,319,320,321,322,

323
THOMAS
  Vitter 176
THOMPSON
  Captain 158
  Dr. 160
  Jackson 158
  Sarah 158
  William 163
THOMSON
  William 162
  Wm, MD 162
TIGER
  Charles 149,150,151,152,153, 154,155,156
  Charley 150
  Charlie 150
  Dave 150,151,152,154,156
  Harry 184,185
  He con con 124
  He con con thla 124,125
  He.co.con.thla 123
  He-co-con-thla 122
  James 122,123,125,126
  Jennetta 149
  Ka-ka-ney 152,154
  Ka-Ka-Ney 156
  Ka-ke-ney 152
  Louisa 251
  Rose 250
  Tom 25,46,52,200,208
  William 233,239
TIMONTHLUBBY
  Nellie 288
TOBLER
  Fred 187,188,189,190
  Mary 190
  Pleasant 187,188,189,190
TOMLIN
  Sylvia 178

U CO DALIE 125
UCODALIA 124

VAN BUSKIRK
  Frank J 2
VANN
  Billy 105,106
  Rena 105
VAUGHAN
  J C 119
VICK
  E G 116
  Eban G. 116
  Even G. 119
WADSWORTH
  B W 48,57,203
  Ben 49
  Ben W 23,27,45,48,51,56,57, 199,203,206,210
  Mr. 24,25,47,51,53,201,207,208
WALKER
  Noodle 270
  Rhoda 155
WASHINGTON
  Isaac 113
WATTS
  Chas G 160,161
WEBSTER
  Chas E 1
WEST
  Josie 182,183
  Thomas 182,183,184,186
  Yamah 182,183
  Yanah 183
WETCHIE 251
WHETSTONE
  Anderson 281
  Eula Pear 169
  Eula Pearl 164,165,166,167,168
  James 164,165,166,167,168,169
  Jude 281
  Nancy Caroline 281
  Theodosia .. 164,165,166,167,168,169
WHITEMAN
  William H 98,99,101,102,103
WILEY
  Melissa 197,198
WILLIA
  George 176
WILLIAM
  Cinda 319,320,323
  Gib 319

WILLIAMS
    Annie 244,245,246,247,248
    Baby 321,322,323
    Bettie 321,322,323
    Big 322,323
    Cinda 90,249,262,271,286,292, 297,313,317,322,323
    John 226,230,235,240,244,245, 246,247,248
    Sinthe.. 322
    Thomas 226,230,235,240,244,245, 246,247,248
    Wilumpka 322
WILLIE 124
WILSON
    Jesse E 156
    John 184,185,186
WILYARME 245
WOLF
    Nancy Davis 85,86,87,88
WOOD
    Wm 40

YAH CON PN CON THLA 124
YARNIE 14
YOU LON WA THLA 124
YOUNG
    (Illegible) 158

www.ingramcontent.com/pod-product-compliance
Lightning Source LLC
Chambersburg PA
CBHW020243030426
42336CB00010B/596